D0428224

The Editor

MARK RAWLINSON is Senior Lecturer in English at the
University of Leicester. His books include *British Writing
of the Second World War* and *Pat Barker.*

A NORTON CRITICAL EDITION

Anthony Burgess
A CLOCKWORK ORANGE

AUTHORITATIVE TEXT
BACKGROUNDS AND CONTEXTS
CRITICISM

Edited by

MARK RAWLINSON
UNIVERSITY OF LEICESTER

W • W • NORTON & COMPANY • *New York* • *London*

W. W. Norton & Company has been independent since its founding in 1923, when William Warder Norton and Mary D. Herter Norton first published lectures delivered at the People's Institute, the adult education division of New York City's Cooper Union. The firm soon expanded its program beyond the Institute, publishing books by celebrated academics from America and abroad. By mid-century, the two major pillars of Norton's publishing program—trade books and college texts—were firmly established. In the 1950s, the Norton family transferred control of the company to its employees, and today—with a staff of four hundred and a comparable number of trade, college, and professional titles published each year—W. W. Norton & Company stands as the largest and oldest publishing house owned wholly by its employees.

The text of this book is composed in Fairfield Medium with the display set in Bernhard Modern.
Book design by Antonina Krass.
Production manager: Eric Pier-Hocking.

Library of Congress Cataloging-in-Publication Data

Burgess, Anthony, 1917–1993.
   A clockwork orange : authoritative text backgrounds and contexts criticism / Anthony Burgess ; edited by Mark Rawlinson.
       p.   cm.—(A Norton critical edition)
   Includes bibliographical references.
   ISBN: 978-0-393-92809-9 (pbk.)
   1. Burgess, Anthony, 1917–1993. Clockwork orange.   2. Teenage boys—Fiction.   3. Criminals—Fiction.   4. Satire.   5. Kubrick, Stanley—Criticism and interpretation.   6. Clockwork orange (Motion picture)
I. Rawlinson, Mark.   II. Title.
   PR6052.U638C5 2011
823' .914—dc22   2010041349

W. W. Norton & Company, Inc., 500 Fifth Avenue, New York, N.Y. 10110
wwnorton.com

W. W. Norton & Company Ltd., Castle House, 75/76 Wells Street, London
W1T 3QT

4 5 6 7 8 9 0

Contents

Preface

Anthony Burgess's *A Clockwork Orange* is internationally famous, an iconic English-language novel of the second half of the twentieth century. But the book was little known when, in 1972, the sensational reception of an extraordinary film by Stanley Kubrick projected it into notoriety. Subsequently, the director withdrew himself, and in Britain also withdrew his film from circulation, in a tacit protest against the controversy-mongering by journalists and politicians. Anthony Burgess found himself defending a work he'd written ten years previously. What is more, the story he'd written was brought to a wider public through a screen adaptation of the twenty-chapter North American version, and not the twenty-one-chapter novel, with a very different ending, which Burgess had published in the UK in 1962. The Norton Critical Edition of *A Clockwork Orange* follows Norton's practice since 1987 of restoring the twenty-first chapter to the North American edition of the novel. Readers of the novel can now, for the first time, interpret decisions about the form of *A Clockwork Orange* (both Norton's, and later Kubrick's) in the context of the author's changing evaluation of his own fiction and of his motives in writing it.

Depending on your point of view, when Burgess found himself sole defender of the integrity of an adapted and truncated work of fiction, he was either being unjustly punished for his authorship or enjoying the opportunity to make authorative interventions in his work's unanticipated afterlife. The film's continuing notoriety was the occasion for the novelist to explain and interpret his fiction, and to reflect on its dissemination in print and on celluloid. Later Burgess would himself adapt the novel for stage performances, and these events were further opportunities to multiply his tangled but illuminating account of the work's genesis, linguistic distinctiveness, publication, and reception.

This edition incorporates contemporary documents that represent some of the cultural and historical concerns—ranging from delinquency to the morality of art—that *A Clockwork Orange* articulated. The selections of literary-critical comment on the novel demonstrate its thematic core—the political, psychological, and

religious meanings of free will—but also Burgess's range as an artist and the work's ramifications with more recent agendas in literary studies. The decision to include critical comment on Kubrick's
film acknowledges the importance of the extra-literary contexts in
which the meanings and significance of *A Clockwork Orange* have
been produced over the last fifty years. Andy Warhol's loose adaptation of the novel in his 1965 film *Vinyl* is one of the earliest examples
of homage to Alex. But it is the design and advertising of Kubrick's
film that has undeniably been the major determinant of the impact
of *A Clockwork Orange* on popular culture, music, and fashion. As
well as illustrating the dialogue between the novel and its industrial
and street-level appropriation, commentary on the film amplifies
more traditional literary analysis by reframing thematic and formal
questions in terms of adaptation, audience, and documented popular
reception.

Burgess declared that the reader's experience of the estranging
"Nadsat" slang spoken by Alex and his "droogs" was a significant
formal complement to the novel's thematic content. He alleged that
by learning Nadsat subliminally, in the context of following both
Alex's story and Alex's narration, his readers were experiencing something akin to the processes of "brain-washing." The analogy may be
weak, but it implies authorial disfavour of the kind of apparatus—
supplying English equivalents for Nadsat terms—which Stanley
Hyman created for the first U.S. paperback edition of *A Clockwork
Orange*, and that was subsequently reproduced in the UK Penguin
edition following the release of *Stanley Kubrick's A Clockwork Orange*.
This edition has a different kind of glossary, one which indicates
the Russian-language roots of the youth lexicon that Burgess invented
for the novel. The juxtaposition of Nadsat and Russian terms is
intended to help the reader appreciate Burgess's auditory and verbal
imagination, rather than to rule on the semantic properties of Nadsat. This glossary draws on the *Collins Gem* dictionary Burgess used
at the time of his visit to the Soviet Union to indicate the sounds that
the author was experimenting with, as well as his dictionary's translations of the Russian words that his Nadsat terms ultimately derive
from.

MARK RAWLINSON

Acknowledgments

I am grateful to the late Liana Burgess for her support for the Norton Critical Edition of *A Clockwork Orange*. Anthony Burgess's biographer Andrew Biswell, together with Alan Roughley of the International Anthony Burgess Centre, Manchester, have offered invaluable help and encouragement throughout the preparation of this edition. I would also like to thank all the delegates at the Burgess conferences in Angers in 2004 and Manchester in 2005 for welcoming me to their international community of Burgess scholarship, and for their generosity with ideas and advice. As ever, I have had great help in finding printed materials from the staff of the David Wilson Library, University of Leicester, and of the Upper Reading Room in the Bodleian Library, University of Oxford. My colleague Martin Stannard first encouraged me to take on this edition (his Norton edition of Ford's *The Good Soldier* was a dauntingly impressive example to follow), and successive Heads of the School of English at the University of Leicester (Richard Foulkes and Martin Halliwell) have supported my work on it. Working with W. W. Norton & Company has been an object lesson in how books should be made. I'd particularly like to thank Alan Cameron (in London), Carol Bemis, Rivka Genesen, Ben Reynolds, and Marian Johnson. Julian North and Marion North offered generous assistance in the last days. I am most thankful for the opportunity that has arisen from this commission by Norton to read and reread the novels and other writings of Anthony Burgess: a rare pleasure.

Abbreviations

AB	Anthony Burgess
OED	*The Oxford English Dictionary*, 2e
TS	Typescript of *A Clockwork Orange*, with marginal insertions in the author's hand. William Ready Division of Archives and Research Collections, McMaster University Library, Hamilton, Ontario, Anthony Burgess, Box 1.
Norton 1987	Anthony Burgess, *A Clockwork Orange* (New York: Norton, 1987)
Norton 1995	Anthony Burgess, *A Clockwork Orange* (New York: Norton, 1995)
Heinemann	Anthony Burgess, *A Clockwork Orange* (London: Heinemann, 1962)

The Text of
A CLOCKWORK ORANGE[1,2]

1. TS i, half title: "*A Clockwork Orange* is the [autograph add. "scarifying"] autobiographi-
   cal confession of Alex, a juvenile delinquent of the unspecified but not very distant
   future, who tells the tale of his own criminal excesses and his 're-education' in the peculiar slang of his generation. It will take the reader no more than fifteen pages to master
   and revel in the expressive language of 'nadsat'; after that he has before him an easily
   digestible feast of picaresque villainy and social satire. The book can be read as a
   straight horror comedy or, on a deeper level, as a fable of good and evil and the importance of human choice. As the genial Alex himself might put it, 'It is a horrorshow story,
   which will either make you smeck like bezoomy or bring the old tears to your glazzies.'"
2. TS iii, title page: line drawing of an orange revealing "clockwork" internal parts.

Part One

I[3]

'What's it going to be then, eh?'

There was me, that is Alex, and my three droogs, that is Pete, Georgie, and Dim, Dim being really dim, and we sat in the Korova Milkbar making up our rassoodocks what to do with the evening, a flip dark chill winter bastard though dry. The Korova Milkbar was a milkplus mesto, and you may, O my brothers, have forgotten what these mestos were like, things changing so skorry these days and everybody very quick to forget, newspapers not being read much neither. Well, what they sold there was milk plus something else. They had no licence for selling liquor, but there was no law yet against prodding some of the new veshches which they used to put into the old moloko, so you could peet it with vellocet or synthemesc or drencrom or one or two other veshches which would give you a nice quiet horrorshow fifteen minutes admiring Bog And All His Holy Angels And Saints in your left shoe with lights bursting all over your mozg.[4] Or you could peet milk with knives in it, as we used to say, and this would sharpen you up and make you ready for a bit of dirty twenty-to-one, and that was what we were peeting this evening I'm starting off the story with.

Our pockets were full of deng, so there was no real need from the point of view of crasting any more pretty polly to tolchock some old veck in an alley and viddy him swim in his blood while we counted the takings and divided by four, nor to do the ultra-violent on some shivering starry grey-haired ptitsa in a shop and go smecking off with the till's guts. But, as they say, money isn't everything.

The four of us were dressed in the heighth[5] of fashion, which in those days was a pair of black very tight tights with the old jelly

---

3. In Heinemann, the 1962 first UK edition, the three sections of the novel are separated by pages bearing a box with an arabic numeral, 1 through 3. The same sized boxes, containing arabic numerals 1 through 7, are employed by analogy with the large, decorated initial capital letters in illuminated manuscripts, on the first page of each chapter.
4. TS 1: autograph marginal gloss: "мозг?"
5. Archaism with which Burgess marks the linguistic distinctiveness of Alex's narrative voice.

mould, as we called it, fitting on the crutch underneath the tights, this being to protect and also a sort of a design you could viddy clear enough in a certain light, so that I had one in the shape of a spider, Pete had a rooker[6] (a hand, that is), Georgie had a very fancy one of a flower, and poor old Dim had a very hound-and-horny one of a clown's litso (face, that is), Dim not ever having much of an idea of things and being, beyond all shadow of a doubting thomas, the dimmest of we four. Then we wore waisty jackets without lapels but with these very big built-up shoulders ('pletchoes' we called them) which were a kind of a mockery of having real shoulders like that. Then, my brothers, we had these off-white cravats which looked like whipped-up kartoffel or spud with a sort of a design made on it with a fork. We wore our hair not too long and we had flip horrorshow boots for kicking.

'What's it going to be then, eh?'

There were three devotchkas sitting at the counter all together, but there were four of us malchicks and it was usually like one for all and all for one. These sharps were dressed in the heighth of fashion too, with purple and green and orange wigs on their gullivers, each one not costing less than three or four weeks of those sharps' wages, I should reckon, and make-up to match (rainbows round the glazzies,[7] that is, and the rot[8] painted very wide). Then they had long black very straight dresses, and on the groody part of them they had little badges of like silver with different malchicks' names on them—Joe and Mike and suchlike. These were supposed to be the names of the different malchicks they'd spatted with before they were fourteen. They kept looking our way and I nearly felt like saying the three of us (out of the corner of my rot, that is) should go off for a bit of pol and leave poor old Dim behind, because it would be just a matter of kupetting[9] Dim a demi-litre of white but this time with a dollop of synthemesc in it, but that wouldn't really have been playing like the game. Dim was very very ugly and like his name, but he was a horrorshow filthy fighter and very handy with the boot.

'What's it going to be then, eh?'

The chelloveck sitting next to me, there being this long big plushy seat that ran round three walls, was well away with his glazzies glazed and sort of burbling slovos like 'Aristotle wishy washy works outing cyclamen get forficulate[1] smartish'. He was in the land all right, well away, in orbit, and I knew what it was like, having tried it like

6. TS 1: autograph marginal gloss: "рукá."
7. TS 2: marginal ink drawing of eye.
8. TS 2: marginal ink drawing of pursed lips.
9. TS 2: reads "koopeeting"
1. *OED*: "*v. intr.* To have a 'creeping' sensation, as if a *forficula* or earwig were crawling over one's skin."

everybody else had done, but at this time I'd got to thinking it was
a cowardly sort of a veshch, O my brothers. You'd lay there after you'd
drunk the old moloko and then you got the messel[2] that everything
all round you was sort of in the past. You could viddy it all right, all
of it, very clear—tables, the stereo,[3] the lights, the sharps and the
malchicks—but it was like some veshch that used to be there but
was not there not no more. And you were sort of hypnotized by your
boot or shoe or a finger-nail as it might be, and at the same time you
were sort of picked up by the old scruff and shook like it might be a
cat. You got shook and shook till there was nothing left. You lost your
name and your body and your self and you just didn't care, and you
waited till your boot or your finger-nail got yellow, then yellower and
yellower all the time. Then the lights started cracking like atomics
and the boot or finger-nail or, as it might be, a bit of dirt on your
trouser-bottom turned into a big big big mesto, bigger than the
whole world, and you were just going to get introduced to old Bog or
God when it was all over. You came back to here and now whimpering sort of, with your rot all squaring up for a boohoohoo. Now,
that's very nice but very cowardly. You were not put on this earth
just to get in touch with God. That sort of thing could sap all the
strength and the goodness out of a chelloveck.

'What's it going to be then, eh?'

voice

The stereo was on and you got the idea that the singer's goloss was
moving from one part of the bar to another, flying up to the ceiling
and then swooping down again and whizzing from wall to wall. It was
Berti Laski[4] rasping a real starry oldie called 'You Blister My Paint'.[5]
One of the three ptitsas[6] at the counter, the one with the green wig,
kept pushing her belly out and pulling it in in time to what they
called the music. I could feel the knives in the old moloko starting
to prick, and now I was ready for a bit of twenty-to-one. So I yelped:
'Out out out out!' like a doggie, and then I cracked this veck who
was sitting next to me and well away and burbling a horrorshow
crack on the ooko or earhole, but he didn't feel it and went on with
his 'Telephonic hardware and when the farfarculule gets rubadub-
dub'. He'd feel it all right when he came to, out of the land.

'Where out?' said Georgie.

2. TS 3: autograph marginal comment, "Check this"
3. Stereo sound (usually binaural) was not new—Disney's *Fantasia* (1940) was exhibited
   using a process called Fantasound—but two-channel recorded discs were not easily
   manufactured, and were not presented to the market before 1958. See Greg Milner,
   Perfecting Sound Forever: An Aural History of Recorded Music (New York: Faber and
   Faber, 2009), 143–44.
4. An allusion to Harold Laski (1893–1950), the Manchester-born Jewish Marxist, Socialist politician, and political theorist.
5. For Burgess's 1987 lyric with this title, see http://theburgessproject.blogspot.com/
   2006/10/you-blister-my-paint.html.
6. TS 3: autograph marginal gloss, "птица птиста (latter word erased) check"

'Oh, just to keep walking,' I said, 'and viddy what turns up, O my little brothers.'

So we scatted out into the big winter nochy and walked down Marghanita Boulevard[7] and then turned into Boothby Avenue[8] and there we found what we were pretty well looking for, a malenky jest to start off the evening with. There was a doddery starry schoolmaster type veck, glasses on and his rot open to the cold nochy air. He had books under his arm and a crappy umbrella and was coming round the corner from the Public Biblio, which not many lewdies used those days. You never really saw many of the older bourgeois type out after nightfall those days, what with the shortage of police and we fine young malchickiwicks about, and this prof type chelloveck was the only one walking in the whole of the street. So we goolied up to him, very polite, and I said: 'Pardon me, brother.'

He looked a malenky bit poogly when he viddied the four of us like that, coming up so quiet and polite and smiling, but he said: 'Yes? What is it?' in a very loud teacher-type goloss, as if he was trying to show us he wasn't poogly. I said:

'I see you have books under your arm, brother. It is indeed a rare pleasure these days to come across somebody that still reads, brother.'

'Oh,' he said, all shaky. 'Is it? Oh, I see.' And he kept looking from one to the other of we four, finding himself now like in the middle of a very smiling and polite square.

'Yes,' I said. 'It would interest me greatly, brother, if you would kindly allow me to see what books those are that you have under your arm. I like nothing better in this world than a good clean book, brother.'

'Clean,' he said. 'Clean, eh?' And then Pete skvatted these three books from him and handed them round real skorry. Being three, we all had one each to viddy at except for Dim. The one I had was called *Elementary Crystallography*,[9] so I opened it up and said: 'Excellent, really first-class,' keeping turning the pages. Then I said in a very shocked type goloss: 'But what is this here? What is this filthy slovo? I blush to look at this word. You disappoint me, brother, you do really.'

'But,' he tried, 'but, but.'

'Now,' said Georgie, 'here is what I should call real dirt. There's one slovo beginning with an f and another with a c.' He had a book called *The Miracle of the Snowflake*.

---

7. TS 4: autograph marginal comment, "How about Laski?" Marghanita Laski (1915–1988), atheist writer and journalist, and panelist on popular BBC television shows; niece of Harold Laski.

8. Allusion to Robert, Lord Boothby (1900–1986), politician, British delegate to the Consultative Assembly of the Council of Europe (later the European Economic Community, then the European Union; 1949–57), made Baron Boothby in 1958.

9. Martin J. Buerger's *Elementary Crystallography: An Introduction to the Fundamental Geometrical Features of Crystals* appeared in 1956 from Chapman & Hall, publisher of Evelyn Waugh's novels. The mineral buergerite was named after the author.

'Oh,' said poor old Dim, smotting over Pete's shoulder and going too far, like he always did, 'it says here what he done to her, and there's a picture and all. Why,' he said, 'you're nothing but a filthy-minded old skitebird.'

'An old man of your age, brother,' I said, and I started to rip up the book I'd got, and the others did the same with the ones they had, Dim and Pete doing a tug-of-war with *The Rhombohedral*[1] *System*. The starry prof type began to creech: 'But those are not mine, those are the property of the municipality, this is sheer wantonness and vandal work,' or some such slovos. And he tried to sort of wrest the books back off of us, which was like pathetic. 'You deserve to be taught a lesson, brother,' I said, 'that you do.' This crystal book I had was very tough-bound and hard to razrez to bits, being real starry and made in days when things were made to last like, but I managed to rip the pages up and chuck them in handfuls of like snowflakes, though big, all over this creeching old veck, and then the others did the same with theirs, old Dim just dancing about like the clown he was. 'There you are,' said Pete. 'There's the mackerel of the cornflake for you, you dirty reader of filth and nastiness.'

'You naughty old veck, you,' I said, and then we began to filly about with him. Pete held his rookers and Georgie sort of hooked his rot wide open for him and Dim yanked out his false zoobies, upper and lower. He threw these down on the pavement and then I treated them to the old bootcrush, though they were hard bastards like, being made of some new horrorshow plastic stuff. The old veck began to make sort of chumbling shooms—'wuf waf wof'—so Georgie let go of holding his goobers apart and just let him have one in the toothless rot with his ringy fist, and that made the old veck start moaning a lot then, then out comes the blood, my brothers, real beautiful. So all we did then was to pull his outer platties off, stripping him down to his vest and long underpants (very starry; Dim smecked his head off near), and then Pete kicks him lovely in his pot, and we let him go. He went sort of staggering off, it not having been too hard of a tol-chock really, going 'Oh oh oh', not knowing where or what was what really, and we had a snigger at him and then riffled through his pockets, Dim dancing round with his crappy umbrella meanwhile, but there wasn't much in them. There were a few starry letters, some of them dating right back to 1960, with 'My dearest dearest' in them and all that chepooka, and a keyring and a starry leaky pen. Old Dim gave up his umbrella dance and of course had to start reading one of the letters out loud, like to show the empty street he could read. 'My darling one,' he recited, in this very high type goloss, 'I shall be thinking of you while you are away and hope you will remember to wrap

---

1. A rhombohedron is a three-dimensional figure with faces of lozenges or diamonds; technically, each face is a rhombus, with four sides of equal length.

up warm when you go out at night.' Then he let out a very shoomny smeck—'Ho ho ho'—pretending to start wiping his yahma with it. 'All right,' I said. 'Let it go, O my brothers.' In the trousers of this starry veck there was only a malenky bit of cutter (money, that is)—not more than three gollies—so we gave all his messy little coin the scatter treatment, it being hen-korm to the amount of pretty polly we had on us already. Then we smashed the umbrella and razrezzed[2] his platties and gave them to the blowing winds, my brothers, and then we'd finished with the starry teacher type veck. We hadn't done much, I know, but that was only like the start of the evening and I make no appy polly loggies to thee or thine for that. The knives in the milk-plus were stabbing away nice and horrorshow now.

The next thing was to do the sammy act, which was one way to unload some of our cutter so we'd have more of an incentive like for some shop-crasting, as well as it being a way of buying an alibi in advance, so we went into the Duke of New York[3] on Amis[4] Avenue and sure enough in the snug there were three or four old baboochkas peeting their black and suds on SA[5] (State Aid). Now we were the very good malchicks, smiling good evensong to one and all, though these wrinkled old lighters started to get all shook, their veiny old rookers all trembling round their glasses and making the suds spill on the table. 'Leave us be, lads,' said one of them, her face all mappy with being a thousand years old, 'we're only poor old women.' But we just made with the zoobies, flash flash flash, sat down, rang the bell, and waited for the boy to come. When he came, all nervous and rubbing his rookers on his grazzy apron, we ordered us four veterans—a veteran being rum and cherry brandy mixed, which was popular just then, some liking a dash of lime in it, that being the Canadian variation. Then I said to the boy:

'Give these poor old baboochkas over there a nourishing something. Large Scotchmen all round and something to take away.' And I poured my pocket of deng all over the table, and the other three did likewise, O my brothers. So double firegolds were brought in for the scared starry lighters, and they knew not what to do or say. One of them got out 'Thanks, lads,' but you could see they thought there was

2. TS 6: autograph marginal gloss, "Check разрез"
3. A title first created in the fourteenth century and usually granted to the second son of the Monarch, the Duke of York is hence a common name for inns, public houses, and other premises licensed for the sale of intoxicating liquor. The futuristic ironies of Burgess's pub name are picked up by the name of the gang leader the Duke of New York, played by the southern soul singer Isaac Hayes in John Carpenter's 1981 film *Escape from New York*.
4. An allusion to Kingsley Amis (1922–1995), a British author whose first novel, *Lucky Jim*, a comedy of provincial academic life, was a popular and critical success in 1954, and became iconic of a literary generation known as The Movement or the Angry Young Men (from John Osborne's 1956 play *Look Back in Anger*).
5. SA is the acronym for the *Sturmabteilung*, Hitler's brownshirts (to distinguish the members of this paramilitary organization from the black-and-brown uniformed SS).

something dirty like coming. Anyway, they were each given a bottle of Yank General,[6] cognac that is, to take away, and I gave money for them to be delivered each a dozen of black and suds that following morning, they to leave their stinking old cheenas' addresses at the counter. Then with the cutter that was left over we did purchase, my brothers, all the meat pies, pretzels, cheese-snacks, crisps and choc-bars in that mesto, and those too were for the old sharps. Then we said: 'Back in a minoota,' and the old ptitsas were still saying: 'Thanks, lads,' and 'God bless you, boys,' and we were going out without one cent of cutter in our carmans.

'Makes you feel real dobby, that does,' said Pete. You could viddy that poor old Dim the dim didn't quite pony all that, but he said nothing for fear of being called gloopy and a domeless wonderboy. Well, we went off now round the corner to Attlee Avenue,[7] and there was this sweets and cancers[8] shop still open. We'd left them alone near three months now and the whole district had been very quiet on the whole, so the armed millicents or rozz[9] patrols weren't round there much, being more north of the river these days. We put our maskies on—new jobs these were, real horrorshow, wonderfully done really; they were like faces of historical personalities (they gave you the name when you bought) and I had Disraeli, Pete had Elvis Presley, Georgie had Henry VIII and poor old Dim had a poet veck called Peebee Shelley;[1] they were a real like disguise, hair and all, and they were some very special plastic veshch so you could roll up when you'd done with it and hide it in your boot—then three of us went in,

6. TS 7: autograph line drawing of the three stars of a Lieutenant-General in the United States Army. The stars on bottles of Cognac indicate the duration of the ageing process: three-star or VS (Very Special) Cognac is the youngest, but must be more than two years old.

7. Clement Attlee (1883–1967), socialist Prime Minister (1945–51) after the Labour Party's landslide election victory following VE (Victory in Europe) Day. Attlee was associated with such policies as the Keynesian ideal of full employment, the nationalization of industry, and the creation of the National Health Service as part of a Welfare State; he was also an atheist.

8. The scientific association of smoking and cancer is sometimes assumed to be more recent than it is, an effect of tobacco industry lobbying. Richard Doll, who would become a leading epidemiologist, coauthored "Smoking and carcinoma of the lung; Preliminary report" in the 1950 *British Medical Journal*, but the correlation had been observed as early as the 1920s. In 1964, a report commissioned by the United States Surgeon General Luther Terry demonstrated a causal link between smoking and both cancer and emphysema, resulting in the introduction of the Surgeon General's health warning on cigarette packaging. *OED* has an example of "cancer-stick" from 1959, in Angry-Young-Man novelist John Braine's second novel, *The Vodi*.

9. *OED* has an example of "rozzer," the English slang term for policeman, from 1893. The etymology is unknown.

1. The masks represent Benjamin Disraeli (1804–1881), the Jewish Victorian Prime Minister who created the Conservative Party; a rock and roll vocalist widely known as The King (1935–1977); a Tudor Monarch (1491–1547); and Percy Bysshe Shelley (1792–1822), Romantic poet notorious for his atheism and radicalism. TS 8: autograph marginal comment, "Will this name [Presley] be known when the book appears?" Presley had a huge impact, creating new musical audiences in the mid-1950s, but his iconic status was not assured by 1962.

Puckle

Pete keeping chasso without, not that there was anything to worry about out there. As soon as we launched on the shop we went for Slouse who ran it, a big portwine jelly of a veck who viddied at once what was coming and made straight for the inside where the telephone was and perhaps his well-oiled pooshka, complete with six dirty rounds. Dim was round that counter skorry as a bird, sending packets of snoutie flying and cracking over a big cut-out showing a sharp with all her zoobies going flash at the customers and her groodies near hanging out to advertise some new brand of cancers. What you could viddy then was a sort of a big ball rolling into the inside of the shop behind the curtain, this being old Dim and Slouse sort of locked in a death struggle. Then you could slooshy panting and snoring and kicking behind the curtain and veshches falling over and swearing and then glass going smash smash smash. Mother Slouse, the wife, was sort of froze behind the counter. We could tell she would creech murder given one chance, so I was round that counter very skorry and had a hold of her, and a horrorshow big lump she was too, all nuking of scent and with flipflop big bobbing groodies on her. I'd got my rooker round her rot to stop her belting out death and destruction to the four winds of heaven, but this lady doggie gave me a large foul big bite on it and it was me that did the creeching, and then she opened up beautiful with a flip yell for the millicents. Well, then she had to be tolchocked proper with one of the weights for the scales, and then a fair tap with a crowbar they had for opening cases, and that brought the red out like an old friend. So we had her down on the floor and a rip of her platties for fun and a gentle bit of the boot to stop her moaning. And, viddying her lying there with her groodies on show, I wondered should I or not, but that was for later on in the evening. Then we cleaned the till, and there was flip horrorshow takings that nochy, and we had a few packs of the very best top cancers apiece, then off we went, my brothers.

'A real big heavy great bastard he was,' Dim kept saying. I didn't like the look of Dim; he looked dirty and untidy, like a veck who'd been in a fight, which he had been, of course, but you should never *look* as though you have been. His cravat was like someone had trampled on it, his maskie had been pulled off and he had floor-dirt on his litso, so we got him in an alleyway and tidied him up a malenky bit, soaking our tashtooks in spit to cheest the dirt off. The things we did for old Dim. We were back in the Duke of New York very skorry, and I reckoned by my watch we hadn't been more than ten minutes away. The starry old baboochkas were still there on the black and suds and Scotchmen we'd bought them, and we said: 'Hallo there, girlies, what's it going to be?' They started on the old 'Very kind, lads, God bless you, boys,' and so we rang the collocoll and brought a different waiter in this time and we ordered beers with rum in, being

sore athirst, my brothers, and whatever the old ptitsas wanted. Then
I said to the old baboochkas: 'We haven't been out of here, have we?
Been here all the time, haven't we?' They all caught on real skorry
and said:

'That's right, lads. Not been out of our sight, you haven't. God bless
you, boys,' drinking.

Not that it mattered much, really. About half an hour went by
before there was any sign of life among the millicents, and then it
was only two very young rozzes that came in, very pink under their
big copper's shlemmies. One said:

'You lot know anything about the happenings at Slouse's shop
this night?'

'Us?' I said, innocent. 'Why, what happened?'

'Stealing and roughing. Two hospitalizations. Where've you lot
been this evening?'

'I don't go for that nasty tone,' I said. 'I don't care much for these
nasty insinuations. A very suspicious nature all this betokeneth, my
little brothers.'

'They've been in here all night, lads,' the old sharps started to
creech out. 'God bless them, there's no better lot of boys living for
kindness and generosity. Been here all the time they have. Not seen
them move we haven't.'

'We're only asking,' said the other young millicent. 'We've got our
job to do like anyone else.' But they gave us the nasty warning look
before they went out. As they were going out we handed them a bit
of lip-music: brrrrzzzzrrrr. But, myself, I couldn't help a bit of disappointment at things as they were those days. Nothing to fight against
really. Everything as easy as kiss-my-sharries. Still, the night was still
very young.[2]

2

When we got outside of the Duke of New York we viddied, by the
main bar's long lighted window, a burbling old pyahnitsa or drunkie,
howling away at the filthy songs of his fathers and going blerp blerp
in between as it might be a filthy old orchestra in his stinking rotten
guts. One veshch I could never stand was that. I could never stand to
see a moodge all filthy and rolling and burping and drunk, whatever
his age might be, but more especially when he was real starry like
this one was. He was sort of flattened to the wall and his platties
were a disgrace, all creased and untidy and covered in cal and mud
and filth and stuff. So we got hold of him and cracked him with a

2. TS 10: autograph sketch of masked head at the foot of the page.

few good horrorshow tolchocks, but he still went on singing. The song went:

> And I will go back to my darling, my darling,
> When you, my darling, are gone.

But when Dim fisted him a few times on his filthy drunkard's rot he shut up singing and started to creech: 'Go on, do me in, you bastard cowards, I don't want to live anyway, not in a stinking world like this one.' I told Dim to lay off a bit then, because it used to interest me sometimes to slooshy what some of these starry decreps had to say about life and the world. I said: 'Oh. And what's stinking about it?'

He cried out: 'It's a stinking world because it lets the young get on to the old like you done, and there's no law nor order no more.' He was creeching out loud and waving his rookers and making real horrorshow with the slovos, only the odd blurp blurp coming from his keeshkas, like something was orbiting within, or like some very rude interrupting sort of a moodge making a shoom, so that this old veck kept sort of threatening it with his fists, shouting: 'It's no world for any old man any longer,[1] and that means that I'm not one bit scared of you, my boyos, because I'm too drunk to feel the pain if you hit me, and if you kill me I'll be glad to be dead.' We smecked and then grinned but said nothing, and then he said: 'What sort of a world is it at all? Men on the moon[2] and men spinning round the earth[3] like it might be midges round a lamp, and there's not no attention paid to earthly law nor order no more. So your worst you may do, you filthy cowardly hooligans.' Then he gave us some lip-music—'Prrrrzzzzrrrr'—like we'd done to those young millicents, and then he started singing again:

> O dear dear land, I fought for thee
> And brought thee peace and victory—

So we cracked into him lovely, grinning all over our litsos, but he still went on singing. Then we tripped him so he laid down flat and heavy and a bucketload of beer-vomit came whooshing out. That was disgusting so we gave him the boot, one go each, and then it was blood, not song nor vomit, that came out of his filthy old rot. Then we went on our way.

---

1. Compare the opening of W. B. Yeats's 1928 poem "Sailing to Byzantium": "That is no country for old men."
2. NASA did not put men on the moon until 1969, but President John F. Kennedy vowed before Congress on May 25, 1961, to put a man on the moon by the end of the decade. While the moon became the Cold-War grail of U.S. science policy, the public imagination was shackled to much earlier visions of lunar exploration: the 1964 film *First Men in the Moon* was based on H. G. Wells's scientific romance from 1901.
3. The first man in earth orbit was the Soviet cosmonaut Yuri Gagarin (1934–1968). News of Gagarin's mission on April 12, 1961, shocked the United States into massive retaliatory investment in space technology.

It was round by the Municipal Power Plant[4] that we came across Billyboy and his five droogs. Now in those days, my brothers, the teaming up was mostly by fours or fives, these being like auto-teams, four being a comfy number for an auto, and six being the outside limit for gang-size. Sometimes gangs would gang up so as to make like malenky armies for big night-war, but mostly it was best to roam in these like small numbers. Billyboy was something that made me want to sick just to viddy his fat grinning litso, and he always had this von of very stale oil that's been used for frying over and over, even when he was dressed in his best platties, like now. They viddied us just as we viddied them, and there was like a very quiet kind of watching each other now. This would be real, this would be proper, this would be the nozh, the oozy, the britva, not just fisties and boots. Billyboy and his droogs stopped what they were doing, which was just getting ready to perform something on a weepy young devotchka they had there, not more than ten, she creeching away but with her platties still on, Billyboy holding her by one rooker and his number-one, Leo, holding the other. They'd probably just been doing the dirty slovo part of the act before getting down to a malenky bit of ultra-violence. When they viddied us a-coming they let go of this boo-hooing little ptitsa, there being plenty more where she came from, and she ran with her thin white legs flashing through the dark, still going 'Oh oh oh'. I said, smiling very wide and droogie: 'Well, if it isn't fat stinking billygoat Billyboy in poison. How art thou, thou globby bottle of cheap stinking chip-oil?[5] Come and get one in the yarbles, if you have any yarbles, you eunuch jelly, thou.' And then we started.

There were four of us to six of them, like I have already indicated, but poor old Dim, for all his dimness, was worth three of the others in sheer madness and dirty fighting. Dim had a real horrorshow length of oozy or chain round his waist, twice wound round, and he unwound this and began to swing it beautiful in the eyes or glazzies. Pete and Georgie had good sharp nozhes, but I for my own part had a fine starry horrorshow cut-throat britva which, at that time, I could flash and shine artistic. So there we were dratsing away in the dark, the old Luna with men on it just coming up, the stars stabbing away as it might be knives anxious to join in the dratsing. With my britva I managed to slit right down the front of one of Billyboy's droog's platties, very very neat and not even touching the plott under the cloth. Then in the dratsing this droog of Billyboy's suddenly found himself all opened up like a peapod, with his belly bare and his poor old yarbles showing, and then he got very very razdraz, waving and screaming and losing his guard and letting in old Dim with his chain snaking

4. Compare T.S. Eliot's *The Waste Land* (1922), line 190, "round behind the gashouse."
5. Animal or vegetable fat in which potatoes are fried.

whissssshhhhhhhhh, so that old Dim chained him right in the glazzies, and this droog of Billyboy's went tottering off and howling his heart out. We were doing very horrorshow, and soon we had Billyboy's number-one down underfoot, blinded with old Dim's chain and crawling and howling about like an animal, but with one fair boot on the gulliver he was out and out and out.

Of the four of us Dim, as usual, came out the worst in point of looks, that is to say his litso was all bloodied and his platties a dirty mess, but the others of us were still cool and whole. It was stinking fatty Billyboy I wanted now, and there I was dancing about with my britva like I might be a barber on board a ship on a very rough sea, trying to get in at him with a few fair slashes on his unclean oily litso. Billyboy had a nozh, a long flick-type, but he was a malenky bit too slow and heavy in his movements to vred anyone really bad. And, my brothers, it was real satisfaction to me to waltz—left two three, right two three—and carve left cheeky and right cheeky, so that like two curtains of blood seemed to pour out at the same time, one on either side of his fat filthy oily snout in the winter starlight. Down this blood poured in like red curtains, but you could viddy Billyboy felt not a thing, and he went lumbering on like a filthy fatty bear, poking at me with his nozh.

Then we slooshied the sirens and knew the millicents were coming with pooshkas pushing out of the police-auto-windows at the ready. That little weepy devotchka had told them, no doubt, there being a box for calling the rozzes not too far behind the Muni Power Plant. 'Get you soon, fear not,' I called, 'stinking billygoat. I'll have your yarbles off lovely.' Then off they ran, slow and panting, except for Number One Leo out snoring on the ground, away north towards the river, and we went the other way. Just round the next turning was an alley, dark and empty and open at both ends, and we rested there, panting fast then slower, then breathing like normal. It was like resting between the feet of two terrific and very enormous mountains, these being the flat-blocks,[6] and in the windows of all of the flats you could viddy like blue dancing light. This would be the telly. Tonight was what they called a worldcast,[7] meaning that the same programme was being viddied by everybody in the world that wanted to, that being mostly the middle-aged middle-class lewdies. There would be

---

6. In Britain, tower blocks or high-rise apartment buildings of between ten and thirty storeys are associated with post–World War II public-housing projects. High rises were a rationalist and modernist architectural solution to the housing shortage—part of a policy of slum clearance as well as of redevelopment of bomb-damaged areas—but they generated rather than solved social problems, some becoming ghettos of poverty.
7. This neologism aniticipates global television audiences: the Apollo 11 moon landing in 1969 is one of the earliest examples of a live broadcast event that synchronized the attention of hundreds of millions of people around the globe.

some big famous stupid comic chelloveck or black singer, and it was all being bounced off the special telly satellites[8] in outer space, my brothers. We waited panting, and we could slooshy the sirening mil-licents going east, so we knew we were all right now. But poor old Dim kept looking up at the stars and planets and the Luna with his rot wide open like a kid who'd never viddied any such thing before, and he said:

'What's on them, I wonder. What would be up there on things like that?'

I nudged him hard, saying: 'Come, gloopy bastard as thou art. Think thou not on them. There'll be life like down here most likely, with some getting knifed and others doing the knifing. And now, with the nochy still molodoy, let us be on our way, O my brothers.' The others smecked at this, but poor old Dim looked at me serious, then up again at the stars and the Luna. So we went on our way down the alley, with the worldcast blueing on on either side. What we needed now was an auto, so we turned left coming out of the alley, knowing right away we were in Priestley[9] Place as soon as we viddied the big bronze statue of some starry poet with an apey upper lip and a pipe stuck in a droopy old rot. Going north we came to the filthy old Film-drome, peeling and dropping to bits through nobody going[1] there much except malchicks like me and my droogs, and then only for a yell or a razrez or a bit of in-out-in-out in the dark. We could viddy from the poster on the Filmdrome's face, a couple of fly-dirted spots trained on it, that there was the usual cowboy riot, with the archan-gels on the side of the US marshal six-shooting at the rustlers out of hell's fighting legions, the kind of hound-and-horny veshch[2] put out by Statefilm[3] in those days. The autos parked by the sinny weren't all that horrorshow, crappy starry veshches most of them, but there was a newish Durango 95[4] that I thought might do. Georgie had one of these polyclefs, as they called them, on his keyring, so we were soon

---

8. The successful launch of the earth satellite Sputnik 1 on October 4, 1957, was the start-ing gun for the Space Race between the Soviet Union and the United States. The first satellite television signal was relayed by the commercial satellite Telstar #1, launched in 1962, and the first national satellite television network was established in Russia in 1967.
9. J.B. Priestley (1894–1984), socialist middle-brow novelist and broadcaster, famous for his wartime, Sunday-evening radio "Postscripts" interpreting the course of the war. Priestley's discussions of the new, planned society to be created after the war were so popular that Churchill reportedly ordered him taken off the air.
1. Cinemagoing in Britain fell from a peak at the end of World War II (1,640 million admissions in 1946) to 395 million admissions in 1962. (Figures drawn from the Brit-ish Film Institute website: www.screenonline.org.uk/film/facts/fact1.html.)
2. TS 15: autograph gloss "Вещ"
3. "Statefilm" has a Soviet air, but a number of western European film industries, includ-ing those in Britain and Germany, were state-supported.
4. Durango is a landlocked state of Mexico. The Ramones song "Durango 95" pays hom-age to Burgess's invention, which is ironically echoed in the automobile names in Martin Amis's novel *Money: A Suicide Note* (1984).

aboard—Dim and Pete at the back, puffing away lordly at their cancers—and I turned on the ignition and started her up and she grumbled away real horrorshow, a nice warm vibraty feeling grumbling all through your guttiwuts. Then I made with the noga, and we backed out lovely, and nobody viddied us take off.

We fillied round what was called the backtown for a bit, scaring old vecks and cheenas that were crossing the roads and zigzagging after cats and that. Then we took the road west. There wasn't much traffic about, so I kept pushing the old noga through the floorboards near, and the Durango 95 ate up the road like spaghetti. Soon it was winter trees and dark, my brothers, with a country dark, and at one place I ran over something big with a snarling toothy rot in the headlamps, then it screamed and squelched under and old Dim at the back near laughed his gulliver off—'Ho ho ho'—at that. Then we saw one young malchick with his sharp, lubbilubbing[5] under a tree, so we stopped and cheered at them, then we bashed into them both with a couple of half-hearted tolchocks, making them cry, and on we went. What we were after now was the old surprise visit. That was a real kick and good for smecks and lashings of the ultra-violent. We came at last to a sort of a village, and just outside this village was a small sort of a cottage on its own with a bit of a garden. The Luna was well up now, and we could viddy this cottage fine and clear as I eased up and put the brake on, the other three giggling like bezoomny, and we could viddy the name on the gate of this cottage veshch was HOME, a gloopy sort of a name. I got out of the auto, ordering my droogs to shush their giggles and act like serious, and I opened this malenky gate and walked up to the front door. I knocked nice and gentle and nobody came, so I knocked a bit more and this time I could slooshy somebody coming, then a bolt drawn, then the door inched open an inch or so, then I could viddy this one glaz looking out at me and the door was on a chain. 'Yes? Who is it?' It was a sharp's goloss, a young-ish devotchka by her sound, so I said in a very refined manner of speech, a real gentleman's goloss:

'Pardon, madam, most sorry to disturb you, but my friend and me were out for a walk, and my friend has taken bad all of a sudden with a very troublesome turn, and he is out there on the road dead out and groaning. Would you have the goodness to let me use your telephone to telephone for an ambulance?'

'We haven't a telephone,' said this devotchka. 'I'm sorry, but we haven't. You'll have to go somewhere else.' From inside this malenky cottage I could slooshy the clack clack clacky clack clack clackity clackclack of some veck typing away, and then the typing stopped and there was this chelloveck's goloss calling: 'What is it, dear?'

5. TS 16: autograph gloss, "Don't like this much."

'Well,' I said, 'could you of your goodness please let him have a cup of water? It's like a faint, you see. It seems as though he's passed out in a sort of a fainting fit.'

The devotchka sort of hesitated and then said: 'Wait.' Then she went off, and my three droogs had got out of the auto quiet and crept up horrorshow stealthy, putting their maskies on now, then I put mine on, then it was only a matter of me putting in the old rooker and undoing the chain, me having softened up this devotchka with my gent's goloss, so that she hadn't shut the door like she should have done, us being strangers of the night. The four of us then went roaring in, old Dim playing the shoot as usual with his jumping up and down and singing out dirty slovos, and it was a nice malenky cottage, I'll say that. We all went smecking into the room with a light on, and there was this devotchka sort of cowering, a young pretty bit of sharp with real horrorshow groodies on her, and with her was this chelloveck who was her moodge, youngish too with hornrimmed otchkies on him, and on a table was a typewriter and all papers scattered everywhere, but there was one little pile of paper like that must have been what he'd already typed, so here was another intelligent type bookman type like that we'd fillied with some hours back, but this one was a writer not a reader. Anyway, he said:

'What is this? Who are you? How dare you enter my house without permission.' And all the time his goloss was trembling and his rookers too. So I said:

'Never fear. If fear thou hast in thy heart, O brother, pray banish it forthwith.' Then Georgie and Pete went out to find the kitchen, while old Dim waited for orders, standing next to me with his rot wide open. 'What is this, then?' I said, picking up the pile like of typing from off of the table, and the horn-rimmed moodge said, dithering:

'That's just what I want to know. What *is* this? What do you want? Get out at once before I throw you out.' So poor old Dim, masked like Peebee Shelley, had a good loud smeck at that, roaring like some animal.

'It's a book,' I said. 'It's a book what you are writing.' I made the old goloss very coarse. 'I have always had the strongest admiration for them as can write books.' Then I looked at its top sheet, and there was the name—A CLOCKWORK ORANGE[6]—and I said: 'That's a fair gloopy title. Who ever heard of a clockwork orange?' Then I read a malenky bit out loud in a sort of very high type preaching goloss: '—The attempt to impose upon man, a creature of growth and capable of sweetness, to ooze juicily at the last round the bearded lips of God, to attempt to impose, I say, laws and conditions appropriate to

6. TS 18: autograph query, "ital?" and line drawing similar to the title page's orange revealing clockwork components.

a mechanical creation, against this I raise my swordpen—'[7] Dim
made the old lip-music at that and I had to smeck myself. Then I
started to tear up the sheets and scatter the bits over the floor, and
this writer moodge went sort of bezoomny and made for me with his
zoobies clenched and showing yellow and his nails ready for me like
claws. So that was old Dim's cue and he went grinning and going er er
and a a a for this veck's dithering rot, crack crack, first left fistie then
right, so that our dear old droog the red—red vino on tap and the
same in all places, like it's put out by the same big firm—started to
pour and spot the nice clean carpet and the bits of his book that I
was still ripping away at, razrez razrez. All this time this devotchka,
his loving and faithful wife, just stood like froze by the fireplace,
and then she started letting out little malenky creeches, like in time
to the like music of old Dim's fisty work. Then Georgie and Pete
came in from the kitchen, both munching away, though with their
maskies on, you could do that with them on and no trouble, Georgie with like a cold leg of something in one rooker and half a loaf of
kleb with a big dollop of maslo[8] on it in the other, and Pete with a
bottle of beer frothing its gulliver off and a horrorshow rookerful of
like plum cake. They went haw haw haw, viddying old Dim dancing
round and fisting the writer veck so that the writer veck started to
platch like his life's work was ruined, going boo hoo hoo with a very
square bloody rot, but it was haw haw haw in a muffled eater's way
and you could see bits of what they were eating. I didn't like that, it
being dirty and slobbery, so I said:
‘Drop that mounch. I gave no permission. Grab hold of this veck
here so he can viddy all and not get away.’ So they put down their
fatty pishcha on the table among all the flying paper and they clopped
over to the writer veck whose horn-rimmed otchkies were cracked
but still hanging on, with old Dim still dancing round and making
ornaments shake on the mantelpiece (I swept them all off then and
they couldn't shake no more, little brothers) while he fillied with the
author of *A Clockwork Orange*, making his litso all purple and dripping away like some very special sort of a juicy fruit. ‘All right, Dim,’
I said. ‘Now for the other veshch, Bog help us all.’ So he did the
strong-man on the devotchka, who was still creech creech creeching
away in very horrorshow four-in-a-bar, locking her rookers from the
back, while I ripped away at this and that and the other, the others
going haw haw haw still, and real good horrorshow groodies they
were that then exhibited their pink glazzies, O my brothers, while
I untrussed and got ready for the plunge. Plunging, I could slooshy

---

7. Cardinal Richelieu in Edward Bulwer-Lytton's 1839 play *Richelieu; Or the Conspiracy*
   delivers the best-known formulation of a proverbial contrast: "The pen is mightier than
   the sword."
8. TS 18: autograph query, "масло butter?"

cries of agony and this writer bleeding veck that Georgie and Pete held on to nearly got loose howling bezoomny with the filthiest of slovos that I already knew and others he was making up. Then after me it was right old Dim should have his turn, which he did in a beasty snorty howly sort of a way with his Peebee Shelley maskie taking no notice, while I held on to her. Then there was a changeover, Dim and me grabbing the slobbering writer veck who was past struggling really, only just coming out with slack sort of slovos like he was in the land in a milk-plus bar, and Pete and Georgie had theirs. Then there was like quiet and we were full of like hate, so smashed what was left to be smashed—typewriter, lamp, chairs—and Dim, it was typical of old Dim, watered the fire out and was going to dung on the carpet, there being plenty of paper, but I said no. 'Out out out out,' I howled. The writer veck and and his zheena[9] were not really there, bloody and torn and making noises. But they'd live.

So we got into the waiting auto and I left it to Georgie to take the wheel, me feeling that malenky bit shagged, and we went back to town, running over odd squealing things on the way.

<h1 style="text-align:center">3</h1>

We yeckated back townwards, my brothers, but just outside, not far from what they called the Industrial Canal, we viddied the fuel needle had like collapsed, like our own ha ha ha needles had, and the auto was coughing kashl kashl kashl. Not to worry overmuch, though, because a rail station kept flashing blue—on off on off—just near. The point was whether to leave the auto to be sobiratted by the rozzes or, us feeling like in a hate and murder mood, to give it a fair tolchock into the starry waters for a nice heavy loud plesk before the death of the evening. This latter we decided on, so we got out and, the brakes off, all four tolchocked it to the edge of the filthy water that was like treacle mixed with human hole products, then one good horrorshow tolchock and in she went. We had to dash back for fear of the filth splashing on our platties, but splussshhhh and glolp she went, down and lovely. 'Farewell, old droog,[1] called Georgie, and Dim obliged with a clowny great guff—'Huh huh huh huh.' Then we made for the station to ride the one stop to Center, as the middle of the town was called. We paid our fares nice and polite and waited gentlemanly and quiet on the platform, old Dim fillying with the slot machines, his carmans being full of small malenky coin, and ready if need be to distribute chocbars to the poor and starving, though

9. TS 20: autograph query, "better word? Жина (sic)"
1. TS 21: autograph query, "should be drook? Друг"

there was none such about, and then the old espresso rapido[2] came lumbering in and we climbed aboard, the train looking to be near empty. To pass the three-minute ride we fillied about with what they called the upholstery, doing some nice horrorshow tearing-out of the seats' guts and old Dim chaining the okno till the glass cracked and sparkled in the winter air, but we were all feeling that bit shagged and fagged and fashed, it having been an evening of some small energy expenditure, my brothers, only Dim, like the clowny animal he was, full of the joys-of, but looking all dirtied over and too much von of sweat on him, which was one thing I had against old Dim.

We got out at Center and walked slow back to the Korova Milkbar, all going yawwwww a malenky bit and exhibiting to moon and star and lamplight our back fillings, because we were still only growing malchicks and had school[3] in the daytime, and when we got into the Korova we found it fuller than when we'd left earlier on. But the chelloveck that had been burbling away, in the land, on white and synthemesc or whatever, was still on at it, going: 'Urchins of deadcast in the way-ho-hay glill platonic time weatherborn.' It was probable that this was his third or fourth lot that evening, for he had that pale inhuman look, like he'd become a *thing*, and like his litso was really a piece of chalk carved. Really, if he wanted to spend so long in the land, he should have gone into one of the private cubies at the back and not stayed in the big mesto, because here some of the malchickies would filly about with him a malenky bit, though not too much because there were powerful bruiseboys hidden away in the old Korova who could stop any riot. Anyway, Dim squeezed in next to this veck and, with his big clown's yawp that showed his hanging grape, he stabbed this veck's foot with his own large filthy sabog. But the veck, my brothers, heard nought, being now all above the body.

It was nadsats mostly milking and coking and fillying around (nadsats were what we used to call the teens),[4] but there were a few of the more starry ones, vecks and cheenas alike (but not of the bourgeois, never them) laughing and govoreeting at the bar. You could tell from their barberings and loose platties (big stringy sweaters mostly) that they'd been on rehearsal at the TV studios round the corner. The devotchkas among them had these very lively litsos and wide big rots, very red, showing a lot of teeth, and smecking away and not caring about the wicked world one whit. And then the disc on the stereo

---

2. The Italian State Railways (Ferrovie dello Stato) operates express (espresso) and non-stop InterCity (rapido) services, as well as stopping trains (locale, diretto). Burgess's slow-moving train is ironically named, but also picks up on the recent vogue for coffee bars in London, in particular for the Gaggia piston espresso machine, introduced to Britain in the early 1950s.

3. In the United Kingdom, the age for legally leaving school (the end of compulsory education) was lifted to fifteen in 1947; the present age of sixteen was established in 1972.

4. TS 22: autograph cancellation of text in parentheses cancelled with "OK, Stet."

twanged off and out (it was Jonny Zhivago,[5] a Russky koshka, singing 'Only Every Other Day'), and in the like interval, the short silence before the next one came on, one of these devotchkas—very fair and with a big smiling red rot and in her late thirties I'd say—suddenly came with a burst of singing, only a bar and a half and as though she was like giving an example of something they'd all been govoreeting about, and it was like for a moment, O my brothers, some great bird had flown into the milkbar, and I felt all the little malenky hairs on my plott standing endwise and the shivers crawling up like slow malenky lizards and then down again. Because I knew what she sang. It was from an opera by Friedrich Gitterfenster called *Das Bettzeug*,[6] and it was the bit where she's snuffing it with her throat cut, and the slovos are 'Better like this maybe'. Anyway, I shivered.

But old Dim, as soon as he'd slooshied this dollop of song like a lomtick of redhot meat plonked on your plate, let off one of his vulgarities, which in this case was a lip-trump followed by a dog-howl followed by two fingers pronging twice at the air followed by a clowny guffaw. I felt myself all of a fever and like drowning in redhot blood, slooshying and viddying Dim's vulgarity, and I said: 'Bastard. Filthy drooling mannerless bastard.' Then I leaned across Georgie, who was between me and horrible Dim, and fisted Dim skorry on the rot. Dim looked very surprised, his rot open, wiping the krovvy off of his goober with his rook and in turn looking surprised at the red flowing krovvy and at me. 'What for did you do that for?' he said in his ignorant way. Not many viddied what I'd done, and those that viddied cared not. The stereo was on again and was playing a very sick electronic guitar veshch. I said:

'For being a bastard with no manners and not the dook of an idea how to comport yourself publicwise, O my brother.'

Dim put on a hound-and-horny look of evil, saying: 'I don't like you should do what you done then. And I'm not your brother no more and wouldn't want to be.' He'd taken a big snotty tashtook from his pocket and was mopping the red flow puzzled, keeping on looking at it frowning as if he thought that blood was for other vecks and not for him. It was like he was singing blood to make up for his vulgarity when that devotchka was singing music. But that devotchka was smecking away ha ha ha now with her droogs at the bar, her red rot working and her zoobies ashine, not having noticed Dim's filthy vulgarity. It was me really Dim had done wrong to. I said:

---

5. The Russian poet Boris Pasternak (1890–1960) is best known for his novel of the Russian Revolution, *Doctor Zhivago*, first published in Italy in 1957; it won him the Nobel Prize for Literature, which Pasternak declined to accept. Zhivago, a doctor and poet, was played by Omar Sharif in David Lean's 1965 film.
6. In German, *Gitterfenster* is a lattice-barred window and *Bettzeug* is bedding.

'If you don't like this and you wouldn't want that, then you know what to do, little brother.' Georgie said, in a sharp way that made me look:

'All right. Let's not be starting.'

'That's clean up to Dim,' I said. 'Dim can't go on all his jeezny being as a little child.' And I looked sharp at Georgie. Dim said, and the red krovvy was easing its flow now:

'What natural right does he have to think he can give the orders and tolchock me whenever he likes? Yarbles is what I say to him, and I'd chain his glazzies out soon as look.'

'Watch that,' I said, as quiet as I could with the stereo bouncing all over the walls and ceiling and the in-the-land veck beyond Dim getting loud now with his 'Spark nearer, ultoptimate'. I said: 'Do watch that, O Dim, if to continue to be on live thou dost wish.'

'Yarbles,' said Dim, sneering, 'great bolshy yarblockos[7] to you. What you done then you had no right. I'll meet you with chain or nozh or britva any time, not having you aiming tolchocks at me reasonless, it stands to reason I won't have it.'

'A nozh scrap any time you say,' I snarled back. Pete said:

'Oh now, don't, both of you malchicks. Droogs, aren't we? It isn't right droogs should behave thiswise. See, there are some loose-lipped malchicks over there smecking at us, leering like. We mustn't let ourselves down.'

'Dim,' I said, 'has got to learn his place. Right?'

'Wait,' said Georgie. 'What's all this about place? This is the first I ever hear about lewdies learning their place.'

Pete said: 'If the truth is known, Alex, you shouldn't have given old Dim that uncalled-for tolchock. I'll say it once and no more. I say it with all respect, but if it had been me you'd given it to you'd have to answer. I say no more.' And he drowned his litso in his milk-glass.

I could feel myself getting all razdraz inside, but I tried to cover it, saying calm: 'There has to be a leader. Discipline there has to be. Right?' None of them skazatted a word or nodded even. I got more razdraz inside, calmer out. 'I,' I said, 'have been in charge long now. We are all droogs, but somebody has to be in charge. Right? Right?' They all like nodded, wary like. Dim was osooshing the last of the krovvy off. It was Dim who said now:

'Right, right. Doobidoob. A bit tired, maybe, everybody is. Best not to say more.' I was surprised and just that malenky bit poogly to sloosh Dim govoreeting that wise. Dim said: 'Bedways is rightways now, so best we go homeways. Right?' I was very surprised. The other two nodded, going right right right. I said:

7. TS 24: autograph gloss, "ЯБЛОКО = apple"

'You understand about that tolchock on the rot, Dim. It was the music, see. I get all bezoomny when any veck interferes with a ptitsa singing, as it might be. Like that then.'

'Best we go off homeways and get a bit of spatchka,' said Dim. 'A long night for growing malchicks. Right?' Right right nodded the other two. I said:

'I think it best we go home now. Dim has made a real horrorshow suggestion. If we don't meet daywise, O my brothers, well then— same time same place tomorrow?'

'Oh yes,' said Georgie. 'I think that can be arranged.'

'I might,' said Dim, 'be just that malenky bit late. But same place and near same time tomorrow surely.' He was still wiping away at his goober, though no krovvy flowed any longer now. 'And,' he said, 'it's to be hoped there won't be no more of them singing ptitsas in here.' Then he gave his old Dim guff, a clowny big hohohohoho. It seemed like he was too dim to take much offence.

So off we went our several ways, me belching arrrgh on the cold coke I'd peeted. I had my cut-throat britva handy in case any of Billyboy's droogs should be around near the flatblock waiting, or for that matter any of the other bandas or gruppas or shaikas that from time to time were at war with one. Where I lived was with my dadda and mum in the flats of Municipal Flatblock 18A, between Kingsley[8] Avenue and Wilsonsway.[9] I got to the big main door with no trouble, though I did pass one young malchick sprawling and creeching and moaning in the gutter, all cut about lovely, and saw in the lamplight also streaks of blood here and there like signatures, my brothers, of the night's fillying. And too I saw just by 18A a pair of devotchka's neezhnies doubtless rudely wrenched off in the heat of the moment, O my brothers. And so in. In the hallway was the good old municipal painting[1] on the walls—vecks and ptitsas very well developed, stern in the dignity of labour, at workbench and machine with not one stitch of platties on their well-developed plotts. But of course some of the malchicks living in 18A had, as was to be expected, embellished and decorated the said big painting with handy pencil and ballpoint, adding hair and stiff rods and dirty ballooning slovos out of the dignified rots of these nagoy (bare, that is) cheenas and vecks. I went to the lift, but there was no need to press the electric knopka to see if it was working or not, because it had been tolchocked real horrorshow this night, the metal doors all buckled, some feat of rare strength

8. An allusion either to Kingsley Amis (see note 4, p. 8) or to Kingsley Martin (1897–1969), who edited the left-wing periodical *New Statesman and Nation* from 1930 to 1960.
9. An allusion to Angus Wilson (1913–1991), British novelist whose futuristic *The Old Men at the Zoo* was published in 1961.
1. An allusion to socialist realism, which Joseph Stalin declared to be the official Soviet state doctrine of pictorial and literary representation in 1932.

indeed, so I had to walk the ten floors up. I cursed and panted climbing, being tired in plott if not so much in brain. I wanted music very bad this evening, that singing devotchka in the Korova having perhaps started me off. I wanted like a big feast of it before getting my passport stamped, my brothers, at sleep's frontier and the stripy shest lifted to let me through.

I opened the door of 10-8 with my own little klootch, and inside our malenky quarters all was quiet, the pee and em both being in sleepland, and mum had laid out on the table my malenky bit of supper—a couple of lomticks of tinned spongemeat with a shive or so of kleb and butter, a glass of the old cold moloko. Hohoho, the old moloko, with no knives or synthemesc or drencrom[2] in it. How wicked, my brothers, innocent milk must always seem to me now. Still, I drank and ate growling, being more hungry than I thought at first, and I got fruit-pie from the larder and tore chunks off it to stuff into my greedy rot. Then I tooth-cleaned and clicked, cleaning out the old rot with my yahzick or tongue, then I went into my own little room or den, easing off my platties as I did so. Here was my bed and my stereo, pride of my jeezny, and my discs in their cupboard, and banners and flags on the wall, these being like remembrances of my corrective school life since I was eleven, O my brothers, each one shining and blazoned with name or number: SOUTH 4; METRO CORSKOL BLUE DIVISION; THE BOYS OF ALPHA.

The little speakers of my stereo were all arranged round the room, on ceiling, walls, floor, so, lying on my bed slooshying the music, I was like netted and meshed in the orchestra. Now what I fancied first tonight was this new violin concerto by the American Geoffrey Plautus,[3] played by Odysseus Choerilos[4] with the Macon (Georgia) Philharmonic, so I slid it from where it was neatly filed and switched on and waited.

Then, brothers, it came. Oh, bliss, bliss and heaven. I lay all nagoy to the ceiling, my gulliver on my rookers on the pillow, glazzies closed, rot open in bliss, slooshying the sluice of lovely sounds. Oh, it was gorgeousness and gorgeosity made flesh. The trombones crunched redgold under my bed, and behind my gulliver the trumpets threewise silverflamed, and there by the door the timps rolling through my guts and out again crunched like candy thunder.[5] Oh, it was wonder of wonders. And then, a bird of like rarest spun heavenmetal, or like silvery wine flowing in a spaceship, gravity all nonsense now,

---

2. TS 26: autograph comment, "Not too happy."
3. Titus Maccius Plautus (c. 254–184 BC), Roman comic playwright.
4. Odysseus is the hero of Homer's *Odyssey* (eighth century BC), which provided the mythic framework for *Ulysses* (1922), the modernist masterpiece of Burgess's literary hero, James Joyce (1882–1941). Three Ancient Greek poets share the name Choerilos.
5. Compare Joyce's *Ulysses*, especially Episode 11, "Sirens," for examples of synaesthetic writing that mingles the senses; also see Burgess's study of Joyce's language, *Joysprick* (1973).

came the violin solo above all the other strings, and those strings were like a cage of silk round my bed. Then flute and oboe bored, like worms of like platinum, into the thick thick toffee gold and silver. I was in such bliss, my brothers. Pee and em in their bedroom next door had learnt now not to knock on the wall with complaints of what they called noise. I had taught them. Now they would take sleep-pills. Perhaps, knowing the joy I had in my night music, they had already taken them.[6] As I slooshied, my glazzies tight shut to shut in the bliss that was better than any synthemesc Bog or God, I knew such lovely pictures. There were vecks and ptitsas, both young and starry, lying on the ground screaming for mercy, and I was smecking all over my rot and grinding my boot in their litsos.[7] And there were devotchkas ripped and creeching against walls and I plunging like a shlaga into them, and indeed when the music, which was one movement only, rose to the top of its big highest tower, then, lying there on my bed with glazzies tight shut and rookers behind my gulliver, I broke and spattered and cried aaaaaaah with the bliss of it. And so the lovely music glided to its glowing close.

After that I had lovely Mozart, the Jupiter,[8] and there were new pictures of different litsos to be ground and splashed, and it was after this that I thought I would have just one last disc only before crossing the border, and I wanted something starry and strong and very firm, so it was J. S. Bach I had, the Brandenburg Concerto just for middle and lower strings.[9] And, slooshying with different bliss than before, I viddied again this name on the paper I'd razrezzed that night, a long time ago it seemed, in that cottage called HOME. The name was about a clockwork orange. Listening to the J. S. Bach, I began to pony better what that meant now, and I thought, slooshying away to the brown gorgeousness of the starry German master, that I would like to have tolchocked them both harder and ripped them to ribbons on their own floor.

4

The next morning I woke up at oh eight oh oh hours, my brothers, and as I still felt shagged and fagged and fashed and bashed and my glazzies were stuck together real horrorshow with sleepglue, I thought

6. TS 27: autograph comment on this sentence (circled), "Too ordinary?"
7. A favorite image of George Orwell's, culminating in O'Brien's invitation to Winston Smith to imagine the future as "a boot stamping on a human face—forever" in *Nineteen Eighty-Four* (1949), part III, chapter III. Burgess interrogates Orwell's dystopia in his book *1985* (1978).
8. Wolfgang Amadeus Mozart (1756–1791) completed his Symphony No. 41 in C Major, K. 551, in 1788. The nickname "Jupiter" was not Mozart's.
9. Bach's Concerto No. 6 in B Flat Major, BWV 1051, presented to the Margrave of Brandenburg-Schwedt in 1721.

I would not go to school. I thought how I would have a malenky bit longer in the bed, an hour or two say, and then get dressed nice and easy, perhaps even having a splosh about in the bath, and then brew a pot of real strong horrorshow chai and make toast for myself and slooshy the radio or read the gazetta, all on my oddy knocky. And then in the afterlunch I might perhaps, if I still felt like it, itty off to the old skolliwoll and see what was vareeting in that great seat of gloopy useless learning, O my brothers. I heard my papapa grumbling and trampling and then ittying off to the dyeworks where he rabbited, and then my mum called in in a very respectful goloss as she did now I was growing up big and strong:

'It's gone eight, son. You don't want to be late again.'

So I called back: 'A bit of a pain in my gulliver. Leave us be and I'll try to sleep it off and then I'll be right as dodgers for this after.' I slooshied her give a sort of a sigh and she said:

'I'll put your breakfast in the oven then, son. I've got to be off myself now.' Which was true, there being this law for everybody not a child nor with child nor ill to go out rabbiting. My mum worked at one of the Statemarts,[1] as they called them, filling up the shelves with tinned soup and beans and all that cal. So I slooshied her clank a plate in the gas-oven like and then she was putting her shoes on and then getting her coat from behind the door and then sighing again, then she said: 'I'm off now, son.' But I let on to be back in sleepland and then I did doze off real horrorshow, and I had a queer and very real like sneety, dreaming for some reason of my droog Georgie. In this sneety he'd got like very much older and very sharp and hard and was govoreeting about discipline and obedience and how all the malchicks under his control had to jump hard at it and throw up the old salute like being in the army, and there was me in line like the rest saying yes sir and no sir, and then I viddied clear that Georgie had these stars on his pletchoes and he was like a general. And then he brought in old Dim with a whip, and Dim was a lot more starry and grey and had a few zoobies missing as you could see when he let out a smeck, viddying me, and then my droog Georgie said, pointing like at me: 'That man has filth and cal all over his platties,' and it was true. Then I creeched: 'Don't hit, please don't, brothers,' and started to run. And I was running in like circles and Dim was after me, smecking his gulliver off, cracking with the old whip, and each time I got a real horrorshow tolchock with this whip there was like a very loud electric bell ringringringing, and this bell was like a sort of a pain too.

Then I woke up real skorry, my heart going bap bap bap, and of course there was really a bell going brrrr, and it was our front-door bell. I let on that nobody was at home, but this brrrr still ittied on, and then I heard a goloss shouting through the door: 'Come on then,

1. Self-service grocery stores were first established in the United Kingdom in the 1950s.

get out of it, I know you're in bed.' I recognized the goloss right away. It was the goloss of P. R. Deltoid[2] (a real gloopy nazz,[3] that one) what they called my Post-Corrective Adviser, an overworked veck with hundreds on his books. I shouted right right right, in a goloss of like pain, and I got out of bed and attired myself, O my brothers, in a very lovely over-gown of like silk, with designs of like great cities all over this over-gown. Then I put my nogas into very comfy woolly toofles, combed my luscious glory, and was ready for P. R. Deltoid. When I opened up he came shambling in looking shagged, a battered old shlapa on his gulliver, his raincoat filthy. 'Ah, Alex boy,' he said to me. 'I met your mother, yes. She said something about a pain somewhere. Hence not at school, yes.'

'A rather intolerable pain in the head, brother, sir,' I said in my gentleman's goloss. 'I think it should clear by this afternoon.'

'Or certainly by this evening, yes,' said P. R. Deltoid. 'The evening is the great time, isn't it, Alex boy? Sit,' he said, 'sit, sit,' as though this was his domy and me his guest. And he sat in this starry rocking-chair of my dad's and began rocking, as if that was all he'd come for. I said:

'A cup of the old chai, sir? Tea, I mean.'

'No time,' he said. And he rocked, giving me the old glint under frowning brows, as if with all the time in the world. 'No time, yes,' he said, gloopy. So I put the kettle on. Then I said:

'To what do I owe the extreme pleasure? Is anything wrong, sir?'

'Wrong?' he said, very skorry and sly, sort of hunched looking at me but still rocking away. Then he caught sight of an advert in the gazetta, which was on the table—a lovely smecking young ptitsa with her groodies hanging out to advertise, my brothers, the Glories of the Jugoslav Beaches.[4] Then, after sort of eating her up in two swallows, he said: 'Why should you think in terms of there being anything wrong? Have you been doing something you shouldn't, yes?'

'Just a manner of speech,' I said, 'sir.'

'Well,' said P. R. Deltoid, 'it's just a manner of speech from me to you that you watch out, little Alex, because next time, as you very well know, it's not going to be the corrective school any more. Next time it's going to be the barry place and all my work ruined. If you have no consideration for your horrible self you at least might have some for me, who have sweated over you. A big black mark, I tell

---

2. The deltoid is the muscle forming the contour of the shoulder.
3. TS 30: autograph gloss "HA3 = name"
4. Under Marshal Josip Broz Tito (1892–1980), the Yugoslav state supported a tourist industry to earn foreign currency from the early 1960s. Yugoslavia developed into a significant Mediterranean destination for Western visitors until the independence movements and civil wars of the early 1990s, which broke up the Socialist Federal Republic (1943–92).

you in confidence, for every one we don't reclaim, a confession of failure for every one of you that ends up in the stripy hole.'

'I've been doing nothing I shouldn't, sir,' I said. 'The millicents have nothing on me, brother, sir I mean.'

'Cut out this clever talk about millicents,' said P. R. Deltoid very weary, but still rocking. 'Just because the police have not picked you up lately doesn't, as you very well know, mean you've not been up to some nastiness. There was a bit of a fight last night, wasn't there? There was a bit of shuffling with nozhes and bike-chains and the like. One of a certain fat boy's friends was ambulanced off late from near the Power Plant and hospitalized, cut about very unpleasantly, yes. Your name was mentioned. The word has got through to me by the usual channels. Certain friends of yours were named also. There seems to have been a fair amount of assorted nastiness last night. Oh, nobody can prove anything about anybody, as usual. But I'm warning you, little Alex, being a good friend to you as always, the one man in this sore and sick community who wants to save you from yourself.'

'I appreciate all that, sir,' I said, 'very sincerely.'

'Yes, you do, don't you?' he sort of sneered. 'Just watch it, that's all, yes. We know more than you think, little Alex.' Then he said, in a goloss of great suffering, but still rocking away: 'What gets into you all? We study the problem and we've been studying it for damn well near a century, yes, but we get no farther with our studies. You've got a good home here, good loving parents, you've got not too bad of a brain. Is it some devil that crawls inside you?'

'Nobody's got anything on me, sir,' I said. 'I've been out of the rookers of the millicents for a long time now.'

'That's just what worries me,' sighed P. R. Deltoid. 'A bit too long of a time to be healthy. You're about due now by my reckoning. That's why I'm warning you, little Alex, to keep your handsome young proboscis out of the dirt, yes. Do I make myself clear?'

'As an unmuddied lake, sir,' I said. 'Clear as an azure sky of deepest summer. You can rely on me, sir.' And I gave him a nice zooby smile.

But when he'd ookadeeted and I was making this very strong pot of chai, I grinned to myself over this veshch that P. R. Deltoid and his droogs worried about. All right, I do bad, what with crasting and tolchocks and carves with the britva and the old in-out-in-out, and if I get loveted, well, too bad for me, O my little brothers, and you can't run a country with every chelloveck comporting himself in my manner of the night. So if I get loveted and it's three months in this mesto and another six in that, and then, as P. R. Deltoid so kindly warns, next time, in spite of the great tenderness of my summers, brothers, it's the great unearthly zoo itself, well, I say: 'Fair, but a pity, my lords, because I just cannot bear to be shut in. My endeavour shall be, in such future as stretches out its snowy and lilywhite arms to me before the nozh overtakes or the blood spatters its final chorus in twisted metal and smashed glass on the highroad, to not get loveted again.' Which is fair speeching. But, brothers, this biting of their toenails over what is the *cause* of badness is what turns me into a fine laughing malchick. They don't go into what is the cause of *goodness*, so why of the other shop? If lewdies are good that's because they like it, and I wouldn't ever interfere with their pleasures, and so of the other shop. And I was patronizing the other shop. More, badness is of the self, the one, the you or me on our oddy knockies, and that self is made by old Bog or God and is his great pride and radosty. But the not-self cannot have the bad, meaning they of the government and the judges and the schools cannot allow the bad because they cannot allow the self. And is not our modern history, my brothers, the story of brave malenky selves fighting these big machines? I am serious with you, brothers, over this. But what I do I do because I like to do.

So now, this smiling winter morning, I drink this very strong chai with moloko and spoon after spoon after spoon of sugar, me having a sladky tooth, and I dragged out of the oven the breakfast my poor old mum had cooked for me. It was an egg fried, that and no more, but I made toast and ate egg and toast and jam, smacking away at it while I read the gazetta. The gazetta was the usual about ultra-violence and bank robberies and strikes and footballers making everybody paralytic with fright by threatening to not play next Saturday if they did not get higher wages,[5] naughty malchickiwicks as they were. Also there were more space-trips and bigger stereo TV screens and offers of free packets of soapflakes in exchange for the labels on soup-tins, amazing offer for one week only, which made me smeck. And there was a bolshy big article on Modern Youth (meaning me, so I gave the old bow, grinning like bezoomny) by some very clever bald chelloveck. I read this with care, my brothers, slurping away at the old chai, cup after tass after chasha, crunching my lomticks of black toast dipped in jammiwam and eggiweg. This learned veck said the usual veshches, about no parental discipline, as he called it, and the shortage of real horrorshow teachers who would lambast bloody beggary out of their innocent poops and make them go boohoohoo for mercy. All this was gloopy and made me smeck, but it was like nice to go on knowing one was making the news all the time, O my brothers. Every day there was something about Modern Youth, but the best veshch they ever had in the old gazetta was by some starry pop in a doggy collar who

---

5. During the 1960–61 soccer (Association Football) season, professional players, led by Jimmy Hill under the auspices of the Professional Footballers' Association, voted for strike action with the aim of abolishing the maximum wage and the retain and transfer contract system (which meant that a player in dispute with his club over wages could not move to another club).

said that in his considered opinion and he was govoreeting as a man of Bog IT WAS THE DEVIL THAT WAS ABROAD and was like ferreting his way into like young innocent flesh, and it was the adult world that could take the responsibility for this with their wars and bombs and nonsense.[6] So that was all right. So he knew what he talked of, being a Godman. So we young innocent malchicks could take no blame. Right right right.

When I'd gone erk erk a couple of razzes on my full innocent stomach, I started to get out day platties from my wardrobe, turning the radio on. There was music playing, a very nice malenky string quartet, my brothers, by Claudius Birdman,[7] one that I knew well. I had to have a smeck, though, thinking of what I'd viddied once in one of these like articles on Modern Youth, about how Modern Youth would be better off if A Lively Appreciation Of The Arts could be like encouraged. Great Music, it said, and Great Poetry would like quieten Modern Youth down and make Modern Youth more Civilized. Civilized my syphilised yarbles. Music always sort of sharpened me up, O my brothers, and made me like feel like old Bog himself, ready to make with the old donner and blitzen and have vecks and ptitsas creeching away in my ha ha power. And when I'd cheested up my litso and rookers a bit and done dressing (my day platties were like student-wear: the old blue pantalonies with sweater with A for Alex) I thought here at least was time to itty off to the disc-bootick (and cutter too, my pockets being full of pretty polly) to see about this long-promised and long-ordered stereo Beethoven Number Nine (the Choral Symphony, that is), recorded on Masterstroke by the Esh Sham Sinfonia under L. Muhaiwir.[8] So out I went, brothers.

The day was very different from the night. The night belonged to me and my droogs and all the rest of the nadsats, and the starry bourgeois lurked indoors drinking in the gloopy worldcasts, but the day was for the starry ones, and there always seemed to be more rozzes or millicents about during the day, too. I got the autobus from the corner and rode to Center, and then I walked back to Taylor Place, and there was the disc-bootick I favoured with my inestimable custom, O my brothers. It had the gloopy name of MELODIA,[9] but it was a real horrorshow mesto and skorry, most times, at getting the new recordings. I walked in and the only other customers were two young ptitsas sucking away at ice-sticks (and this, mark, was dead cold win-

---

6. An irony explored by the British novelist William Golding (1911–1993) in his first published novel, *Lord of the Flies* (1954).
7. See Phillips, p. 237 in this Norton Critical Edition.
8. See Phillips, p. 237 in this Norton Critical Edition. The German composer Ludwig van Beethoven (1770–1827), completed his Symphony No. 9 in D Minor, Op. 125, in 1824; its final movement includes a chorus based on "Ode to Joy," a poem by Friedrich Schiller.
9. There is no connection with the Soviet state-owned recording organization Grammplastt-rest, which did not change its name to Melodiya until 1964.

ter) and sort of shuffling through the new popdiscs—Johnny Burn-
away, Stash Kroh, The Mixers, Lay Quiet Awhile With Ed And Id
Molotov,[1] and all the rest of that cal. These two ptitsas couldn't have
been more than ten, and they too, like me, it seemed, evidently, had
decided to take a morning off from the old skolliwoll. They saw themselves, you could see, as real grown-up devotchkas already, what with
the old hipswing when they saw your Faithful Narrator, brothers, and
padded groodies and red all ploshed on their goobers. I went up to
the counter, making with the polite zooby smile at old Andy behind it
(always polite himself, always helpful, a real horrorshow type of a
veck, though bald and very very thin). He said:
'Aha, I know what you want, I think. Good news, good news. It has
arrived.'[2] And with like big conductor's rookers beating time he went
to get it. The two young ptitsas started giggling, as they will at that
age, and I gave them a like cold glazzy. Andy was back real skorry,
waving the great shiny white sleeve of the Ninth, which had on it,
brothers, the frowning beetled like thunderbottled litso of Ludwig
van himself. 'Here,' said Andy. 'Shall we give it the trial spin?' But I
wanted it back home on my stereo to slooshy on my oddy knocky,
greedy as hell. I fumbled out the deng to pay and one of the little ptitsas said:
'Who you getten, bratty? What biggy, what only?' These young
devotchkas had their own like way of govoreeting. 'The Heaven Sev-
enteen? Luke Sterne? Goggly Gogol?'[3] And both giggled, rocking
and hippy. Then an idea hit me and made me near fall over with the
anguish and ecstasy of it, O my brothers, so I could not breathe for
near ten seconds. I recovered and made with my new-clean zoobies
and said:
'What you got back home, little sisters, to play your fuzzy warbles
on?' Because I could viddy the discs they were buying were these
teeny pop veshches. 'I bet you got little save tiny portable like picnic
spinners.' And they sort of pushed their lower lips out at that. 'Come
with uncle,' I said, 'and hear all proper. Hear angel trumpets and
devil trombones. You are invited.' And I like bowed. They giggled
again and one said:

1. The name of the Bolshevik Vyacheslav Mikhailovich Molotov (1890–1986) has become
   associated with a makeshift bomb, usually containing a flammable liquid such as petrol and a fuse of impregnated cloth.
2. TS 35: autograph additions, so that text reads, "'Aha, I know what thou wantest, I
   thinkest. Good news, good news. It have arrived.'"
3. Of these fictional preteen bands invented by Burgess, the first was incarnated as the
   New Romantic band Heaven 17 by former members of the Human League, and their
   first album *Penthouse and Pavement* entered the U.K. Top 20 in 1981. The English
   writer Laurence Sterne (1713–1768) is best known for the anti-novel *The Life and
   Opinions of Tristram Shandy, Gentleman* (1759–67). Nikolai Vasilievich Gogol (1809–
   1852), a Ukrainian author writing in Russian, is famous for the novel *Dead Souls* (1842)
   and his story "The Overcoat" (1842), which, according to the novelist Dostoyevsky, initiated modern Russian literature.

'Oh, but we're so hungry. Oh, but we could so eat.' The other said: 'Yah, she can say that, can't she just.' So I said:

'Eat with uncle. Name your place.'

Then they viddied themselves as real sophistoes, which was like pathetic, and started talking in big-lady golosses about the Ritz and the Bristol and the Hilton and Il Ristorante Granturco. But I stopped that with 'Follow uncle', and I led them to the Pasta Parlour just round the corner and let them fill their innocent young litsos on spaghetti and sausages and cream-puffs and banana-splits and hot choc-sauce, till I near sicked with the sight of it, I, brothers, lunching but frugally off a cold ham-slice and a growling dollop of chilli. These two young ptitsas were much alike, though not sisters. They had the same ideas or lack of, and the same colour hair—a like dyed strawy. Well, they would grow up real today. Today I would make a day of it. No school this afterlunch, but education certain, Alex as teacher. Their names, they said, were Marty and Sonietta, bezoomny enough and in the heighth of their childish fashion, so I said:

'Righty right, Marty and Sonietta. Time for the big spin. Come.' When we were outside on the cold street they thought they would not go by autobus, oh no, but by taxi, so I gave them the humour, though with a real horrorshow in-grin, and I called a taxi from the rank near Center. The driver, a starry whiskery veck in very stained platties, said:

'No tearing up, now. No nonsense with them seats. Just re-upholstered they are.' I quieted his gloopy fears and off we spun to Municipal Flatblock 18A, these two bold little ptitsas giggling and whispering. So, to cut all short, we arrived, O my brothers, and I led the way up to 10-8, and they panted and smecked away the way up, and then they were thirsty, they said, so I unlocked the treasure-chest in my room and gave these ten-year-young devotchkas a real horror-show Scotchman apiece, though well filled with sneezy pins-and-needles soda. They sat on my bed (yet unmade) and leg-swung, smecking and peeting their highballs, while I spun their like pathetic malenky discs through my stereo. Like peeting some sweet scented kid's drink, that was, in like very beautiful and lovely and costly gold goblets. But they went oh oh oh and said, 'Swoony' and 'Hilly' and other weird slovos that were the heighth of fashion in that youth group. While I spun this cal for them I encouraged them to drink and have another, and they were nothing loath, O my brothers. So by the time their pathetic pop-discs had been twice spun each (there were two: 'Honey Nose', sung by Ike Yard, and 'Night After Day After Night', moaned by two horrible yarbleless like eunuchs whose names I forget) they were getting near the pitch of like young ptitsa's hysterics, what with jumping all over my bed and me in the room with them.

What was actually done that afternoon there is no need to
describe, brothers, as you may easily guess all. Those two were
unplattied and smecking fit to crack in no time at all, and they
thought it the bolshiest fun to viddy old Uncle Alex standing there
all nagoy and pan-handled, squirting the hypodermic like some
bare doctor, then giving myself the old jab of growling jungle-cat
secretion in the rooker. Then I pulled the lovely Ninth out of its
sleeve, so that Ludwig van was now nagoy too, and I set the needle
hissing on to the last movement, which was all bliss. There it was
then, the bass strings like govoreeting away from under my bed at
the rest of the orchestra, and then the male human goloss coming
in and telling them all to be joyful, and then the lovely blissful tune
all about Joy being a glorious spark like of heaven, and then I felt
the old tigers leap in me and then I leapt on these two young ptitsas. This time they thought nothing fun and stopped creeching
with high mirth, and had to submit to the strange and weird desires
of Alexander the Large which, what with the Ninth and the hypo
jab, were choodessny and zammechat and very demanding, O my
brothers. But they were both very very drunken and could hardly
feel very much.

When the last movement had gone round for the second time with
all the banging and creeching about Joy Joy Joy Joy, then these two
young ptitsas were not acting the big lady sophisto no more. They
were like waking up to what was being done to their malenky persons
and saying that they wanted to go home and like I was a wild beast.
They looked like they had been in some big bitva, as indeed they had,
and were all bruised and pouty. Well, if they would not go to school
they must still have their education. And education they had had.
They were creeching and going ow ow ow as they put their platties
on, and they were like punchipunching me with their teeny fists as
I lay there dirty and nagoy and fair shagged and fagged on the bed.
This young Sonietta was creeching: 'Beast and hateful animal.
Filthy horror.' So I let them get their things together and get out,
which they did, talking about how the rozzes should be got on to me
and all that cal. Then they were going down the stairs and I dropped
off to sleep, still with the old Joy Joy Joy Joy crashing and howling
away.

5

What happened, though, was that I woke up late (near seven-thirty
by my watch) and, as it turned out, that was not so clever. You can
viddy that everything in this wicked world counts. You can pony

that one thing always leads to another.[1] Right right right. My stereo was no longer on about Joy and I Embrace Ye O Ye Millions, so some veck had dealt it the off, and that would be either pee or em, both of them now being quite clear to the slooshying in the living-room and, from the clink clink of plates and slurp slurp of peeting tea from cups, at their tired meal after the day's rabbiting in factory the one, store the other. The poor old. The pitiable starry. I put on my over-gown and looked out, in guise of loving only son, to say:

'Hi hi hi, there. A lot better after the day's rest. Ready now for evening work to earn that little bit.' For that's what they said they believed I did these days. 'Yum yum, mum. Any of that for me?' It was like some frozen pie[2] that she'd unfroze and then warmed up and it looked not so very appetitish, but I had to say what I said. Dad looked at me with a not-so-pleased suspicious like look but said nothing, knowing he dared not, and mum gave me a tired like little smeck, to thee fruit of my womb my only son sort of. I danced to the bathroom and had a real skorry cheest all over, feeling dirty and gluey, then back to my den for the evening's platties. Then, shining, combed, brushed and gorgeous, I sat to my lomtick of pie. Papapa said:

'Not that I want to pry, son, but where exactly is it you go to work of evenings?'

'Oh,' I chewed, 'it's mostly odd things, helping like. Here and there, as it might be.' I gave him a straight dirty glazzy, as to say to mind his own and I'd mind mine. 'I never ask for money, do I? Not money for clothes or for pleasures? All right, then, why ask?'

My dad was like humble mumble chumble. 'Sorry, son,' he said. 'But I get worried sometimes. Sometimes I have dreams. You can laugh if you like, but there's a lot in dreams. Last night I had this dream with you in it and I didn't like it one bit.'

'Oh?' He had gotten me interessovatted now, dreaming of me like that. I had like a feeling I had had a dream, too, but I could not remember proper what. 'Yes?' I said, stopping chewing my gluey pie.

'It was vivid,' said my dad. 'I saw you lying on the street and you had been beaten by other boys. These boys were like the boys you used to go around with before you were sent to that last Corrective School.'

'Oh?' I had an in-grin at that, papapa believing I had real reformed or believing he believed. And then I remembered my own dream, which was a dream of that morning, of Georgie giving his general's orders and old Dim smecking around toothless as he wielded the

---

1. Pierre-Simon Laplace (1749–1827), mathematician and astronomer, is often identified with strong causal determinism, which holds that the present state of the universe is the cause of its future states, and therefore that a complete knowledge of that present state permits the calculation of future states. Alongside other determinisms, such as B. F. Skinner's behaviorism, such ideas are inimical to free will.
2. In Britain, frozen food—in particular, meals that required only reheating—made their first significant impact on a newly affluent middle-class market in the 1950s.

whip. But dreams go by opposites I was once told. 'Never worry about
thine only son and heir, O my father,' I said. 'Fear not. He canst
taketh care of himself, verily.'

'And,' said my dad, 'you were like helpless in your blood and you
couldn't fight back.' That was real opposites, so I had another quiet
malenky grin within and then I took all the deng out of my carmans
and tinkled it on the saucy table-cloth. I said:

'Here, dad, it's not much. It's what I earned last night. But perhaps
for the odd peet of Scotchman in the snug somewhere for you and
mum.'

'Thanks, son,' he said. 'But we don't go out much now. We daren't
go out much, the streets being what they are. Young hooligans and so
on. Still, thanks. I'll bring her home a bottle of something tomorrow.'
And he scooped this ill-gotten pretty into his trouser carmans, mum
being at the cheesting of the dishes in the kitchen. And I went out
with loving smiles all round.

When I got to the bottom of the stairs of the flatblock I was somewhat surprised. I was more than that. I opened my rot like wide in
the old stony gapes. They had come to meet me. They were waiting
by the all scrawled-over municipal wall-painting of the nagoy dignity of labour, bare vecks and cheenas stern at the wheels of industry, like I said, with all this dirt pencilled from their rots by naughty
malchicks. Dim had a big thick like stick of black greasepaint and
was tracing filthy slovos real big over our municipal painting and
doing the old Dim guff—wuh huh huh—while he did it. But he
turned round when Georgie and Pete gave me the well hello, showing their shining droogy zoobies, and he horned out: 'He are here,
he have arrived, hooray,' and did a clumsy turnitoe bit of dancing.

'We got worried,' said Georgie. 'There we were, awaiting and peeting away at the old knify moloko, and you had not turned up. So
then Pete here thought how you might have been like offended by
some veshch or other, so round we come to your abode. That's right,
Pete, right?'

'Oh, yes, right,' said Pete.

'Appy polly loggies,' I said, careful. 'I had something of a pain in
the gulliver so had to sleep. I was not wakened when I gave orders
for wakening. Still, here we all are, ready for what the old nochy
offers, yes?' I seemed to have picked up that yes? from P. R. Deltoid,
my Post-Corrective Adviser. Very strange.

'Sorry about the pain,' said Georgie, like very concerned. 'Using
the gulliver too much like, maybe. Giving orders and discipline and
such, perhaps. Sure the pain is gone? Sure you'll not be happier
going back to the bed?' And they all had a bit of a malenky grin.[3]

3. TS 41: autograph emendation to "smeck," cancelled and replaced by "grin."

'Wait,' I said. 'Let's get things nice and sparkling clear. This sarcasm, if I may call it such, does not become you, O my little friends. Perhaps you have been having a bit of a quiet govoreet behind my back, making your own little jokes and such-like. As I am your droog and leader, surely I am entitled to know what goes on, eh? Now then, Dim, what does that great big horsy gape of a grin portend?' For Dim had his rot open in a sort of bezoomny soundless smeck. Georgie got in very skorry with:

'All right, no more picking on Dim, brother. That's part of the new way.'

'New way?' I said. 'What's this about a new way? There's been some very large talk behind my sleeping back and no error. Let me slooshy more.' And I sort of folded my rookers and leaned comfortable to listen against the broken banister-rail, me being still higher than them, droogs as they called themselves, on the third stair.

'No offence, Alex,' said Pete, 'but we wanted to have things more democratic like. Not like you like saying what to do and what not all the time. But no offence.' Georgie said:

'Offence is neither here nor elsewhere. It's a matter of who has ideas. What ideas has he had?' And he kept his very bold glazzies turned full on me. 'It's all the small stuff, malenky veshches like last night. We're growing up, brothers.'

'More,' I said, not moving. 'Let me slooshy more.'

'Well,' said Georgie, 'if you must have it, have it then. We itty round, shop-crasting and the like, coming out with a pitiful rookerful of cutter each. And there's Will the English in the Muscleman coffee mesto saying he can fence anything that any malchick cares to try to crast. The shiny stuff, the ice,' he said, still with these like cold glazzies on me. 'The big big big money is available is what Will the English says.'

'So,' I said, very comfortable out but real razdraz within. 'Since when have you been consorting and comporting with Will the English?'

'Now and again,' said George, 'I get around all on my oddy knocky. Like last Sabbath for instance. I can live my own jeezny,[4] droogie, right?'

I didn't really care for any of this, my brothers. 'And what will you do,' I said, 'with the big big big deng or money as you so highfaluting call it? Have you not every veshch you need? If you need an auto you pluck it from the trees. If you need pretty polly you take it. Yes? Why this sudden shilarny for being the big bloated capitalist?'

'Ah,' said Georgie, 'you think and govoreet sometimes like a little child.' Dim went huh huh huh at that. 'Tonight,' said Georgie, 'we pull a mansize crast.'

4. TS 42: autograph gloss, "Check жизнь"

So my dream had told truth, then. Georgie the general saying what we should do and what not do, Dim with the whip as mindless grinning bulldog. But I played with care, with great care, the greatest, saying, smiling: 'Good. Real horrorshow. Initiative comes to them as wait. I have taught you much, little droogie. Now tell me what you have in mind, Georgieboy.'

'Oh,' said Georgie, cunning and crafty in his grin, 'the old moloko-plus first, would you not say? Something to sharpen us up, boy, but you especially, we having the start of you.'

'You have govoreeted my thoughts for me,' I smiled away. 'I was about to suggest the dear old Korova. Good good good. Lead, little Georgie.' And I made with a like deep bow, smiling like bezoomny but thinking all the time. But when we got into the street I viddied that thinking is for the gloopy ones and that the oomny ones use like inspiration and what Bog sends. For now it was lovely music that came to my aid. There was an auto ittying by and it had its radio on, and I could just slooshy a bar or so of Ludwig van (it was the Violin Concerto,[5] last movement), and I viddied right at once what to do. I said, in like a thick deep goloss: 'Right, Georgie, now,' and I whished out my cut-throat britva. Georgie said: 'Uh?' but he was skorry enough with his nozh, the blade coming sloosh out of the handle, and we were on to each other. Old Dim said: 'Oh, no, not right that isn't,' and made to uncoil the chain round his tally, but Pete said, putting his rooker firm on old Dim: 'Leave them. It's right like that.' So then Georgie and Your Humble did the old quiet cat-stalk,[6] looking for openings, knowing each other's style a bit too horrorshow really, Georgie now and then going lurch lurch with his shining nozh but not no wise connecting. And all the time lewdies passed by and viddied all this but minded their own, it being perhaps a common street-sight. But then I counted odin dva tree[7] and went ak ak ak with the britva, though not at litso or glazzies but at Georgie's nozh-holding rooker and, my little brothers, he dropped. He did. He dropped his nozh with a tinkle tankle on the hard winter sidewalk. I had just ticklewickled his fingers with my britva, and there he was looking at the malenky dribble of krovvy that was redding out in the lamplight. 'Now,' I said, and it was me that was starting, because Pete had given old Dim the soviet not to uncoil the oozy from round his tally and Dim had taken it, 'now, Dim, let's thou and me have all this now, shall us?' Dim went, 'Aaaaaaarhgh,' like some bolshy bezoomny animal, and snaked out the chain from his waist real horrorshow and skorry, so you had to admire. Now the right style for me here was to keep low like in frog-dancing to protect litso and glazzies, and this I

5. Beethoven wrote his Violin Concerto in D Major, Op. 61, in 1806; the third movement is allegro.
6. TS 43: autograph gloss, "cat-stalk not catstalk"
7. Russian: one, two, three.

did, brothers, so that poor old Dim was a malenky bit surprised, him
being accustomed to the straight face-on lash lash lash. Now I will
say that he whished me horrible on the back so that it stung like
bezoomny, but that pain told me to dig in skorry once and for all and
be done with old Dim. So I swished with the britva at his left noga
in its very tight tight and I slashed two inches of cloth and drew a
malenky drop of krovvy to make Dim real bezoomny. Then while he
went hauwwww hauwww hauwww like a doggie I tried the same style
as for Georgie, banking all on one move—up, cross, cut—and I felt
the britva go just deep enough in the meat of old Dim's wrist and he
dropped his snaking oozy yelping like a little child. Then he tried to
drink in all the blood from his wrist and howl at the same time, and
there was too much krovvy to drink and he went bubble bubble bubble, the red like fountaining out lovely, but not for very long. I said:

'Right, my droogies, now we should know. Yes, Pete?'

'I never said anything,' said Pete. 'I never govoreeted one slovo.
Look, old Dim's bleeding to death.'

'Never,' I said. 'One can die but once. Dim died before he was
born. That red red krovvy will soon stop.' Because I had not cut into
the like main cables. And I myself took a clean tashtook from my
carman[8] to wrap round poor old dying Dim's rooker, howling and
moaning as he was, and the krovvy stopped like I said it would, O
my brothers. So they knew now who was master and leader, sheep,
thought I.

It did not take long to quieten these two wounded soldiers down in
the snug of the Duke of New York, what with large brandies (bought
with their own cutter, me having given all to my dad) and a wipe with
tashtooks dipped in the water-jug. The old ptitsas we'd been so horrorshow to last night were there again, going, 'Thanks, lads' and 'God
bless you, boys' like they couldn't stop, though we had not repeated
the old sammy act with them. But Pete said: 'What's it to be, girls?'
and bought black and suds for them, him seeming to have a fair
amount of pretty polly in his carmans, so they were on louder than
ever with their 'God bless and keep you all, lads' and 'We'd never split
on you, boys' and 'The best lads breathing, that's what you are'. At
last I said to Georgie:

'Now we're back to where we were, yes? Just like before and all
forgotten, right?'

'Right right right,' said Georgie. But old Dim still looked a bit
dazed and he even said: 'I could have got that big bastard, see, with
my oozy, only some veck got in the way,' as though he'd been dratsing not with me but with some other malchick. I said:

'Well, Georgieboy, what did you have in mind?'

8. TS 44: autograph gloss, "карман"

'Oh,' said Georgie, 'not tonight. Not this nochy, please.'

'You're a big strong chelloveck,' I said, 'like us all. We're not little children, are we, Georgieboy? What, then, didst thou in thy mind have?'

'I could have chained his glazzies real horrorshow,' said Dim, and the old baboochkas were still on with their 'Thanks, lads'.

'It was this house, see,' said Georgie. 'The one with the two lamps outside. The one with the gloopy name, like.'

'What gloopy name?'

'The Mansion or the Manse or some such piece of gloop. Where this very starry ptitsa lives with her cats and all these very starry valuable veshches.'

'Such as?'

'Gold and silver and like jewels. It was Will the English who like said.'

'I viddy,' I said. 'I viddy horrorshow.' I knew where he meant—Oldtown, just beyond Victoria Flatblock.[9] Well, the real horrorshow leader knows always when like to give and show generous to his like unders. 'Very good, Georgie,' I said. 'A good thought, and one to be followed. Let us at once itty.' And as we were going out the old baboochkas said: 'We'll say nothing, lads. Been here all the time you have, boys.' So I said: 'Good old girls. Back to buy more in ten minutes.' And so I led my three droogs out to my doom.

6

Just past the Duke of New York going east was offices and then there was the starry beat-up biblio and then was the bolshy flatblock called Victoria Flatblock after some victory or other, and then you came to the like starry type houses of the town in what was called Oldtown. You got some of the real horrorshow ancient domies here, my broth-ers, with starry lewdies living in them, thin old barking like colonels with sticks and old ptitsas who were widows and deaf starry damas with cats who, my brothers, had felt not the touch of any chelloveck in the whole of their pure like jeeznies. And here, true, there were starry veshches that would fetch their share of cutter on the tourist market—like pictures and jewels and other starry pre-plastic cal[1] of that type. So we came nice and quiet to this domy called the Manse, and there were globe lights outside on iron stalks, like guarding the front door on each side, and there was a light like dim on in one of the rooms on the ground level, and we went to a nice patch of street

---

9. In Orwell's *Nineteen Eighty-Four*, the hero Winston Smith lives in Victory Mansions.
1. TS 47: autograph gloss, "кал"

dark to watch through the window what was ittying on. This window had iron bars in front of it, like the house was a prison, but we could viddy nice and clear what was ittying on.

What was ittying on was that this starry ptitsa, very grey in the voloss and with a very liny like litso, was pouring the old moloko from a milk-bottle into saucers and then setting these saucers down on the floor, so you could tell there were plenty of mewing kots and koshkas writhing about down there. And we could viddy one or two, great fat scoteenas, jumping up on to the table with their rots open going mare mare mare. And you could viddy this old baboochka talking back to them, govoreeting in like scoldy language to her pussies. In the room you could viddy a lot of old pictures on the walls and starry very elaborate clocks, also some like vases and ornaments that looked starry and dorogoy. Georgie whispered: 'Real horrorshow deng to be gotten for them, brothers. Will the English is real anxious.' Pete said: 'How in?' Now it was up to me, and skorry, before Georgie started telling us how. 'First veshch,' I whispered, 'is to try the regular way, the front. I will go very polite and say that one of my droogs has had a like funny fainting turn on the street. Georgie can be ready to show, when she opens, thatwise. Then to ask for water or to phone the doc. Then in easy.' Georgie said:

'She may not open.' I said:

'We'll try it, yes?' And he sort of shrugged his pletchoes, making with a frog's rot. So I said to Pete and old Dim: 'You two droogies get either side of the door. Right?' They nodded in the dark right right right. 'So,' I said to Georgie, and I made bold straight for the front door. There was a bellpush and I pushed, and brrrrrr brrrrrr sounded down the hall inside. A like sense of slooshying followed, as though the ptitsa and her koshkas all had their ears back at the brrrrr brrrrrr, wondering. So I pushed the old zvonock a malenky bit more urgent. I then bent down to the letter-slit and called through in a refined like goloss: 'Help, madam, please. My friend has just had a funny turn on the street. Let me phone a doctor, please.' Then I could viddy a light being put on in the hall, and then I could hear the old baboochka's nogas going flip flap in flip-flap slippers to nearer the front door, and I got the idea, I don't know why, that she had a big fat pussycat under each arm. Then she called out in a very surprising deep like goloss:

'Go away. Go away or I shoot.' Georgie heard that and wanted to giggle. I said, with like suffering and urgency in my gentleman's goloss:

'Oh, please help, madam. My friend's very ill.'

'Go away,' she called. 'I know your dirty tricks, making me open the door and then buy things I don't want. Go away, I tell you.' That was real lovely innocence, that was. 'Go away,' she said again, 'or I'll

set my cats on to you.' A malenky bit bezoomny she was, you could
tell that, through spending her jeezny all on her oddy knocky. Then
I looked up and I viddied that there was a sash-window above the
front door and that it would be a lot more skorry to just do the old
pletcho climb and get in that way. Else there'd be this argument all
the long nochy. So I said:

'Very well, madam. If you won't help I must take my suffering
friend elsewhere.' And I winked my droogies all away quiet, only
me crying out: 'All right, old friend, you will surely meet some good
samaritan some place other. This old lady perhaps cannot be blamed
for being suspicious with so many scoundrels and rogues of the night
about. No, indeed not.' Then we waited again in the dark and I whispered: 'Right. Return to door. Me stand on Dim's pletchoes. Open
that window and me enter, droogies. Then to shut up that old ptitsa
and open up for all. No trouble.' For I was like showing who was
leader and the chelloveck with the ideas. 'See,' I said. 'Real horrorshow bit of stonework over that door, a nice hold for my nogas.' They
viddied all that, admiring perhaps I thought, and said and nodded
Right right right in the dark.

So back tiptoe to the door. Dim was our heavy strong malchick
and Pete and Georgie like heaved me up on to Dim's bolshy manly
pletchoes. All this time, O thanks to worldcasts on the gloopy TV
and, more, lewdies' night-fear through lack of night-police, dead lay
the street. Up there on Dim's pletchoes I viddied that this stonework
above the door would take my boots lovely. I kneed up, brothers, and
there I was. The window, as I had expected, was closed, but I outed
with my britva and cracked the glass of the window smart with the
bony handle thereof. All the time below my droogies were hard
breathing. So I put in my rooker through the crack and made the
lower half of the window sail up open silver-smooth and lovely. And
I was, like getting into the bath, in. And there were my sheep down
below, their rots open as they looked up, O brothers.

I was in bumpy darkness, with beds and cupboards and bolshy
heavy stoolies and piles of boxes and books about. But I strode man-
ful towards the door of the room I was in, seeing a like crack of light
under it. The door went squeeeeeeeeeeeak and then I was on a dusty
corridor with other doors. All this waste, brothers, meaning all these
rooms and but one starry sharp and her pussies, but perhaps the kots
and koshkas had like separate bedrooms, living on cream and fish-
heads like royal queens and princes. I could hear the like muffled
goloss of this old ptitsa down below saying: 'Yes yes yes, that's it,' but
she would be govoreeting to these mewing sidlers going maaaaaaah
for more moloko. Then I saw the stairs going down to the hall and
I thought to myself that I would show these fickle and worthless
droogs of mine that I was worth the whole three of them and more.

I would do all on my oddy knocky. I would perform the old ultra-violence on the starry ptitsa and on her pusspots if need be, then I would take fair rookerfuls of what looked like real polezny stuff and go waltzing to the front door and open up showering gold and silver on my waiting droogs. They must learn all about leadership.

So down I ittied, slow and gentle, admiring in the stairwell grahzny pictures of old time—devotchkas with long hair and high collars, the like country with trees and horses, the holy bearded veck all nagoy hanging on a cross. There was a real musty von of pussies and pussy-fish and starry dust in this domy, different from the flatblocks. And then I was downstairs and I could viddy the light in this front room where she had been doling moloko to the kots and koshkas. More, I could viddy these great overstuffed scoteenas going in and out with their tails waving and like rubbing themselves on the door-bottom. On a like big wooden chest in the dark hall I could viddy a nice malenky statue that shone in the light of the room, so I crasted this for my own self, it being like of a young thin devotchka standing on one noga with her rookers out, and I could see this was made of sil-ver. So I had this when I ittied into the lit-up room, saying: 'Hi hi hi. At last we meet. Our brief govoreet through the letter-hole was not, shall we say, satisfactory, yes? Let us admit not, oh verily not, you stinking starry old sharp.' And I like blinked in the light at this room and the old ptitsa in it. It was full of kots and koshkas all crawling to and fro over the carpet, with bits of fur floating in the lower air, and these fat scoteenas were all different shapes and colours, black, white, tabby, ginger, tortoise-shell, and of all ages, too, so that there were kittens fillying about with each other and there were pussies full-grown and there were real dribbling starry ones very bad-tempered. Their mistress, this old ptitsa, looked at me fierce like a man and said:

'How did you get in? Keep your distance, you villainous young toad, or I shall be forced to strike you.'

I had a real horrorshow smeck at that, viddying that she had in her veiny rooker a crappy wood walking-stick which she raised at me threatening. So, making with my shiny zoobies, I ittied a bit nearer to her, taking my time, and on the way I saw on a like sideboard a lovely little veshch, the loveliest malenky veshch any malchick fond of music like myself could ever hope to viddy with his own two glazzies, for it was like the gulliver and pletchoes of Ludwig van himself, what they call a bust, a like stone veshch with stone long hair and blind glazzies and the big flowy cravat. I was off for that right away, saying: 'Well, how lovely and all for me.' But ittying towards it with my glazzies like full on it and my greedy rooker held out, I did not see the milk saucers on the floor and into one I went and sort of lost balance.

'Whoops,' I said, trying to steady, but this old ptitsa had come up behind me very sly and with great skorriness for her age and then she went crack crack on my gulliver with her bit of a stick. So I found myself on my rookers and knees trying to get up and saying: 'Naughty naughty naughty.' And then she was going crack crack again, saying: 'Wretched little slummy bedbug, breaking into *real* people's houses.' I didn't like this crack crack eegra, so I grasped hold of one end of her stick as it came down again and then she lost her balance and was trying to steady herself against the table, but then the table-cloth came off with a milk-jug and a milk-bottle going all drunk then scattering white splosh in all directions, then she was down on the floor grunting, going: 'Blast you, boy, you shall suffer.' Now all the cats were getting spoogy and running and jumping in a like cat-panic, and some were blaming each other, hitting out cat-tolchocks with the old lapa[2] and ptaaaa and grrrr and kraaaaark. I got up on to my nogas, and there was this nasty vindictive starry forella[3] with her wattles ashake and grunting as she like tried to lever herself up from the floor, so I gave her a malenky fair kick in the litso, and she didn't like that, crying: 'Waaaaah,' and you could viddy her veiny mottled litso going purplewurple where I'd landed the old noga.

As I stepped back from the kick I must have like trod on the tail of one of these dratsing creeching pusspots, because I slooshied a gromky yauuuuuuuuw and found that like fur and teeth and claws had like fastened themselves round my leg, and there I was cursing away and trying to shake it off holding this silver malenky statue in one rooker and trying to climb over this old ptitsa on the floor to reach lovely Ludwig van in frowning like stone. And then I was into another saucer brimful of creamy moloko and near went flying again, the whole veshch really a very humorous one if you could imagine it sloochatting to some other veck and not to Your Humble Narrator. And then the starry ptitsa on the floor reached over all the dratsing yowling pusscats and grabbed at my noga, still going 'Waaaaah' at me, and, my balance being a bit gone, I went really crash this time, on to sploshing moloko and skriking koshkas, and the old forella started to fist me on the litso, both of us being on the floor, creeching: 'Thrash him, beat him, pull out his finger-nails, the poisonous young beetle,' addressing her pusscats only, and then, as if like obeying the starry old ptitsa, a couple of koshkas got on to me and started scratching like bezoomny. So then I got real bezoomny myself,

---

2. TS 52 reads "naga" for "lapa," suggesting that Burgess made further changes at the proof stage. "Noga" (нога, pronounced na-ga) is the usual nadsat term for foot or leg.
3. Trout, as in the denigratory slang phrase "old trout." Note that Trout is also the popular name for Franz Schubert's Piano Quintet in A Major, D. 667, because its last movement consists of variations on Schubert's song "Die Forelle" (The Trout).

brothers, and hit out at them, but this baboochka said: 'Toad, don't touch my kitties,' and like scratched my litso. So then I creeched: 'You filthy old soomka,' and upped with the little malenky like silver statue and cracked her a fine fair tolchock on the gulliver and that shut her up real horrorshow and lovely.

Now as I got up from the floor among all the craring kots and koshkas what should I slooshy but the shoom of the old police-auto siren in the distance, and it dawned on me skorry that the old forella of the pusscats had been on the phone to the millicents when I thought she'd been govoreeting to the mewlers and mowlers, her having got her suspicions skorry on the boil when I'd rung the old zvonock pretending for help. So now, slooshying this fearsome shoom of the rozz-van, I belted for the front door and had a rabbiting time undoing all the locks and chains and bolts and other protective veshches. Then I got it open, and who should be on the doorstep but old Dim, me just being able to viddy the other two of my so-called droogs belting off. 'Away,' I creeched to Dim. 'The rozzes are coming.' Dim said: 'You stay to meet them huh huh huh,' and then I viddied that he had his oozy out, and then he upped with it and it snaked whishhhhh and he chained me gentle and artistic like on the glazlids, me just closing them up in time. Then I was howling around trying to viddy with this howling great pain, and Dim said: 'I don't like you should do what you done, old droogy. Not right it wasn't to get on to me like the way you done, brat.' And then I could slooshy his bolshy lumpy boots beating off, him going huh huh huh into the darkmans, and it was only about seven seconds after that I slooshied the millicent-van draw up with a filthy great dropping siren-howl, like some bezoomny animal snuffing it. I was howling too and like yawing about and I banged my gulliver smack on the hall-wall, my glazzies being tight shut and the juice astream from them, very agonizing. So there I was like groping in the hallway as the millicents arrived. I couldn't viddy them, of course, but I could slooshy and damn near smell the von of the bastards, and soon I could feel the bastards as they got rough and did the old twist-arm act, carrying me out. I could also slooshy one millicent goloss saying from like the room I'd come out of with all the kots and koshkas in it: 'She's been nastily knocked but she's breathing,' and there was loud mewing all the time.

'A real pleasure this is,' I heard another millicent goloss say as I was tolchocked very rough and skorry into the auto. 'Little Alex all to our own selves.' I creeched out:

'I'm blind, Bog bust and bleed you, you grahzny bastards.'

'Language, language,' like smecked a goloss, and then I got a like backhand tolchock with some ringy rooker or other full on the rot. I said:

'Bog murder you, you vonny stinking bratchnies. Where are the others? Where are my stinking traitorous droogs? One of my cursed grahzny bratties chained me on the glazzies. Get them before they get away. It was all their idea, brothers. They like forced me to do it. I'm innocent, Bog butcher you.' By this time they were all having like a good smeck at me with the heighth of like callousness, and they'd tolchocked me into the back of the auto, but I still kept on about these so-called droogs of mine and then I viddied it would be no good, because they'd all be back now in the snug of the Duke of New York forcing black and suds and double Scotchmen down the unprotesting gorloes of those stinking starry ptitsas and they saying: 'Thanks, lads. God bless you, boys. Been here all the time you have, lads. Not been out of our sight you haven't.'

All the time we were sirening off to the rozz-shop, me being wedged between two millicents and being given the odd thump and malenky tolchock by these smecking bullies. Then I found I could open up my glaz-lids a malenky bit and viddy like through all tears a kind of a streamy city going by, all the lights like having run into one another. I could viddy now through smarting glazzies these two smecking millicents at the back with me and the thin-necked driver and the fat-necked bastard next to him, this one having a sarky like govoreet at me, saying: 'Well, Alex boy, we all look forward to a pleasant evening together, don't we not?' I said:

'How do you know my name, you stinking vonny bully? May Bog blast you to hell, grahzny bratchny as you are, you sod.' So they all had a smeck at that and I had my ooko like twisted by one of these stinking millicents at the back with me. The fat-necked not-driver said:

'Everybody knows little Alex and his droogs. Quite a famous young boy our Alex has become.'

'It's those others,' I creeched. 'Georgie and Dim and Pete. No droogs of mine, the bastards.'

'Well,' said the fat-neck, 'you've got the evening in front of you to tell the whole story of the daring exploits of those young gentlemen and how they led poor little innocent Alex astray.' Then there was the shoom of another like police siren passing this auto but going the other way.

'Is that for those bastards?' I said. 'Are they being picked up by you bastards?'

'That,' said fat-neck, 'is an ambulance. Doubtless for your old lady victim, you ghastly wretched scoundrel.'

'It was all their fault,' I creeched, blinking my smarting glazzies. 'The bastards will be peeting away in the Duke of New York. Pick them up, blast you, you vonny sods.' And then there was more smecking and another malenky tolchock, O my brothers, on my poor smarting rot. And then we arrived at the stinking rozz-shop and they helped me get out of the auto with kicks and pulls and they tolchocked me up the steps and I knew I was going to get nothing like fair play from these stinky grahzny bratchnies, Bog blast them.[4]

7

They dragged me into this very bright-lit whitewashed cantora, and it had a strong von that was a mixture of like sick and lavatories and beery rots and disinfectant, all coming from the barry places near by. You could hear some of the plennies in their cells cursing and singing and I fancied I could slooshy one belting out:

> 'And I will go back to my darling, my darling,
> When you, my darling, are gone.'

But there were the golosses of millicents telling them to shut it and you could even slooshy the zvook of like somebody being tolchocked real horrorshow and going owwwwwwwww, and it was like the goloss of a drunken starry ptitsa, not a man. With me in this cantora were four millicents, all having a good loud peet of chai, a big pot of it being on the table and they sucking and belching away over their dirty bolshy mugs. They didn't offer me any. All that they gave me, my brothers, was a crappy starry mirror to look into, and indeed I was not your handsome young Narrator any longer but a real strack of a sight, my rot swollen and my glazzies all red and my nose bumped a bit also. They all had a real horrorshow smeck when they viddied my like dismay, and one of them said: 'Love's young nightmare like.' And then a top millicent came in with like stars on his pletchoes to show he was high high high, and he viddied me and said: 'Hm.' So then they started. I said:

'I won't say one single solitary slovo unless I have my lawyer here. I know the law, you bastards.' Of course they all had a good gromky smeck at that and the stellar top millicent said:

'Righty right, boys, we'll start off by showing him that we know the law, too, but that knowing the law isn't everything.' He had a like gentleman's goloss and spoke in a very weary sort of a way, and he nodded with a like droogy smile at one very big fat bastard. This big fat bastard took off his tunic and you could viddy he had a real big starry pot on him, then he came up to me not too skorry and I could get the von of the milky chai he'd been peeting when he opened his rot in a like very tired leery grin at me. He was not too well shaved for a rozz and you could viddy like patches of dried

4. TS 54a: autograph sketch of policeman's head, wearing a peaked cap.

sweat on his shirt under the arms, and you could get this von of like earwax from him as he came close. Then he clenched his stinking red rooker and let me have it right in the belly, which was unfair, and all the other millicents smecked their gullivers off at that, except the top one and he kept on with this weary like bored grin. I had to lean against the whitewashed wall so that all the white got on to my platties, trying to drag the old breath back and in great agony, and then I wanted to sick up the gluey pie I'd had before the start of the evening. But I couldn't stand that sort of veshch, sicking all over the floor, so I held it back. Then I saw that this fatty bruiseboy was turning to his millicent droogs to have a real horrorshow smeck at what he'd done, so I raised my right noga and before they could creech at him to watch out I'd kicked him smart and lovely on the shin. And he creeched murder, hopping around.

But after that they all had a turn, bouncing me from one to the other like some very weary bloody ball, O my brothers, and fisting me in the yarbles and the rot and the belly and dealing out kicks, and then at last I had to sick up on the floor and, like some real bezoomny veck, I even said: 'Sorry, brothers, that was not the right thing at all. Sorry sorry sorry.' But they handed me starry bits of gazetta and made me wipe it, then they made me make with the sawdust. And then they said, almost like dear old droogs, that I was to sit down and we'd all have a quiet like govoreet. And then P. R. Deltoid came in to have a viddy, his office being in the same building, looking very tired and grahzny, to say: 'So it's happened, Alex boy, yes? Just as I thought it would. Dear dear dear, yes.' Then he turned to the millicents to say: 'Evening, inspector. Evening, sergeant. Evening, evening, all. Well, this is the end of the line for me, yes. Dear dear, this boy does look messy, doesn't he? Just look at the state of him.'

'Violence makes violence,' said the top millicent in a very holy type goloss. 'He resisted his lawful arresters.'

'End of the line, yes,' said P. R. Deltoid again. He looked at me with very cold glazzies like I had become a thing and was no more a bleeding very tired battered chelloveck. 'I suppose I'll have to be in court tomorrow.'

'It wasn't me, brother, sir,' I said, a malenky bit weepy. 'Speak up for me, sir, for I'm not so bad. I was led on by the treachery of the others, sir.'

'Sings like a linnet,' said the top rozz, sneery. 'Sings the roof off lovely, he does that.'

'I'll speak,' said cold P. R. Deltoid. 'I'll be there tomorrow, don't worry.'

'If you'd like to give him a bash in the chops, sir,' said the top millicent, 'don't mind us. We'll hold him down. He must be another great disappointment to you.'

P. R. Deltoid then did something I never thought any man like him who was supposed to turn us baddiwads into real horrorshow malchicks would do, especially with all those rozzes around. He came a bit nearer and he spat. He spat. He spat full in my litso and then wiped his wet spitty rot with the back of his rooker. And I wiped and wiped and wiped my spat-on litso with my bloody tash-took, saying: 'Thank you, sir, thank you very much, sir, that was very kind of you, sir, thank you.' And then P. R. Deltoid walked out without another slovo.

The millicents now got down to making this long statement for me to sign, and I thought to myself, Hell and blast you all, if all you bastards are on the side of the Good then I'm glad I belong to the other shop. 'All right,' I said to them, 'you grahzny bratchnies as you are, you vonny sods. Take it, take the lot. I'm not going to crawl around on my brooko any more, you merzky[1] gets. Where do you want it taken from, you cally vonning animals? From my last corrective? Horrorshow, horrorshow, here it is, then.' So I gave it to them, and I had this shorthand millicent, a very quiet and scared type chelloveck, no real rozz at all, covering page after page after page after. I gave them the ultra-violence, the crasting, the dratsing, the old in-out in-out, the lot, right up to this night's veshch with the bugatty starry ptitsa with the mewing kots and koshkas. And I made sure my so-called droogs were in it, right up to the shiyah. When I'd got through the lot the shorthand millicent looked a bit faint, poor old veck. The top rozz said to him, in a kind type goloss:

'Right, son, you go off and get a nice cup of chai for yourself and then type all that filth and rottenness out with a clothes-peg on your nose, three copies. Then they can be brought to our handsome young friend here for signature. And you,' he said to me, 'can now be shown to your bridal suite with running water and all conveniences. All right,' in this weary goloss to two of the real tough rozzes, 'take him away.'

So I was kicked and punched and bullied off to the cells and put in with about ten or twelve other plennies, a lot of them drunk. There were real oozhassny animal type vecks among them, one with his nose all ate away and his rot open like a big black hole, one that was lying on the floor snoring away and all like slime dribbling all the time out of his rot, and one that had like done all cal in his pantalonies. Then there were two like queer ones who both took a fancy to me, and one of them made a jump on to my back, and I had a real nasty bit of dratsing with him and the von on him, like of meth[2] and cheap scent, made me want to sick again, only my belly was empty

1. TS 57: autograph gloss, "мерзкий"
2. Methylated spirit, ethanol (alcohol) that has been "denatured" and dyed (pink in the United Kingdom) to prevent its use as a beverage. As it carries no excise duty, meths is cheap. Proverbially, meths is the drink of choice of tramps and the indigent. (Not to be confused with methamphetamine, as in crystal meth.)

now, O my brothers. Then the other queer one started putting his rookers on to me, and then there was a snarling bit of dratsing between these two, both of them wanting to get at my plott. The shoom became very loud, so that a couple of millicents came along and cracked into these two with like truncheons, so that both sat quiet then, looking like into space, and there was the old krovvy going drip drip drip down the litso of one of them. There were bunks in this cell, but all filled. I climbed up to the top one of one tier of bunks, there being four in a tier, and there was a starry drunken veck snoring away, most probably heaved up there to the top by the millicents. Anyway, I heaved him down again, him not being all that heavy, and he collapsed on top of a fat drunk chelloveck on the floor, and both woke and started creeching and punching pathetic at each other. So I lay down on this vonny bed, my brothers, and went to very tired and exhausted and hurt sleep. But it was not really like sleep, it was like passing out to another better world. And in this other better world, O my brothers, I was in like a big field with all flowers and trees, and there was a like goat with a man's litso playing away on a like flute. And then there rose like the sun Ludwig van himself with thundery litso and cravat and wild windy voloss, and then I heard the Ninth, last movement, with the slovos all a bit mixed-up like they knew themselves they had to be mixed-up, this being a dream:

> Boy, thou uproarious shark of heaven,
>> Slaughter of Elysium,
> Hearts on fire, aroused, enraptured,
>> We will tolchock you on the rot and kick
>> your grahzny vonny bum.[3]

But the tune was right, as I knew when I was being woke up two or ten minutes or twenty hours or days or years later, my watch having been taken away. There was a millicent like miles and miles down below and he was prodding at me with a long stick with a spike on the end, saying:

'Wake up, son. Wake up, my beauty. Wake to real trouble.' I said:

'Why? Who? Where? What is it?' And the tune of the Joy ode in the Ninth was singing away real lovely and horrorshow within. The millicent said:

'Come down and find out. There's some real lovely news for you, my son.' So I scrambled down, very stiff and sore and not like real

---

3. A parody of Schiller's "Ode to Joy." Burgess, in *A Clockwork Orange: A Play with Music*, p. 10, offers the following translation of Schiller's strophe:

> Joy thou glorious spark of heaven,
>> Daughter of Elysium,
> Hearts on fire, aroused, enraptured,
>> To thy sacred shrine we come.

awake, and this rozz, who had a strong von of cheese and onions on him, pushed me out of the filthy snoring cell, and then along corridors, and all the time the old tune Joy Thou Glorious Spark Of Heaven was sparking away within. Then we came to a very neat like cantora with typewriters and flowers on the desks, and at the like chief desk the top millicent was sitting, looking very serious and fixing a like very cold glazzy on my sleepy litso. I said:

'Well well well. What makes, bratty? What gives, this fine bright middle of the nochy?' He said:

'I'll give you just ten seconds to wipe that stupid grin off of your face. Then I want you to listen.'

'Well, what?' I said, smecking. 'Are you not satisfied with beating me near to death and having me spat upon and making me confess to crimes for hours on end and then shoving me among bezoomnies and vonny perverts in that grahzny cell? Have you some new torture for me, you bratchny?'

'It'll be your own torture,' he said, serious. 'I hope to God it'll torture you to madness.'

And then, before he told me, I knew what it was. The old ptitsa who had all the kots and koshkas had passed on to a better world in one of the city hospitals. I'd cracked her a bit too hard, like. Well, well, that was everything. I thought of all those kots and koshkas mewing for moloko and getting none, not any more from their starry forella of a mistress. That was everything. I'd done the lot, now. And me still only fifteen.[4]

---

4. TS 60: autograph sketch of Alex in cravat at the foot of the page.

Part Two

'What's it going to be then, eh?'

I take it up now, and this is the real weepy and like tragic part of the story beginning, my brothers and only friends, in Staja (State Jail, that is) Number 84F.[1] You will have little desire to slooshy all the cally and horrible raskazz of the shock that sent my dad beating his bruised and krovvy rookers against unfair like Bog in His Heaven, and my mum squaring her rot for owwwww owwwww owwwww in her mother's grief at her only child and son of her bosom like letting everybody down real horrorshow. Then there was the starry very grim magistrate in the lower court govoreeting some very hard slovos against your Friend and Humble Narrator, after all the cally and grahzny slander spat forth by P. R. Deltoid and the rozzes, Bog blast them. Then there was being remanded in filthy custody among vonny perverts and prestoopnicks. Then there was the trial in the higher court with judges and a jury, and some very very nasty slovos indeed govoreeted in a very like solemn way, and then Guilty and my mum boohoohooing when they said Fourteen Years, O my brothers. So here I was now, two years just to the day of being kicked and clanged into Staja 84F, dressed in the heighth of prison fashion, which was a one-piece suit of a very filthy like cal colour, and the number sewn on the groody part just above the old tick-tocker and on the back as well, so that going and coming I was 6655321 and not your little droog Alex not no longer.

'What's it going to be then, eh?'

It had not been like edifying, indeed it had not, being in this grahzny hellhole and like human zoo for two years, being kicked and tolchocked by brutal bully warders and meeting vonny leering like criminals, some of them real perverts and ready to dribble all over a luscious young malchick like your story-teller. And there was having to rabbit in the workshop at making matchboxes and itty round and round and round the yard for like exercise, and in the evenings

---

1. Numerological connection with Orwell's dystopia, in his *Nineteen Eighty-Four*.

sometimes some starry prof type veck would give a talk on beetles or
the Milky Way or the Glorious Wonders of the Snowflake, and I had
a good smeck at this last one, because it reminded me of that time of
the tolchocking and Sheer Vandalism with that ded coming from the
public biblio on a winter's night when my droogs were still not traitors and I was like happy and free. Of those droogs I had slooshied
but one thing, and that was one day when my pee and em came to
visit and I was told that Georgie was dead. Yes, dead, my brothers.
Dead as a bit of dog-cal on the road. Georgie had led the other two
into a like very rich[2] chelloveck's house, and there they had kicked
and tolchocked the owner on the floor, and then Georgie had started
to razrez the cushions and curtains, and then old Dim had cracked at
some very precious ornaments, like statues and so on, and this rich
beat-up chelloveck had raged like real bezoomny and gone for them
all with a very heavy iron bar. His being all razdraz had given him
like gigantic strength, and Dim and Pete had got out through the
window but Georgie had tripped on the carpet and then bought this
terrific swinging iron bar crack and splooge on the gulliver, and that
was the end of traitorous Georgie. The starry murderer had got off
with Self Defence, as was really right and proper. Georgie being
killed, though it was more than one year after me being caught by
the millicents, it all seemed right and proper and like Fate.

'What's it going to be then, eh?'
I was in the Wing Chapel, it being Sunday morning, and the
prison charlie was govoreeting the Word of the Lord. It was my rabbit
to play the starry stereo, putting on solemn music before and after
and in the middle too when hymns were sung. I was at the back of
the Wing Chapel (there were four altogether in Staja 84F) near where
the warders or chassos were standing with their rifles and their dirty
bolshy blue brutal jowls, and I could viddy all the plennies sitting
down slooshying the Slovo of the Lord in their horrible cal-coloured
prison platties, and a sort of filthy von rose from them, not like real
unwashed, not grazzy, but like a special real stinking von which you
only got with the criminal types, my brothers, a like dusty, greasy,
hopeless sort of a von. And I was thinking that perhaps I had this von
too, having become a real plenny myself, though still very young. So
it was very important to me, O my brothers, to get out of this stinking
grahzny zoo as soon as I could. And, as you will viddy if you keep
reading on, it was not long before I did.

'What's it going to be then, eh?' said the prison charlie for the third
raz. 'Is it going to be in and out and in and out of institutions like
this, though more in than out for most of you, or are you going to
attend to the Divine Word and realize the punishments that await

2. TS 62: autograph query, "bugatty?"

the unrepentant sinner in the next world, as well as in this? A lot of blasted idiots you are, most of you, selling your birthright for a saucer of cold porridge. The thrill of theft, of violence, the urge to live easy—is it worth it when we have undeniable proof, yes yes, incontrovertible evidence that hell exists? I know, I know, my friends, I have been informed in visions that there is a place, darker than any prison, hotter than any flame of human fire, where souls of unrepentant criminal sinners like yourselves—and don't leer at me, damn you, don't laugh—like yourselves, I say, scream in endless and intolerable agony, their noses choked with the smell of filth, their mouths crammed with burning ordure, their skin peeling and rotting, a fireball spinning in their screaming guts.[3] Yes, yes, yes, I know.'

At this point, brothers, a plenny somewhere or other near the back row let out a shoom of lip-music—'Prrrrrp'—and then the brutal chassos were on the job right away, rushing real skorry to what they thought was the scene of the shoom, then hitting out nasty and delivering tolchocks left and right. Then they picked out one poor trembling plenny, very thin and malenky and starry too, and dragged him off, but all the time he kept creeching: 'It wasn't me, it was him, see,' but that made no difference. He was tolchocked real nasty and then dragged out of the Wing Chapel creeching his gulliver off.

'Now,' said the prison charlie, 'listen to the Word of the Lord.' Then he picked up the big book and flipped over the pages, keeping on wetting his fingers to do this by licking them splurge splurge. He was a bolshy great burly bastard with a very red litso, but he was very fond of myself, me being young and also now very interested in the big book. It had been arranged as part of my like further education to read in the book and even have music on the chapel stereo while I was reading, O my brothers. And that was real horrorshow. They would like lock me in and let me slooshy holy music by J. S. Bach and G. F. Handel, and I would read of these starry yahoodies tolchocking each other and then peeting their Hebrew vino and getting on to the bed with their wives' like handmaidens, real horrorshow. That kept me going, brothers. I didn't so much kopat the later part of the book, which is more like all preachy govoreeting than fighting and the old in-out.[4] But one day the charles said to me, squeezing me like tight with his bolshy beefy rooker: 'Ah, 6655321, think on the divine suffering. Meditate on that, my boy.' And all the time he had this rich manny von of Scotch on him, and then he went off to

3. The prison charlie's sermon is a pale echo of the sermon on hell to which Stephen Dedalus listens in Joyce's *A Portrait of the Artist as a Young Man* (1916).
4. Note the parallel between Alex's account of the relationship between the Old Testament and the New Testament, and that between the twenty-chapter version of *A Clockwork Orange* and the twenty-first chapter.

his little cantora to peet some more. So I read all about the scourging and the crowning with thorns and then the cross veshch and all that cal, and I viddied better that there was something in it. While the stereo played bits of lovely Bach I closed my glazzies and viddied myself helping in and even taking charge of the tolchocking and the nailing in, being dressed in a like toga that was the heighth of Roman fashion. So being in Staja 84F was not all that wasted, and the Governor himself was very pleased to hear that I had taken to like Religion, and that was where I had my hopes.

This Sunday morning the charlie read out from the book about chellovecks who slooshied the slovo and didn't take a blind bit being like a domy built upon sand,[5] and then the rain came splash and the old boomaboom cracked the sky and that was the end of that domy. But I thought that only a very dim veck would build his domy upon sand, and a right lot of real sneering droogs and nasty neighbours a veck like that would have, them not telling him how dim he was doing that sort of building. Then the charles creeched: 'Right, you lot. We'll end with Hymn Number 435 in the Prisoners' Hymnal.' Then there was a crash and plop and a whish whish whish while the plennies picked up and dropped and lickturned the pages of their grazzy malenky hymnbooks, and the bully fierce warders creeched: 'Stop talking there, bastards. I'm watching you, 920537.' Of course I had the disc ready on the stereo, and then I let the simple music for organ only come belting out with a growwwwow-wwwowwww. Then the plennies started to sing real horrible:

> Weak tea are we, new brewed
>> But stirring make all strong.
> We eat no angel's food,
> ·   Our times of trial are long.[6]

They sort of howled and wept these stupid slovos with the charlie like whipping them on with 'Louder, damn you, sing up,' and the warders creeching: 'Just you wait, 7749222', and 'One on the turnip coming up for you, filth.' Then it was all over and the charlie said: 'May the Holy Trinity keep you always and make you good, amen,' and the shamble out began to a nice choice bit of Symphony No. 2 by Adrian Schweigselber,[7] chosen by your Humble Narrator, O my brothers. What a lot they were, I thought, as I stood there by the starry chapel stereo, viddying them all shuffle out going marrrrre

---

5. Jesus' parable of the rock and sand from Matthew 7.24–29.
6. TS 65: autograph staves with melodic line for "Weak tea are we, new brewed." Andrew Biswell, in *The Real Life of Anthony Burgess* (2005), p. 251, suggests reasons of expense for the omission of Burgess's music from lines in the Heinemann edition.
7. The composer Adrian Schweigselber is ironically named. The German verb *schweigen* means to be silent.

and baaaaaa like animals and up-your-piping with their grahzny
fingers at me, because it looked like I was very special favoured.
When the last one had slouched out, his rookers hanging like an
ape and the one warder left giving him a fair loud tolchock on the
back of the gulliver, and when I had turned off the stereo, the charlie came up to me, puffing away at a cancer, still in his starry bog-
man's platties, all lacy and white like a devotchka's. He said:

'Thank you as always, little 6655321. And what news have you
got for me today?' The idea was, I knew, that this charlie was after
becoming a very great holy chelloveck in the world of Prison Religion, and he wanted a real horrorshow testimonial from the Governor, so he would go and govoreet quietly to the Governor now and
then about what dark plots were brewing among the plennies, and
he would get a lot of this cal from me. A lot of it would be all like
made up, but some of it would be true, like for instance the time it
had come through to our cell on the waterpipes knock knock
knockiknockiknock knockknock that big Harriman was going to
break. He was going to tolchock the warder at slop-time and get out in
the warder's platties. Then there was going to be a big throwing
about of the horrible pishcha we got in the dining-hall, and I knew
about that and told. Then the charlie passed it on and was compli-
mented like by the Governor for his Public Spirit and Keen Ear. So
this time I said, and this was not true:

'Well, sir, it has come through on the pipes that a consignment of
cocaine has arrived by irregular means and that a cell somewhere
along Tier 5 is to be the centre of distribution.' I made all that up as
I went along, like I made up so many of these stories, but the prison
charlie was very grateful, saying: 'Good, good, good. I shall pass
that on to Himself,' this being what he called the Governor. Then
I said:

'Sir, I have done my best, have I not?' I always used my very polite
gentleman's goloss govoreeting with those at the top. 'I've tried, sir,
haven't I?'

'I think,' said the charlie, 'that on the whole you have, 6655321.
You've been very helpful and, I consider, shown a genuine desire to
reform. You will, if you continue in this manner, earn your remission with no trouble at all.'

'But sir,' I said, 'how about this new thing they're talking about?
How about this new like treatment that gets you out of prison in no
time at all and makes sure that you never get back in again?'

'Oh,' he said, very like wary. 'Where did you hear this? Who's
been telling you these things?'

'These things get around, sir,' I said. 'Two warders talk, as it
might be, and somebody can't help hearing what they say. And then
somebody picks up a scrap of newspaper in the workshops and the

newspaper says all about it. How about you putting me in for this thing, sir, if I may make so bold as to make the suggestion?'

You could viddy him thinking about that while he puffed away at his cancer, wondering how much to say to me about what he knew about this veshch I'd mentioned. Then he said: 'I take it you're referring to Ludovico's Technique.' He was still very wary.

'I don't know what it's called, sir,' I said. 'All I know is that it gets you out quickly and makes sure that you don't get in again.'

'That is so,' he said, his eyebrows like all beetling while he looked down at me. 'That is quite so, 6655321. Of course, it's only in the experimental stage at the moment. It's very simple but very drastic.'

'But it's being used here, isn't it, sir?' I said. 'Those new like white buildings by the South Wall, sir. We've watched those being built, sir, when we've been doing our exercise.'

'It's not been used yet,' he said, 'not in this prison, 6655321. Himself has grave doubts about it. I must confess I share those doubts. The question is whether such a technique can really make a man good. Goodness comes from within, 6655321. Goodness is something chosen. When a man cannot choose he ceases to be a man.' He would have gone on with a lot more of this cal, but we could slooshy the next lot of plennies marching clank clank down the iron stairs to come for their bit of Religion. He said: 'We'll have a little chat about this some other time. Now you'd better start the voluntary.' So I went over to the starry stereo and put on J. S. Bach's *Wachet Auf* Choral Prelude[8] and in these grahzny vonny bastard criminals and perverts came shambling like a lot of broke-down apes, the warders or chassos like barking at them and lashing them. And soon the prison charlie was asking them: 'What's it going to be then, eh?' And that's where you came in.

We had four of these lomticks of like Prison Religion that morning, but the charles said no more to me about this Ludovico's Technique, whatever it was, O my brothers. When I'd finished my rabbit with the stereo he just govoreeted a few slovos of thanks and then I was privodeeted back to the cell on Tier 6 which was my very vonny and crammed home. The chasso was not really too bad of a veck and he did not tolchock or kick me in when he'd opened up, he just said: 'Here we are, sonny, back to the old waterhole.' And there I was with my new type droogs, all very criminal but, Bog be praised, not given to perversions of the body. There was Zophar on his bunk, a very thin and brown veck who went on and on and on in his like cancery goloss, so that nobody bothered to slooshy. What he

8. The first of J. S. Bach's six Schübler Chorales for organ, a transcription of the central chorale of the Church Cantata "Wachet auf, ruft uns die Stimme" (Awake, we are called by the voice of the watchman), BWV 140, composed for the twenty-seventh Sunday after Trinity 1731.

was saying now like to nobody was 'And at that time you couldn't get hold of a poggy' (whatever that was, brothers), 'not if you was to hand over ten million archibalds, so what do I do eh, I goes down to Turkey's and says I've got this sproog on that morrow, see, and what can he do?' It was all this very old-time real criminal's slang he spoke. Also there was Wall, who had only one glazzy, and he was tearing bits of his toe-nails off in honour of Sunday. Also there was Big Jew, a very fat sweaty veck lying flat on his bunk like dead. In addition there were Jojohn and The Doctor. Jojohn was very mean and keen and wiry and had specialized in like Sexual Assault, and The Doctor had pretended to be able to cure syph and gon and gleet but he had only injected water, also he had killed off two devotchkas instead, like he had promised, of getting rid of their unwanted loads for them. They were a terrible grahzny lot really, and I didn't enjoy being with them, O my brothers, any more than you do now, but it won't be for much longer.

Now what I want you to know is that this cell was intended for only three when it was built, but there were six of us there, all jammed together sweaty and tight. And that was the state of all the cells in all the prisons in those days, brothers, and a dirty cally disgrace it was, there not being decent room for a chelloveck to stretch his limbs. And you will hardly believe what I say now, which is that on this Sunday they brosatted in another plenny. Yes, we had had our horrible pishcha of dumplings and vonny stew and were smoking a quiet cancer each on our bunks when this veck was thrown into our midst. He was a chinny starry veck and it was him who started creeching complaints before we even had a chance to viddy the position. He tried to like shake the bars, creeching: 'I demand my sodding rights, this one's full-up, it's a bleeding imposition, that's what it is.' But one of the chassos came back to say that he had to make the best of it and share a bunk with whoever would let him, otherwise it would have to be the floor. 'And,' said the warder, 'it's going to get worse, not better. A right dirty criminal world you lot are trying to build.'

2

Well, it was the letting-in of this new chelloveck that was really the start of my getting out of the old Staja, for he was such a nasty quarrelsome type of plenny, with a very dirty mind and filthy intentions, that trouble nachinatted that very same day. He was also very boastful and started to make with a very sneery litso at us all and a loud proud goloss. He made out that he was the only real horrorshow prestoopnick in the whole zoo, going on that he'd done this and done the other and killed ten rozzes with one crack of his

rooker and all that cal. But nobody was very impressed, O my brothers. So then he started on me, me being the youngest there, trying to
say that as the youngest I ought to be the one to zasnoot on the floor
and not him. But all the others were for me, creeching: 'Leave him
alone, you grahzny bratchny,' and then he began the old whine about
how nobody loved him. So that same nochy I woke up to find this
horrible plenny actually lying with me on my bunk, which was on the
bottom of the three-tier and also very narrow, and he was govoreeting dirty like love-slovos and stroke stroke stroking away. So then
I got real bezoomny and lashed out, though I could not viddy all that
horrorshow, there being only this malenky little red light outside on
the landing. But I knew it was this one, the vonny bastard, and then
when the trouble really got under way and the lights were turned on
I could viddy his horrible litso with all krovvy dripping from his rot
where I'd hit out with my clawing rooker.

What sloochatted then, of course, was that my cellmates woke up
and started to join in, tolchocking a bit wild in the near-dark, and the
shoom seemed to wake up the whole tier, so that you could slooshy
a lot of creeching and banging about with tin mugs on the wall, as
though all the plennies in all the cells thought a big break was about
to commence, O my brothers. So then the lights came on and the
chassos came along in their shirts and trousers and caps, waving big
sticks. We could viddy each other's flushed litsos and the shaking of
fisty rookers, and there was a lot of creeching and cursing. Then I put
in my complaint and every chasso said it was probably Your Humble
Narrator, brothers, that started it all anyway, me having no mark of a
scratch on me but this horrible plenny dripping red red krovvy from
the rot where I'd got him with my clawing rooker. That made me real
bezoomny. I said I would not sleep another nochy in that cell if the
Prison Authorities were going to allow horrible vonny stinking per-
verted prestoopnicks to leap on my plott when I was in no position to
defend myself, being asleep. 'Wait till the morning,' they said. 'Is it a
private room with bath and television that your honour requires?
Well, all that will be seen to in the morning. But for the present, little
droog, get your bleeding gulliver down on your straw-filled podooshka
and let's have no more trouble from anyone. Right right right?' Then
off they went with stern warnings for all, then soon after the lights
went out, and then I said I would sit up all the rest of the nochy, saying first to this horrible prostoopnick: 'Go on, get on my bunk if you
wish it. I fancy it no longer. You have made it filthy and cally with
your horrible vonny plott lying on it already.' But then the others
joined in. Big Jew said, still sweating from the bit of a bitva we'd had
in the dark:

'Not having that we're not, brotherth. Don't give in to the thquirt.'
So this new one said:

'Crash your dermott, yid,' meaning to shut up, but it was very insulting. So then Big Jew got ready to launch a tolchock. The Doctor said:

'Come on, gentlemen, we don't want any trouble, do we?' in his very high-class goloss, but this new prestoopnick was really asking for it. You could viddy that he thought he was a very big bolshy veck and it was beneath his dignity to be sharing a cell with six and having to sleep on the floor till I made this gesture at him. In his sneery way he tried to take off The Doctor, saying:

'Owwww, yew wahnt noo moor trabble, is that it, Archiballs?' So Jojohn, mean and keen and wiry, said:

'If we can't have sleep let's have some education. Our new friend here had better be taught a lesson.' Although he like specialized in Sexual Assault he had a nice way of govoreeting, quiet and like precise. So the new plenny sneered:

'Kish and kosh and koosh, you little terror.' So then it all really started, but in a queer like gentle way, with nobody raising his goloss much. The new plenny creeched a malenky bit at first, but then Wall fisted his rot while Big Jew held him up against the bars so that he could be viddied in the malenky red light from the landing, and he just went oh oh oh. He was not a very strong type of veck, being very feeble in his trying to tolchock back, and I suppose he made up for this by being shoomny in the goloss and very boastful. Anyway, seeing the old krovvy flow red in the red light, I felt the old joy like rising up in my keeshkas and I said:

'Leave him to me, go on, let me have him now, brothers.' So Big Jew said:

'Yeth, yeth, boyth, that'th fair. Thlosh him then, Alekth.' So they all stood around while I cracked at this prestoopnick in the near dark. I fisted him all over, dancing about with my boots on though unlaced, and then I tripped him and he went crash crash on to the floor. I gave him one real horrorshow kick on the gulliver and he went ohhhhh, then he sort of snorted off to like sleep, and The Doctor said:

'Very well, I think that will be enough of a lesson,' squinting to viddy this downed and beaten-up veck on the floor. 'Let him dream perhaps about being a better boy in the future.' So we all climbed back into our bunks, being very tired now. What I dreamt of, O my brothers, was of being in some very big orchestra, hundreds and hundreds strong, and the conductor was a like mixture of Ludwig van and G. F. Handel,[1] looking very deaf and blind and weary of the

---

1. G. F. Handel (1685–1759), German composer who settled in London, and is best known for the oratorio *Messiah* (based on the Bible in English), which premiered in Dublin in 1742.

world. I was with the wind instruments, but what I was playing was like a white pinky bassoon made of flesh and growing out of my plott, right in the middle of my belly, and when I blew into it I had to smeck ha ha ha very loud because it like tickled, and then Ludwig van G. F. got very razdraz and bezoomny. Then he came right up to my litso and creeched loud in my ooko, and then I woke up like sweating. Of course, what the loud shoom really was was the prison buzzer going brrrrr brrrrr brrrrr. It was winter morning and my glazzies were all cally with sleepglue, and when I opened up they were very sore in the electric light that had been switched on all over the zoo. Then I looked down and viddied this new prestoopnick lying on the floor, very bloody and bruisy and still out out out. Then I remembered about last night and that made me smeck a bit.

But when I got off the bunk and moved him with my bare noga, there was a feel of like stiff coldness, so I went over to The Doctor's bunk and shook him, him always being very slow at waking up in the morning. But he was off his bunk skorry enough this time, and so were the others, except for Wall who slept like dead meat. 'Very unfortunate,' The Doctor said. 'A heart attack, that's what it must have been.' Then he said, looking round at us all: 'You really shouldn't have gone for him like that. It was most ill-advised really.' Jojohn said:

'Come come, doc, you weren't all that backward yourself in giving him a sly bit of fist.' Then Big Jew turned on me, saying:

'Alekth, you were too impetuouth. That latht kick wath a very very nathty one.' I began to get razdraz about this and said:

'Who started it, eh? I only got in at the end, didn't I?' I pointed at Jojohn and said: 'It was your idea.' Wall snored a bit loud, so I said: 'Wake that vonny bratchny up. It was him that kept on at his rot while Big Jew here had him up against the bars.' The Doctor said:

'Nobody will deny having a gentle little hit at the man, to teach him a lesson so to speak, but it's apparent that you, my dear boy, with the forcefulness and, shall I say, heedlessness of youth, dealt him the coo de grass. It's a great pity.'

'Traitors,' I said. 'Traitors and liars,' because I could viddy it was all like before, two years before, when my so-called droogs had left me to the brutal rookers of the millicents. There was no trust anywhere in the world, O my brothers, the way I could see it. And Jojohn went and woke up Wall, and Wall was only too ready to swear that it was Your Humble Narrator that had done the real dirty tolchocking and brutality. When the chassos came along, and then the Chief Chasso, and then the Governor himself, all these cell-droogs of mine were very shoomny with tales of what I'd done to oobivat this worthless pervert whose krovvy-covered plott lay sacklike on the floor.

That was a very queer day, O my brothers. The dead plott was carried off, and then everybody in the whole prison had to stay locked
up till further orders, and there was no pishcha given out, not even a
mug of hot chai. We just all sat there, and the warders or chassos sort
of strode up and down the tier, now and then creeching 'Shut it' or
'Close that hole' whenever they slooshied even a whisper from any of
the cells. Then about eleven o'clock in the morning there was a sort
of like stiffening and excitement and like the von of fear spreading
from outside the cell, and then we could viddy the Governor and the
Chief Chasso and some very bolshy important-looking chellovecks
walking by real skorry, govoreeting like bezoomny. They seemed to
walk right to the end of the tier, then they could be slooshied walking
back again, more slow this time, and you could slooshy the Governor,
a very sweaty fatty fair-haired veck, saying slovos like 'But, sir—' and
'Well, what can be done, sir?' and so on. Then the whole lot stopped
at our cell and the Chief Chasso opened up. You could viddy who was
the real important veck right away, very tall and with blue glazzies
and with real horrorshow platties on him, the most lovely suit, brothers, I had ever viddied, absolutely in the heighth of fashion. He just
sort of looked right through us poor plennies, saying, in a very beautiful real educated goloss: 'The Government cannot be concerned
any longer with outmoded penological theories. Cram criminals
together and see what happens. You get concentrated criminality,
crime in the midst of punishment. Soon we may be needing all our
prison space for political offenders.' I didn't pony this at all, brothers,
but after all he was not govoreeting to me. Then he said: 'Common
criminals like this unsavoury crowd'—(that meant me, brothers, as
well as the others, who were real prestoopnicks and treacherous with
it)—'can best be dealt with on a purely curative basis. Kill the criminal reflex, that's all. Full implementation in a year's time. Punishment means nothing to them, you can see that. They enjoy their
so-called punishment. They start murdering each other.' And he
turned his stern blue glazzies on me. So I said, bold:
'With respect, sir, I object very strongly to what you said then. I
am not a common criminal, sir, and I am not unsavoury. The others
may be unsavoury but I am not.' The Chief Chasso went all purple
and creeched:
'You shut your bleeding hole, you. Don't you know who this is?'
'All right, all right,' said this big veck. Then he turned to the Governor and said: 'You can use him as a trailblazer. He's young, bold,
vicious. Brodsky will deal with him tomorrow and you can sit in
and watch Brodsky. It works all right, don't worry about that. This
vicious young hoodlum will be transformed out of all recognition.'
And those hard slovos, brothers, were like the beginning of my
freedom.

3

That very same evening I was dragged down nice and gentle by brutal tolchocking chassos to viddy the Governor in his holy of holies holy office. The Governor looked very weary at me and said: 'I don't suppose you know who that was this morning, do you, 6655321?' And without waiting for me to say no he said: 'That was no less a personage than the Minister of the Interior, the new Minister of the Interior and what they call a very new broom. Well, these new ridiculous ideas have come at last and orders are orders, though I may say to you in confidence that I do not approve. I most emphatically do not approve. An eye for an eye, I say.[1] If someone hits you you hit back, do you not? Why then should not the State, very severely hit by you brutal hooligans, not hit back also? But the new view is to say no. The new view is that we turn the bad into the good. All of which seems to me grossly unjust. Hm?' So I said, trying to be like respectful and accommodating:

'Sir.' And then the Chief Chasso, who was standing all red and burly behind the Governor's chair, creeched:

'Shut your filthy hole, you scum.'

'All right, all right,' said the like tired and fagged-out Governor. 'You, 6655321, are to be reformed. Tomorrow you go to this man Brodsky. It is believed that you will be able to leave State Custody in a little over a fortnight. In a little over a fortnight you will be out again in the big free world, no longer a number. I suppose,' and he snorted a bit here, 'that prospect pleases you?' I said nothing so the Chief Chasso creeched:

'Answer, you filthy young swine, when the Governor asks you a question.' So I said:

'Oh, yes, sir. Thank you very much, sir. I've done my best here, really I have. I'm very grateful to all concerned.'

'Don't be,' like sighed the Governor. 'This is not a reward. This is far from being a reward. Now, there is a form here to be signed. It says that you are willing to have the residue of your sentence commuted to submission to what is called here, ridiculous expression, Reclamation Treatment. Will you sign?'

'Most certainly I will sign,' I said, 'sir. And very many thanks.' So I was given an ink-pencil and I signed my name nice and flowy. The Governor said:

'Right. That's the lot, I think.' The Chief Chasso said:

'The Prison Chaplain would like a word with him, sir.' So I was marched out and off down the corridor towards the Wing Chapel,

1. Exodus 21.23–25.

tolchocked on the back and the gulliver all the way by one of the chassos, but in a very like yawny and bored manner. And I was marched across the Wing Chapel to the little cantora of the charles and then made to go in. The charles was sitting at his desk, smelling loud and clear of a fine manny von of expensive cancers and Scotch. He said:

'Ah, little 6655321, be seated.' And to the chassos: 'Wait outside, eh?' Which they did. Then he spoke in a very like earnest way to me, saying: 'One thing I want you to understand, boy, is that this is nothing to do with me. Were it expedient, I would protest about it, but it is not expedient. There is the question of my own career, there is the question of the weakness of my own voice when set against the shout of certain more powerful elements in the polity. Do I make myself clear?' He didn't, brothers, but I nodded that he did. 'Very hard ethical questions are involved,' he went on. 'You are to be made into a good boy, 6655321. Never again will you have the desire to commit acts of violence or to offend in any way whatsoever against the State's Peace. I hope you take all that in. I hope you are absolutely clear in your own mind about that.' I said:

'Oh, it will be nice to be good, sir.' But I had a real horrorshow smeck at that inside, brothers. He said:

'It may not be nice to be good, little 6655321. It may be horrible to be good. And when I say that to you I realize how self-contradictory that sounds. I know I shall have many sleepless nights about this. What does God want? Does God want goodness or the choice of goodness? Is a man who chooses the bad perhaps in some way better than a man who has the good imposed upon him? Deep and hard questions, little 6655321. But all I want to say to you now is this: if at any time in the future you look back to these times and remember me, the lowest and humblest of all God's servitors, do not, I pray, think evil of me in your heart, thinking me in any way involved in what is now about to happen to you. And now, talking of praying, I realize sadly that there will be little point in praying for you. You are passing now to a region where you will be beyond the reach of the power of prayer. A terrible terrible thing to consider. And yet, in a sense, in choosing to be deprived of the ability to make an ethical choice, you have in a sense really chosen the good. So I shall like to think. So, God help us all, 6655321, I shall like to think.' And then he began to cry. But I didn't really take much notice of that, brothers, only having a bit of a quiet smeck inside, because you could viddy that he had been peeting away at the old whisky, and now he took a bottle from a cupboard in his desk and started to pour himself a real horrorshow bolshy slog into a very greasy and grahzny glass. He downed it and then said: 'All may be well, who knows? God works in a mysterious way.' Then he began to sing away at a hymn in a real loud rich goloss. Then the door opened and the chassos came in to tolchock me back to my vonny cell, but the old charles still went on singing this hymn.

Well, the next morning I had to say goodbye to the old Staja, and I felt a malenky bit sad as you always will when you have to leave a place you've like got used to. But I didn't go very far, O my brothers. I was punched and kicked along to the new white building just beyond the yard where we used to do our bit of exercise. This was a very new building and it had a new cold like sizy smell which gave you a bit of the shivers. I stood there in the horrible bolshy bare hall and I got new vons, sniffing away there with my like very sensitive morder or sniffer. These were like hospital vons, and the chelloveck the chassos handed me over to had a white coat on, as he might be a hospital man. He signed for me, and one of the brutal chassos who had brought me said: 'You watch this one, sir. A right brutal bastard he has been and will be again, in spite of all his sucking up to the Prison Chaplain and reading the Bible.' But this new chelloveck had real horrorshow blue glazzies which like smiled when he govoreeted. He said:

'Oh, we don't anticipate any trouble. We're going to be friends, aren't we?' And he smiled with his glazzies and his fine big rot which was full of shining white zoobies and I sort of took to this veck right away. Anyway, he passed me on to a like lesser veck in a white coat, and this one was very nice too, and I was led off to a very nice white clean bedroom with curtains and a bedside lamp, and just the one bed in it, all for Your Humble Narrator. So I had a real horrorshow inner smeck at that, thinking I was really a very lucky young malchickiwick. I was told to take off my horrible prison platties and I was given a really beautiful set of pyjamas, O my brothers, in plain green, the heighth of bedwear fashion. And I was given a nice warm dressing-gown too and lovely toofles to put my bare nogas in, and I thought: 'Well, Alex boy, little 6655321 as was, you have copped it lucky and no mistake. You are really going to enjoy it here.'

After I had been given a nice chasha of real horrorshow coffee and some old gazettas and mags to look at while peeting it, this first veck in white came in, the one who had like signed for me, and he said: 'Aha, there you are,' a silly sort of a veshch to say but it didn't sound silly, this veck being so like nice. 'My name,' he said, 'is Dr Branom. I'm Dr Brodsky's assistant. With your permission, I'll just give you the usual brief overall examination.' And he took the old stetho out of his right carman. 'We must make sure you're quite fit, mustn't we? Yes indeed, we must.' So while I lay there with my pyjama top off and he did this, that and the other, I said:

'What exactly is it, sir, that you're going to do?'

'Oh,' said Dr Branom, his cold stetho going all down my back, 'it's quite simple, really. We just show you some films.'

'Films?' I said. I could hardly believe my ookos, brothers, as you may well understand. 'You mean,' I said, 'it will be just like going to the pictures?'

'They'll be special films,' said this Dr Branom. 'Very special films. You'll be having the first session this afternoon. Yes,' he said, getting up from bending over me, 'you seem to be quite a fit young boy. A bit under-nourished, perhaps. That will be the fault of the prison food. Put your pyjama top back on. After every meal,' he said, sitting on the edge of the bed, 'we shall be giving you a shot in the arm. That should help.' I felt really grateful to this very nice Dr Branom. I said:

'Vitamins, sir, will it be?'

'Something like that,' he said, smiling real horrorshow and friendly. 'Just a jab in the arm after every meal.' Then he went out. I lay on the bed thinking this was like real heaven, and I read some of the mags they'd given me—*Worldsport*, *Sinny* (this being a film mag) and *Goal*. Then I lay back on the bed and shut my glazzies and thought how nice it was going to be out there again, Alex with perhaps a nice easy job during the day, me being now too old for the old skolliwoll, and then perhaps getting a new like gang together for the nochy, and the first rabbit would be to get old Dim and Pete, if they had not been got already by the millicents. This time I would be very careful not to get loveted. They were giving another like chance, me having done murder and all, and it would not be like fair to get loveted again, after going to all this trouble to show me films that were going to make me a real good malchick. I had a real horrorshow smeck at everybody's like innocence, and I was smecking my gulliver off when they brought in my lunch on a tray. The veck who brought it was the one who'd led me to this malenky bedroom when I came into the mesto, and he said:

'It's nice to know somebody's happy.' It was really a very nice appetizing bit of pishcha they'd laid out on the tray—two or three lomticks of like hot roastbeef with mashed kartoffel and vedge, then there was also ice-cream and a nice hot chasha of chai. And there was even a cancer to smoke and a matchbox with one match in. So this looked like it was the life, O my brothers. Then, about half an hour after while I was lying a bit sleepy on the bed, a woman nurse came in, a real nice young devotchka with real horrorshow groodies (I had not seen such for two years) and she had a tray and a hypodermic. I said:

'Ah, the old vitamins, eh?' And I clickclicked at her but she took no notice. All she did was to slam the needle into my left arm, and then swishhhh in went the vitamin stuff. Then she went out again, clack clack on her high-heeled nogas. Then the white-coated veck who was like a male nurse came in with a wheelchair. I was a malenky bit surprised to viddy that. I said:

'What giveth then, brother? I can walk, surely, to wherever we have to itty to.' But he said:

'Best I push you there.' And indeed, O my brothers, when I got off the bed I found myself a malenky bit weak. It was the under-nourishment like Dr Branom had said, all that horrible prison pish-cha. But the vitamins in the after-meal injection would put me right. No doubt at all about that, I thought.

4

Where I was wheeled to, brothers, was like no sinny I had ever viddied before. True enough, one wall was all covered with silver screen, and direct opposite was a wall with square holes in for the projector to project through, and there were stereo speakers stuck all over the mesto. But against the right-hand one of the other walls was a bank of all like little meters, and in the middle of the floor facing the screen was like a dentist's chair with all lengths of wire running from it, and I had to like crawl from the wheelchair to this, being given some help by another like male nurse veck in a white coat. Then I noticed that underneath the projection holes was like all frosted glass and I thought I viddied shadows of like people moving behind it and I thought I slooshied somebody cough kashl kashl kashl. But then all I could like notice was how weak I seemed to be, and I put that down to changing over from prison pishcha to this new rich pishcha and the vitamins injected into me. 'Right,' said the wheelchair-wheeling veck, 'now I'll leave you. The show will commence as soon as Dr Brodsky arrives. Hope you enjoy it.' To be truthful, brothers, I did not really feel that I wanted to viddy any film-show this afternoon. I was just not in the mood. I would have liked much better to have a nice quiet spachka on the bed, nice and quiet and all on my oddy knocky. I felt very limp.

What happened now was that one white-coated veck strapped my gulliver to a like head-rest, singing to himself all the time some vonny cally pop-song. 'What's this for?' I said. And this veck replied, inter-rupting his like song an instant, that it was to keep my gulliver still and make me look at the screen. 'But,' I said, 'I *want* to look at the screen. I've been brought here to viddy films and viddy films I shall.' And then the other white-coat veck (there were three altogether, one of them a devotchka who was like sitting at the bank of meters and twiddling with knobs) had a bit of a smeck at that. He said:

'You never know. Oh, you never know. Trust us, friend. It's better this way.' And then I found they were strapping my rookers to the chair-arms and my nogas were like stuck to a foot-rest. It seemed a bit bezoomny to me but I let them get on with what they wanted to get on with. If I was to be a free young malchick again in a fortnight's time I would put up with much in the meantime, O my brothers. One veshch I did not like, though, was when they put like clips on the skin of my forehead, so that my top glaz-lids were pulled up and up and up and I could not shut my glazzies no matter how I tried. I tried to smeck and said: 'This must be a real horrorshow film if you're so keen on my viddying it.' And one of the white-coat vecks said, smecking:

'Horrorshow is right, friend. A real show of horrors.' And then I had like a cap stuck on my gulliver and I could viddy all wires running away from it, and they stuck a like suction pad on my belly and one on the old tick-tocker, and I could just about viddy wires running away from those. Then there was the shoom of a door opening and you could tell some very important chelloveck was coming in by the way the white-coated under-vecks went all stiff. And then I viddied this Dr Brodsky. He was a malenky veck, very fat, with all curly hair curling all over his gulliver, and on his spuddy nose he had very thick ochkies. I could just viddy that he had a real horrorshow suit on, absolutely the heighth of fashion, and he had a like very delicate and subtle von of operating-theatres coming from him. With him was Dr Branom, all smiling like as though to give me confidence. 'Everything ready?' said Dr Brodsky in a very breathy goloss. Then I could slooshy voices saying Right right right from like a distance, then nearer to, then there was a quiet like humming shoom as though things had been switched on. And then the lights went out and there was Your Humble Narrator And Friend sitting alone in the dark, all on his frightened oddy knocky, not able to move nor shut his glazzies nor anything. And then, O my brothers, the film-show started off with some very gromky atmosphere music coming from the speakers, very fierce and full of discord. And then on the screen the picture came on, but there was no title and no credits. What came on was a street, as it might have been any street in any town, and it was a real dark nochy and the lamps were lit. It was a very good like professional piece of sinny, and there were none of these flickers and blobs you get, say, when you viddy one of these dirty films in somebody's house in a back street. All the time the music bumped out, very like sinister. And then you could viddy an old man coming down the street, very starry, and then there leaped out on this starry veck two malchicks dressed in the heighth of fashion, as it was at this time (still thin trousers but no like cravat any more, more of a real tie), and then they started to filly with him.

You could slooshy his screams and moans, very realistic, and you could even get the like heavy breathing and panting of the two tolchocking malchicks. They made a real pudding out of this starry veck, going crack crack crack at him with their fisty rookers, tearing his platties off and then finishing up by booting his nagoy plott (this lay all krovvy-red in the grahzny mud of the gutter) and then running off very skorry. Then there was the close-up gulliver of this beaten-up starry veck, and the krovvy flowed beautiful red. It's funny how the colours of the like real world only seem really real when you viddy them on the screen.

Now all the time I was watching this I was beginning to get very aware of a like not feeling all that well, and this I put down to the under-nourishment and my stomach not quite ready for the rich pishcha and vitamins I was getting here. But I tried to forget this, concentrating on the next film which came on at once, my brothers, without any break at all. This time the film like jumped right away on a young devotchka who was being given the old in-out by first one malchick then another then another then another, she creeching away very gromky through the speakers and like very pathetic and tragic music going on at the same time. This was real, very real, though if you thought about it properly you couldn't imagine lewdies actually agreeing to having all this done to them in a film, and if these films were made by the Good or the State you couldn't imagine them being allowed to take these films without like interfering with what was going on. So it must have been very clever what they call cutting or editing or some such veshch. For it was very real. And when it came to the sixth or seventh malchick leering and smecking and then going into it and the devotchka creeching on the soundtrack like bezoomny, then I began to feel sick. I had like pains all over and felt I could sick up and at the same time not sick up, and I began to feel like in distress, O my brothers, being fixed rigid too on this chair. When this bit of film was over I could slooshy the goloss of this Dr Brodsky from over by the switchboard saying: 'Reaction about twelve point five? Promising, promising.'

Then we shot straight into another lomtick of film, and this time it was of just a human litso, a very like pale human face held still and having different nasty veshches done to it. I was sweating a malenky bit with the pain in my guts and a horrible thirst and my gulliver going throb throb throb, and it seemed to me that if I could not viddy this bit of film I would perhaps be not so sick. But I could not shut my glazzies, and even if I tried to move my glaz-balls about I still could not get like out of the line of fire of this picture. So I had to go on viddying what was being done and hearing the most ghastly creechings coming from this litso. I knew it could not really be *real*, but that made no difference. I was heaving away but could not sick, viddying first a britva cut out an eye,[1] then slice down the cheek, then go rip rip rip all over, while red krovvy shot on to the camera lens. Then all the teeth were like wrenched out with a pair of pliers, and the creeching and the blood were terrific. Then I slooshied this very pleased goloss of Dr Brodsky going: 'Excellent, excellent, excellent.'

The next lomtick of film was of an old woman who kept a shop being kicked about amid very gromky laughter by a lot of malchicks, and these malchicks broke up the shop and then set fire to it. You could viddy this poor starry ptitsa trying to crawl out of the flames, screaming and creeching, but having had her leg broke by these malchicks kicking her she could not move. So then all the flames went roaring round her, and you could viddy her agonized litso like appealing through the flames and then disappearing in the flames, and then you could slooshy the most gromky and agonized and agonizing screams that ever came from a human goloss. So this time I knew I had to sick up, so I creeched:

'I want to be sick. Please let me be sick. Please bring something for me to be sick into.' But this Dr Brodsky called back:

'Imagination only. You've nothing to worry about. Next film coming up.' That was perhaps meant to be a joke, for I heard a like smeck coming from the dark. And then I was forced to viddy a most nasty film about Japanese torture. It was the 1939–45 War, and there were soldiers being fixed to trees with nails and having fires lit under them and having their yarbles cut off, and you even viddied a gulliver being sliced off a soldier with a sword, and then with his head rolling about and the rot and the glazzies looking alive still, the plott of this soldier actually ran about, krovvy like a fountain out of the neck, and then it dropped, and all the time there was very very loud laughter from the Japanese. The pains I felt now in my belly and the headache and the thirst were terrible, and they all seemed to be coming out of the screen. So I creeched:

'Stop the film! Please, please stop it! I can't stand any more.' And then the goloss of this Dr Brodsky said:

'Stop it? *Stop it*, did you say? Why, we've hardly started.' And he and the others smecked quite loud.

---

1. A sequence in which a razor is used to cut an eyeball is central to the effect and the reputation of the surrealist film *Un Chien Andalou* (1929), directed by Luis Buñuel and Salvador Dalí.

5

I do not wish to describe, brothers, what other horrible veshches I
was like forced to viddy that afternoon. The like minds of this Dr
Brodsky and Dr Branom and the others in white coats, and remember there was this devotchka twiddling with the knobs and watching the meters, they must have been more cally and filthy than any
prestoopnick in the Staja itself. Because I did not think it was possible for any veck to even think of making films of what I was forced
to viddy, all tied to this chair and my glazzies made to be wide open.
All I could do was to creech very gromky for them to turn it off,
turn it off, and that like part drowned the noise of dratsing and fillying and also the music that went with it all. You can imagine it
was a like a terrible relief when I'd viddied the last bit of film and
this Dr Brodsky said, in a very yawny and bored like goloss: 'I think
that should be enough for Day One, don't you, Branom?' And there
I was with the lights switched on, my gulliver throbbing like a bolshy big engine that makes pain, and my rot all dry and cally inside,
and feeling I could like sick up every bit of pishcha I had ever eaten,
O my brothers, since the day I was like weaned. 'All right,' said this
Dr Brodsky, 'he can be taken back to his bed.' Then he like patted
me on the pletcho and said: 'Good, good. A very promising start,'
grinning all over his litso, then he like waddled out, Dr Branom after
him, but Dr Branom gave me a like very droogy and sympathetic type
smile as though he had nothing to do with all this veshch but was
like forced into it as I was.

Anyhow, they freed my plott from the chair and they let go the
skin above my glazzies so that I could open and shut them again,
and I shut them, O my brothers, with the pain and throb in my
gulliver, and then I was like carried to the old wheelchair and taken
back to my malenky bedroom, the under-veck who wheeled me
singing away at some hound-and-horny popsong so that I like snarled:
'Shut it, thou,' but he only smecked and said: 'Never mind, friend,'
and then sang louder. So I was put into the bed and still felt bolnoy
but could not sleep, but soon I started to feel that soon I might start
to feel that I might soon start feeling just a malenky bit better, and
then I was brought some nice hot chai with plenty of moloko and
sakar and, peeting that, I knew that that like horrible nightmare
was in the past and all over. And then Dr Branom came in, all nice
and smiling. He said:

'Well, by my calculations you should be starting to feel all right
again. Yes?'

'Sir,' I said, like wary. I did not quite kopat what he was getting at
govoreeting about calculations, seeing that getting better from feel-

ing bolnoy is like your own affair and nothing to do with calcula-
tions. He sat down, all nice and droogy, on the bed's edge and said:
   'Dr Brodsky is pleased with you. You had a very positive response.
Tomorrow, of course, there'll be two sessions, morning and afternoon, and I should imagine that you'll be feeling a bit limp at the
end of the day. But we have to be hard on you, you have to be
cured.' I said:
   'You mean I have to sit through—? You mean I have to look at—?
Oh, no,' I said. 'It was horrible.'
   'Of course it was horrible,' smiled Dr Branom. 'Violence is a very
horrible thing. That's what you're learning now. Your body is learning it.'
   'But,' I said, 'I don't understand. I don't understand about feeling
sick like I did. I never used to feel sick before. I used to feel like very
the opposite. I mean, doing it or watching it I used to feel real horrorshow. I just don't understand why or how or what—'
   'Life is a very wonderful thing,' said Dr Branom in a like very holy
goloss. 'The processes of life, the make-up of the human organism,
who can fully understand these miracles? Dr Brodsky is, of course,
a remarkable man. What is happening to you now is what should
happen to any normal healthy human organism contemplating the
actions of the forces of evil, the workings of the principle of destruction. You are being made sane, you are being made healthy.'
   'That I will not have,' I said, 'nor can understand at all. What
you've been doing is to make me feel very very ill.'[1]
   'Do you feel ill now?' he said, still with the old droogy smile on
his litso. 'Drinking tea, resting, having a quiet chat with a friend—
surely you're not feeling anything but well?'
   I like listened and felt for pain and sickness in my gulliver and
plott, in a like cautious way, but it was true, brothers, that I felt real
horrorshow and even wanting my dinner. 'I don't get it,' I said. 'You
must be doing something to me to make me feel ill.' And I sort of
frowned about that, thinking.
   'You felt ill this afternoon,' he said, 'because you're getting better.
When we're healthy we respond to the presence of the hateful with
fear and nausea. You're becoming healthy, that's all. You'll be healthier still this time tomorrow.' Then he patted me on the noga and
went out, and I tried to puzzle the whole veshch out as best I could.
What it seemed to me was that the wires and other veshches that
were fixed to my plott perhaps were making me feel ill, and that
it was all a trick really. I was still puzzling out all this and wondering whether I should refuse to be strapped down to this chair

---

1. The Hippocratic Oath sworn by doctors, said to date back to the Greek physician Hip-
   pocrates (late fifth century BC), includes the vow never to "do harm to anyone."

tomorrow and start a real bit of dratsing with them all, because I had
my rights, when another chelloveck came in to see me. He was a like
smiling starry veck who said he was what he called the Discharge
Officer, and he carried a lot of bits of paper with him. He said:

'Where will you go when you leave here?' I hadn't really thought
about that sort of veshch at all, and it only now really began to
dawn on me that I'd be a fine free malchick very soon, and then I
viddied that would only be if I played it everybody's way and did not
start any dratsing and creeching and refusing and so on. I said:

'Oh, I shall go home. Back to my pee and em.'

'Your—?' He didn't get nadsat-talk at all, so I said:

'To my parents in the dear old flatblock.'

'I see,' he said. 'And when did you last have a visit from your
parents?'

'A month,' I said, 'very near. They like suspended visiting-day for
a bit because of one prestoopnick getting some blasting-powder
smuggled in across the wires from his ptitsa. A real cally trick to
play on the innocent, like punishing them as well. So it's like near a
month since I had a visit.'

'I see,' said this veck. 'And have your parents been informed of
your transfer and impending release?' That had a real lovely zvook
that did, that slovo *release*. I said:

'No.' Then I said: 'It will be a nice surprise for them, that, won't
it? Me just walking in through the door and saying: "Here I am,
back, a free veck again." Yes, real horrorshow.'

'Right,' said the Discharge Officer veck, 'we'll leave it at that. So
long as you have somewhere to live. Now, there's the question of your
having a job, isn't there?' And he showed me this long list of jobs I
could have, but I thought, well, there would be time enough for that.
A nice malenky holiday first. I could do a crasting job soon as I got
out and fill the old carmans with pretty polly, but I would have to be
very careful and I would have to do the job all on my oddy knocky. I
did not trust so-called droogs any more. So I told this veck to leave it
a bit and we would govoreet about it again. He said right right right,
then got ready to leave. He showed himself to be a very queer sort of
a veck, because what he did now was to like giggle and then say:
'Would you like to punch me in the face before I go?' I did not think
I could possibly have slooshied that right, so I said:

'Eh?'

'Would you,' he giggled, 'like to punch me in the face before I go?'
I frowned like at that, very puzzled, and said:

'Why?'

'Oh,' he said, 'just to see how you're getting on.' And he brought
his litso real near, a fat grin all over his rot. So I fisted up and went
smack at this litso, but he pulled himself away real skorry, grinning
still, and my rooker just punched air. Very puzzling, this was, and

I frowned as he left, smecking his gulliver off. And then, my brothers, I felt real sick again, just like in the afternoon, just for a couple of minootas. It then passed off skorry, and when they brought my dinner in I found I had a fair appetite and was ready to crunch away at the roast chicken. But it was funny that starry chelloveck asking for a tolchock in the litso. And it was funny feeling sick like that.

What was even funnier was when I went to sleep that night, O my brothers. I had a nightmare, and, as you might expect, it was of one of those bits of film I'd viddied in the afternoon. A dream or nightmare is really only like a film inside your gulliver, except that it is as though you could walk into it and be part of it. And this is what happened to me. It was a nightmare of one of the bits of film they showed me near the end of the afternoon like session, all of smecking malchicks doing the ultra-violent on a young ptitsa who was creeching away in her red red krovvy, her platties all razrezzed real horrorshow. I was in this fillying about, smecking away and being like the ringleader, dressed in the heighth of nadsat fashion. And then at the heighth of all this dratsing and tolchocking I felt like paralysed and wanting to be very sick, and all the other malchicks had a real gromky smeck at me. Then I was dratsing my way back to being awake all through my own krovvy, pints and quarts and gallons of it, and then I found myself in my bed in this room. I wanted to be sick, so I got out of the bed all trembly so as to go off down the corridor to the old vaysay. But, behold, brothers, the door was locked. And turning round I viddied for like the first raz that there were bars on the window. And so, as I reached for the like pot in the malenky cupboard beside the bed, I viddied that there would be no escaping from any of all this. Worse, I did not dare to go back into my own sleeping gulliver. I soon found I did not want to be sick after all, but then I was poogly of getting back into bed to sleep. But soon I fell smack into sleep and did not dream any more.

6

'Stop it, stop it, stop it,' I kept on creeching out. 'Turn it off, you grahzny bastards, for I can stand no more.' It was the next day, brothers, and I had truly done my best morning and afternoon to play it their way and sit like a horrorshow smiling co-operative malchick in the chair of torture while they flashed nasty bits of ultra-violence on the screen, my glazzies clipped open to viddy all, my plott and rookers and nogas fixed to the chair so I could not get away. What I was being made to viddy now was not really a veshch I would have thought to be too bad before, it being only three or four malchicks crasting in a shop and filling their carmans with cutter, at the same time fillying about with the creeching starry ptitsa running the shop, tolchocking her and letting the red red krovvy flow. But the throb and like crash crash crash crash in my gulliver and the wanting to sick and the terrible dry rasping thirstiness in my rot, all were worse than yesterday. 'Oh, I've had enough,' I cried. 'It's not fair, you vonny sods,' and I tried to struggle out of the chair but it was not possible, me being as good as stuck to it.

'First-class,' creeched out this Dr Brodsky. 'You're doing really well. Just one more and then we're finished.'

What it was now was the starry 1939–45 War again, and it was a very blobby and liny and crackly film you could viddy had been made by the Germans. It opened with German eagles and the Nazi flag with that like crooked cross that all malchicks at school love to draw, and then there were very haughty and nadmenny like German officers walking through streets that were all dust and bomb-holes and broken buildings. Then you were allowed to viddy lewdies being shot against walls, officers giving the orders, and also horrible nagoy plotts left lying in gutters, all like cages of bare ribs and white thin nogas. Then there were lewdies being dragged off creeching though not on the sound-track, my brothers, the only sound being music, and being tolchocked while they were dragged off. Then I noticed, in all my pain and sickness, what music it was that like crackled and boomed on the sound-track, and it was Ludwig van, the last movement of the Fifth Symphony, and I creeched like bezoomny at that. 'Stop!' I creeched. 'Stop, you grahzny disgusting sods. It's a sin, that's what it is, a filthy unforgivable sin, you bratchnies!' They didn't stop right away, because there was only a minute or two more to go—lewdies being beaten up and all krovvy, then more firing squads, then the old Nazi flag and THE END. But when the lights came on this Dr Brodsky and also Dr Branom were standing in front of me, and Dr Brodsky said:

'What's all this about sin, eh?'

'That,' I said, very sick. 'Using Ludwig van like that. He did no harm to anyone. Beethoven just wrote music.' And then I was really sick and they had to bring a bowl that was in the shape of like a kidney.

'Music,' said Dr Brodsky, like musing. 'So you're keen on music. I know nothing about it myself. It's a useful emotional heightener, that's all I know. Well, well. What do you think about that, eh, Branom?'

'It can't be helped,' said Dr Branom. 'Each man kills the thing he loves, as the poet-prisoner said.[1] Here's the punishment element, perhaps. The Governor ought to be pleased.'

---

1. This line is from "The Ballad of Reading Gaol," the poem Oscar Wilde (1854–1900) wrote on his release from prison in May 1897. In the preface to his novel *The Picture of*

'Give me a drink,' I said, 'for Bog's sake.'

'Loosen him,' ordered Dr Brodsky. 'Fetch him a carafe of ice-cold water.' So then these under-vecks got to work and soon I was peeting gallons and gallons of water and it was like heaven, O my brothers. Dr Brodsky said:

'You seem a sufficiently intelligent young man. You seem, too, to be not without taste. You've just got this violence thing, haven't you? Violence and theft, theft being an aspect of violence.' I didn't govoreet a single slovo, brothers. I was still feeling sick, though getting a malenky bit better now. But it had been a terrible day. 'Now, then,' said Dr Brodsky, 'how do you think this is done? Tell me, what do you think we're doing to you?'

'You're making me feel ill,' I said. 'I'm ill when I look at those filthy pervert films of yours. But it's not really the films that's doing it. But I feel that if you'll stop these films I'll stop feeling ill.'

'Right,' said Dr Brodsky. 'It's association, the oldest educational method in the world.[2] And what really causes you to feel ill?'

'These grahzny sodding veshches that come out of my gulliver and my plott,' I said, 'that's what it is.'

'Quaint,' said Dr Brodsky, like smiling, 'the dialect of the tribe.[3] Do you know anything of its provenance, Branom?'

'Odd bits of old rhyming slang,' said Dr Branom, who did not look quite so much like a friend any more. 'A bit of gipsy talk, too. But most of the roots are Slav. Propaganda. Subliminal penetration.'[4]

'All right, all right, all right,' said Dr Brodsky, like impatient and not interested any more. 'Well,' he said to me, 'it isn't the wires. It's

Dorian Gray (1891), Wilde, wrote that "there is no such thing as a moral or immoral book," a polemical rejection of the supposed linkage between art and morality, which is a leading theme in *A Clockwork Orange*.

2. In philosophy, the Associationism of John Locke, David Hartley, and David Hume is concerned with the associations between sensations and ideas, that is, the connection between experience and its mental representation. Associationism acquired a scientific dimension in the hands of the Russian physiologist Ivan Petrovich Pavlov (1849–1936), who provided an account of "conditional" reflexes, behaviors conditional on specific experiences.

3. "To purify the dialect of the tribe," wrote T. S. Eliot in his poem *Little Gidding* (1942), alluding to the French symbolist Stéphane Mallarmé (1842–1898), who wrote in *Le Tombeau d'Edgar Poe* (1875), "Donner un sens plus pur aux mots de la tribu." The phrase is often associated with the idea of the necessity of a programme of linguistic or cultural paternalism. See Morag Shiach, "To purify the dialect of the tribe: Modernism and Language Reform," *Modernism/Modernity* 14.1 (January 2007), 21–34.

4. The market researcher James Vicary (1915–1977) coined the term "subliminal advertising" in 1957; see Vance Packard, *The Hidden Persuaders* (New York: Penguin, 1957). Subliminal advertising was banned in the United Kingdom in 1958. Despite the lack of evidence for its effectiveness, subliminal persuasion has been a staple of the folk psychology of popular culture, for instance in moral panics over back-masking (the supposed insertion of messages recorded backwards into popular music). In *The Manchurian Candidate*, a 1959 novel by Richard Condon, a United States soldier captured in the Korean War is brainwashed by Chinese Communists and returned to the country, later to be activated as an assassin when he is presented with the learned stimulus.

nothing to do with what's fastened to you. Those are just for measuring your reactions. What is it, then?'

I viddied then, of course, what a bezoomny shoot I was not to notice that it was the hypodermic shots in the rooker. 'Oh,' I creeched, 'oh, I viddy all now. A filthy cally vonny trick. An act of treachery, sod you, and you won't do it again.'

'I'm glad you've raised your objections now,' said Dr Brodsky. 'Now we can be perfectly clear about it. We can get this stuff of Ludovico's into your system in many different ways. Orally, for instance. But the subcutaneous method is the best. Don't fight against it, please. There's no point in your fighting. You can't get the better of us.'

'Grahzny bratchnies,' I said, like snivelling. Then I said: 'I don't mind about the ultra-violence and all that cal. I can put up with that. But it's not fair on the music. It's not fair I should feel ill when I'm slooshying lovely Ludwig van and G. F. Handel and others. All that shows you're an evil lot of bastards and I shall never forgive you, sods.'

They both looked a bit like thoughtful. Then Dr Brodsky said: 'Delimitation is always difficult. The world is one, life is one. The sweetest and most heavenly of activities partake in some measure of violence—the act of love, for instance; music, for instance. You must take your chance, boy. The choice has been all yours.' I didn't understand all these slovos, but now I said:

'You needn't take it any further, sir.' I'd changed my tune a malenky bit in my cunning way. 'You've proved to me that all this dratsing and ultra-violence and killing is wrong wrong and terribly wrong. I've learned my lesson, sirs. I see now what I've never seen before. I'm cured, praise God.' And I raised my glazzies in a like holy way to the ceiling. But both these doctors shook their gullivers like sadly and Dr Brodsky said:

'You're not cured yet. There's still a lot to be done. Only when your body reacts promptly and violently to violence, as to a snake, without further help from us, without medication, only then—' I said:

'But, sir, sirs, I *see* that it's wrong. It's wrong because it's against like society, it's wrong because every veck on earth has the right to live and be happy without being beaten and tolchocked and knifed. I've learned a lot, oh really I have.' But Dr Brodsky had a loud long smeck at that, showing all his white zoobies, and said:

'The heresy of an age of reason,' or some such slovos. 'I see what is right and approve, but I do what is wrong. No, no, my boy, you must leave it all to us. But be cheerful about it. It will soon be all over. In less than a fortnight now you'll be a free man.' Then he patted me on the pletcho.[5]

5. TS 95: autograph gloss in margin of this paragraph, "Cal! Cal! Кал!"

Less than a fortnight. O my brothers and friends, it was like an age. It was like from the beginning of the world to the end of it. To finish the fourteen years with remission in the Staja would have been nothing to it. Every day it was the same. When the devotchka with the hypodermic came round, though, four days after this govoreeting with Dr Brodsky and Dr Branom, I said: 'Oh, no you won't,' and tolchocked her on the rooker, and the syringe went tinkle clatter on to the floor. That was like to viddy what they would do. What they did was to get four or five real bolshy white-coated bastards of undervecks to hold me down on the bed, tolchocking me with grinny litsos close to mine, and then this nurse ptitsa said: 'You wicked naughty little devil, you,' while she jabbed my rooker with another syringe and squirted this stuff in real brutal and nasty. And then I was wheeled off exhausted to this like hell sinny as before.

Every day, my brothers, these films were like the same, all kicking and tolchocking and red red krovvy dripping off of litsos and plotts and spattering all over the camera lenses. It was usually grinning and smecking malchicks in the heighth of nadsat fashion, or else teeheeheeing Jap torturers or brutal Nazi kickers and shooters. And each day the feeling of wanting to die with the sickness and gulliver pains and aches in the zoobies and horrible horrible thirst grew really worse. Until one morning I tried to defeat the bastards by crash crash crashing my gulliver against the wall so that I should tolchock myself unconscious, but all that happened was I felt sick with viddying that this kind of violence was like the violence in the films, so I was just exhausted and was given the injection and was wheeled off like before.

And then there came a morning when I woke up and had my breakfast of eggs and toast and jam and very hot milky chai, and then I thought: 'It can't be much longer now. Now must be very near the end of the time. I have suffered to the heighths and cannot suffer any more.' And I waited and waited, brothers, for this nurse ptitsa to bring in the syringe, but she did not come. And then the white-coated underveck came and said:

'Today, old friend, we are letting you walk.'

'Walk?' I said. 'Where?'

'To the usual place,' he said. 'Yes, yes, look not so astonished. You are to walk to the films, me with you of course. You are no longer to be carried in a wheelchair.'

'But,' I said, 'how about my horrible morning injection?' For I was really surprised at this, brothers, they being so keen on pushing this Ludovico veshch into me, as they said. 'Don't I get that horrible sicky stuff rammed into my poor suffering rooker any more?'

'All over,' like smecked this veck. 'For ever and ever amen. You're on your own now, boy. Walking and all to the chamber of horrors.

But you're still to be strapped down and made to see. Come on then, my little tiger.' And I had to put my over-gown and toofles on and walk down the corridor to the like sinny mesto.

Now this time, O my brothers, I was not only very sick but very puzzled. There it was again, all the old ultra-violence and vecks with their gullivers smashed and torn krovvy-dripping ptitsas creeching for mercy, the like private and individual fillying and nastiness. Then there were the prison-camps and the Jews and the grey like foreign streets full of tanks and uniforms and vecks going down in withering rifle-fire, this being the public side of it. And this time I could blame nothing for me feeling sick and thirsty and full of aches except what I was forced to viddy, my glazzies still being clipped open and my nogas and plott fixed to the chair but this set of wires and other veshches no longer coming out of my plott and gulliver. So what could it be but the films I was viddying that were doing this to me? Except, of course, brothers, that this Ludovico stuff was like a vaccination and there it was cruising about in my krovvy, so that I would be sick always for ever and ever amen whenever I viddied any of this ultra-violence. So now I squared my rot and went boo hoo hoo, and the tears like blotted out what I was forced to viddy in like all blessed runny silvery dewdrops. But these white-coat bratchnies were skorry with their tashtooks to wipe the tears away, saying: 'There there, wazzums all weepy-weepy den?' And there it was again all clear before my glazzies, these Germans prodding like beseeching and weeping Jews—vecks and cheenas and malchicks and devotchkas—into mestos where they would all snuff it of poison gas.[6] Boo hoo hoo I had to go again, and along they came to wipe the tears off, very skorry, so I should not miss one solitary veshch of what they were showing. It was a terrible and horrible day, O my brothers and only friends.

I was lying on the bed all alone that nochy after my dinner of fat thick mutton stew and fruit-pie and ice-cream, and I thought to myself: 'Hell hell hell, there might be a chance for me if I get out now.'[7] I had no weapon, though. I was allowed no britva here, and I had been shaved every other day by a fat bald-headed veck who came to my bed before breakfast, two white-coated bratchnies standing by to viddy I was a good non-violent malchick. The nails on my rookers had been scissored and filed real short so I could not scratch. But I was still skorry on the attack, though they had weakened me down, brothers, to a like shadow of what I had been in the old free days. So now I got off the bed and went to the locked door

---

6. The moving images which climax Alex's reeducation, images of the Nazi death camps, strikingly anticipate a later disagreement over the ethics of the representation of what we now know as the Holocaust.
7. TS 98: cancels single quotes around phrase.

and began to fist it real horrorshow and hard, creeching at the same time: 'Oh, help help. I'm sick, I'm dying. Doctor doctor doctor, quick. Please. Oh, I'll die, I know I shall. Help.' My gorlo was real dry and sore before anyone came. Then I heard nogas coming down the corridor and a like grumbling goloss, and then I recognized the goloss of the white-coated veck who brought my pishcha and like escorted me to my daily doom. He like grumbled:

'What is it? What goes on? What's your little nasty game in there?'

'Oh, I'm dying,' I like moaned. 'Oh, I have a ghastly pain in my side. Appendicitis, it is. Ooooooh.'

'Appendy shitehouse,' grumbled this veck, and then to my joy, brothers, I could slooshy the like clank of keys. 'If you're trying it, little friend, my friends and me will beat and kick you all through the night.' Then he opened up and brought in like the sweet air of the promise of my freedom. Now I was like behind the door when he pushed it open, and I could viddy him in the corridor light looking round for me puzzled. Then I raised my two fisties to tolchock him on the neck nasty, and then, I swear, as I sort of viddied him in advance lying moaning or out out out and felt the like joy rise in my guts, it was then that this sickness rose in me as it might be a wave and I felt a horrible fear as if I was really going to die. I like tottered over to the bed going urgh urgh urgh, and the veck, who was not in his white coat but an over-gown, viddied clear enough what I had had in my mind for he said:

'Well, everything's a lesson, isn't it? Learning all the time, as you could say. Come on, little friend, get up from that bed and hit me. I want you to, yes, really. A real good crack across the jaw. Oh, I'm dying for it, really I am.' But all I could do, brothers, was to just lay there sobbing boo hoo hoo. 'Scum,' like sneered this veck now. 'Filth.' And he pulled me up by like the scruff of my pyjama-top, me being very weak and limp, and he raised and swung his right rooker so that I got a fair old tolchock clean on the litso. 'That,' he said, 'is for getting me out of my bed, you young dirt.' And he wiped his rookers against each other swish swish and went out. Crunch crunch went the key in the lock.

And what, brothers, I had to escape into sleep from then was the horrible and wrong feeling that it was better to get the hit than give it. If that veck had stayed I might even have like presented the other cheek.[8]

---

8. In the Sermon on the Mount, Matthew 5.38–39, Jesus preaches: "Ye have heard that it hath been said, An eye for an eye, and a tooth for a tooth: But I say unto you, That ye resist not evil: but whosoever shall smite thee on thy right cheek, turn to him the other also."

7

I could not believe, brothers, what I was told. It seemed that I had been in that vonny mesto for near ever and would be there for near ever more. But it had always been a fortnight and now they said the fortnight was near up. They said:

'Tomorrow, little friend, out out out.' And they made with the old thumb, like pointing to freedom. And then the white-coated veck who had tolchocked me and who had still brought me my trays of pishcha and like escorted me to my everyday torture said: 'But you still have one real big day in front of you. It's to be your passing-out day.' And he had a leery smeck at that.

I expected this morning that I would be ittying as usual to the sinny mesto in my pyjamas and toofles and overgown. But no. This morning I was given my shirt and underveshches and my platties of the night and my horrorshow kick-boots, all lovely and washed or ironed or polished. And I was even given my cut-throat britva that I had used in those old happy days for fillying and dratsing. So I gave with the puzzled frown at this as I got dressed, but the white-coated under-veck just like grinned and would govoreet nothing, O my brothers.

I was led quite kindly to the same old mesto, but there were changes there. Curtains had been drawn in front of the sinny screen and the frosted glass under the projection holes was no longer there, it having perhaps been pushed up or folded to the sides like blind or shutters. And where there had been just the noise of coughing kashl kashl kashl and like shadows of lewdies was now a real audience, and in this audience there were litsos I knew. There was the Staja Governor and the holy man, the charlie or charles as he was called, and the Chief Chasso and this very important and well-dressed chelloveck who was the Minister of the Interior or Inferior. All the rest I did not know. Dr Brodsky and Dr Branom were there, though not now white-coated, instead they were dressed as doctors would dress who were big enough to want to dress in the heighth of fashion. Dr Branom just stood, but Dr Brodsky stood and govoreeted in a like learned manner to all the lewdies assembled. When he viddied me coming in he said: 'Aha. At this stage, gentlemen, we introduce the subject himself. He is, as you will perceive, fit and well nourished. He comes straight from a night's sleep and a good breakfast, undrugged, unhypnotized. Tomorrow we send him with confidence out into the world again, as decent a lad as you would meet on a May morning, unvicious, unviolent, if anything—as you will observe—inclined to the kindly word and the helpful act. What a change is here, gentlemen, from the wretched hoodlum the State committed to unprofitable punishment some two years ago, unchanged after two years. Unchanged, do I say? Not quite. Prison taught him the false smile, the rubbed hands of hypocrisy, the fawning greased obsequious leer. Other vices it taught him, as well as confirming him in those he had long practised before. But, gentlemen, enough of words. Actions speak louder than. Action now. Observe, all.'

I was a bit dazed by all this govoreeting and I was trying to grasp in my mind that like all this was about me. Then all the lights went out and then there came on two like spotlights shining from the projection-squares, and one of them was full on Your Humble and Suffering Narrator. And into the other spotlight there walked a bolshy big chelloveck I had never viddied before. He had a lardy like litso and a moustache and like strips of hair pasted over his near-bald gulliver. He was about thirty or forty or fifty, some old age like that, starry. He ittied up to me and the spotlight ittied with him, and soon the two spotlights had made like one big pool. He said to me, very sneery: 'Hello, heap of dirt. Pooh, you don't wash much, judging from the horrible smell.' Then, as if he was like dancing, he stamped on my nogas, left, right, then he gave me a finger-nail flick on the nose that hurt like bezoomny and brought the old tears to my glazzies, then he twisted at my left ooko like it was a radio dial. I could slooshy titters and a couple of real horrorshow hawhawhaws coming from like the audience. My nose and nogas and ear-hole stung and pained like bezoomny, so I said:

'What do you do that to me for? I've never done wrong to you, brother.'

'Oh,' this veck said, 'I do this'—flickflicked nose again—'and that'—twisted smarting ear-hole—'and the other'—stamped nasty on right noga—'because I don't care for your horrible type. And if you want to do anything about it, start, start, please do.' Now I knew that I'd have to be real skorry and get my cut-throat britva out before this horrible killing sickness whooshed up and turned the like joy of battle into feeling I was going to snuff it. But, O brothers, as my rooker reached for the britva in my inside carman I got this like picture in my mind's glazzy of this insulting chelloveck howling for mercy with the red red krovvy all streaming out of his rot, and hot after this picture the sickness and dryness and pains were rushing to overtake, and I viddied that I'd have to change the way I felt about this rotten veck very very skorry indeed, so I felt in my carmans for cigarettes or for pretty polly, and, O my brothers, there was not either of these veshches. I said, like all howly and blubbery:

'I'd like to give you a cigarette, brother, but I don't seem to have any.' This veck went:

'Wah wah. Boohoohoo. Cry, baby.' Then he flickflickflicked with his bolshy horny nail at my nose again, and I could slooshy very loud smecks of like mirth coming from the dark audience. I said, real desperate, trying to be nice to this insulting and hurtful veck to stop the pains and sickness coming up:

'Please let me do something for you, please.' And I felt in my carmans but could find only my cut-throat britva, so I took this out and handed it to him and said: 'Please take this, please. A little present. Please have it.' But he said:

'Keep your stinking bribes to yourself. You can't get round me that way.' And he banged at my rooker and my cut-throat britva fell on the floor. So I said:

'Please, I must do something. Shall I clean your boots? Look, I'll get down and lick them.' And, my brothers, believe it or kiss my sharries, I got down on my knees and pushed my red yahzick out a mile and a half to lick his grahzny vonny boots. But all this veck did was to kick me not too hard on the rot. So then it seemed to me that it would not bring on the sickness and pain if I just gripped his ankles with my rookers tight round them and brought this grahzny bratchny down to the floor. So I did this and he got a real bolshy surprise, coming down crack amid loud laughter from the vonny audience. But viddying him on the floor I could feel the whole horrible feeling coming over me, so I gave him my rooker to lift him up skorry and up he came. Then just as he was going to give me a real nasty and earnest tolchock on the litso Dr Brodsky said:

'All right, that will do very well.' Then this horrible veck sort of bowed and danced off like an actor while the lights came up on me blinking and with my rot square for howling. Dr Brodsky said to the audience: 'Our subject is, you see, impelled towards the good by, paradoxically, being impelled towards evil. The intention to act violently is accompanied by strong feelings of physical distress. To counter these the subject has to switch to a diametrically opposed attitude. Any questions?'[1]

'Choice,' rumbled a rich deep goloss. I viddied it belonged to the prison charlie. 'He has no real choice, has he? Self-interest, fear of physical pain, drove him to that grotesque act of self-abasement. Its insincerity was clearly to be seen. He ceases to be a wrongdoer. He ceases also to be a creature capable of moral choice.'

'These are subtleties,' like smiled Dr Brodsky. 'We are not concerned with motive, with the higher ethics. We are concerned only with cutting down crime—'

'And,' chipped in this bolshy well-dressed Minister, 'with relieving the ghastly congestion in our prisons.'

---

1. Aversion therapy is the recognized term for treatments in which a patient is simultaneously presented with a stimulus and something unpleasant. The coincidence conditions an aversive association between the stimulus and some discomfort or pain, which in turn modifies behavior.

'Hear hear,' said somebody.

There was a lot of govoreeting and arguing then and I just stood there, brothers, like completely ignored by all these ignorant bratchnies, so I creeched out:

'Me, me, me. How about me? Where do I come into all this? Am I like just some animal or dog?'[2] And that started them off govoreeting real loud and throwing slovos at me. So I creeched louder still, creeching: 'Am I just to be like a clockwork orange?' I didn't know what made me use those slovos, brothers, which just came like without asking into my gulliver. And that shut all those vecks up for some reason for a minoota or two. Then one very thin starry professor type chelloveck stood up, his neck like all cables carrying like power from his gulliver to his plott, and he said:

'You have no cause to grumble, boy. You made your choice and all this is a consequence of your choice. Whatever now ensues is what you yourself have chosen.' And the prison charlie creeched out:

'Oh, if only I could believe that.' And you could viddy the Governor give him a look like meaning that he would not climb so high in like Prison Religion as he thought he would. Then loud arguing started again, and then I could slooshy the slovo Love being thrown around, the prison charles himself creeching as loud as any about Perfect Love Casteth Out Fear[3] and all that cal. And now Dr Brodsky said, smiling all over his litso:

'I am glad, gentlemen, this question of Love has been raised. Now we shall see in action a manner of Love that was thought to be dead with the Middle Ages.'[4] And then the lights went down and the spotlights came on again, one on your poor and suffering Friend and Narrator, and into the other there like rolled or sidled the most lovely young devotchka you could ever hope in all your jeezny, O my brothers, to viddy. That is to say, she had real horrorshow groodies all of which you could like viddy, she having on platties which came down down down off her pletchoes. And her nogas were like Bog in His Heaven, and she walked like to make you groan in your keeshkas, and yet her litso was a sweet smiling young like innocent litso. She came up towards me with the light like it was the like light of heavenly grace and all that cal coming with her, and the first thing that flashed into my gulliver was that I would like to have her right down there on the floor with the old in-out real savage, but skorry as a shot came the sickness, like a like detective that had been

2. Pavlov's work on conditioned reflexes to sensory stimuli involved investigating the gastric system of dogs and measuring the production of saliva.
3. First Epistle of John 4.18: "There is no fear in love; but perfect love casteth out fear; because fear hath torment."
4. Courtly love, or *fin'amor*, as found in the stories of Sir Lancelot (as told, for instance, by Chrétien de Troyes or Sir Thomas Malory) is an ennobling sexual love in which the mistress is the idealized object of the knight's fealty.

watching round a corner and now followed to make his grahzny arrest. And now the von of lovely perfume that came off her made me want to think of starting to like heave in my keeshkas, so I knew I had to think of some new like way of thinking about her before all the pain and thirstiness and horrible sickness come over me real horrorshow and proper. So I creeched out:

'O most beautiful and beauteous of devotchkas, I throw like my heart at your feet for you to like trample all over. If I had a rose I would give it to you. If it was all rainy and cally now on the ground you could have my platties to walk on so as not to cover your dainty nogas with filth and cal.' And as I was saying all this, O my brothers, I could feel the sickness like slinking back. 'Let me,' I creeched out, 'worship you and be like your helper and protector from the wicked like world.' Then I thought of the right slovo and felt better for it, saying: 'Let me be like your true knight,' and down I went again on the old knees, bowing and like scraping.

And then I felt real shooty and dim, it having been like an act again, for this devotchka smiled and bowed to the audience and like danced off, the lights coming up to a bit of applause. And the glazzies of some of these starry vecks in the audience were like popping out at this young devotchka with dirty and like unholy desire, O my brothers.

'He will be your true Christian,' Dr Brodsky was creeching out, 'ready to turn the other cheek, ready to be crucified rather than crucify, sick to the very heart at the thought even of killing a fly.' And that was right, brothers, because when he said that I thought of killing a fly and felt just that tiny bit sick, but I pushed the sickness and pain back by thinking of the fly being fed with bits of sugar and looked after like a bleeding pet and all that cal. 'Reclamation,' he creeched. 'Joy before the Angels of God.'

'The point is,' this Minister of the Inferior was saying real gromky, 'that it works.'

'Oh,' the prison charlie said, like sighing, 'it works all right, God help the lot of us.'

Part Three

'What's it going to be then, eh?'

That, my brothers, was me asking myself the next morning, stand-ing outside this white building that was like tacked on to the old Staja, in my platties of the night of two years back in the grey light of dawn, with a malenky bit of a bag with my few personal veshches in and a bit of cutter kindly donated by the vonny Authorities to like start me off in my new life.

The rest of the day before had been very tiring, what with inter-views to go on tape for the telenews and photographs being took flash flash flash and more like demonstrations of me folding up in the face of ultra-violence and all that embarrassing cal. And then I had like fallen into the bed and then, as it looked to me, been wak-ened up to be told to get off out, to itty off home, they did not want to viddy Your Humble Narrator never not no more, O my brothers. So there I was, very very early in the morning, with just this bit of pretty polly in my left carman, jingle-jangling it and wondering:

'What's it going to be then, eh?'

Some breakfast some mesto, I thought, me not having eaten at all that morning, every veck being so anxious to tolchock me off out to freedom. A chasha of chai only I had peeted. This Staja was in a very like gloomy part of the town, but there were malenky workers' caffs all around and I soon found one of those, my brothers. It was very cally and vonny, with one bulb in the ceiling with fly-dirt like obscuring its bit of light, and there were early rabbiters slurping away at chai and horrible-looking sausages and slices of kleb which they like wolfed, going wolf wolf wolf[1] and then creeching for more. They were served by a very cally devotchka but with very bolshy groodies on her, and some of the eating vecks tried to grab her, going haw haw haw while she went he he he, and the sight of them near made me want to sick, brothers. But I asked for some toast and jam

---

1. Compare Joyce's treatment of animal appetites in the Laestrygonians episode of *Ulysses*, where similar verbal techniques are used to present Leopold Bloom's entrance to a similar establishment.

and chai very politely and with my gentleman's goloss, then I sat in a dark corner to eat and peet.

While I was doing this, a malenky little dwarf of a veck ittied in, selling the morning's gazettas, a twisted and grahzny prestoopnick type with thick glasses on with steel rims, his platties like the colour of very starry decaying currant pudding. I kupetted a gazetta, my idea being to get ready for plunging back into normal jeezny again by viddying what was ittying on in the world. This gazetta I had seemed to be like a Government gazetta, for the only news that was on the front page was about the need for every veck to make sure he put the Government back in again on the next General Election, which seemed to be about two or three weeks off. There were very boastful slovos about what the Government had done, brothers, in the last year or so, what with increased exports and a real horrorshow foreign policy and improved social services and all that cal. But what the Government was really most boastful about was the way in which they reckoned the streets had been made safer for all peace-loving night-walking lewdies in the last six months, what with better pay for the police and the police getting like tougher with young hooligans and perverts and burglars and all that cal. Which interessovatted Your Humble Narrator some deal. And on the second page of the gazetta there was a blurry like photograph of somebody who looked very familiar, and it turned out to be none other than me me me. I looked very gloomy and like scared, but that was really with the flashbulbs going pop pop all the time. What it said underneath my picture was that here was the first graduate from the new State Institute for Reclamation of Criminal Types, cured of his criminal instincts in a fortnight only, now a good law-fearing citizen and all that cal. Then I viddied there was a very boastful article about this Ludovico's Technique and how clever the Government was and all that cal. Then there was another picture of some veck I thought I knew, and it was this Minister of the Inferior or Interior. It seemed that he had been doing a bit of boasting, looking forward to a nice crime-free era in which there would be no more fear of cowardly attacks from young hooligans and perverts and burglars and all that cal. So I went arghhhhhh and threw this gazetta on the floor, so that it covered up stains of spilled chai and horrible spat gobs from the cally animals that used this caff.

'What's it going to be then, eh?'

What it was going to be now, brothers, was homeways and a nice surprise for dadada and mum, their only son and heir back in the family bosom. Then I could lay back on the bed in my own malenky den and slooshy some lovely music, and at the same time I could think over what to do now with my jeezny. The Discharge Officer had given me a long list the day before of jobs I could try for, and he had telephoned to different vecks about me, but I had no intention, my brothers, of going off to rabbit right away. A malenky bit of a rest first, yes, and a quiet think on the bed to the sound of lovely music.

And so the autobus to Center, and then the autobus to Kingsley Avenue, the flats of Flatblock 18A being just near. You will believe me, my brothers, when I say that my heart was going clopclopclop with the like excitement. All was very quiet, it still being early winter morning, and when I ittied into the vestibule of the flatblock there was no veck about, only the nagoy vecks and cheenas of the Dignity of Labour. What surprised me, brothers, was the way that had been cleaned up, there being no longer any dirty ballooning slovos from the rots of the Dignified Labourers, not any dirty parts of the body added to their naked plotts by dirty-minded pencilling malchicks. And what also surprised me was that the lift was working. It came purring down when I pressed the electric knopka, and when I got in I was surprised again to viddy all was clean inside the like cage.

So up I went to the tenth floor, and there I saw 10-8 as it had been before, and my rooker trembled and shook as I took out of my carman the little klootch I had for opening up. But I very firmly fitted the klootch in the lock and turned, then opened up then went in, and there I met three pairs of surprised and almost frightened glazzies looking at me, and it was pee and em having their breakfast, but it was also another veck that I had never viddied in my jeezny before, a bolshy thick veck in his shirt and braces, quite at home, brothers, slurping away at the milky chai and munch-munching at his eggiweg and toast. And it was this stranger veck who spoke first, saying:

'Who are you, friend? Where did you get hold of a key? Out, before I push your face in. Get out there and knock. Explain your business, quick.'

My dad and mum sat like petrified, and I could viddy they had not yet read the gazetta, then I remembered that the gazetta did not arrive till papapa had gone off to his work. But then mum said: 'Oh, you've broken out. You've escaped. Whatever shall we do? We shall have the police here, oh oh oh. Oh, you bad and wicked boy, disgracing us all like this.' And, believe it or kiss my sharries, she started to go boo hoo. So I started to try and explain, they could ring up the Staja if they wanted, and all the time this stranger veck sat there like frowning and looking as if he could push my litso in with his hairy bolshy beefy fist. So I said:

'How about you answering a few, brother? What are you doing here and for how long? I didn't like the tone of what you said just

then. Watch it. Come on, speak up.' He was a working-man type
veck, very ugly, about thirty or forty, and he sat now with his rot
open at me, not govoreeting one single slovo. Then my dad said:

'This is all a bit bewildering, son. You should have let us know you
were coming. We thought it would be at least another five or six years
before they let you out. Not,' he said, and he said it very like gloomy,
'that we're not very pleased to see you again and a free man, too.'

'Who is this?' I said. 'Why can't he speak up? What's going on in
here?'

'This is Joe,' said my mum. 'He lives here now. The lodger, that's
what he is. Oh, dear dear dear,' she went.

'You,' said this Joe. 'I've heard all about you, boy. I know what
you've done, breaking the hearts of your poor grieving parents. So
you're back, eh? Back to make life a misery for them once more, is
that it? Over my dead corpse you will, because they've let me be more
like a son to them than like a lodger.' I could nearly have smecked
loud at that if the old razdraz within me hadn't started to wake up the
feeling of wanting to sick, because this veck looked about the same
age as my pee and em, and there he was like trying to put a son's
protecting rooker round my crying mum, O my brothers.

'So,' I said, and I near felt like collapsing in all tears myself. 'So
that's it, then. Well, I give you five large minootas to clear all your
horrible cally veshches out of my room.' And I made for this room,
this veck being a malenky bit too slow to stop me. When I opened
the door my heart cracked to the carpet, because I viddied it was no
longer like my room at all, brothers. All my flags had gone off the
walls and this veck had put up pictures of boxers, also like a team
sitting smug with folded rookers and a silver like shield in front.
And then I viddied what else was missing. My stereo and my disc-
cupboard were no longer there, nor was my locked treasure-chest
that contained bottles and drugs and two shining clean syringes.
'There's been some filthy vonny work going on here,' I creeched.
'What have you done with my own personal veshches, you horrible
bastard?' This was to this Joe, but it was my dad that answered,
saying:

'That was all took away, son, by the police. This new regulation,
see, about compensation for the victims.'

I found it very hard not to be very ill, but my gulliver was aching
shocking and my rot was so dry that I had to take a skorry swig
from the milk-bottle on the table, so that this Joe said: 'Filthy pig-
gish manners.' I said:

'But she died. That one died.'

'It was the cats, son,' said my dad like sorrowful, 'that were left
with nobody to look after them till the will was read, so they had
to have somebody in to feed them. So the police sold your things,

clothes and all, to help with the looking after of them. That's the law, son. But you were never much of a one for following the law.'

I had to sit down then, and this Joe said: 'Ask permission before you sit, you mannerless young swine,' so I cracked back skorry with a 'Shut your dirty big fat hole, you,' feeling sick. Then I tried to be all reasonable and smiling for my health's sake like, so I said: 'Well, that's my room, there's no denying that. This is my home also. What suggestions have you, my pee and em, to make?' But they just looked very glum, my mum shaking a bit, her litso all lines and wet with like tears, and then my dad said:

'All this needs thinking about, son. We can't very well just kick Joe out, not just like that, can we? I mean, Joe's here doing a job, a con-tract it is, two years, and we made like an arrangement, didn't we, Joe? I mean, son, thinking you were going to stay in prison a long time and that room going begging.' He was a bit ashamed, you could viddy that from his litso. So I just smiled and like nodded, saying:

'I viddy all. You got used to a bit of peace and you got used to a bit of extra pretty polly. That's the way it goes. And your son has just been nothing but a terrible nuisance.' And then, my brothers, believe me or kiss my sharries, I started to like cry, feeling very like sorry for myself. So my dad said:

'Well, you see, son, Joe's paid next month's rent already. I mean, whatever we do in the future we can't say to Joe to get out, can we, Joe?' This Joe said:

'It's you two I've got to think of, who've been like a father and mother to me. Would it be right or fair to go off and leave you to the tender mercies of this young monster who has been like no real son at all? He's weeping now, but that's his craft and artfulness. Let him go off and find a room somewhere. Let him learn the error of his ways and that a bad boy like he's been doesn't deserve such a good mum and dad as what he's had.'

'All right,' I said, standing up in all like tears still. 'I know how things are now. Nobody wants or loves me. I've suffered and suffered and suffered and everybody wants me to go on suffering. I know.'

'You've made others suffer,' said this Joe. 'It's only right you should suffer proper. I've been told everything that you've done, sitting here at night round the family table, and pretty shocking it was to listen to. Made me real sick a lot of it did.'

'I wish,' I said, 'I was back in the prison. Dear old Staja as it was. I'm ittying off now,' I said. 'You won't ever viddy me no more. I'll make my own way, thank you very much. Let it lie heavy on your consciences.' My dad said:

'Don't take it like that, son,' and my mum just went boo hoo hoo, her litso all screwed up real ugly, and this Joe put his rooker round her again, patting her and going there there there like bezoomny.

And so I just sort of staggered to the door and went out, leaving them to their horrible guilt, O my brothers.

2

Ittying down the street in a like aimless sort of a way, brothers, in these night platties which lewdies like stared at as I went by, cold too, it being a bastard cold winter day, all I felt I wanted was to be away from all this and not to have to think any more about any sort of veshch at all. So I got the autobus to Center, then I walked back to Taylor Place, and there was the disc-bootick MELODIA I had used to favour with my inestimable custom, O my brothers, and it looked much the same sort of mesto as it always had, and walking in I expected to viddy old Andy there, that bald and very very thin helpful like veck from whom I had kupetted discs in the old days. But there was no Andy there now, brothers, only a scream and a creech of nadsat (teenage, that is) malchicks and ptitsas slooshying some new horrible popsong and dancing to it as well, and the veck behind the counter not much more than a nadsat himself, clicking his rooker-bones and smecking like bezoomny. So I went up and waited till he like deigned to notice me, then I said:

'I'd like to hear a disc of the Mozart Number Forty.'[1] I don't know why that should have come into my gulliver, but it did. The counter-veck said:

'Forty what, friend?'

I said: 'Symphony. Symphony Number Forty in G Minor.'

'Ooooh,' went one of the dancing nadsats, a malchick with his hair all over his glazzies, 'seemfunnah. Don't it seem funny? He wants a seemfunnah.'

I could feel myself growing all razdraz within, but I had to watch that, so I like smiled at the veck who had taken over Andy's place and at all the dancing and creeching nadsats. This counter-veck said: 'You go into that listen-booth over there, friend, and I'll pipe something through.'

So I went over to the malenky box where you could slooshy the discs you wanted to buy, and then this veck put a disc on for me, but it wasn't the Mozart Forty, it was the Mozart 'Prague'[2]—he seemingly having just picked up any Mozart he could find on the shelf—and that should have started making me real razdraz and I had to watch that for fear of the pain and sickness, but what I'd forgotten

1. Mozart's Symphony No. 40 in G Minor, K. 550, written in 1788, one of only two minor-key symphonies by the composer.
2. Mozart's Symphony No. 38 in D Major, K. 504, first performed in Prague in 1787.

was something I shouldn't have forgotten and now made me want to snuff it. It was that these doctor bratchnies had so fixed things that any music that was like for the emotions would make me sick just like viddying or wanting to do violence. It was because all those violence films had music with them. And I remembered especially that horrible Nazi film with the Beethoven Fifth, last movement. And now here was lovely Mozart made horrible. I dashed out of the box like bezoomny to get away from the sickness and pain that were coming on, and I dashed out of the shop with these nadsats smecking after me and the counter-veck creeching: 'Eh eh eh!' But I took no notice and went staggering almost like blind across the road and round the corner to the Korova Milkbar. I knew what I wanted.

The mesto was near empty, it being still morning. It looked strange too, having been painted with all red mooing cows, and behind the counter was no veck I knew. But when I said: 'Milk plus, large,' the veck with a like lean litso very newly shaved knew what I wanted. I took the large moloko plus to one of the little cubies that were all round this mesto, there being like curtains to shut them off from the main mesto, and there I sat down in the plushy chair and sipped and sipped. When I'd finished the whole lot I began to feel that things were happening. I had my glazzies like fixed on a malenky bit of silver paper from a cancer packet that was on the floor, the sweeping-up of this mesto not being all that horrorshow, brothers. This scrap of silver began to grow and grow and grow and it was so like bright and fiery that I had to squint my glazzies at it. It got so big that it became not only this whole cubie I was lolling in but like the whole Korova, the whole street, the whole city. Then it was the whole world, then it was the whole everything, brothers, and it was like a sea washing over every veshch that had ever been made or thought of even. I could sort of slooshy myself making special sort of shooms and govoreeting slovos like 'Dear dead idlewilds, rot not in variform guises' and all that cal. Then I could like feel the vision beating up in all this silver, and then there were colours like nobody had ever viddied before, and then I could viddy like a group of statues a long long long way off that was like being pushed nearer and nearer and nearer, all lit up by very bright light from below and above alike, O my brothers. This group of statues was of God or Bog and all His Holy Angels and Saints, all very bright like bronze, with beards and bolshy great wings that waved about in a kind of wind, so that they could not really be of stone or bronze, really, and the eyes or glazzies like moved and were alive. These bolshy big figures came nearer and nearer and nearer till they were like going to crush me down, and I could slooshy my goloss going 'Eeeeee'. And I felt I had got rid of everything—platties, body, brain, name, the lot—and felt real horrorshow, like in heaven. Then there was the shoom of like crumbling and crumpling, and Bog and the Angels and Saints sort of shook their gullivers at me, as though to govoreet that there wasn't quite time now but I must try again, and then everything like leered and smecked and collapsed and the big warm light grew like cold, and then there I was as I was before, the empty glass on the table and wanting to cry and feeling like death was the only answer to everything.

And that was it, that was what I viddied quite clear was the thing to do, but how to do it I did not properly know, never having thought of that before, O my brothers. In my little bag of personal veshches I had my cut-throat britva, but I at once felt very sick as I thought of myself going swishhhh at myself and all my own red red krovvy flowing. What I wanted was not something violent but something that would make me like just go off gentle[3] to sleep and that be the end of Your Humble Narrator, no more trouble to anybody any more. Perhaps, I thought, if I ittied off to the Public Biblio round the corner I might find some book on the best way of snuffing it with no pain. I thought of myself dead and how sorry everybody was going to be, pee and em and that cally vonny Joe who was a like usurper, and also Dr Brodsky and Dr Branom and that Inferior Interior Minister and every veck else. And the boastful vonny Government too. So out I scatted into the winter, and it was afternoon now, near two o'clock, as I could viddy from the bolshy Center timepiece, so that me being in the land with the old moloko plus must have took like longer than I thought. I walked down Marghanita Boulevard and then turned into Boothby Avenue, then round the corner again, and there was the Public Biblio.

It was a starry cally sort of a mesto that I could not remember going into since I was a very very malenky malchick, no more than about six years old, and there were two parts to it—one part to borrow books and one part to read in, full of gazettas and mags and like the von of very starry old men with their plotts stinking of like old age and poverty. These were standing at the gazetta stands all round the room, snuffling and belching and govoreeting to themselves and turning over the pages to read the news very sadly, or else they were sitting at the tables looking at the mags or pretending to, some of them asleep and one or two of them snoring real gromky. I couldn't like remember what it was I wanted at first, then I remembered with a bit of shock that I had ittied here to find out how to snuff it without pain, so I goolied over to the shelf full of reference veshches. There were a lot of books, but there was none with a title, brothers, that would really do. There was a medical book that I took down, but when I opened it it was full of drawings

---

3. Contrast the 1951 villanelle by Dylan Thomas (1914–1953): "Do not go gentle into that good night."

and photographs of horrible wounds and diseases, and that made me want to sick just a bit. So I put that back and then took down the big book or Bible, as it was called, thinking that might give me like comfort as it had done in the old Staja days (not so old really, but it seemed a very very long time ago), and I staggered over to a chair to read in it. But all I found was about smiting seventy times seven and a lot of Jews cursing and tolchocking each other, and that made me want to sick, too. So then I near cried, so that a very starry ragged moodge opposite me said:

'What is it, son? What's the trouble?'

'I want to snuff it,' I said. 'I've had it, that's what it is. Life's become too much for me.'

A starry reading veck next to me said: 'Shhhh,' without looking up from some bezoomny mag he had full of drawings of like bolshy geometrical veshches. That rang a bell somehow. This other moodge said:

'You're too young for that, son. Why, you've got everything in front of you.'

'Yes,' I said, bitter. 'Like a pair of false groodies.' This mag-reading veck said: 'Shhhh' again, looking up this time, and something clicked for both of us. I viddied who it was. He said, real gromky:

'I never forget a shape, by God. I never forget the shape of anything. By God, you young swine, I've got you now.' Crystallography, that was it. That was what he'd been taking away from the Biblio that time. False teeth crunched up real horrorshow. Platties torn off. His books razrezzed, all about Crystallography. I thought I had best get out of here real skorry, brothers. But this starry old moodge was on his feet, creeching like bezoomny to all the starry old coughers at the gazettas round the walls and to them dozing over mags at the tables. 'We have him,' he creeched. 'The poisonous young swine who ruined the books on Crystallography, rare books, books not to be obtained ever again, anywhere.' This had a terrible mad shoom about it, as though this old veck was really off his gulliver. 'A prize specimen of the cowardly brutal young,' he creeched. 'Here in our midst and at our mercy. He and his friends beat me and kicked me and thumped me. They stripped me and tore out my teeth. They laughed at my blood and my moans. They kicked me off home, dazed and naked.' All this wasn't quite true, as you know, brothers. He had some platties on, he hadn't been completely nagoy.

I creeched back: 'That was over two years ago. I've been punished since then. I've learned my lesson. See over there—my picture's in the papers.'

'Punishment, eh?' said one starry like ex-soldier type. 'You lot should be exterminated. Like so many noisome pests. Punishment, indeed.'

'All right, all right,' I said. 'Everybody's entitled to his opinion. For-give me, all. I must go now.' And I started to itty out of this mesto of bezoomny old men. Aspirin, that was it. You could snuff it on a hun-dred aspirin. Aspirin from the old drugstore. But the crystallography veck creeched:

'Don't let him go. We'll teach him all about punishment, the murderous young pig. Get him.' And, believe it, brothers, or do the other veshch, two or three starry dodderers, about ninety years old apiece, grabbed me with their trembly old rookers, and I was like made sick by the von of old age and disease which came from these near-dead moodges. The crystal veck was on to me now, starting to deal me malenky weak tolchocks on my litso, and I tried to get away and itty out, but these starry rookers that held me were stronger than I had thought. Then other starry vecks came hobbling from the gazettas to have a go at Your Humble Narrator. They were creech-ing veshches like: 'Kill him, stamp on him, murder him, kick his teeth in,' and all that cal, and I could viddy what it was clear enough. It was old age having a go at youth, that's what it was. But some of them were saying: 'Poor old Jack, near killed poor old Jack he did, this is the young swine' and so on, as though it had all happened yesterday. Which to them I suppose it had. There was now like a sea of vonny runny dirty old men trying to get at me with their like feeble rookers and horny old claws, creeching and panting on to me, but our crystal droog was there in front, dealing out tolchock after tol-chock. And I daren't do a solitary single veshch, O my brothers, it being better to be hit at like that than to want to sick and feel that horrible pain, but of course the fact that there was violence going on made me feel that the sickness was peeping round the corner to viddy whether to come out into the open and roar away.

Then an attendant veck came along, a youngish veck, and he creeched: 'What goes on here? Stop it at once. This is a reading-room.' But nobody took any notice. So the attendant veck said: 'Right, I shall phone the police.' So I creeched, and I never thought I would ever do that in all my jeezny:

'Yes yes yes, do that, protect me from these old madmen.' I noticed that the attendant veck was not too anxious to join in the dratsing and rescue me from the rage and madness of these starry vecks' claws; he just scatted off to his like office or wherever the telephone was. Now these old men were panting a lot now, and I felt I could just flick at them and they would all fall over, but I just let myself be held, very patient, by these starry rookers, my glazzies closed, and feel the feeble tolchocks on my litso, also slooshy the panting breathy old golosses creeching: 'Young swine, young murderer, hoo-ligan, thug, kill him.' Then I got such a real painful tolchock on the nose that I said to myself to hell to hell, and I opened my glazzies up and started to struggle to get free, which was not hard, brothers, and I tore off creeching to the sort of hallway outside the reading-room. But these starry avengers still came after me, panting like dying, with their animal claws all trembling to get at your friend and Humble Narrator. Then I was tripped up and was on the floor and was being kicked at, then I slooshied golosses of young vecks creeching: 'All right, all right, stop it now,' and I knew the police had arrived.

3

I was like dazed, O my brothers, and could not viddy very clear, but I was sure I had met these millicents some mesto before. The one who had hold of me, going: 'There there there,' just by the front door of the Public Biblio, him I did not know at all, but it seemed to me he was like very young to be a rozz. But the other two had backs that I was sure I had viddied before. They were lashing into these starry old vecks with great bolshy glee and joy, swishing away with malenky whips, creeching: 'There, you naughty boys. That should teach you to stop rioting and breaking the State's Peace, you wicked villains, you.' So they drove these panting and wheezing and near dying starry avengers back into the reading-room, then they turned round, smecking with the fun they'd had, to viddy me. The older one of the two said:

'Well well well well well well well. If it isn't little Alex. Very long time no viddy, droog. How goes?' I was like dazed, the uniform and the shlem or helmet making it hard to viddy who this was, though litso and goloss were very familiar. Then I looked at the other one, and about him, with his grinning bezoomny litso, there was no doubt. Then, all numb and growing number, I looked back at the well well welling one. This one was then fatty old Billyboy, my old enemy. The other was, of course, Dim, who had used to be my droog and also the enemy of stinking fatty goaty Billyboy, but was now a millicent with uniform and shlem and whip to keep order. I said:

'Oh no.'

'Surprise, eh?' And old Dim came out with the old guff I remembered so horrorshow: 'Huh huh huh.'

'It's impossible,' I said. 'It can't be so. I don't believe it.'

'Evidence of the old glazzies,' grinned Billyboy. 'Nothing up our sleeves. No magic, droog. A job for two who are now of job-age. The police.'

'You're too young,' I said. 'Much too young. They don't make rozzes of malchicks of your age.'

'Was young,' went old millicent Dim. I could not get over it, brothers, I really could not. 'That's what we was, young droogie. And you it was that was always the youngest. And here now we are.'

'I still can't believe it,' I said. Then Billyboy, rozz Billyboy that I couldn't get over, said to this young millicent that was like holding on to me and that I did not know:

'More good would be done, I think, Rex, if we doled out a bit of the old summary.[1] Boys will be boys, as always was. No need to go through the old station routine. This one here has been up to his old tricks, as we can well remember though you, of course, can't. He has been attacking the aged and defenceless, and they have properly been retaliating. But we must have our say in the State's name.'

'What is all this?' I said, not able hardly to believe my ookos. 'It was them that went for me, brothers. You're not on their side and can't be. You can't be, Dim. It was a veck we fillied with once in the old days trying to get his own malenky bit of revenge after all this long time.'

'Long time is right,' said Dim. 'I don't remember them days too horrorshow. Don't call me Dim no more, either. Officer call me.'

'Enough is remembered, though,' Billyboy kept nodding. He was not so fatty as he had been. 'Naughty little malchicks handy with cut-throat britvas—these must be kept under.' And they took me in a real strong grip and like walked me out of the Biblio. There was a millicent patrolcar waiting outside, and this veck they called Rex was the driver. They like tolchocked me into the back of this auto, and I couldn't help feeling it was all really like a joke, and that Dim anyway would pull his shlem off his gulliver and go haw haw haw. But he didn't. I said, trying to fight the strack inside me:

'And old Pete, what happened to old Pete? It was sad about Georgie,' I said. 'I slooshied all about that.'

'Pete, oh yes, Pete,' said Dim. 'I seem to remember like the name.' I could viddy we were driving out of town. I said:

'Where are we supposed to be going?'

Billyboy turned round from the front to say: 'It's light still. A little drive into the country, all winter-bare but lonely and lovely. It is not right, not always, for lewdies in the town to viddy too much of our summary punishment. Streets must be kept clean in more than one way.' And he turned to the front again.

'Come,' I said. 'I just don't get this at all. The old days are dead and gone days. For what I did in the past I have been punished. I have been cured.'

'That was read out to us,' said Dim. 'The Super read all that out to us. He said it was a very good way.'

---

1. Summary justice may refer either to justice meted out under military law by an officer rather than at the direction of a court martial, or to vigilantism, in which case judgment and punishment are carried out by persons acting outside the law and the legal apparatus.

'Read to you,' I said, a malenky bit nasty. 'You still too dim to read for yourself, O brother?'

'Ah, no,' said Dim, very like gentle and like regretful. 'Not to speak like that. Not no more, droogie.' And he launched a bolshy tolchock right on my cluve, so that all red red nose-krovvy started to drip drip drip.

'There was never any trust,' I said, bitter, wiping off the krovvy with my rooker. 'I was always on my oddy knocky.'

'This will do,' said Billyboy. We were now in the country and it was all bare trees and a few odd distant like twitters, and in the distance there was some like farm machine making a whirring shoom. It was getting all dusk now, this being the heighth of winter. There were no lewdies about, nor no animals. There was just the four. 'Get out, Alex boy,' said Dim. 'Just a malenky bit of summary.'

All through what they did this driver veck just sat at the wheel of the auto, smoking a cancer, reading a malenky bit of a book. He had the light on in the auto to viddy by. He took no notice of what Billyboy and Dim did to your Humble Narrator. I will not go into what they did, but it was all like panting and thudding against this like background of whirring farm engines and the twittwittwittering in the bare or nagoy branches. You could viddy a bit of smoky breath in the auto light, this driver turning the pages over quite calm. And they were on to me all the time, O my brothers. Then Billyboy or Dim, I couldn't say which one, said: 'About enough, droogie, I should think, shouldn't you?' Then they gave me one final tolchock on the litso each and I fell over and just laid there on the grass. It was cold but I was not feeling the cold. Then they dusted their rookers and put back on their shlems and tunics which they had taken off, and then they got back into the auto. 'Be viddying you some more sometime, Alex,' said Billyboy, and Dim just gave one of his old clowny guffs. The driver finished the page he was reading and put his book away, then he started the auto and they were off townwards, my ex-droog and ex-enemy waving. But I just laid there, fagged and shagged.

After a bit I was hurting bad, and then the rain started, all icy. I could viddy no lewdies in sight, nor no lights of houses. Where was I to go, who had no home and not much cutter in my carmans? I cried for myself boo hoo hoo. Then I got up and began walking.

4

Home, home, home, it was home I was wanting, and it was HOME I came to, brothers. I walked through the dark and followed not the town way but the way where the shoom of a like farm machine had been coming from. This brought me to a sort of village I felt I had viddied before, but was perhaps because all villages look the same, in the dark especially. Here were houses and there was a like drinking mesto, and right at the end of the village there was a malenky cottage on its oddy knocky, and I could viddy its name shining white on the gate. HOME, it said. I was all dripping wet with this icy rain, so that my platties were no longer in the heighth of fashion but real miserable and like pathetic, and my luscious glory was a wet tangled cally mess all spread over my gulliver, and I was sure there were cuts and bruises all over my litso, and a couple of my zoobies sort of joggled loose when I touched them with my tongue or yahzick. And I was sore all over my plott and very thirsty, so that I kept opening my rot to the cold rain, and my stomach growled grrrrr all the time with not having had any pishcha since morning and then not very much, O my brothers.

HOME, it said, and perhaps here would be some veck to help. I opened the gate and sort of slithered down the path, the rain like turning to ice, and then I knocked gentle and pathetic on the door. No veck came, so I knocked a malenky bit longer and louder, and then I heard the shoom of nogas coming to the door. Then the door opened and a male goloss said: 'Yes, what is it?'

'Oh,' I said, 'please help. I've been beaten up by the police and just left to die on the road. Oh, please give me a drink of something and a sit by the fire, please, sir.'

The door opened full then, and I could viddy like warm light and a fire going crackle crackle within. 'Come in,' said this veck, 'who-ever you are. God help you, you poor victim, come in and let's have a look at you.' So I like staggered in, and it was no big act I was put-ting on, brothers, I really felt done and finished. This kind veck put his rookers round my pletchoes and pulled me into this room where the fire was, and of course I knew right away now where it was and why HOME on the gate looked so familiar. I looked at this veck and he looked at me in a kind sort of way, and I remembered him well now. Of course he would not remember me, for in those carefree days I and my so-called droogs did all our bolshy dratsing and fillying and crasting in maskies which were real horrorshow disguises. He was a shortish veck in middle age, thirty, forty, fifty, and he had ochkies on. 'Sit down by the fire,' he said, 'and I'll get you some whisky and warm water. Dear dear dear, somebody *has* been beating you up.' And he gave a like tender look at my gulliver and litso.

'The police,' I said. 'The horrible ghastly police.'

'Another victim,' he said, like sighing. 'A victim of the modern age. I'll go and get you that whisky and then I must clean up your wounds a little.' And off he went. I had a look round this malenky comfortable room. It was nearly all books now and a fire and a couple of chairs, and you could viddy somehow that there wasn't a woman living there. On the table was a typewriter and a lot of like tumbled papers, and I remembered that this veck was a writer veck. *A Clockwork Orange*, that had been it. It was funny that that stuck in my mind. I must not let on, though, for I needed help and kindness now. Those horrible grahzny bratchnies in that terrible white mesto had done that to me, making me need help and kindness now and forcing me to want to give help and kindness myself, if anybody would take it.

'Here we are, then,' said this veck returning. He gave me this hot stimulating glassful to peet, and it made me feel better, and then he cleaned up these cuts on my litso. Then he said: 'You have a nice hot bath, I'll draw it for you, and then you can tell me all about it over a nice hot supper which I'll get ready while you're having the bath.' O my brothers, I could have wept at his kindness, and I think he must have viddied the old tears in my glazzies, for he said: 'There there there,' patting me on the pletcho.

Anyway, I went up and had this hot bath, and he brought in pyjamas and an over-gown for me to put on, all warmed by the fire, also a very worn pair of toofles. And now, brothers, though I was aching and full of pains all over, I felt I would soon feel a lot better. I ittied downstairs and viddied that in the kitchen he had set the table with knives and forks and a fine big loaf of kleb, also a bottle of PRIMA SAUCE, and soon he served out a nice fry of eggiwegs and lomticks of ham and bursting sausages and big bolshy mugs of hot sweet milky chai. It was nice sitting there in the warm, eating, and I found I was very hungry, so that after the fry I had to eat lomtick after lomtick of kleb and butter spread with strawberry jam out of a bolshy great pot. 'A lot better,' I said. 'How can I ever repay?'

'I think I know who you are,' he said. 'If you are who I think you are, then you've come, my friend, to the right place. Wasn't that your picture in the papers this morning? Are you the poor victim of this horrible new technique? If so, then you have been sent here by Providence. Tortured in prison, then thrown out to be tortured by the police. My heart goes out to you, poor poor boy.' Brothers, I could not get a slovo in, though I had my rot wide open to answer his questions. 'You are not the first to come here in distress,' he said. 'The police are fond of bringing their victims to the outskirts of this village. But it is providential that you, who are also another kind of victim, should come here. Perhaps, then, you have heard of me?'

I had to be very careful, brothers. I said: 'I have heard of *A Clockwork Orange*. I have not read it, but I have heard of it.'[1]

---

1. Alex's words here anticipate the situation created for Burgess by the notoriety of Kubrick's film: many had heard of his book, few had read it. Roger Lewis, in *Anthony Burgess* (2002, p. 286), reports that the Heinemann archive shows that the first hardback edition sold only 3,872 copies.

'Ah,' he said, and his litso shone like the sun in its flaming morning glory. 'Now tell me about yourself.'

'Little enough to tell, sir,' I said, all humble. 'There was a foolish and boyish prank, my so-called friends persuading or rather forcing me to break into the house of an old ptitsa—lady, I mean. There was no real harm meant. Unfortunately the lady strained her good old heart in trying to throw me out, though I was quite ready to go of my own accord, and then she died. I was accused of being the cause of her death. So I was sent to prison, sir.'

'Yes yes yes, go on.'

'Then I was picked out by the Minister of the Inferior or Interior to have this Ludovico's veshch tried out on me.'

'Tell me all about it,' he said, leaning forward eager, his pullover elbows with all strawberry jam on them from the plate I'd pushed to one side. So I told him all about it. I told him the lot, all, my brothers. He was very eager to hear all, his glazzies like shining and his goobers apart, while the grease on the plates grew harder harder harder. When I had finished he got up from the table, nodding a lot and going hm hm hm, picking up the plates and other veshches from the table and taking them to the sink for washing up. I said:

'I will do that, sir, and gladly.'

'Rest, rest, poor lad,' he said, turning the tap on so that all steam came burping out. 'You've sinned, I suppose, but your punishment has been out of all proportion. They have turned you into something other than a human being. You have no power of choice any longer. You are committed to socially acceptable acts, a little machine capable only of good. And I see that clearly—that business about the marginal conditionings. Music and the sexual act, literature and art, all must be a source now not of pleasure but of pain.'

'That's right, sir,' I said, smoking one of this kind man's cork-tipped cancers.

'They always bite off too much,' he said, drying a plate like absent-mindedly. 'But the essential intention is the real sin. A man who cannot choose ceases to be a man.'

'That's what the charles said, sir,' I said. 'The prison chaplain, I mean.'

'Did he, did he? Of course he did. He'd have to, wouldn't he, being a Christian? Well, now then,' he said, still wiping the same plate he'd been wiping ten minutes ago, 'we shall have a few people in to see you tomorrow. I think you can be used, poor boy. I think that you can help dislodge this overbearing Government. To turn a decent young man into a piece of clockwork should not, surely, be seen as any triumph for any government, save one that boasts of its repressiveness.' He was still wiping this same plate. I said:

'Sir, you're still wiping that same plate. I agree with you, sir, about boasting. This Government seems to be very boastful.'

'Oh,' he said, like viddying this plate for the first time and then putting it down. 'I'm still not too handy,' he said, 'with domestic chores. My wife used to do them all and leave me to my writing.'

'Your wife, sir?' I said. 'Has she gone and left you?' I really wanted to know about his wife, remembering very well.

'Yes, left me,' he said, in a like loud and bitter goloss. 'She died, you see. She was brutally raped and beaten. The shock was very great. It was in this house,' his rookers were trembling, holding a wiping-up cloth, 'in that room next door. I have had to steel myself to continue to live here, but she would have wished me to stay where her fragrant memory still lingers. Yes yes yes. Poor little girl.' I viddied all clearly, my brothers, what had happened that far-off nochy, and viddying myself on that job, I began to feel I wanted to sick and the pain started up in my gulliver. This veck viddied this, because my litso felt it was all drained of red red krovvy, very pale, and he would be able to viddy this. 'You go to bed now,' he said kindly. 'I've got the spare room ready. Poor poor boy, you must have had a terrible time. A victim of the modern age, just as she was. Poor poor poor girl.'

5

I had a real horrorshow night's sleep, brothers, with no dreams at all, and the morning was very clear and like frosty, and there was the very pleasant like von of breakfast frying away down below. It took me some little time to remember where I was, as it always does, but it soon came back to me and then I felt like warmed and protected. But, as I laid there in the bed, waiting to be called down to breakfast, it struck me that I ought to get to know the name of this kind protecting and like motherly veck, so I had a pad round in my nagoy nogas looking for *A Clockwork Orange*, which would be bound to have his eemya in, he being the author. There was nothing in my bedroom except a bed and a chair and a light, so I ittied next door to this veck's own room, and there I viddied his wife on the wall, a bolshy blown-up photo, so I felt a malenky bit sick remembering. But there were two or three shelves of books there too, and there was, as I thought there must be, a copy of *A Clockwork Orange*, and on the back of the book, like on the spine, was the author's eemya— F. Alexander. Good Bog, I thought, he is another Alex. Then I leafed through, standing in my pyjamas and bare nogas but not feeling one malenky bit cold, the cottage being warm all through, and I could not viddy what the book was about. It seemed written in a very bezoomny like style, full of Ah and Oh and that cal, but what seemed to come out of it was that all lewdies nowadays were being turned into machines and that they were really—you and me and him and kiss-my-sharries—more like a natural growth like a fruit. F. Alexander seemed to think that we all like grow on what he called the world-tree in the world-orchard that like Bog or God planted, and we were there because Bog or God had need of us to quench his thirsty love, or some such cal. I didn't like the shoom of this at all, O my brothers, and wondered how bezoomny this F. Alexander really was, perhaps driven bezoomny by his wife's snuffing it. But then he called me down in a like sane veck's goloss, full of joy and love and all that cal, so down Your Humble Narrator went.

'You've slept long,' he said, ladling out boiled eggs and pulling black toast from under the grill. 'It's nearly ten already. I've been up hours, working.'

'Writing another book, sir?' I said.

'No no, not that now,' he said, and we sat down nice and droogy to the old crack crack crack of eggs and crackle crunch crunch of this black toast, very milky chai standing by in bolshy great morning mugs. 'No, I've been on the phone to various people.'

'I thought you didn't have a phone,' I said, spooning egg in and not watching out what I was saying.

'Why?' he said, very alert like some skorry animal with an egg-spoon in its rooker. 'Why shouldn't you think I have a phone?'

'Nothing,' I said, 'nothing, nothing.' And I wondered, brothers, how much he remembered of the earlier part of that distant nochy, me coming to the door with the old tale and saying to phone the doctor and she saying no phone. He took a very close smot at me but then went back to being like kind and cheerful and spooning up the old eggiweg. Munching away, he said:

'Yes, I've rung up various people who will be interested in your case. You can be a very potent weapon, you see, in ensuring that this present evil and wicked Government is not returned in the forthcoming election. The Government's big boast, you see, is the way it has dealt with crime these last months.' He looked at me very close again over his steaming egg, and I wondered again if he was viddying what part I had so far played in his jeezny. But he said: 'Recruiting brutal young roughs for the police. Proposing debilitating and will-sapping techniques of conditioning.' All these long slovos, brothers, and a like mad or bezoomny look in his glazzies. 'We've seen it all before,' he said, 'in other countries. The thin end of the wedge. Before we know where we are we shall have the full apparatus of totalitarianism.'[1]

---

1. A concept initially developed to identify the specific character of Italian Fascism in the 1920s.

'Dear dear dear,' I thought, egging away and toast-crunching. I
said:

'Where do I come into all this, sir?'

'You,' he said, still with this bezoomny look, 'are a living witness
to these diabolical proposals. The people, the common people must
know, must see.' He got up from his breakfast and started to walk
up and down the kitchen, from the sink to the like larder, saying very
gromky: 'Would they like their sons to become what you, poor victim, have become? Will not the Government itself now decide what
is and what is not crime and pump out the life and guts and will of
whoever sees fit to displease the Government?' He became quieter
but did not go back to his egg. 'I've written an article,' he said, 'this
morning, while you were sleeping. That will be out in a day or so,
together with your unhappy picture. You shall sign it, poor boy, a
record of what they have done to you.' I said:

'And what do you get out of all this, sir? I mean, besides the pretty
polly you'll get for the article, as you call it? I mean, why are you so
hot and strong against this Government, if I may make like so bold
as to ask?'

He gripped the edge of the table and said, gritting his zoobies,
which were very cally and all stained with cancer-smoke: 'Some of
us have to fight. There are great traditions of liberty to defend. I am
no partisan man. Where I see the infamy I seek to erase it. Party
names mean nothing. The tradition of liberty means all. The common people will let it go, oh yes. They will sell liberty for a quieter
life. That is why they must be prodded, *prodded*—' And here, brothers, he picked up a fork and stuck it two or three razzes into the wall,
so that it all got bent. Then he threw it on the floor. Very kindly he
said: 'Eat well, poor boy, poor victim of the modern world,' and I
could viddy quite clear he was going off his gulliver. 'Eat, eat. Eat my
egg as well.' But I said:

'And what do I get out of this? Do I get cured of the way I am? Do
I find myself able to slooshy the old Choral Symphony without
being sick once more? Can I live like a normal jeezny again? What,
sir, happens to me?'

He looked at me, brothers, as if he hadn't thought of that before
and, anyway, it didn't matter compared with Liberty and all that cal,
and he had a look of surprise at me saying what I said, as though
I was being like selfish in wanting something for myself. Then he said:
'Oh, as I say, you're a living witness, poor boy. Eat up all your breakfast and then come and see what I've written, for it's going into *The
Weekly Trumpet* under your name, you unfortunate victim.'

Well, brothers, what he had written was a very long and very
weepy piece of writing, and as I read it I felt very sorry for the poor
malchick who was govoreeting about his sufferings and how the

Government had sapped his will and how it was up to all lewdies to not let such a rotten and evil Government rule them again, and then of course I realized that the poor suffering malchick was none other than Y.H.N. 'Very good,' I said. 'Real horrorshow. Written well thou hast, O sir.' And then he looked at me very narrow and said:

'What?' It was like he had not slooshied me before.

'Oh, that,' I said, 'is what we call nadsat talk. All the teens use that, sir.' So then he ittied off to the kitchen to wash up the dishes, and I was left in these borrowed night platties and toofles, waiting to have done to me what was going to be done to me, because I had no plans for myself. O my brothers.

While the great F. Alexander was in the kitchen a dingalingaling came at the door. 'Ah,' he creeched, coming out wiping his rookers, 'it will be these people. I'll go.' So he went and let them in, a kind of rumbling hahaha of talk and hallo and filthy weather and how are things in the hallway, then they ittied into the room with the fire and the books and the article about how I had suffered, viddying me and going Aaaaah as they did it. There were three lewdies, and F. Alex gave me their eemyas. Z. Dolin was a very wheezy smoky kind of a veck, coughing kashl kashl kashl with the end of a cancer in his rot, spilling ash all down his platties and then brushing it away with like very impatient rookers. He was a malenky round veck, fat, with big thick-framed ochkies on. Then there was Something Something Rubinstein, a very tall and polite chelloveck with a real gentleman's goloss, very starry with a like eggy beard. And lastly there was D. B. da Silva who was like skorry in his movements and had this strong von of scent coming from him. They all had a real horrorshow look at me and seemed like overjoyed with what they viddied. Z. Dolin said:

'All right, all right, eh? What a superb device he can be, this boy. If anything, of course, he could for preference look even iller and more zombyish than he does. Anything for the cause. No doubt we can think of something.'

I did not like that crack about zombyish, brothers, and so I said: 'What goes on, bratties? What dost thou in mind for thy little droog have?' And then F. Alexander swooshed in with:

'Strange, strange, that manner of voice pricks me. We've come into contact before, I'm sure we have.' And he brooded, like frowning. I would have to watch this, O my brothers. D. B. da Silva said:

'Public meetings, mainly. To exhibit you at public meetings will be a tremendous help. And, of course, the newspaper angle is all tied up. A ruined life is the approach. We must inflame all hearts.' He showed his thirty-odd zoobies, very white against his dark-coloured litso, he looking a malenky bit like some foreigner. I said:

'Nobody will tell me what I get out of all this. Tortured in jail, thrown out of my home by my own parents and their filthy overbearing lodger, beaten by old men and near-killed by the millicents—what is to become of me?' The Rubinstein veck came in with:

'You will see, boy, that the Party will not be ungrateful. Oh, no. At the end of it all there will be some very acceptable little surprise for you. Just you wait and see.'

'There's only one veshch I require,' I creeched out, 'and that's to be normal and healthy as I was in the starry days, having my malenky bit of fun with *real* droogs and not those who just call themselves that and are really more like traitors. Can you do that, eh? Can any veck restore me to what I was? That's what I want and that's what I want to know.'

Kashl kashl kashl, coughed this Z. Dolin. 'A martyr to the cause of Liberty,' he said. 'You have your part to play and don't forget it. Meanwhile, we shall look after you.' And he began to stroke my left rooker as if I was like an idiot, grinning in a bezoomny way. I creeched:

'Stop treating me like a thing that's like got to be just used. I'm not an idiot you can impose on, you stupid bratchnies. Ordinary prestoopnicks are stupid, but I'm not ordinary and nor am I dim. Do you slooshy?'

'Dim,' said F. Alexander, like musing. 'Dim. That was a name somewhere. Dim.'

'Eh?' I said. 'What's Dim got to do with it? What do *you* know about Dim?' And then I said: 'Oh, Bog help us.' I didn't like the like look in F. Alexander's glazzies. I made for the door, wanting to go upstairs and get my platties and then itty off.

'I could almost believe,' said F. Alexander, showing his stained zoobies, his glazzies mad. 'But such things are impossible. For, by Christ, if he were I'd tear him. I'd split him, by God, yes yes, so I would.'

'There,' said D. B. da Silva, stroking his chest like he was a doggie to calm him down. 'It's all in the past. It was other people altogether. We must help this poor victim. That's what we must do now, remembering the Future and our Cause.'

'I'll just get my platties,' I said, at the stair-foot, 'that is to say clothes, and then I'll be ittying off all on my oddy knocky. I mean, my gratitude for all, but I have my own jeezny to live.' Because, brothers, I wanted to get out of here real skorry. But Z. Dolin said:

'Ah, no. We have you, friend, and we keep you. You come with us. Everything will be all right, you'll see.' And he came up to me like to grab hold of my rooker again. Then, brothers, I thought of fight, but thinking of fight made me like want to collapse and sick, so I just stood. And then I saw this like madness in F. Alexander's glazzies and said:

'Whatever you say. I am in your rookers. But let's get it started and all over, brothers.' Because what I wanted now was to get out of this mesto called HOME. I was beginning not to like the like look of the glazzies of F. Alexander one malenky bit.

'Good,' said this Rubinstein. 'Get dressed and let's get started.'

'Dim dim dim,' F. Alexander kept saying in a like low mutter. 'What or who was this Dim?' I ittied upstairs real skorry and dressed in near two seconds flat. Then I was out with these three and into an auto, Rubinstein one side of me and Z. Dolin coughing kashl kashl kashl the other side, D. B. da Silva doing the driving, into the town and to a flatblock not really all that distant from what had used to be my own flatblock or home. 'Come, boy, out,' said Z. Dolin, coughing to make the cancer-end in his rot glow red like some malenky furnace. 'This is where you shall be installed.' So we ittied in, and there was like another of these Dignity of Labour veshches on the wall of the vestibule, and we upped in the lift, brothers, and then went into a flat like all the flats of all the flatblocks of the town. Very very malenky, with two bedrooms and one live-eat-work-room, the table of this all covered with books and papers and ink and bottles and all that cal. 'Here is your new home,' said D. B. da Silva. 'Settle here, boy. Food is in the food-cupboard. Pyjamas are in a drawer. Rest, rest, perturbed spirit.'[2]

'Eh?' I said, not quite ponying that.

'All right,' said Rubinstein, with his starry goloss. 'We are now leaving you. Work has to be done. We'll be with you later. Occupy yourself as best you can.'

'One thing,' coughed Z. Dolin kashl kashl kashl. 'You saw what stirred in the tortured memory of our friend F. Alexander. Was it, by any chance—? That is to say, did you—? I think you know what I mean. We won't let it go any further.'

'I've paid,' I said. 'Bog knows I've paid for what I did. I've paid not only like for myself but for those bratchnies too that called themselves my droogs.' I felt violent so then I felt a bit sick. 'I'll lay down a bit,' I said. 'I've been through terrible terrible times.'

'You have,' said D. B. da Silva, showing all his thirty zoobies. 'You do that.'

So they left me, brothers. They ittied off about their business, which I took to be about politics and all that cal, and I was on the bed, all on my oddy knocky with everything very very quiet. I just laid there with my sabogs kicked off my nogas and my tie loose, like all bewildered and not knowing what sort of a jeezny I was going to live now. And all sorts of like pictures kept like passing through my gulliver, of the different chellovecks I'd met at school and in the Staja, and the different veshches that had happened to me, and how there was not one veck you could trust in the whole bolshy world. And then I like dozed off, brothers.

---

2. Shakespeare, *Hamlet* 1.5.182.

When I woke up I could slooshy music coming out of the wall, real gromky, and it was that that had dragged me out of my bit of like sleep. It was a symphony that I knew real horrorshow but had not slooshied for many a year, namely the Symphony Number Three of the Danish veck Otto Skadelig,[3] a very gromky and violent piece, especially in the first movement, which was what was playing now. I slooshied for two seconds in like interest and joy, but then it all came over me, the start of the pain and the sickness, and I began to groan deep down in my keeshkas. And then there I was, me who had loved music so much, crawling off the bed and going oh oh oh to myself, and then bang bang banging on the wall creeching: 'Stop, stop it, turn it off!' But it went on and it seemed to be like louder. So I crashed at the wall till my knuckles were all red red krovvy and torn skin, creeching and creeching, but the music did not stop. Then I thought I had to get away from it, so I lurched out of the malenky bedroom and ittied skorry to the front door of the flat, but this had been locked from the outside and I could not get out. And all the time the music got more and more gromky, like it was all a deliberate torture, O my brothers. So I stuck my little fingers real deep in my ookos, but the trombones and kettledrums blasted through gromky enough. So I creeched again for them to stop and went hammer hammer hammer on the wall, but it made not one malenky bit of difference. 'Oh, what am I to do?' I boohooed to myself. 'Oh, Bog in Heaven help me.' I was like wandering all over the flat in pain and sickness, trying to shut out the music and like groaning deep out of my guts, and then on top of the pile of books and papers and all that cal that was on the table in the living-room I viddied what I had to do and what I had wanted to do until those old men in the Public Biblio and then Dim and Billyboy disguised as rozzes stopped me, and that was to do myself in, to snuff it, to blast off for ever out of this wicked and cruel world. What I viddied was the slovo DEATH on the cover of a like pamphlet, even though it was only DEATH TO THE GOVERNMENT. And like it was Fate there was another like malenky booklet which had an open window on the cover, and it said: 'Open the window to fresh air, fresh ideas, a new way of living.' And so I knew that was like telling me to finish it all off by jumping out. One moment of pain, perhaps, and then sleep for ever and ever and ever.

The music was still pouring in all brass and drums and the violins miles up through the wall. The window in the room where I had laid down was open. I ittied to it and viddied a fair drop to the autos and buses and walking chellovecks below. I creeched out to the world: 'Goodbye, goodbye, may Bog forgive you for a ruined

3. The Danish word *skadelig* means harmful.

life.' Then I got on to the sill, the music blasting away to my left, and I shut my glazzies and felt the cold wind on my litso, then I jumped.

6

I jumped, O my brothers, and I fell on the sidewalk hard, but I did not snuff it, oh no. If I had snuffed it I would not be here to write what I written have. It seems that the jump was not from a big enough heighth to kill. But I cracked my back and my wrists and nogas and felt very bolshy pain before I passed out, brothers, with astonished and surprised litsos of chellovecks in the streets looking at me from above. And just before I passed out I viddied clear that not one chelloveck in the whole horrid world was for me and that that music through the wall had all been like arranged by those who were supposed to be my like new droogs and that it was some veshch like this that they wanted for their horrible selfish and boastful politics. All that was in like a million millionth part of one minoota before I threw over the world and the sky and the litsos of the staring chellovecks that were above me.

Where I was when I came back to jeezny after a long black black gap of it might have been a million years was a hospital, all white and with this von of hospitals you get, all like sour and smug and clean. These antiseptic veshches you get in hospitals should have a real horrorshow von of like frying onions or of flowers. I came very slow back to knowing who I was and I was all bound up in white and I could not feel anything in my plott, pain nor sensation nor any veshch at all. All round my gulliver was a bandage and there were bits of stuff like stuck to my litso, and my rookers were all in bandages and like bits of stick were like fixed to my fingers like on it might be flowers to make them grow straight, and my poor old nogas were all straightened out too, and it was all bandages and wire cages and into my right rooker, near the pletcho, was red red krovvy dripping from a jar upside down. But I could not feel anything, O my brothers. There was a nurse sitting by my bed and she was reading some book that was all like very dim print and you could viddy it was a story because of a lot of inverted commas, and she was like breathing hard uh uh uh over it, so it must have been a story about the old in-out in-out. She was a real horrorshow devotchka, this nurse, with a very red rot and like long lashes over her glazzies, and under her like very stiff uniform you could viddy she had very horrorshow groodies. So I said to her: 'What gives, O my little sister? Come thou and have a nice lay-down with your malenky droog in this bed.' But the slovos didn't come out horrorshow at all, it being as though my rot was all stiffened up, and I could feel with my yahzick that some of my zoobies were no longer there. But this nurse like jumped and dropped her book on the floor and said:

'Oh, you've recovered consciousness.'

That was like a big rotful for a malenky ptitsa like her, and I tried to say so, but the slovos came out only like er er er. She ittied off and left me on my oddy knocky, and I could viddy now that I was in a malenky room of my own, not in one of these long wards like I had been in as a very little malchick, full of coughing dying starry vecks all round to make you want to get well and fit again. It had been like diphtheria I had had then, O my brothers.

It was like now as though I could not hold to being conscious all that long, because I was like asleep again almost right away, very skorry, but in a minoota or two I was sure that this nurse ptitsa had come back and had brought chellovecks in white coats with her and they were viddying me very frowning and going hm hm hm at Your Humble Narrator. And with them I was sure there was the old charles from the Staja govoreeting: 'Oh my son, my son,' breathing a like very stale von of whisky on to me and then saying: 'But I would not stay, oh no. I could not in no wise subscribe to what those bratchnies are going to do to other poor prestoopnicks. So I got out and am preaching sermons now about it all, my little beloved son in J.C.'

I woke up again later on and who should I viddy there round the bed but the three from whose flat I had jumped out, namely D. B. da Silva and Something Something Rubinstein and Z. Dolin. 'Friend,' one of these vecks was saying, but I could not viddy or slooshy horrorshow which one, 'friend, little friend,' this goloss was saying, 'the people are on fire with indignation. You have killed those horrible boastful villains' chances of re-election. They will go and will go for ever and ever. You have served Liberty well.' I tried to say:

'If I had died it would have been even better for you political bratchnies, would it not, pretending and treacherous droogs as you are.' But all that came out was er er er. Then one of these three seemed to hold out a lot of bits cut from gazettas and what I could viddy was a horrible picture of me all krovvy on a stretcher being carried off and I seemed to like remember a kind of a popping of lights which must have been photographer vecks. Out of one glazz I could read like headlines which were sort of trembling in the rooker of the chelloveck that held them, like BOY VICTIM OF CRIMINAL REFORM SCHEME and GOVERNMENT AS MURDERER and then there was like a picture of a veck that looked familiar to me and it said OUT OUT OUT, and that would be the Minister of the Inferior or Interior. Then the nurse ptitsa said:

'You shouldn't be exciting him like that. You shouldn't be doing anything that will make him upset. Now come on, let's have you out.' I tried to say:

'Out out out,' but it was er er er again. Anyway, these three political vecks went. And I went, too, only back to the land, back to all blackness lit up by like odd dreams which I didn't know whether they were dreams or not, O my brothers. Like for instance I had this idea of my whole plott or body being like emptied of as it might be dirty water and then filled up again with clean. And then there were really lovely and horrorshow dreams of being in some veck's auto that had been crasted by me and driving up and down the world all on my oddy knocky running lewdies down and hearing them creech they were dying, and in me no pain and no sickness. And also there were dreams of doing the old in-out in-out with devotchkas, forcing like them down on the ground and making them have it and everybody standing round clapping their rookers and cheering like bezoomny. And then I woke up again and it was my pee and em come to viddy their ill son, my em boohooing real horrorshow. I could govoreet a lot better now and could say:

'Well well well well well, what gives? What makes you think you are like welcome?' My papapa said, in a like ashamed way:

'You were in the papers, son. It said they had done great wrong to you. It said how the Government drove you to try and do yourself in. And it was our fault too, in a way, son. Your home's your home, when all's said and done, son.' And my mum kept on going boohoohoo and looking ugly as kiss-my-sharries. So I said:

'And how beeth thy new son Joe? Well and healthy and prosperous, I trust and pray.' My mum said:

'Oh, Alex Alex. Owwwwwwww.' My papapa said:

'A very awkward thing, son. He got into a bit of trouble with the police and was done by the police.'

'Really?' I said. 'Really? Such a good sort of chelloveck and all. Amazed proper I am, honest.'

'Minding his own business he was,' said my pee. 'And the police told him to move on. Waiting at a corner he was, son, to see a girl he was going to meet. And they told him to move on and he said he had rights like everybody else, and then they sort of fell on top of him and hit him about cruel.'

'Terrible,' I said. 'Really terrible. And where is the poor boy now?'

'Owwwww,' boohooed my mum. 'Gone back owwwwwwme.'

'Yes,' said dad. 'He's gone back to his own home town to get better. They've had to give his job here to somebody else.'

'So now,' I said, 'you're willing for me to move back in again and things be like they were before.'

'Yes, son,' said my papapa. 'Please, son.'

'I'll consider it,' I said. 'I'll think about it real careful.'

'Owwwww,' went my mum.

'Ah, shut it,' I said, 'or I'll give you something proper to yowl and creech about. Kick your zoobies in I will.' And, O my brothers, saying that made me feel a malenky bit better, as if all like fresh red red krovvy was flowing all through my plott. That was something I had to think about. It was like as though to get better I had had to get worse.

'That's no way to speak to your mother, son,' said my papapa. 'After all, she brought you into the world.'

'Yes,' I said, 'and a right grahzny vonny world too.' I shut my glazzies tight in like pain and said: 'Go away now. I'll think about coming back. But things will have to be very different.'

'Yes, son,' said my pee. 'Anything you say.'

'You'll have to make up your mind,' I said, 'who's to be boss.'

'Owwwwww,' my mum went on.

'Very good, son,' said my papapa. 'Things will be as you like. Only get well.'

When they had gone I laid and thought a bit about different veshches, like all different pictures passing through my gulliver, and when the nurse ptitsa came back in and like straightened the sheets on the bed I said to her:

'How long is it I've been in here?'

'A week or so,' she said.

'And what have they been doing to me?'

'Well,' she said, 'you were all broken up and bruised and had sustained severe concussion and had lost a lot of blood. They've had to put all that right, haven't they?'

'But,' I said, 'has anyone been doing anything with my gulliver? What I mean is, have they been playing around with inside like my brain?'

'Whatever they've done,' she said, 'it'll all be for the best.'

But a couple of days later a couple of like doctor vecks came in, both youngish vecks with these very sladky smiles, and they had like a picture book with them. One of them said: 'We want you to have a look at these and to tell us what you think about them. All right?'

'What giveth. O little droogies?' I said. 'What new bezoomny idea dost thou in mind have?' So they both had a like embarrassed smeck at that and then they sat down either side of the bed and opened up this book. On the first page there was like a photograph of a bird-nest full of eggs.

'Yes?' one of these doctor vecks said.

'A bird-nest,' I said, 'full of like eggs. Very very nice.'

'And what would you like to do about it?' the other one said.

'Oh,' I said, 'smash them. Pick up the lot and like throw them against a wall or a cliff or something and then viddy them all smash up real horrorshow.'

'Good good,' they both said, and then the page was turned. It was like a picture of one of these bolshy great birds called peacocks with all its tail spread out in all colours in a very boastful way. 'Yes?' said one of these vecks.

'I would like.' I said, 'to pull out like all those feathers in its tail and slooshy it creech blue murder. For being so like boastful.'

'Good,' they both said, 'good good good.' And they went on turning the pages. There were like pictures of real horrorshow devotchkas, and I said I would like to give them the old in-out in-out with lots of ultra-violence. There were like pictures of chellovecks being given the boot straight in the litso and all red red krovvy everywhere and I said I would like to be in on that. And there was a picture of the old nagoy droog of the prison charlie's carrying his cross up a hill, and I said I would like to have the old hammer and nails. Good good good. I said:

'What is all this?'

'Deep hypnopaedia,' or some such slovo, said one of these two vecks. 'You seem to be cured.'

'Cured?' I said. 'Me tied down to this bed like this and you say cured? Kiss my sharries is what I say.'

'Wait,' the other said. 'It won't be long now.'

So I waited and, O my brothers, I got a lot better, munching away at eggiwegs and lomticks of toast and peeting bolshy great mugs of milky chai, and then one day they said I was going to have a very very very special visitor.

'Who?' I said, while they straightened the bed and combed my luscious glory for me, me having the bandage off now from my gulliver and the hair growing again.

'You'll see, you'll see,' they said. And I viddied all right. At two-thirty of the afternoon there were like all photographers and men from gazettas with notebooks and pencils and all that cal. And, brothers, they near trumpeted a bolshy fanfare for this great and important veck who was coming to viddy Your Humble Narrator. And in he came, and of course it was none other than the Minister of the Interior or Inferior, dressed in the heighth of fashion and with this very upper-class haw haw haw goloss. Flash flash bang went the cameras when he put out his rooker to me to shake it. I said:

'Well well well well well. What giveth then, old droogie?' Nobody seemed to quite pony that, but somebody said in a like harsh goloss:

'Be more respectful, boy, in addressing the Minister.'

'Yarbles,' I said, like snarling like a doggie. 'Bolshy great yarblockos to thee and thine.'

'All right, all right,' said the Interior Inferior one very skorry. 'He speaks to me as a friend, don't you, son?'

'I am everyone's friend,' I said. 'Except to my enemies.'

'And who are your enemies?' said the Minister, while all the gazetta vecks went scribble scribble scribble. 'Tell us that, my boy.'

'All who do me wrong,' I said, 'are my enemies.'

'Well,' said the Int Inf Min, sitting down by my bed. 'I and the Government of which I am a member want you to regard us as friends. Yes, friends. We have put you right, yes? You are getting the best of treatment. We never wished you harm, but there are some who did and do. And I think you know who those are.'

'All who do me wrong,' I said, 'are my enemies.'

'Yes yes yes,' he said. 'There are certain men who wanted to use you, yes, use you for political ends. They would have been glad, yes, glad for you to be dead, for they thought they could then blame it all on the Government. I think you know who those men are.'

'I did not,' I said, 'like the look of them.'

'There is a man,' said the Intinfmin, 'called F. Alexander, a writer of subversive literature, who has been howling for your blood. He has been mad with desire to stick a knife in you. But you're safe from him now. We put him away.'

'He was supposed to be like a droogie,' I said. 'Like a mother to me was what he was.'

'He found out that you had done wrong to him. At least,' said the Min very very skorry, 'he believed you had done wrong. He formed this idea in his mind that you had been responsible for the death of someone near and dear to him.'

'What you mean,' I said, 'is that he was told.'

'He had this idea,' said the Min. 'He was a menace. We put him away for his own protection. And also,' he said, 'for yours.'

'Kind,' I said. 'Most kind of thou.'

'When you leave here,' said the Min, 'you will have no worries. We shall see to everything. A good job on a good salary. Because you are helping us.'

'Am I?' I said.

'We always help our friends, don't we?' And then he took my rooker and some veck creeched: 'Smile!' and I smiled like bezoomny without thinking, and then flash flash crack flash bang there were pictures being taken of me and the Intinfmin all droogy together. 'Good boy,' said this great chelloveck. 'Good good boy. And now, see, a present.'

What was brought in now, brothers, was a big shiny box, and I viddied clear what sort of a veshch it was. It was a stereo. It was put down next to the bed and opened up and some veck plugged its lead into the wall-socket. 'What shall it be?' asked a veck with ochkies on his nose, and he had in his rookers lovely shiny sleeves full of music. 'Mozart? Beethoven? Schoenberg? Carl Orff?'[1]

---

1. Arnold Schoenberg (1874–1951), composer best known as the instigator of serialism, and Carl Orff (1895–1982), whose cantata *Carmina Burana* (1937) revived medieval song rediscovered at the beginning of the nineteeth century.

'The Ninth,' I said. 'The glorious Ninth.'

And the Ninth it was, O my brothers. Everybody began to leave nice and quiet while I laid there with my glazzies closed, slooshying the lovely music. The Min said: 'Good good boy,' patting me on the pletcho, then he ittied off. Only one veck was left, saying: 'Sign here, please.' I opened my glazzies up to sign, not knowing what I was signing and not, O my brothers, caring either. Then I was left alone with the glorious Ninth of Ludwig van.

Oh, it was gorgeosity and yumyumyum. When it came to the Scherzo I could viddy myself very clear running and running on like very light and mysterious nogas, carving the whole litso of the creeching world with my cut-throat britva.[2] And there was the slow movement and the lovely last singing movement still to come. I was cured all right.[3]

7

'What's it going to be then, eh?'

There was me, Your Humble Narrator, and my three droogs, that is Len, Rick, and Bully, Bully being called Bully because of his bolshly big neck and very gromky goloss which was just like some bolshy great bull bellowing auuuuuuuuh. We were sitting in the Korova Milkbar making up our rassoodocks what to do with the evening, a flip dark chill winter bastard though dry. All round were chellovecks well away on milk plus vellocet and synthemesc and drencrom and other veshches which take you far far far away from this wicked and real world into the land to viddy Bog And All His Holy Angels And Saints in your left sabog with lights bursting and spurting all over your mozg. What we were peeting was the old moloko with knives in it, as we used to say, to sharpen you up and make you ready for a bit of dirty twenty-to-one, but I've told you all that before.

We were dressed in the heighth of fashion, which in those days was these very wide trousers and a very loose black shiny leather like jerkin over an open-necked shirt with a like scarf tucked in. At this time too it was the heighth of fashion to use the old britva on the gulliver, so that most of the gulliver was like bald and there was hair

2. In E. M. Forster's *Howards End* (1910), Chapter V, a performance of Beethoven's Fifth Symphony is the occasion for a famous study of the sympathetic imaginations of the characters, beginning, "It will be generally admitted that Beethoven's Fifth Symphony is the most sublime noise that has ever penetrated into the ear of man." The progressive heroine, Helen Schlegel, hears, or rather imagines, "a goblin walking quietly over the universe"—a scenario echoed in Alex's fantasy.

3. TS 147: autograph comment, "Should we end here? An optional 'Epilogue' follows." See p. 203.

only on the sides. But it was always the same on the old nogas—real horrorshow bolshy big boots for kicking litsos in.

'What's it going to be then, eh?'

I was like the oldest of we four, and they all looked up to me as their leader, but I got the idea sometimes that Bully had the thought in his gulliver that he would like to take over, this being because of his bigness and the gromky goloss that bellowed out of him when he was on the warpath. But all the ideas came from Your Humble, O my brothers, and also there was this veshch that I had been famous and had had my picture and articles and all that cal in the gazettas. Also I had by far the best job of all we four, being in the National Gramo-disc Archives on the music side with a real horrorshow carman full of pretty polly at the week's end and a lot of nice free discs for my own malenky self on the side.

This evening in the Korova there was a fair number of vecks and ptitsas and devotchkas and malchicks smecking and peeting away, and cutting through their govoreeting and the burbling of the in-the-landers with their 'Gorgor fallatuke and the worm sprays in filltip slaughterballs' and all that cal you could slooshy a popdisc on the stereo, this being Ned Achimota singing 'That Day, Yeah, That Day'. At the counter were three devotchkas dressed in the heighth of nadsat fashion, that is to say long uncombed hair dyed white and false groodies sticking out a metre or more and very very tight short skirts with all like frothy white underneath, and Bully kept saying: 'Hey, get in there we could, three of us. Old Len is not interested. Leave old Len alone with his God.' And Len kept saying: 'Yarbles yarbles. Where is the spirit of all for one and one for all, eh boy?' Suddenly I felt both very very tired and also full of tingly energy, and I said:

'Out out out out out.'

'Where to?' said Rick, who had a litso like a frog's.

'Oh, just to viddy what's doing in the great outside,' I said. But somehow, my brothers, I felt very bored and a bit hopeless, and I had been feeling that a lot these days. So I turned to the chelloveck nearest me on the big plush seat that ran right round the whole mesto, a chelloveck, that is, who was burbling away under the influence, and I fisted him real skorry ack ack ack in the belly. But he felt it not, brothers, only burbling away with his 'Cart cart virtue, where in toptails lieth the poppoppicorns?' So we scatted out into the big winter nochy.

We walked down Marghanita Boulevard and there were no millicents patrolling that way, so when we met a starry veck coming away from a news-kiosk where he had been kupetting a gazetta I said to Bully: "All right, Bully boy, thou canst if thou like wishest.' More and more these days I had been just giving the orders and standing back to viddy them being carried out. So Bully cracked into him er er er, and the other two tripped him and kicked at him, smecking away, while he was down and then let him crawl off to where he lived, like whimpering to himself. Bully said:

'How about a nice yummy glass of something to keep out the cold, O Alex?' For we were not too far from the Duke of New York. The other two nodded yes yes yes but all looked at me to viddy whether that was all right. I nodded too and so off we ittied. Inside the snug there were these starry ptitsas or sharps or baboochkas you will remember from the beginning and they all started on their: 'Evening, lads, God bless you, boys, best lads living, that's what you are,' waiting for us to say: 'What's it going to be, girls?' Bully rang the collocoll and a waiter came in rubbing his rookers on his grazzy apron. 'Cutter on the table, droogies,' said Bully, pulling out his own rattling and chinking mound of deng. 'Scotchmen for us and the same for the old baboochkas, eh?' And then I said:

'Ah, to hell. Let them buy their own.' I didn't know what it was, but these last days I had become like mean. There had come into my gulliver a like desire to keep all my pretty polly to myself, to like hoard it all up for some reason. Bully said:

'What gives, bratty? What's coming over old Alex?'

'Ah, to hell,' I said. 'I don't know. I don't know. What it is is I don't like just throwing away my hard-earned pretty polly, that's what it is.'

'Earned?' said Rick. 'Earned? It doesn't have to be earned, as well thou knowest, old droogie. Took, that's all, just took, like.' And he smecked real gromky and I viddied one or two of his zoobies weren't all that horrorshow.

'Ah,' I said, 'I've got some thinking to do.' But viddying these baboochkas looking all eager like for some free alc, I like shrugged my pletchoes and pulled out my own cutter from my trouser carman, notes and coin all mixed together, and plonked it tinkle crackle on the table.

'Scotchmen all round, right,' said the waiter. But for some reason I said:

'No, boy, for me make it one small beer, right.' Len said:

'This I do not much go for,' and he began to put his rooker on my gulliver, like kidding I must have fever, but I like snarled doggy-wise for him to give over skorry. 'All right, all right, droog,' he said. 'As thou like sayest.' But Bully was having a smot with his rot open at something that had come out of my carman with the pretty polly I'd put on the table. He said:

'Well well well. And we never knew.'

'Give me that,' I snarled and grabbed it skorry. I couldn't explain how it had got there, brothers, but it was a photograph I had scis-

sored out of the old gazetta and it was of a baby. It was of a baby
gurgling goo goo goo with all like moloko dribbling from its rot and
looking up and like smecking at everybody, and its was all nagoy
and its flesh was like in all folds with being a very fat baby. There
was then like a bit of haw haw haw struggling to get hold of this bit
of paper from me, so I had to snarl again at them and I grabbed the
photo and tore it up into tiny teeny pieces and let it fall like a bit
of snow on to the floor. The whisky came in then and the starry
baboochkas said: 'Good health, lads, God bless you, boys, the best
lads living, that's what you are,' and all that cal. And one of them
who was all lines and wrinkles and no zoobies in her shrunken old
rot said: 'Don't tear up money, son. If you don't need it give it them
as does,' which was very bold and forward of her. But Rick said:

'Money that was not, O baboochka. It was a picture of a dear little itsy witsy bitsy bit of a baby.' I said:

'I'm getting just that bit tired, that I am. It's you who's the babies,
you lot. Scoffing and grinning and all you can do is smeck and give
people bolshy cowardly tolchocks when they can't give them back.'
Bully said:

'Well now, we always thought it was you who was the king of that
and also the teacher. Not well, that's the trouble with thou, old
droogie.'

I viddied this sloppy glass of beer I had on the table in front of me
and felt like all vomity within, so I went 'Aaaaah' and poured all the
frothy vonny cal all over the floor. One of the starry ptitsas said:

'Waste not want not.' I said:

'Look, droogies. Listen. Tonight I am somehow just not in the
mood. I know not why or how it is, but there it is. You three go your
own ways this nightwise, leaving me out. Tomorrow we shall meet
same place same time, me hoping to be like a lot better.'

'Oh,' said Bully, 'right sorry I am.' But you could viddy a like gleam
in his glazzies, because now he would be taking over for this nochy.
Power power, everybody like wants power. 'We can postpone till
tomorrow,' said Bully. 'what we in mind had. Namely, that bit of
shop-crasting in Gagarin Street.[1] Flip horrorshow takings there,
droog, for the having.'

'No,' I said. 'You postpone nothing. You just carry on in your own
like style. Now,' I said, 'I itty off.' And I got up from my chair.

'Where to, then?' asked Rick.

'That know I not,' I said. 'Just to be on like my own and sort
things out.' You could viddy the old baboochkas were real puzzled
at me going out like that and like all morose and not the bright and

1. See note 3 on p. 12.

smecking malchickiwick you will remember. But I said: 'Ah, to hell, to hell,' and scatted out all on my oddy knocky into the street.

It was dark and there was a wind sharp as a nozh getting up, and there were very very few lewdies about. There were these patrol cars with brutal rozzes inside them like cruising about, and now and then on the corner you would viddy a couple of very young millicents stamping against the bitchy cold and letting out steam breath on the winter air, O my brothers. I suppose really a lot of the old ultra-violence and crasting was dying out now, the rozzes being so brutal with who they caught, though it had become like a fight between naughty nadsats and the rozzes who could be more skorry with the nozh and the britva and the stick and even the gun. But what was the matter with me these days was that I didn't like care much. It was like something soft getting into me and I could not pony why. What I wanted these days I did not know. Even the music I liked to slooshy in my own malenky den was what I would have smecked at before, brothers. I was slooshying more like malenky romantic songs, what they call *Lieder*, just a goloss and a piano, very quiet and like yearny, different from when it had been all bolshy orchestras and me lying on the bed between the violins and the trombones and kettledrums. There was something happening inside me, and I wondered if it was like some disease or if it was what they had done to me that time upsetting my gulliver and perhaps going to make me real bezoomny.

So thinking like this with my gulliver bent and my rookers stuck in my trouser carmans I walked the town, brothers, and at last I began to feel very tired and also in great need of a nice bolshy cha-sha of milky chai. Thinking about this chai, I got a sudden like picture of me sitting before a bolshy fire in an armchair peeting away at this chai, and what was funny and very very strange was that I seemed to have turned into a very starry chelloveck, about seventy years old, because I could viddy my own voloss, which was very grey, and I also had whiskers, and these were very grey too. I could viddy myself as an old man, sitting by a fire, and then the like picture vanished. But it was very like strange.

I came to one of these tea-and-coffee mestos, brothers, and I could viddy through the long long window that it was full of very dull lewdies, like ordinary, who had these very patient and expressionless litsos and would do no harm to no one, all sitting there and govoreet-ing like quietly and peeting away at their nice harmless chai and cof-fee. I ittied inside and went up to the counter and bought me a nice hot chai with plenty of moloko, then I ittied to one of these tables and sat down to peet it. There was a like young couple at this table, peeting and smoking filter-tip cancers, and govoreeting and smeck-ing very quietly between themselves, but I took no notice of them and just went on peeting away and like dreaming and wondering what it was in me that was like changing and what was going to happen to me. But I viddied that the devotchka at this table who was with this chelloveck was real horrorshow, not the sort you would want to like throw down and give the old in-out in-out to, but with a horrorshow plott and litso and a smiling rot and very very fair voloss and all that cal. And then the veck with her, who had a hat on his gulliver and had his litso like turned away from me, swivelled round to viddy the bolshy big clock they had on the wall in this mesto, and then I viddied who he was and then he viddied who I was. It was Pete, one of my three droogs from those days when it was Georgie and Dim and him and me. It was Pete like looking a lot older though he could not now be more than nineteen and a bit, and he had a bit of a moustache and an ordinary day-suit and this hat on. I said:

'Well well well, droogie, what gives? Very very long time no viddy.' He said:

'It's little Alex, isn't it?'

'None other,' I said. 'A long long long time since those dead and gone good days. And now poor Georgie, they told me, is underground and old Dim is a brutal millicent, and here is thou and here is I, and what news hast thou, old droogie?'

'He talks funny, doesn't he?' said this devotchka, like giggling.

'This,' said Pete to the devotchka, 'is an old friend. His name is Alex. May I,' he said to me, 'introduce my wife?'

My rot fell wide open then. 'Wife?' I like gaped. 'Wife wife wife? Ah no, that cannot be. Too young art thou to be married, old droog. Impossible impossible.'

This devotchka who was like Pete's wife (impossible impossible) giggled again and said to Pete: 'Did you used to talk like that too?'

'Well,' said Pete, and he liked smiled. 'I'm nearly twenty. Old enough to be hitched, and it's been two months already. You were very young and very forward, remember.'

'Well,' I liked gaped still. 'Over this get can I not, old droogie. Pete married. Well well well.'

'We have a small flat,' said Pete. 'I am earning very small money at State Marine Insurance, but things will get better, that I know. And Georgina here—'

'What again is that name?' I said, rot still open like bezoomny. Pete's wife (wife, brothers) like giggled again.

'Georgina,' said Pete. 'Georgina works too. Typing, you know. We manage, we manage.' I could not, brothers, take my glazzies off him, really. He was like grown up now, with a grown-up goloss and all. 'You must,' said Pete, 'come and see us sometime. You still,' he said, 'look very young, despite all your terrible experiences. Yes yes yes, we've read all about them. But, of course, you *are* very young still.'

'Eighteen,' I said, 'just gone.'

'Eighteen, eh?' said Pete. 'As old as that. Well well well. Now,' he said, 'we have to be going.' And he like gave this Georgina of his a like loving look and pressed one of her rookers between his and she gave him one of these looks back, O my brothers. 'Yes,' said Pete, turning back to me, 'we're off to a little party at Greg's.'

'Greg?' I said.

'Oh, of course,' said Pete, 'you wouldn't know Greg, would you? Greg is after your time. While you were away Greg came into the picture. He runs little parties, you know. Mostly wine-cup and word-games. But very nice, very pleasant, you know. Harmless, if you see what I mean.'

'Yes,' I said. 'Harmless. Yes yes, I viddy that real horrorshow.' And this Georgina devotchka giggled again at my slovos. And then these two ittied off to their vonny word-games at this Greg's, whoever he was. I was left all on my oddy knocky with my milky chai, which was getting cold now, like thinking and wondering.

Perhaps that was it, I kept thinking. Perhaps I was getting too old for the sort of jeezny I had been leading, brothers. I was eighteen now, just gone. Eighteen was not a young age. At eighteen old Wolfgang Amadeus had written concertos and symphonies and operas and oratorios and all that cal, no, not cal, heavenly music. And then there was old Felix M.[1] with his *Midsummer Night's Dream* Overture. And there were others. And there was this like French poet set by old Benjy Britt,[2] who had done all his best poetry by the age of fifteen, O my brothers. Arthur, his first name. Eighteen was not all that young an age, then. But what was I going to do?

Walking the dark chill bastards of winter streets after ittying off from this chai and coffee mesto, I kept viddying like visions, like these cartoons in the gazettas. There was Your Humble Narrator Alex coming home from work to a good hot plate of dinner, and there was this ptitsa all welcoming and greeting like loving. But I could not viddy her all that horrorshow, brothers, I could not think who it might be. But I had this sudden very strong idea that if I walked into the room next to this room where the fire was burning away and my hot dinner laid on the table, there I should find what I really wanted, and now it all tied up, that picture scissored out of the gazetta and meeting old Pete like that. For in that other room in a cot was laying gurgling goo goo goo my son. Yes yes yes, brothers, my son. And now I felt this bolshy big hollow inside my plott, feel-

1. Felix Mendelssohn (1809–1847), German Romantic composer.
2. The poet is Arthur Rimbaud (1854–1891), whose *Illuminations* was set to music by the English composer Benjamin Britten (1913–1976) in 1941.

ing very surprised too at myself. I knew what was happening, O my brothers. I was like growing up.

Yes yes yes, there it was. Youth must go, ah yes. But youth is only being in a way like it might be an animal. No, it is not just like being an animal so much as being like one of these malenky toys you viddy being sold in the streets, like little chellovecks made out of tin and with a spring inside and then a winding handle on the outside and you wind it up grrr grrr grrr and off it itties, like walking, O my brothers. But it itties in a straight line and bangs straight into things bang bang and it cannot help what it is doing. Being young is like being like one of these malenky machines.

My son, my son. When I had my son I would explain all that to him when he was starry enough to like understand. But then I knew he would not understand or would not want to understand at all and would do all the veshches I had done, yes perhaps even killing some poor starry forella surrounded with mewing kots and koshkas, and I would not be able to really stop him. And nor would he be able to stop his own son, brothers. And so it would itty on to like the end of the world, round and round and round, like some bolshy gigantic like chelloveck, like old Bog Himself (by courtesy of Korova Milkbar) turning and turning and turning a vonny grahzny orange in his gigantic rookers.

But first of all, brothers, there was this veshch of finding some devotchka or other who would be a mother to this son. I would have to start on that tomorrow, I kept thinking. That was something like new to do. That was something I would have to get started on, a new like chapter beginning.

That's what it's going to be then, brothers, as I come to the like end of this tale. You have been everywhere with your little droog Alex, suffering with him, and you have viddied some of the most grahzny bratchnies old Bog ever made, all on to your old droog Alex. And all it was was that I was young. But now as I end this story, brothers, I am not young, not no longer, oh no. Alex like groweth up, oh yes.

But where I itty now, O my brothers, is all on my oddy knocky, where you cannot go. Tomorrow is all like sweet flowers and the turning vonny earth and the stars and the old Luna up there and your old droog Alex all on his oddy knocky seeking like a mate. And all that cal. A terrible grahzny vonny world, really, O my brothers. And so farewell from your little droog. And to all others in this story profound shooms of lip-music brrrrrr. And they can kiss my sharries. But you, O my brothers, remember sometimes thy little Alex that was. Amen. And all that cal.

Notes on the Text

The text in this edition is based on the first U.K. edition (Heinemann, 1962) of twenty-one chapters. The following notes indicate variants between that edition and the first U.S. edition to print the twenty-first chapter of the novel (Norton, 1987), as well as the current U.S. edition (Norton, 1995). Lineation in brackets refers to this Norton Critical Edition.

Heinemann "gullivers, each"; Norton 1987 "gullivers. each"; Norton 1995 "gullivers, each" [4:19]

Heinemann "us, leering"; Norton 1987 "us. leering"; Norton 1995 "us, leering" [22:19]

Heinemann "cat-stalk"; Norton 1987 "cat-stalk" (across line end); Norton 1995 "catstalk" [37:25]

Heinemann "more than than"; Norton 1987 "more than"; Norton 1995 "more than" [52:21]

Heinemann "ochkies"; Norton 1987 "otchkies"; Norton 1995 "otch-kies" (TS 83 reads "ochkies"; TS 17 "otchkies"; TS 126 "ochkies", TS 133 "otchkies" corrected to "ochkies") [67:22]

Heinemann "normal jeezny"; Norton 1987 "normal jeezny"; Norton 1995 "text jeezny" [103:32]

Heinemann "say: 'What's"; Norton 1987 "say 'What's"; Norton 1995 "say 'What's" [116:12]

Heinemann "was what"; Norton 1987 "what what"; Norton 1995 "what what" [118:16]

Heinemann "wife (wife"; Norton 1987 "wife. (wife"; Norton 1995 "wife. (wife" [119:39]

Heinemann "Yes yes yes"; Norton 1987 "Yes yes, yes"; Norton 1995 "Yes yes, yes" [119:44]

Heinemann "just"; Norton 1987 "Just"; Norton 1995 "Just" [209:21]

Heinemann "Yes yes"; Norton 1987 "Yes, yes"; Norton 1995 "Yes, yes" [120:1]

Heinemann "chai and coffee"; Norton 1987 "chai-and-coffee"; Norton 1995 "chai-and-coffee" [120:29]

Heinemann "lip-music"; Norton 1987 "lipmusic"; Norton 1995 "lip-music" [121:40]

A Glossary of Nadsat Terms

This Glossary of the Russian-origin terms in Alex's version of "nadsat" is supplied not in the expectation that the reader will require "translations" of Alex's vocabulary, but to illustrate the process by which Burgess arrived at the distinctive style of his novel. The list is based on the *Collins Gem Russian-English, English-Russian Dictionary*; Burgess's copy is held in the Anthony Burgess Collection at the University of Angers, France.[1]

Nadsat term	"Soviet Orthography," together with the bracketed guide to pronunciation and Shapiro's English definition of the Russian word whose *sound* and *sense* Burgess was playing with in his creation of this faux English teen argot
baboochka	бабушка [baā-bŏŏsh-ka] *n.* grandma; granny
baddiwad	бедовый [bye-do-vay] *adj.* mischievous; naughty
banda	банда [bān-da] *n.* gang
bezoomny	безумный [byez-ōōm-năy] *adj.* crazy; frantic; mad
bitva	битва [b'ēt- va] *n.* battle; fight
bog	Бог [bog] *n.* God; Lord; Almighty
bolnoy	больной [bal'-nóy] *adj.* ill; sick
bolshy	большой [bal'-shóy] *adj.* bulky; great; large
bratchny	брачный [brāch-năy] *adj.* conjugal; nuptial
bratty	брат [brāt] *n.* brother
britva	бритва [brit-va] *n.* razor
brooko	брюхо [bryōō-chŏ] *n.* abdomen; paunch
brosay	бросать [bra-sāt] *vt.* to fling; to throw
bugatty	богачи [ba-ga-ch] *n. pl.* the rich, cf. Bugatti, marque of an exclusive sports car company founded by Ettore Bugatti (1881–1947)

---

1. Roger Lewis, in *Anthony Burgess* (London: Faber, 2002), 85, notes: "The flyleaf of Burgess's copy of Waldemar Shapiro's *Collins Russian Gem Dictionary* (1958) is inscribed 'Ivan Vilson' in perfect Cyrillic."

cal	кал [kal] *n.* excrement
cantora	контора [kon-tó-ra] *n.* bureau; countinghouse; office
carman	карман [kar-mān] *n.* pocket
chai	чай [chāy] *n.* tea
chasha	чаша [chā-sha] *n.* beaker; bowl
chasso	часовой [cha-sa-vóy] *n.* sentinel; sentry
cheena	жéнщина [zhen-shchi-na] *n.* woman
cheest	чистить [chis-t'it] *vt.* to clean; to cleanse
chelloveck	человек [che-la-vyék] *n.* creature; human being; individual; person
chepooka	чепуха [che-pŏŏ-chā] *n.* nonsense
choodessny	чудесный [choo-dyes-nay] *adj.* wonderful; miraculous; beautiful; lovely
cluve	клюв [klyoov] *n.* beak; bill
collocoll	кólокол [kó-la-kŏl] *n.* bell
crast	красть [krāst] *vt.* to steal
creech	кричать [kri-chāt] *vi.* to call out; to shout
dama	дама [dā-ma] *n.* lady
ded	дед [dyed] *n.* grandfather
deng	деньги [dyén'-gi] *n.* money; currency
devotchka	девочка [dyé-vach-ka] *n.* little girl
dobby	добро [da-bró] *n.* well-being; goods; property
domy	дом [dom] *n.* house; home
dorogoy	дорогой [da-ra-goy] *adj.* dear, expensive; darling, dear
drat	драть [drāt'] *vt.* to tear; to flog; to thrash
droog	друг [drōog] *n.* friend
dva	два [dvā] *num.* two
eegra	игра [i-grā] *n.* game; sport
eemya	имя [ē-mya] *n.* name; noun
gazetta	газета [ga-zyé-ta] *n.* journal; newspaper
glazz	глаз [glāz] *n.* eye
gloopy	глупец [glŏŏ-pyéts] *n.* fool; simpleton
goloss	голос [gó-lŏs] *n.* voice; tone; vote
goober	губа [gŏŏ-bā] *n.* lip
gooly	гулять [gŏŏ-lyāt] *vi.* to walk
gorlo	горло [gór-lŏ] *n.* throat
govoreet	говорить [ga-va-r'et] *vt.* to say; to speak; to tell
grazzy, grahzny	грязнить [gryaz-n'ēt] *vt.* to dirty; to soil
gromky	громкий [gróm-ki] *adj.* loud; boisterous
groody	грудь [grōod] *n.* breast; chest; bosom
gruppa	группа [grōo-pa] *n.* group
gulliver	голова [ga-la-vā] *n.* head
horrorshow	хорошо [cha-ra-shó] *adj.* all right; very well

itty	идти [i-t'ē] *vi.* to go
jeezny	жизнь [zhizn'] *n.* life, lifetime; existence; living
keeshkas	кишка [kish-kā] *n.* gut, intestine; garden hose
kleb	хлеб [chlyéb] *n.* bread; loaf; corn
klootch	ключ [klyooch] *n.* key
knopka	кнопка [knóp-ka] *n.* button; knob; press stud
kopat	копать [ka-pāt] *vt.* to dig; to excavate
koshka	кошка [kósh-ka] *n.* cat
kot	кот [kot] *n.* tomcat
krovvy	кровь [krov] *n.* blood
kupet	купить [kŏŏ-p'ēt] *vt.* to buy
lapa	лапа [lá-pa] *n.* paw; pad
lewdies	люди [lyōō-d'i] *n.* people
litso	лицо [l'i-tsó] *n.* face; person
lomtick	лóмтик [given in English-Russian section of *Collins Gem*] *n.* slice
loveted	ловить [la-v'ēt] *vt.* to catch; to hunt
malchick	мальчик [māl-chik] *n.* boy; youngster
malenky	маленький [mā-lyen-ki] *adj.* little; small; diminutive
maslo	масло [mās-lŏ] *n.* butter
merzky	мерзкий [English-Russian] *adj.* filthy
messel	мысль [māsl'] *n.* conception; reflection; thought
mesto	место [myés-tŏ] *n.* place
millicent	милиция [not in Collins] *n.* from the Workers' and Peasants' Militsiya (1917); i.e. an officer of the regional police force
minoota	минута [m'i-nōō-ta] *n.* minute; instant; moment
molodoy	молодой [ma-la-dóy] *adj.* young
moloko	молоко [ma-la-kó] *n.* milk
moodge	мужик [mŏŏ-zhik] *n.* peasant
morder	морда [mór-da] *n.* muzzle; snout; ugly face
mozg	мозг [mozg] *n.* brain
nachinat	начинать [na-chi-nāt] *vt.* to begin; to initiate
nadmenny	надменный [nad-myén-năy] *adj.* haughty; supercilious
nadsat	ending of the numerals eleven to nineteen in Russian, e.g. одиннадсать, eleven
nagoy	нагой [na-góy] *adj.* bare, nude
nazz	according to Burgess's manuscript addition to the TS, the word here is наз [naz], name, and not fool, derived from *adv.* назад, [na-zād]

neezhnies   *n.*, from ни́жний белье [English-Russian], underwear: ни́жний [n'ēzh-ni] literally means inferior, lower

nochy   ночь [noch'] *n.* night

noga   нога [na-gā] *n.* foot; leg

nozh   нож [nozh] *n.* knife

oddy-knocky   одинокий [a-d'i-nó-ki] *adj.* lonely; solitary; single

odin   один [a-d'ēn] *num., pron.* a; an; one

okno   окно [ak-nó] *n.* window

oobivat   убивать [ŏŏ-b'i-vāt] *vt.* to kill; to murder

ookadeet   уходить [ŏŏ-cha-d'ēt] *vi.* to go away; to leave

ooko   ухо [ŏŏ-chŏ] *n.* ear

oomny   умный [ōōm-năy] *adj.* intelligent; sensible; wise

oozhassny   ужасный [ŏŏ-zhās-năy] *adj.* dreadful; ghastly; horrid

oozy   узы [English-Russian] *n.* chain

osoosh   очищать [a-chi-shchāt] *vt.* to clean; to cleanse; to purify; to refine; to clear

otchkies / ochkies   очки [ach-kē] *n.* eyeglasses; spectacles

peet   пить [p'ēt] *vt.* to drink

pishcha   пища [p'ē-shcha] *n.* food

platch   плакать [plā-kat] *vi.* to cry; to weep

platties   платье [plā-tye] *n.* dress; clothes

plenny   пленник [plyén-n'ik] *n.* captive; prisoner

plesk   плескать [plyes-kāt] *vi.* to splash

pletcho   плечо [plye-chó] *n.* shoulder

plott   плоть [plot'] *n.* flesh

podooshka   подушка [pa-dōōsh-ka] *n.* cushion; pillow

pol   пол [pol] *n.* floor; ground; sex

polezny   полезный [pa-lyéz-năy] *adj.* beneficial; useful; utilitarian

pony   понимать [pa-n'i-māt] *vt.* to understand

poogly   пугать [pŏŏ-gāt] *vt.* to frighten; to scare

pooshka   пушка [pōōsh-ka] *n.* cannon; gun

prestoopnick   преступник [prye-stōōp-n'ik] *n.* criminal; delinquent; offender

privodeet   приводить [pr'i-va-d'ēt] *vt.* to bring; to lead up; to bring forward; to set

ptitsa   птица [pt'ē-tsa] *n.* bird [i.e., English slang for a young woman]

pyahnitsa   пьяница [pyā-n'i-tsa] *n.* drunkard

rabbit   работа [ra-bó-ta] *n.* labor; task; work; job

radosty   радость [rā-dŏst] *n.* delight; gladness; joy

raskazz	рассказ [ras-skāz] *n.* story; tale
rasoodock	рассудок [ras-sōo-dǒk] *n.* mind; reason; sense; understanding
raz	раз [rāz] *n.* time; *adv.* once; one day
razdraz	раздражать [raz-dra-zhāt] *vt.* to annoy; to irritate; to exasperate
razrez	разрез [raz-ryéz] *n.* cut; rip; gash; slash; slit
rooker	рука [rōo-kā] *n.* hand; arm; forearm
rot	рот [rot] *n.* mouth
sakar	сахар [sā-*ch*ar] *n.* sugar
scoteena	скотина [ska-t'ē-na] *n.* beast, brute
shaika	шайка[shāy-ka] *n.* band, gang
sharries	шарик [English-Russian] *n.* marbles
shest	шест [shest] *n.* perch; pole
shiyah	шейка [shéy-ka] *n.* neck of stringed instruments; slender neck
shlapa	шляпа [shlyā-pa] *n.* hat
shlem	шлем [English-Russian] *n.* helmet
shoom	шум [shōōm] *n.* clamor; noise; riot
shoot	шутка [shōōt-ka] *n.* banter; joke
skazat	сказать [ska-zāt] *vt.* to tell; to say
skorry	скоро [skó-rǒ] *adv.* quickly; rapidly
sladky	сладкий [slād-ki] *adj.* sugary; sweet
sloochat	случаться [slōo-chāt-sya] *vi.* to happen
slooshy	слушать [slōo-shat] *vt.* to listen
slovo	слово [sló-vǒ] *n.* word; speech
smeck	смех [smyech] *n.* laughter
smot	смотр [smotr] *n.* inspection
sneety	сниться [sn'ēt'-sya] *vi.* to dream
sobirat	собирать [sa-b'i-rāt] *vt.* to collect; to gather; to assemble
soomka	сумка [sōōm-ka] *n.* handbag; bag is disparaging slang for a female, especially elderly or unattractive
soviet	совет [sa-vyét] *n.* council; advice, counsel
spat	спать [spāt] *vi.* to sleep
spoogy	спугивать [spōō-gi-vat'] *vt.* to frighten away
starry	старый [stā-rǎy] *adj.* old
strack	страх [strāch] *n.* fear; scare; terror
tally	талия [tā-lya] *n.* waist
tolchock	толчок [tal-chók] *n.* jerk; jolt; impulse
toofles	туфля [tōōf-lya] *n.* slipper
tree	три [trē] *num.* three
vareet	варить [va-r'ēt] *vt.* to boil; to cook; to poach; to brew

veck	*see* chelloveck
veshch	вещь [vyeshch] *n.* object, thing
viddy	видеть [v'ē-dyet] *vt.* to perceive; to see
voloss	волос [vó-lŏs] *n.* hair
von	вонь [von'] *n.* stench
vred	вред [vryéd] *n.* harm; hurt; damage; injury
yahma	яма [ya-ma] *n.* pit
yahzick	язык [ya-zak] *n.* tongue
yeckate	ехать [yé-chat] *vi.* to drive; to ride
zammechat	замечательный [za-mye-chā-tyel'-năy] *adj.* remarkable; striking
zasnoot	заснуть [English-Russian] *vi.* to sleep
zheena	жена [zhe-nā] *n.* wife
zoobies	зуб [zōōb] *n.* tooth
zvonok	звонок [zva-nók] *n.* bell
zvook	звук [zvōōk] *n.* sound; tone

BACKGROUNDS AND CONTEXTS

Anthony Burgess on
A Clockwork Orange

[Writing A Clockwork Orange][†]

* * * In despair I typed a new title—*A Clockwork Orange*—and wondered what story might match it. I had always liked the Cockney expression and felt there might be a meaning in it deeper than a bizarre metaphor of, not necessarily sexual, queerness. Then a story began to stir.

Lynne and I had come home to a new British phenomenon—the violence of teenage gangs. We had, on our leaves of 1957 and 1958, seen teddy boys in coffee bars. These were youths dressed very smartly in neo-Edwardian suits with heavy-soled boots and distinctive coiffures. They seemed too elegant to be greatly given to violence, but they were widely feared by the faint-hearted. They were a personification of the *Zeitgeist* in that they seemed to express a brutal disappointment with Britain's post-war decline as a world power and evoked the age of Edwardian expansion in their clothes if nothing else. They had originally been called Edwardian Strutters. They had been briefly influential even in Malaya, where national servicemen had worn the attire off duty, and we had seen young Malays and Chinese sweating in heavy serge. Now, in 1960, they were being superseded by hooligans more casually dressed. The Mods and Rockers were so called because the first group wore modern clothes, whatever they were, and the others had motorcycles with rockers or parking prongs. The second edition of the *Oxford English Dictionary* is right in pointing to the leather jackets of the Rockers as a sartorial mark, but it is wrong in supposing that they got their name from a love of rock 'n' roll. Lynne and I saw Mods and Rockers knocking hell out of each other when we made a trip to Hastings.

These young people seemed to love aggression for its own sake. They were expressing the Manichean principle of the universe,

† From *You've Had Your Time: Being the Second Part of the Confessions of Anthony Burgess* (New York: Weidenfeld, 1991), 26–27; 37–38; 59. Reprinted by permission of the Estate of Anthony Burgess, in care of the International Anthony Burgess Foundation.

opposition as an end in itself, *yin* versus *yang*, X against Y. I foresaw that the Queen's Peace was going to be greatly disrupted by the aimless energy of these new young, well-fed with money in their pockets. They were not, of course, all that new. The apprentices of Queen Elizabeth I's time used to riot, but they were dealt with in a very summary way—sometimes hanged on the spot. I at first thought of making my new novel a historical one, dealing with a particular apprentices' riot in the 1590s, when young thugs beat up the women who sold eggs and butter at prices considered too high, with perhaps William Shakespeare breaking his hip when slithering on a pavement greasy with blood and eggyolk. But I finally decided to be prophetic, positing a near future—1970, say—in which youthful aggression reached so frightful a pitch that the government would try to burn it out with Pavlovian techniques of negative reinforcement. I saw that the novel would have to have a metaphysical or theological base—youthful free will having the choice of good and evil although generally choosing evil; the artificial extirpation of free will through scientific conditioning; the question as to whether this might not, in theological terms, be a greater evil than the free choice of evil.

My problem in writing the novel was not one that would have worried Nevil Shute: it was wholly stylistic. The story had to be told by a young thug of the future, and it had to be told in his own version of English. This would be partly the slang of his group, partly his personal idiolect. It was pointless to write the book in the slang of the early sixties: it was ephemeral like all slang and might have a lavender smell by the time the manuscript got to the printers. It seemed, at the time, an insoluble problem. A slang for the 1970s would have to be invented, but I shrank from making it arbitrary. I shut the half-completed draft, whose sixties slang clearly would not do, in a drawer and got down to the writing of something else.

Lynne and I now felt that we ought to take a holiday. There were Russian ships sailing from Tilbury to Leningrad, calling at Copenhagen and Stockholm, and then sailing back, calling at Stockholm and Copenhagen with Helsinki added. There was a brief stay in a Leningrad hotel between voyages. The Russians were known to be good drinkers, and Lynne knew she would feel at home among them. When I had finished my day's stint of novelising, reviewing, and assessing the exotic, I started to relearn Russian. I tried to persuade Lynne that she should at least learn the Cyrillic alphabet, so as to know where the ladies' toilets were, and to master a few sweeteners of social intercourse, such as *dobriy dyen* and *spasibo*. But she was above going back to school, unless she could take a time-trip to being once more head girl and outstanding athlete at Bedwellty. She watched *Emergency Ward Ten* on television instead. Her lack of linguistic curiosity worried me, as also the assumption that it was a husband's duty to be a dragoman, as well as an earner, lover and protector. I wrote out TUALET large in Cyrillic but she gave it to Haji to chew up growling. I sighed and slogged away at my word lists and frequentative verbs, and soon it flashed upon me that I had found a solution to the stylistic problem of *A Clockwork Orange*. The vocabulary of my space-age hooligans could be a mixture of Russian and demotic English, seasoned with rhyming slang and the gipsy's bolo. The Russian suffix for -teen was *nadsat*, and that would be the name of the teenage dialect, spoken by *drugi* or droogs or friends in violence.

Russian loanwords fit better into English than those from German, French, or Italian. English, anyway, is already a kind of mélange of French and German. Russian has polysyllables like *zhevotnoye* for beast, and *ostanovka avtobusa* is not so good as bus stop. But it also has brevities like *brat* for brother and *grud* for breast. The English word, in which four consonants strangle one short vowel, is inept for that glorious smooth roundness. *Groodies* would be right. In the manner of Eastern languages, Russian makes no distinction between leg and foot—*noga* for both—or hand and arm, which are alike *ruka*. This limitation would turn my horrible young narrator into a clockwork toy with inarticulated limbs. As there was much violence in the draft smouldering in my drawer, and would be even more in the finished work, the strange new lingo would act as a kind of mist half-hiding the mayhem and protecting the reader from his own baser instincts. And there was a fine irony in the notion of a teenage race untouched by politics, using totalitarian brutality as an end in itself, equipped with a dialect which drew on the two chief political languages of the age.

I ended up with a Russian loanword vocabulary of around two hundred words. As the book was about brainwashing, it was appropriate that the text itself should be a brainwashing device. The reader would be brainwashed into learning minimal Russian. The novel was to be an exercise in linguistic programming, with the exoticisms gradually clarified by context: I would resist to the limit any publisher's demand that a glossary be provided. A glossary would disrupt the programme and nullify the brainwashing. It turned out to be a considerable pleasure to devise new rhythms and resurrect old ones, chiefly from the King James Bible, to accommodate the weird patois. The novel was nearly finished by the time we were ready to travel to Tilbury and board the *Alexander Radishchev*, a well-found ship of the Baltic Line.

In May 1962 *A Clockwork Orange* appeared. One anonymous summation in a trade paper was not untypical: 'An off-beat and violent tale about teenage gangs in Britain, written in out-of-this-world

gibberish.' The *Times Literary Supplement* was more specific: 'A viscous verbiage . . . which is the swag-bellied offspring of decay . . .
English is being slowly killed by her practitioners.' I was considered
an accomplished writer who had set out deliberately to murder the
language. It was comforting to remember that the same thing had
been said about Joyce. My taste was questionable. 'The author seems
content to use a serious social challenge for frivolous purposes, but
himself to stay neutral.' Robert Taubman, in the *New Statesman*,
said: 'The book, written in a combination of Jacobean English and
nadsat, is a great strain to read,' adding: 'There's not much fantasy
here.' No British reviewer liked it, but the producers of the BBC
television programme *Tonight* were interested enough to invite me
to be interviewed by Derek Hart. They did more. They dramatised
much of the first chapter of the book very effectively and made more
of the language than the theme. I showed myself to be an adequate
television performer. The BBC even paid a small fee, more than
French or American television does, the view of both being that one
should be delighted to publicise one's work for nothing.

In 1962 there was only one BBC television channel. Though
most viewers preferred the offerings of the independent network, it
was said that a good nine million people watched *Tonight*. I took
the train from Charing Cross back to Etchingham in cautious ela-
tion. Surely at least one per cent of those who had had this superfi-
cial exposure to *A Clockwork Orange* would buy the book. I would
become moderately rich; I had had the accolade of a television
appearance and would now be a sort of public personality. But the
book sold badly, rather worse if anything than previous novels of
mine. I learned the great lesson of the dangers of over-exposure.
Viewers had been told enough about the book to be able to discuss
it at cocktail parties: the reading of it would be wearisome, as the
press had already announced, as well as supererogatory. The British
were, I considered, stuffy and desperately conservative. They did not
want experimental fiction and they hated ideas. I began more and
more to look to America.

A Clockwork Orange was published in New York by W. W. Norton
Inc. later in the year. Eric Swenson, Norton's vice-president, insisted
that the book lose its final chapter. I had to accede to this lopping
because I needed the advance, but I was not happy about it. I had
structured the work with some care. It was divided into three sections of seven chapters each, the total figure being, in traditional
arithmology, the symbol of human maturity. My young narrator, the
music-loving thug Alex, ends the story by growing up and renounc-
ing violence as a childish toy. This was the subject of the final chapter, and it was the capacity of this character to accept change which,
in my view, made the work into a genuine if brief novel. But Swen-

son wanted only the reversible artificial change imposed by state conditioning. He wished Alex to be a figure in a fable, not a novel. Alex ends Chapter 20 saying: 'I was cured all right,' and he resumes joy in evil. The American and European editions of the novel are thus essentially different. The tough tradition of American popular fiction ousted what was termed British blandness.

Though they were reading a somewhat different book, American reviewers understood what I was trying to do rather better than their British counterparts. *Time* said: 'It may look like a nasty little shocker, but Burgess has written that rare thing in English letters—a philosophical novel. The point may be overlooked because the hero tells all in nadsat which serves to put him where he belongs—half in and half out of the human race. The pilgrim's progress of a beatnik Stavogrin is a serious and successful moral essay. Burgess argues quite simply that Alex is more of a man as an evil man than as a good zombie. The clockwork of a mechanical society can never counterfeit the organic vitality of moral choice. Goodness is nothing if evil is not accepted as a possibility.' Robert Gorham Davis in the *Hudson Review* said that the novel clearly turned Alex into an inarticulate apostle of existential or even Christian freedom and 'by a perverse logic, images of violence are put at the service of a dreadful, dead-end concept of freedom.' David Talbot in the *New York Herald Tribune* wrote: 'Love cannot exist without the possibility of hate, and by forcing men to abdicate their right to choose one over the other, society turns men into automata. Thus Burgess points his stunning moral: in a clockwork society, human redemption will have to arise out of evil.'

[Pelagian versus Augustinian][†]

While Beatrice-Joanna was going down, her husband Tristram Foxe was ascending. He was humming up to the thirty-second floor of the South London (Channel) Unitary School (Boys) Division Four. A sixty-strong Fifth Form (Stream 10) awaited him. He was to give a lesson in Modern History. On the rear wall of the lift, half-hidden by the bulk of Jordan, an art-master, was a map of Great Britain, a new one, a new school issue. Interesting. Greater London, bounded by sea to south and east, had eaten further into Northern Province and Western Province: the new northern limit was a line running from Lowestoft to Birmingham; to the west the boundary dropped from Birmingham to Bournemouth. Intending migrants from the

† From *The Wanting Seed* (New York: Norton, 1962), 8–12. Copyright © 1962 by Anthony Burgess. Used by permission of W. W. Norton & Company, Inc. and the Estate of Anthony Burgess, care of the International Anthony Burgess Foundation.

Provinces to Greater London had, it was said, no need to move; they merely had to wait. The Provinces themselves still showed their ancient county divisions, but, owing to diaspora, immigration and miscegenation, the old national designations of 'Wales' and 'Scotland' no longer had any precise significance.

Beck, who taught mathematics to the junior forms, was saying to Jordan, 'They ought to wipe out one or the other. Compromise, that's always been our trouble, the liberal vice of compromise. Seven septs to a guinea, ten tanners to a crown, eight tosheroons to a quid. The poor young devils don't know where they are. We can't bear to throw anything away, that's our big national sin—' Tristram got off, leaving old bald Beck to continue his invective. He marched to the Fifth Form classroom, entered, blinked at his boys. May light shone from the seaward window on their blank faces, on the blank walls. He started his lesson.

'—The gradual subsumption of the two main opposing political ideologies under essentially theologico-mythical concepts.' Tristram was not a good teacher. He went too fast for his pupils, used words they found hard to spell, tended to mumble. Obediently the class tried to take down his words in their notebooks. 'Pelagianism,' he said, 'was once known as a heresy. It was even called the British Heresy. Can anybody tell me Pelagius's other name?'

'Morgan,' said a boy called Morgan, a spotty boy.

'Correct. Both names mean "man of the sea".' The boy behind Morgan whistled a kind of hornpipe through his teeth, digging Morgan in the back. 'Stop that,' said Morgan.

'Yes,' continued Tristram. 'Pelagius was of the race that at one time inhabited Western Province. He was what, in the old religious days, used to be called a monk. A monk.' Tristram rose vigorously from his desk and yellowed this word, as if he were fearful that his pupils would not be able to spell it, on the blueboard. Then he sat down again. 'He denied the doctrine of Original Sin and said that man was capable of working out his own salvation.' The boys looked very blank. 'Never mind about that for the moment,' said Tristram kindly. 'What you have to remember is that all this suggests human perfectibility. Pelagianism was thus seen to be at the heart of liberalism and its derived doctrines, especially Socialism and Communism. Am I going too fast?'

'Yes, sir.' Barks and squeals from sixty breaking voices.

'Right.' Tristram had a mild face, blank as the boys', and his eyes gleamed feverishly from behind their contact-lenses. His hair had a negroid kink; his cuticles half-hid blue half-moons. He was thirty-five and had been a schoolmaster for nearly fourteen years. He earned just over two hundred guineas a month but was hoping, since Newick's death, to be promoted to the headship of the Social Studies Department. That would mean a substantial increase in salary, which would mean a bigger flat, a better start in the world for young Roger. Roger, he then remembered, was dead. 'Right,' he repeated, like a sergeant-instructor of the days before Perpetual Peace had set in. 'Augustine, on the other hand, had insisted on man's inherent sinfulness and the need for his redemption through divine grace. This was seen to be at the bottom of Conservatism and other *laissez-faire* and non-progressive political beliefs.' He beamed at his class. 'The opposed thesis, you see,' he said, encouragingly. 'The whole thing is quite simple, really.'

'I don't get it, sir,' boomed a big bold boy named Abney-Hastings.

'Well, you see,' said Tristram amiably, 'the old Conservatives expected no good out of man. Man was regarded as naturally acquisitive, wanting more and more possessions for himself, an uncooperative and selfish creature, not much concerned about the progress of the community. Sin is really only another word for selfishness, gentlemen. Remember that.' He leaned forward, his hands joined, sliding his forearms into the yellow chalk-powder that covered the desk like wind-blown sand. 'What would you do with a selfish person?' he asked. 'Tell me that.'

'Knock him about a bit,' said a very fair boy called Ibrahim ibn Abdullah.

'No.' Tristram shook his head. 'No Augustinian would do that sort of thing. If you expect the worst from a person, you can't ever be disappointed. Only the disappointed resort to violence. The pessimist, which is another way of saying the Augustinian, takes a sort of gloomy pleasure in observing the depths to which human behaviour can sink. The more sin he sees, the more his belief in Original Sin is confirmed. Everyone likes to have his deepest convictions confirmed: that is one of the most abiding of human satisfactions.' Tristram suddenly seemed to grow bored with this trite exposition. He surveyed his sixty, row by row, as if seeking the diversion of bad behaviour; but all sat still and attentive, good as gold, as if bent on confirming the Pelagian thesis. The microradio on Tristram's wrist buzzed thrice. He lifted it to his ear. A gnat-song like the voice of conscience said, '*Please see the Principal at the end of the present period*'—a tiny plopping of plosives. Good. This would be it, then, this would be it. Soon he would be standing in poor dead Newick's place, the salary perhaps back-dated. He now literally stood, his hands clutching in advocate-style his jacket where, in the days of lapels, the lapels would have been. He resumed with renewed vigour.

'Nowadays,' he said, 'we have no political parties. The old dichotomy, we recognize, subsists in ourselves and requires no naïve projection into sects or factions. We are both God and the Devil, though not at the same time. Only Mr Livedog can be that, and Mr Livedog, of course, is a mere fictional symbol.' All the boys smiled. They

all loved *The Adventures of Mr Livedog* in the *Cosmicomic*. Mr Livedog was a big funny fubsy demiurge who, *sufflaminandus* like Shakespeare, spawned unwanted life all over the earth. Overpopulation
was his doing. In none of his adventures, however, did he ever win:
Mr Homo, his human boss, always brought him to heel. 'The theology subsisting in our opposed doctrines of Pelagianism and Augustinianism has no longer any validity. We use these mythical symbols
because they are peculiarly suited to our age, an age relying more
and more on the perceptual, the pictorial, the pictographic. Pettman!'
Tristram shouted, with sudden joy. 'You're eating something. Eating
in class. That won't do, will it?'

※   ※   ※

[Aesthetics versus Ethics][†]

Sir,—I apologize for coming so belatedly to the defence of William
Burroughs. My excuse is the best possible. I have been spending some
time in Tangier with that courteous, hospitable, erudite, gifted and
dedicated writer and, preoccupied with the man himself and the
work he is at present engaged on, have neglected to read till now
what others have been saying about him. Dame Edith will have to
accept, whether she likes it or not, that Mr. Burroughs is a serious
artist trying to extend the boundaries of the novel-form and that his
devotion to the craft of writing is not inferior to her own. If any
writer is likely to rehabilitate an effete form and show us what can
still be done with a language that Joyce seemed to have wrung dry,
it is William Burroughs.

Unfortunately, too many people who should know better protract
a squeamishness about subject-matter that sickens their capacity to
make purely literary judgments. I do not like what Mr. Burroughs
writes about; for that matter I do not always like what I myself write
about: I was nauseated by the content of my *A Clockwork Orange*.
There is, I can assure Dame Edith, no lip-smacking on the part of
Mr. Burroughs when he works at the refining of his raw material
into art. Life is, unfortunately, life. Out of life we must choose, for
our writing, what will best stimulate us to write well. Mr. Burroughs
recognizes that Jane Austen (whom he greatly admires) is not to be
disparaged for the limitations of her subject-matter. The world of
the country parsonage is not necessarily more wholesome than that
of pederastic Morocco—not, anyway, to the artist or the literary

---

† Burgess, letter to the *Times Literary Supplement*, January 2, 1964, 9. Reprinted by
permission of the Estate of Anthony Burgess, in care of the International Anthony
Burgess Foundation. Burgess's defense of Beat Generation experimental writer William Burroughs (1914–1997), and in particular his cut-up novel *Naked Lunch* that was
reviewed in the *TLS* in November 1963, provides a context for the handling of the
relationship of art and morality in *A Clockwork Orange*.

critic who is content with aesthetic judgments and not moral ones. "Everything that lives is holy." This may not be morally true, but it is true of the subject-matter of literature. For heaven's sake, let us leave morals to the moralists and carry on with the job of learning to evaluate art as art.

Anthony Burgess
Applegarth, Etchingham, East Sussex

"Review" of Stanley Kubrick's Film[†]

I went to see Stanley Kubrick's *A Clockwork Orange* in New York, fighting to get in like everybody else. It was worth the fight, I thought—very much a Kubrick movie, technically brilliant, thoughtful, relevant, poetic, mind-opening. It was possible for me to see the work as a radical remaking of my own novel, not as a mere interpretation, and this—the feeling that it was no impertinence to blazon it as *Stanley Kubrick's Clockwork Orange*—is the best tribute I can pay to the Kubrickian mastery. The fact remains, however, that the film sprang out of a book, and some of the controversy which has begun to attach to the film is controversy in which I, inevitably, feel myself involved. In terms of philosophy and even theology, the Kubrick *Orange* is a fruit from my tree.

I wrote *A Clockwork Orange* in 1961, which is a very remote year, and I experience some difficulty in empathising with that long-gone writer who, concerned with making a living, wrote as many as five novels in 14 months. The title is the least difficult thing to explain. In 1945, back from the army, I heard an 80-year-old Cockney in a London pub say that somebody was 'as queer as a clockwork orange'. The 'queer' did not mean homosexual: it meant mad. The phrase intrigued me with its unlikely fusion of demotic and surrealistic. For nearly twenty years I wanted to use it as the title of something. During those twenty years I heard it several times more—in Underground stations, in pubs, in television plays—but always from aged Cockneys, never from the young. It was a traditional trope, and it asked to entitle a work which combined a concern with tradition and a bizarre technique. The opportunity to use it came when I conceived the notion of writing a novel about brainwashing. Joyce's Stephen Dedalus (in *Ulysses*) refers to the world as an 'oblate orange'; man is a microcosm or little world; he is a growth as organic as a fruit; capable of colour, fragrance and sweetness; to meddle with him, condition him, is to turn him into a mechanical creation.

[†] Burgess, "Clockwork Marmalade," *The Listener* 87.2238 (February 17, 1972), 197–99. Reprinted by permission of the Estate of Anthony Burgess, in care of the International Anthony Burgess Foundation.

There had been some talk in the British press about the problems of growing criminality. The youth of the late Fifties were restless and naughty, dissatisfied with the post-war world, violent and destructive, and they—being more conspicuous than mere old-time crooks and hoods—were what many people meant when they talked about growing criminality. Looking back from a peak of violence, we can see that the British teddy-boys and mods and rockers were mere tyros in the craft of anti-social aggression: nevertheless, they were a portent, and the man in the street was right to be scared. How to deal with them? Prison or reform school made them worse: why not save the taxpayer's money by subjecting them to an easy course in conditioning, some kind of aversion therapy which should make them associate the act of violence with discomfort, nausea, or even intimations of mortality? Many heads nodded at this proposal (not, at the time, a governmental proposal, but one put out by private though influential theoreticians). Heads still nod at it. On *The Frost Show* it was suggested to me that it might have been a good thing if Adolf Hitler had been forced to undergo aversion therapy, so that the very thought of a new *putsch* or pogrom would make him sick up his cream cakes.

Hitler was, unfortunately, a human being, and if we could have countenanced the conditioning of one human being we would have to accept it for all. Hitler was a great nuisance but history has known others disruptive enough to make the state's fingers itch—Christ, Luther, Bruno, even D. H. Lawrence. One has to be genuinely philosophical about this, however much one has suffered. I don't know how much free will man really possesses (Wagner's Hans Sachs[1] said: *Wir sind ein wenig frei*—'we are a little free'), but I do know that what little he seems to have is too precious to encroach on, however good the intentions of the encroacher may be.

A Clockwork Orange was intended to be a sort of tract, even a sermon, on the importance of the power of choice. My hero or anti-hero, Alex, is very vicious, perhaps even impossibly so, but his viciousness is not the product of genetic or social conditioning: it is his own thing, embarked on in full awareness. Alex is evil, not merely misguided, and in a properly run society such evil as he enacts must be checked and punished. But his evil is a human evil, and we recognise in his deeds of aggression potentialities of our own—worked out for the non-criminal citizen in war, sectional injustice, domestic unkindness, armchair dreams. In three ways Alex is an exemplar of human-

---

1. Hans Sachs is a character in Richard Wagner's *Die Meistersinger von Nürnberg* (1868). Sachs is a spokesman in the opera for Wagner's interpretation of the philosophy of Arthur Schopenhauer (1788–1860), in particular the idea that music, and aesthetic contemplation in general, is a source of solace in a world characterized by the suffering caused by desire.

ity: he is aggressive, he loves beauty, he is a language-user. Ironically, his name can be taken to mean 'wordless' though he has plenty of words of his own—invented, group-dialect. He has, though, no word to say in the running of his community or the managing of the state: he is, to the state, a mere object, something 'out there' like the Moon, though not so passive.

Theologically, evil is not quantifiable. Yet I posit the notion that one act of evil may be greater than another, and that perhaps the ultimate act of evil is dehumanisation, the killing of the soul—which is as much as to say the capacity to choose between good and evil acts. Impose on an individual the capacity to be good and only good, and you kill his soul for, presumably, the sake of social stability. What my, and Kubrick's, parable tries to state is that it is preferable to have a world of violence undertaken in full awareness—violence chosen as an act of will—than a world conditioned to be good or harmless. I recognise that the lesson is already becoming an old-fashioned one. B. F. Skinner, with his ability to believe that there is something *beyond* freedom and dignity, wants to see the death of autonomous man. He may or may not be right, but in terms of the Judaeo-Christian ethic that *A Clockwork Orange* tries to express, he is perpetrating a gross heresy. It seems to me in accordance with the tradition that Western man is not yet ready to jettison, that the area in which human choice is a possibility should be extended, even if one comes up against new angels with swords and banners emblazoned *No*. The wish to diminish free will is, I should think, the sin against the Holy Ghost.

In both film and book, the evil that the state performs in brainwashing Alex is seen spectacularly in its own lack of self-awareness as regards non-ethical values. Alex is fond of Beethoven, and he has used the Ninth Symphony as a stimulus to dreams of violence. This has been his choice, but there has been nothing to prevent his choosing to use that music as a mere solace or image of divine order. That, by the time his conditioning starts, he has not yet made the better choice does not mean that he will never do it. But, with an aversion therapy which associates Beethoven and violence, that choice is taken away from him for ever. It is an unlooked-for punishment and it is tantamount to robbing a man—stupidly, casually—of his right to enjoy the divine vision. For there is a good beyond mere ethical good, which is always existential: there is the *essential* good, that aspect of God which we can prefigure more in the taste of an apple or the sound of music than in mere right action or even charity.

What hurts me, as also Kubrick, is the allegation made by some viewers and readers of *A Clockwork Orange* that there is a gratuitous indulgence in violence which turns an intended homiletic work into a pornographic one. It was certainly no pleasure to me to describe

acts of violence when writing the novel: I indulged in excess, in caricature, even in an invented dialect with the purpose of making the
violence more symbolic than realistic, and Kubrick found remarkable
cinematic equivalents for my own literary devices. It would have been
pleasanter, and would have made more friends, if there had been no
violence at all, but the story of Alex's reclamation would have lost
force if we weren't permitted to see what he was being reclaimed
from. For my own part, the depiction of violence was intended as
both an act of catharsis and an act of charity, since my own wife was
the subject of vicious and mindless violence in blacked-out London
in 1942, when she was robbed and beaten by three GI deserters.
Readers of my book may remember that the author whose wife is
raped is the author of a work called A Clockwork Orange.

Viewers of the film have been disturbed by the fact that Alex,
despite his viciousness, is quite likeable. It has required a deliberate self-administered act of aversion therapy on the part of some to
dislike him, and to let righteous indignation get in the way of
human charity. The point is that, if we are going to love mankind,
we will have to love Alex as a not unrepresentative member of it.
The place where Alex and his mirror-image F. Alexander are most
guilty of hate and violence is called HOME and it is here, we are told,
that charity ought to begin. But towards that mechanism, the state,
which, first, is concerned with self-perpetuation and, second, is
happiest when human beings are predictable and controllable, we
have no duty at all, certainly no duty of charity.

I have a final point to make, and this will not interest many who
like to think of Kubrick's Orange rather than Burgess's. The language
of both movie and book (called Nadsat—the Russian 'teen' suffix as
in pyatnadsat, meaning fifteen) is no mere decoration, nor is it a sinister indication of the subliminal power that a Communist super-
state may already be exerting on the young. It was meant to turn
A Clockwork Orange into, among other things, a brainwashing primer.
You read the book or see the film, and at the end you should find
yourself in possession of a minimal Russian vocabulary—without
effort, with surprise. This is the way brainwashing works. I chose
Russian words because they blend better into English than those
of French or even German (which is already a kind of English, not
exotic enough). But the lesson of the Orange has nothing to do with
the ideology or repressive techniques of Soviet Russia: it is wholly
concerned with what can happen to any of us in the West, if we do
not keep on our guard. If Orange, like 1984, takes its place as one of
the salutary literary warnings—or cinematic warnings—against
flabbiness, sloppy thinking, and overmuch trust in the state, then it
will have done something of value. For my part, I do not like the book
as much as others I have written: I have kept it, till recently, in an

unopened jar—marmalade, a preserve on a shelf, rather than an orange on a dish. What I would really like to see is a film of one of my other novels, all of which are singularly unaggressive, but I fear that this is too much to hope for. It looks as though I must go through life as the fountain and origin of a great film, and as a man who has to insist, against all opposition, that he is the most unviolent creature alive. Just like Stanley Kubrick.

[The American *A Clockwork Orange*]†

When it was first proposed about eight years ago, that a film be made of *A Clockwork Orange*, it was the Rolling Stones who were intended to appear in it, with Mick Jagger playing the role that Malcolm McDowell eventually filled. Indeed, it was somebody with the physical appearance and mercurial temperament of Jagger that I had in mind when writing the book, although pop groups as we know them had not yet come on the scene. The book was written in 1961, when England was full of skiffle. If I'd thought of giving Alex, the hero, a surname at all (Kubrick gives him two, one of them mine), Jagger would have been as good a name as any: it means "hunter," a person who goes on jags, a person who doesn't keep in line, a person who inflicts jagged rips on the face of society. I did use the name eventually, but it was in a very different novel—*Tremor of Intent*—and meant solely a hunter, and a rather holy one.

I've no doubt that a lot of people will want to read the story because they've seen the movie—far more than the other way around—and I can say at once that the story and the movie are very like each other. Indeed, I can think of only one other film which keeps as painfully close to the book it's based on—Polanski's *Rosemary's Baby*.[1] The plot of the film is that of the book, and so is the language, although naturally there's both more language and more plot in the book than in the film. The language used by Alex, my delinquent hero, is called *Nadsat*—the Russian suffix used in making words like fourteen, fifteen, sixteen—and a lot of the terms he employs are derived from Russian. As these words are filtered through an English-speaking mind, they take on meanings and associations unknown to Russians. Thus, Alex uses the word *horrorshow* to designate anything good—the Russian root for good is horosh—and "fine, splendid, all right then" is the neuter form we ought really to spell as *chorosho* (the *ch* is guttural, as in *Bach*). But good to Alex is tied up with per-

---

† Burgess, "Juice from *A Clockwork Orange*," *Rolling Stone* 110, June 8, 1972, 52–53. Reprinted by permission.
1. Roman Polanski (1933–) wrote the screenplay for his horror movie *Rosemary's Baby* (1968), based on the novel of the same title by Ira Levin (1929–2007).

forming horrors, and when he is made what the State calls good it is through the witnessing of violent films—genuine horror shows. The Russian *golova*—meaning head—is domesticated into *gulliver*, which reminds the reader he is taking in a piece of social satire, like *Gulliver's Travels*. The fact that Russian doesn't distinguish between foot and leg (*noga* for both) and arm and hand (*ruka*) serves—by suggesting a mechanical doll—to emphasise the clockwork-view of life that Alex has: first he is self-geared to be bad, next he is state-geared to be good.

The title of the book comes from an old London expression, which I first heard from a very old Cockney in 1945: "He's as queer as a clockwork orange" (queer meaning mad, not faggish). I liked the phrase because of its yoking of tradition and surrealism, and I determined some day to use it. It has rather specialised meanings for me. I worked in Malaya, where *orang* means a human being, and this connotation is attached to the word, as well as more obvious anagrams, like *organ* and *organise* (an *orange* is, a man is, but the State wants the living organ to be turned into a mechanical emanation of itself). Alex uses some Cockney expressions, also Lancashire ones (like *snuff it*, meaning to die), as well as Elizabethan locutions but his language is essentially Slav-based. It was essential for me to invent a slang of the future, and it seemed best to come from combining the two major political languages of the world—irony here, since Alex is very far from being a political animal. The American paperback edition of *A Clockwork Orange* has a glossary of Nadsat terms, but this was no idea of mine. As the novel is about brainwashing, so it is also a little device of brainwashing in itself or at least a carefully programmed series of lessons on the Russian language. You learn the words without noticing, and a glossary is unnecessary. More—because it's there, you tend to use it, and this gets in the way of the programming.

As the novel was written over ten years ago (and planned nearly 30 years ago), and the age of violence and scientific conditioning it depicts is already here, some people have been tempted to see it as a work of prophecy. But the work merely describes certain tendencies I observed in Anglo-American society in 1961 (and even earlier). True, there was not much drug-taking then, and my novel presents a milk-bar where you can freely ingest hallucinogens and stimulants, but I had only just come back from living in the Far East, where I smoked opium regularly (and without apparent ill effects), and drug-taking was so much part of my scene that it automatically went into the book. Alex is very unmodern in rejecting "synthemesc": his aim is to strengthen the will to violence, not enervate it. I think he is ahead of his time in preferring Beethoven to "teeny pop veshches," but Kubrick's film shows a way (especially in the record-store scene) to bridging the gap between rock music and "the glorious Ninth"—it is a clockwork way, the way of the Moog synthesizer.

* * *

Apart from being gratified that my book has been filmed by one of the best living English-speaking producer-directors, instead of by some pornhound or pighead or other camera-carrying cretin, I cannot say that my life has been changed in any way by Stanley Kubrick's success. I seem to have less rather than more money, but I have always seemed to have less. I get odd letters from cranks, accusing me of sin against the Holy Ghost; invariably, I should think, masturbators, who, having seen the film, have discovered the book, used it as a domestic instrument of auto-erotic release, and then fastened their post-coital guilt onto me. Generally I am filled with a vague displeasure that the gap between a literary impact and a cinematic one should be so great, not only a temporal gap (book published 1962, film released ten years after) but an aesthetic one. Man's greatest achievement is language, and the greatest linguistic achievement is to be found in the dramatic poems or other fictional work in which language is a live, creative, infinitely suggestive force. But such works are invariably ignored by all but a few. Spell a thing to the eye, that most crass and obvious of organs, and behold—a revelation.

I fear, like any writer in my position, that the film may supersede the novel. This is not fair since the film is only a brilliant transference of an essentially literary experience to the screen. Writers like Mailer and Gore Vidal—who have seen novels of theirs turned into abominable pieces of film craft—are not in this position. But I can console myself by saying that *A Clockwork Orange* is not my favourite book, and that the works of mine that I like best are so essentially literary that no film could be made out of them.

As Kubrick's next film is to be about Napoleon, I find myself now writing a novel about Napoleon.[1] God knows why I am doing this; there is no guarantee that he will use it, or even that the book will be published. Just the fascination of what's difficult, or an expression of masochism that lies in all authors, or a certain pride in attacking the impossible. My Napoleon novel will be very brief, and to write a brief novel on Napoleon is far more difficult than to write *War and Peace*. But you can take this present labour as a product of the *Orange* film, and by God it is a labour.

Otherwise, my life is unchanged. What really enrages me is two minor dimensions—it is people referring to both film and book as THE *Clockwork Orange*. Can't the bastards read? No, they can't, and that's what all the trouble is about.

1. *Napoleon Symphony: A Novel in Four Movements* (New York: Knopf, 1974).

* * *

All works of art are dangerous. My little son tried to fly after seeing Disney's *Peter Pan*. I grabbed his legs just as he was about to take off from a fourth story window. A man in New York State sacrificed 67 infants to the God of Jacob; he just loved the Old Testament. A boy in Oklahoma stabbed his mother's second husband after seeing *Hamlet*. A man in Kansas City copulated with his wife after reading *Lady Chatterley's Lover*. After seeing *A Clockwork Orange*, a lot of boys will take up rape and pillage and even murder—The point is, I suppose, that human beings are good and innocent before they come into contact with works of art. Therefore all art should be banned. Hitler would never have dreamed of world conquest if he hadn't read Nietzsche in the *Reader's Digest*. The excesses of Robespierre stemmed from reading Rousseau. Even music is dangerous. The works of Delius have led more than one adolescent to suicide. Wagner's *Tristan and Isolde* used to promote crafty masturbation in the opera house. And look what Beethoven's Ninth Symphony does to Alex in *A Clockwork Orange*. If I were President of the United States, I should at once enact a total prohibition of films, plays, books and music. My book intended to be a delicious dream, not a nightmare of terror, beauty and concupiscence. Burn films—they make marvellous bonfires. Burn books. Burn this issue of *Rolling Stone*.

Take the story as a kind of moral parable, and you won't go far wrong. Alex is a very nasty, young man, and he deserves to be punished, but to rid him of the capacity of choosing between good and evil is the sin against the Holy Ghost, for which—so we're told—there's no forgiveness. And although he's nasty, he's also very human. In other words, he's ourselves, but a bit more so. He has the three main human attributes—love of aggression, love of language, love of beauty. But he's young and has not yet learned the true importance of the free will he so violently delights in. In a sense he's in Eden, and only when he falls (as he does: from a window) does he become capable of being a full human being. In the American edition of the book—the one you have here—we leave Alex dreaming up new acts of violence. We ought to feel pleased about this, since he's now exhibiting a renewal of the capacity for free choice which the State took away from him. The fact that he's not yet chosen to be good is neither here nor there. But in the final chapter of the British edition, Alex is already growing up. He has a new gang, but he's tired of leading it; what he really wants is to have a son of his own—the libido is being tamed and turned social—and the first thing he now has to do is to find a mate, which means sexual love, not just the old in-out in-out. Here, for a bonus, is how that very British ending ends:

That's what it's going to be then, brothers, as I come to the like end of this tale. You have been everywhere with your little droog Alex, suffering with him, and you have viddied some of the most grahzny bratchnies old Bog ever made, all on to your old droog Alex. And all it was was that I was young. But now as I end this story, brothers, I am not young, not no longer, oh no. Alex like groweth up, oh yes.

But where I itty now, O my brothers, is all on my oddy knocky, where you cannot go. Tomorrow is like all sweet flowers and the turning vonny earth and the stars and the old Luna up there and your old droog Alex all on his oddy knocky seeking like a mate. And all that cal. A terrible grahzny vonny world really, O my brothers. And so farewell from your little droog. And to all others in this story profound shooms of lip-music brrrrrr. And they can kiss my sharries. But you, O my brothers, remember sometimes thy little Alex what was. Amen. And all that cal.

America prefers the other, more violent, ending. Who am I to say America is wrong? It's all a matter of choice.

[Print versus Cinema][†]

I had just rolled a piece of paper (this) into the typewriter in order to start a new novel, when the reminder came from the *Scholar* about summer deadlines and the need for me to write my letter from Europe. Naturally, I'm always delighted to put off the agony of throwing people and dialogue and action onto paper—the Flaubertian agony, I mean, of knowing that one is embarking on a Work of Art. H. G. Wells, rightly or wrongly, began his novels as though he were writing a letter from Europe: "I am sitting here at my table in my apartment on the Piazza Santa Cecilia, wondering how to begin . . . There is so much to say about the events and personalities involved in what has become, for better or worse, a major issue of our time, particularly my friend Fozdick, the prime initiator. . . . Meanwhile the Roman rain is whitening the baroque cherubim on the façade opposite, and the ink congeals on my nib . . ." Writers with that easy, hesitant, improvisatory style or nonstyle have always been preferred, at least in England, to us more costive writers. Why not, then, write one's own novels that way? The answer isn't easy. For me, I know, it has something to do with another art I practiced many years ago, that of musical composition. One cannot (unless one is Gustav Mahler) approach a page of scoring paper—fifty cents

† Burgess, "Letter from Europe," *American Scholar* 41.3 (Summer 1972); 425–28. Copyright © 1972 by The Phi Beta Kappa Society.

the sheet—in a Wellsian manner: I don't know whether I should really be giving this theme to the bassoon, and I'm not sure whether it's really the theme I intended, anyway. Writing a novel is more a matter of carving than of letting words flow. But, so I gather from my sculptor friend Milton Hebald, even carving isn't as irreversible as many of us think. The figure you sculpt is the mere scratch on a block big enough to accommodate your David lying down. Mess up the nose and you can always excavate deeper. But if, like myself, you write a single copy of your symphony in ink, there is no such sense of freedom. You're scared of committing yourself to even a single semiquaver on the piccolo. The habit dies hard, as they say. Writing this letter is different: it's not art but phatic communication.

Communication of a sort, since I receive no replies. In this respect, writing a letter for the scholar is not much different from composing a short story. I gain the impression that this letter is *indulged*. Nobody ever complains—which they have a perfect right to do—about my ignoring the great public events that surround me and concentrating instead on the petty grievances and hard-won ecstasies of the free-lance writer's life. This is not a letter from anywhere except myself. The nomadic sort of existence that, at an age proper for settling down, I find suits me best, militates against a decent interest in local politics, the grindings of literary cliques, the taking of sides in general. I am a lost soul. I start the day with three pints of extra-strong tea, sit down to write, rise aching in the early evening, cook for the family (such a relief to stand up and do something comparatively mindless), go to the movies, sleep. A life that harms nobody and can be carried on anywhere. But not a life that anybody should be interested in reading about.

The last few months have, however, taken me out of this seclusion and thrown me into the arena of controversy. They also took me back to England, a country I have ceased to know much about since going into exile in the autumn of 1968. Stanley Kubrick, the film producer and director, completed the filming of a novel of mine a little before Christmas, 1971, and invited me over to London to see a preview. As a great film company was behind it all, my wife, my son and I were installed in a suite in Claridge's, conceivably the best hotel in the world. It is also perhaps the best place in which to observe the more admirable aspects of the British psyche—that efficiency without fuss, for example, which used to be so wonderful a characteristic of the old prenationalized railways. For instance, the Queen, and indeed the entire royal family, came to Claridge's to take luncheon with the King of Afghanistan, and, sitting in the bar, one was not aware that anything unusual was happening. Traffic was not impeded, taxis came and went, men at the reception desk even yawned. No shrieking of sirens, roar of motorcycle escorts, menace of polished holsters and oiled guns. This is the old England, but not many people can afford it.

Who, indeed, can afford anything in a country whose monetary decimalization has been an excuse for turning solidities like half-crowns and florins and shillings into mere, and excessively liquid, pence? A ten-shilling note was once called "half a bar"; it has been replaced by an eccentric fifty-pence coin that has no link with gleaming ingots. Nothing, except a pound and a penny, has a name any more. The inventive Cockneys are probably too depressed to find poetic nominations for the new flimsy pence-clusters. A thing costs 15p or 35½p, not a bob or a tanner or an Oxford scholar or a tosheroon. And on television commercials the price is spelt out as ten pee or twenty pee, making the shameful liquidity all the more obvious. That victory at Waterloo was, after all, a Pyrrhic one. The Continental system has gone through its first phase without protest: now come the liters and kilometers. Old men in the public bars, like the old man in *Nineteen Eighty-Four*, will soon be complaining that half a liter of beer isn't enough and a whole liter sends you bleeding well running to the toilet all the bleeding time. But nobody up there cares and, indeed, why should anybody care when there are no stomachic protests, only little whines? It is the submission to what is called progress that makes England so worrying these days. And progress doesn't solely mean entering that Europe which England once fought so valiantly to keep out of; it means also a subtle deterioriation in public morality, a weakening of the old concern with what was called "national" decency.

I met this when being interviewed by a reporter from the London *Evening News*. He asked me about the meaning of the film Kubrick has made from one of my novels, and I referred to the novel itself—a book I wrote nearly twelve years ago. I said that one of my purposes in composing what seemed a very violent work of literature was to purge my own mind of an event that had been troubling it for nearly twenty years—the assault on my wife in the London blackout by a gang of G.I. deserters who were after money more than kicks. The assault, I suggested, might have had something to do with my wife's subsequent poor health and her eventual comparatively early death. All over London, the day after the interview, posters proclaimed: "CLOCKWORK ORANGE GANG KILLED MY WIFE—AUTHOR." I appeared a day or so later on a radio talk show in which the moderator, a former disc jockey noted for his tricolor-dyed hair, asked blatantly: "Is it true that a gang raped your wife?" and then, to the female star of *Straw Dogs*, "What's it like to be raped—in a film, that is, ha ha, of course?" The program, needless to say, had a strong moral, even religious, bias. It was a *serious* program, and it was interrupted every ten minutes or so by a pop group. The franchise of this B.B.C. feature was, I was told, essentially musical, and everybody was very lucky to get talk in at all, especially *serious* talk. I have had considerable experience of American talk shows, and I have still to meet such puerility and such complaisance in the face of enforced compromise.

Any author must, I suppose, be irritated by the resurrection of issues that seemed sufficiently disposed of when he raised and then aired them ten years previously. What was depressing in London—and, to a lesser extent, on a just previous trip to New York—was the journalistic assumption that the issues had become genuine at last because they were now being conveyed through the great popular medium of cinema. Even more depressing was the unquestioned aesthetic tenet, whose falseness sticks out a mile, which permits more candor in one artistic medium than in another. All the British journalists I met assumed that the written word is, when corruptive, less so than the word publicly enunciated or converted into a visual image. This is not merely philosophically unsound; it is also hypocritical in a country that has a remarkable record for persecuting writers but honoring mere artistic executants. During a more recent stay in London, subjected as I was to journalistic battering as the original conceptor of a piece of controversial (or obscene, or pornographic) cinematic fiction, it was ironic that the only major public defense of the film *A Clockwork Orange* came from the retired chairman of the British Board of Film Censors, John Trevelyan. The Home Secretary (or Minister of the Interior) was persuaded to see the film with a view to governmental suppression, thus almost turning himself into the Minister of the Interior in the film and book. The most enlightened member of the House of Commons, Maurice Edelman—a man of large culture and a brilliant novelist—fell into a double-standard trap like any moronic backbencher, saying that a book is one thing and a film another. In other words, we can tolerate dangerous books because nobody reads them, but nearly everybody goes to the movies. This is implied but never stated: stated, it would cast doubt on the literacy of the electorate.

Of England, despite the above grouses, one thing can be said, and that is that the channels for publicizing public and private wrongs—fancied or otherwise—remain healthily open. Let a lonely old woman have her electric light cut off, or a man have his roses bulldozed over by the drain-laying county council, and the grievance is at once cried aloud—on the very day of suffering—by the evening papers and the television local news programs. Returning to Italy, one becomes strongly aware of how little the man in the street matters in the news media. The political parties and the syndicates get all the publicity, as well as the Sicilian *crime passionel* murderers and the pop stars, and I find it hard to imagine Italy in a rage over a landlord's commanding the eviction of a pet canary. Perhaps the fault with the

British—a fault, naturally, I find in myself—is the inability to see wrong very clearly at any level higher than that of the ancient widow whose cat has been killed by roadhogs. And it is usually pet animals and gardens and trees that call forth the protective, meaning the aggressive, instinct. I should feel happier about my own people if they could feel more strongly about the bloody mess in Northern Ireland. But, having written "my own people," I remember that I am one-quarter Irish and wholly Catholic and wonder where my true allegiances lie.

Perhaps the British avoid major ethical issues because they tend to see too much virtue in both sides of an argument. (And thus they thank God when it's just a matter of a maltreated kitten, where there's no argument at all.) A highly disruptive national coal strike has just ended, one in which aggressive picketing succeeded in blocking access to alternative forms of fuel, such as oil. There would have been large anger if a crippled pensioner's hothouse blooms had been ruined, but there seemed to be only muted grumbling about the state of the hospitals, where all major operations were suspended, and the disruption of commuter travel. The striking miners, it was generally thought, needed higher wages, and the public suffering was, after all, not as bad as that of London under the blitz. Anyway, the British genuinely like hardship, if it does not go on too long. Returning from January Minneapolis to meet the strike, I wondered what the British would have felt about a cessation of indoor heat with the temperature (as it regularly had been in Minneapolis) at–33 degrees Fahrenheit. The British climate makes just about tolerable the killing of electric radiators in winter and of refrigerators in summer. Dare one have fuel strikes at all in cities like Minneapolis? There's something wrong with political and labor principles if they have to be qualified by grossly material factors such as climate.

* * *

On Stanley Kubrick[†]

Ladies and gentlemen, I don't know whether you are entitled to call me a colleague. I was a film critic many years ago. Indeed, I was a film critic on the oldest European newspaper *The Gibraltar Chronicle*, which in 1943–44, when I worked for it, was the only non-fascist newspaper in continental Europe, even though it was run by the British army. We soldiers in this fortress had been informed, through Washington, by your great, dead president, President Roosevelt, that we had a duty to perform, and that was to protect the Rock. On behalf of a very large American insurance company . . . We were told that if we let this rock fall into fascist hands, the future of the American civilisation would be in jeopardy. And as an earnest of this American civilisation that was in jeopardy, we were allowed to see many American 'B' films. It was my . . . It was my task to criticize these films, or praise them. I was rather bored with the job, and went to very few of them and ended up by inventing my own films, my own cinemas. The Rock is a very cavernous place, and there may be the odd cinema lurking somewhere in St Michael's cave in the water, not like anybody had actually ever been to, but thought they might someday. You know, I was fired from this job, and never did film criticism again.

In 1966, which was my *Annus Mirabilis*, for the benefit of any drama critics who may be present, a wonderful year. I had many jobs: I was drama critic for *The Spectator*, and simultaneously I was opera critic for *Queen*, a great . . . great heterosexual magazine. I was television critic for a magazine, ironically called, *The Listener*. And I was food and wine critic for a left-wing paper that eventually folded up. It was generally recognised that I couldn't do all these jobs efficiently at the same time; and I noticed one night at a particular theater during the first act there were other critics who'd been deputed by their newspapers to sit behind me and see if I genuinely walked out after the first act. My normal procedure was to see one act of a play, the second act of an opera, and have some food and wine afterwards. It was assumed by everybody that I would never get up early enough to see films, so I never became a film critic.

Now as for my connections with the cinema, this is equally tenuous: my father was a cinema pianist. He played in those days which most of you are too young to remember, when there was no soundtrack,

† Acceptance Speech for the New York Film Critics Best Picture Award for Stanley Kubrick's A Clockwork Orange, at Sardi's Restaurant, New York, 1972. Reprinted in Emmanuel Vernadakis and Graham Woodroffe, eds., *Portraits of the Artist in* A Clockwork Orange (Angers: Presses de 'Université d'Angers, 2003), 257–60. Reprinted by permission of the Estate of Anthony Burgess, in care of the International Anthony Burgess Foundation.

and the accompaniment had to be provided by an orchestra in the evenings, by pianists during the day for matinees. My father never saw any films before he accompanied them. He did it all by ear, memory, instinct, intuition, and he had a very much foreshortened view when he accompanied. He told me on one occasion that he worked in a cinema for six months, where the piano didn't work above middle C, so all the music was somewhat Wagnerian. He was fired from this job because, without his knowing it, the film he was looking up at one afternoon, foreshortened, was a religious film; and he saw what looked like a scene of great festivity among men proceeding, and he started playing 'Hail, hail, the gang's all here!'. This turned out, of course to be the Last Supper. I'm sorry I've been allowed a blasphemous note to intrude; but this is, after all, a New York Sunday!

If I . . . If I continue just for a second with a blasphemy, I suppose my own relationship with this film, is that of primal creator with ultimate interpretor, which finds its most megalomaniacal, if I may use the term, or a most mythical metaphor in, say, the relationship between God and Cecil B. DeMille, or maybe the other way round. God wrote a marvellous book, best-seller—marvellous title called *The Old Testament*. I don't think he's ever received a penny's royalties for it; but God is a spirit, and I am merely a consumer of spirits. In my case, rather than God's, this masterpiece, which I think will make a lot of money, is somewhat different. As far as Kubrick is concerned, I knew little about him. I was told over the telephone that Stanley Kubrick wished to make my book *A Clockwork Orange* into a film; and I would get no money from it. Well, I said: 'I'm not ignorant, I know this already; you needn't tell me!' But he said: 'Would you rather he made it and get no money, or somebody else make it?' Well, I had a vision of Ken Russell making it, so I said I was prepared to pay Kubrick to make the film. It turned out to my surprise that Kubrick didn't actually need the money at the time. Kubrick reappeared in my life, or very nearly (he hadn't really appeared at all, had he?). He reappeared by name, very nearly, when I was in Australia. And I was summoned to London to see Kubrick because of two lines in the book. He wasn't sure whether it was a copyright or not, whether they were quotations of an existing song, or whether I had actually written them. So I rushed from Australia to New Zealand, to Hawaii, San Francisco, New York, eventually I ended up in London and appeared for lunch at that old English tavern called 'Trader Vick's'. After a couple of old English nogging of Maïtaï, Kubrick did not turn up.

Then Kubrick used the Australian vernacular and nearly gave birth to a set of diesel engines, when he discovered that the British edition of the book was different from the American edition. Indeed, the American edition, if anyone is interested, has twenty chapters, whereas the British edition has twenty-one. There's a cartoon in the British *Daily Express* which shows a man and a woman leaving the cinema, having seen Kubrick's film, and saying: 'George, dear, I do hope they don't make 'Son of *A Clockwork Orange*.' Well, this is no joke because chapter 21, in the British edition, is precisely that: it's the account of the son of *A Clockwork Orange*, and anybody who wishes to make this movie as a follow up is welcome to see me afterwards.

Well, as you know he doesn't travel, God—I mean, *Kubrick* doesn't travel, and he is stuck there in Boreham Wood, about two miles from Pinewood Studios outside London, and if I may use again a dramatic allusion, it was no question of Boreham Wood coming to 'Dunce' inane, 'Dunce' is here. So all I can say now is that I know you're a little droogie, a little malenky droogie back there in Boreham Wood, we'll shmeck down to his very keeshkas or even his yarbels, and then I'll place this horrorshow peguylok into his rookers.

On his behalf, ladies and gentlemen, I say 'thank you' for your generosity, on his and my behalf I say 'thank you' for your perspicacity, on my own behalf, my fellow writers, I say 'thank you' for your hospitality.

Interview[†]

INTERVIEWER   You mentioned that *A Clockwork Orange* has a concluding chapter in the British edition that isn't available in the American ones. Does this bother you?

BURGESS   Yes, I hate having two different versions of the same book. The U.S. edition has a chapter short, and hence the arithmological plan is messed up. Also, the implied view of juvenile violence as something to go through and then grow out of is missing in the American edition; and this reduces the book to a mere parable, whereas it was intended to be a novel.

INTERVIEWER   What happens in that twenty-first chapter?

BURGESS   In Chapter 21 Alex grows up and realizes that ultra-violence is a bit of a bore and it's time he had a wife and a malenky googoogooing malchickiwick to call him dadada. This was meant to be a mature conclusion but nobody in America has ever liked the idea.

INTERVIEWER   Did Stanley Kubrick consider filming the Heinemann version?

† John Cullinan, "The Art of Fiction XLVIII," interview with Anthony Burgess, *The Paris Review* 56 (1973): 136–39; 162. Copyright © 1973 by The Paris Review; used with permission of The Wiley Agency, LLC.

BURGESS   Kubrick discovered the existence of this final chapter when he was halfway through the film, but it was too late to think of altering the concept. Anyway, he too, an American, thought it too milk-and-watery. I don't know what to think now. After all, it's twelve years since I wrote the thing.

INTERVIEWER   Did you attempt to get the complete novel published here?

BURGESS   Yes—well, I was very dubious about the book itself. When I wrote the book my agent was not willing to present it to a publisher, which is rather unusual; and the sort of publishers in England were very dubious about the book. So when the American publisher made this objection to the final chapter, I didn't feel myself to be in a very strong position. I was a little hesitant to judge the book; I was a little too close to it. I thought: "Well, they may be right." Because authors do tend to be (especially after the completion of a book) very uncertain about the value of the book; and perhaps I gave in a little too weakly, but my concern was partly a financial one. I wanted it to be published in America, and I wanted some money out of it. So I said, "Yes." Whether I'd say "Yes" now I don't know; but I've been persuaded by so many critics that the book is better in its American form that I say, "All right, they know best."

INTERVIEWER   Would it be possible for an American press to put out a limited, hard-bound edition which includes the excluded chapter as a sort of appendix?[1]

BURGESS   I think this should be possible. The best way of doing it is to bring out an annotated edition of the book with this final chapter—an idea which is being resisted by my publishers for some reason, I don't know why. I would be very interested in the comments of the average, say, American student on the differences between the two versions. Because I'm not able to judge myself very clearly now, as to whether I was right or wrong. What is *your* opinion, what do you feel about that?

INTERVIEWER   I find the last chapter problematical in that while it creates an entirely different context for the work, it seems anti-climactic after the neat resurrection of the old Alex, in the twentieth chapter.

BURGESS   Yes.

INTERVIEWER   Still it should remain, because your meaning is altered by the cutting off of the context.

BURGESS   Well, the worst example I know of unjustified translation is to be found in Ford Madox Ford's *Parade's End*, where in

---

1. The twenty-first chapter of *A Clockwork Orange* was restored in the 1987 Norton reprinting of the novel.

the British edition under the imprint of Bodley Head, Graham Greene has taken upon himself to present *Parade's End* as a trilogy, saying he doesn't think the final novel, *The Last Post*, works and he feels perhaps Ford would have agreed with him; and therefore he has taken the liberty of getting rid of the final book. I think Greene is wrong; I think that whatever Ford said, the work is a tetralogy, and the thing is severely maimed with the loss of his final book. An author is not to be trusted in his judgment of this sort of thing. Authors very frequently try to be indifferent to their books. Certainly they are so sick of their books that they don't want to make any serious judgment on them. The problem comes up, you see, when one reads Evelyn Waugh's *A Handful of Dust*, because this frightful ending (where Tony Last spends all his time reading Dickens to this half-breed in the jungle), appeared previously as a short story; and knowing the short story one has a strange attitude to the book. Which makes us feel that here is a deliberate pasting together, where this giant figure at the end that turns up does not spring automatically out of the book but is just taken arbitrarily from another work. Perhaps one shouldn't know too much about these things. Of course one can't avoid it. These two versions of Samuel Butler's *Way of All Flesh*—this raises the problem. Which version would we like better, which is the right version? It's better to know only one thing, to be fairly ignorant of what was going on. You know, behind the version we know.

INTERVIEWER   Isn't this an argument against publishing a complete *A Clockwork Orange*, since a twenty-chapter version is embedded in everyone's mind?

BURGESS   I don't know; they're both relevant. They seem to me to express in a sense the difference between the British approach to life and the American approach to life. There may be something very profound to say about this difference in these different presentations of the novel. I don't know; I'm not able to judge.

INTERVIEWER   In *A Clockwork Orange* and *Enderby* especially there's a persistent strain of mockery toward youth culture and its music. Is there anything good about them?

BURGESS   I despise whatever is obviously ephemeral and yet is shown as possessing some kind of ultimate value. The Beatles, for instance. Most youth culture, especially music, is based on so little knowledge of tradition, and it often elevates ignorance into a virtue. Think of the musically illiterate who set themselves up as "arrangers." And youth is so conformist, so little concerned with maverick values, so proud of being rather than making, so bloody sure that it and it alone *knows*.

*   *   *

INTERVIEWER   Do film versions help or hinder novels?

BURGESS   Films help the novels they're based on, which I both resent and am grateful for. My *Clockwork Orange* paperback has sold over a million in America, thanks to dear Stanley. But I don't like being beholden to a mere film maker. I want to prevail through pure literature. Impossible, of course.

[Human Perfectibility, Dystopias, and Violence]†

The terms Pelagian and Augustinian, though theological, are useful for describing the poles of man's belief as to his own nature. The British monk Pelagius,[1] or Morgan (both names mean "man of the sea"), was responsible for a heresy condemned by the Church in A.D. 416, which, nevertheless, has never ceased to exercise an influence on Western moral thought. The view of man which it opposes appears, to most people, monstrously implausible, even though it is part of traditional Christian doctrine. This view states that man enters the world in a state of "original sin," which he is powerless to overcome by his own efforts alone: he needs Christ's redemption and God's grace. Original sin relates a certain human predisposition to evil to the crime of disobedience committed by Adam in the Garden of Eden. As Zamyatin reminds us, Adam did not wish to be happy; he wished to be "free." He desired free will, meaning the right to choose between courses of action—in effect, between courses on which a moral judgment could be made. He did not realize that, once free, he was more likely to choose the wrong than the right. He would consult the gratification of his own ego rather than what was pleasing to God. He thus condemned himself to divine punishment, which only God's mercy could rescind.

Pelagius denied this terrible endowment. Man was free to choose salvation as much as damnation: he was not predisposed to evil, there was no original sin. Nor was he necessarily predisposed to good: the fact of total freedom of choice rendered him neutral. But he certainly possessed the capability, with no hindrance from unregenerate forces within, to live the good life and, by his own efforts, to achieve salvation at the end. Saint Augustine, Bishop of Hippo, reaffirming the orthodox doctrine of original sin and the need to pray for divine grace, loudly condemned Pelagius. But Pelagius has, in more than fifteen hundred years, refused to be silent.

---

† From *1985* (Boston: Little, Brown, 1978), 52–55; 89–92; 94–97. Reprinted by permission of the Estate of Anthony Burgess, in care of the International Anthony Burgess Foundation.

1. Pelagius (c. 354 BCE–after 418 BCE), monk, probably born in Britain, who was declared a heretic for denying the doctrine of original sin.

In secularizing these views of man, we tend to forget about sin and concentrate on what is good for society and what is not. The Wellsian brand of Pelagianism blamed criminal impulses on environment. What priests called "original sin" was a reaction to poverty, slum tenements, enforced ignorance and squalor. A scientific socialism would extirpate what was called crime. Man was not just morally neutral: being a social animal, he wanted to be a "good," or responsible, member of society; it was his environment that had been getting in the way. But, if there are secular Pelagians (though not so many as before about 1933), there seem to be no secular Augustinians. Those who deny the possibility of moral progress, who insist on the destructive, libidinous urges in man as an unregenerable aspect of his condition, take, of necessity, a traditional theological stance. If anything can be done to improve man, it must come from without— from God, or the Life Force, or a miraculous extraterrestrial virus brought in by a UFO.

The polarity is, however, not all that rigid. We are all both Pelagian and Augustinian, either in cyclical phases, or, through a kind of doublethink, at one and the same time. Orwell was Pelagian in that he was a Socialist, Augustinian in that he created Ingsoc. It sometimes seems that the political life of a free community moves in the following cycle: a Pelagian belief in progress produces a kind of liberal regime that wavers when men are seen not to be perfectible and fail to live up to the liberal image; the regime collapses and is succeeded by an authoritarianism in which men are made to be good; men are seen not to be so bad as the Augustinian philosophy teaches; the way is open for liberalism to return. We tend to Augustinianism when we are disgusted with our own selfishness, to Pelagianism when we seem to have behaved well. Free will is of the essence of Pelagianism; determinism (original sin makes us not altogether responsible for our actions) of Augustinianism. None of us are sure how free we really are.

Invoking two opposed, but interpenetrating, kinds of theology, we find ourselves flirting with terms like *good* and *evil*. These, cut off from their base, tend to become semantically vague though strongly emotive. It is embarrassing to hear a politician use them, less embarrassing—though still disturbing—to hear him juggling with *right* and *wrong*. Strictly, the moral duality which these words represent is within the province of the State, while good and evil relate to theological permanencies. What is right, what is wrong? Whatever the State says. It is right to hate Eastasia and then, in the next breath, wrong. It is right to eat potatoes in a time of glut, wrong to eat them in a time of shortage. The Conservatives are wrong and we, the Socialists, are right—a matter of premises. The laws of the State are always changing and, with them, the values of right and wrong. The need to oppose unchanging values to the State's flighty judgments makes us ready to say that this enactment is good, even though it is wrong, and that one, though right, evil.

It has always been easier to point to examples of evil than of good. An Augustinian might say: inevitably, since evil is in our nature, and good not. *Good*, anyway, is a word with a wide spectrum of meaning: we are liable to confuse ethical good with what, for want of a better term, we must call aesthetic good. One of the great human mysteries is supposed to be provided by the Nazi death camps. A commandant who had supervised the killing of a thousand Jews went home to hear his daughter play a Schubert sonata and cried with holy joy. How was this possible? How could a being so dedicated to evil move without difficulty into a world so divinely good? The answer is that the good of music has nothing to do with ethics. Art does not elevate us into beneficence. It is morally neutral, like the taste of an apple. Instead of recognizing a verbal confusion we ponder an anomaly, or, like George Steiner, assert that a devotion to art renders men less sensitive to moral imperatives. "Men who wept at Werther or Chopin moved, unrealizing, through literal hell." There is no real mystery.

When we say "God is good," what do we mean? Presumably that God is beneficent and works directly on his creation to secure its happiness. But it is difficult to imagine and harder to believe. It is far easier to conceive of God's goodness as somehow analogous to the goodness of a grilled steak or of a Mozart symphony—eternally gratifying and of an infinite intensity; self-sufficient, moreover, with the symphony hearing itself and the eaten also the eater. The goodness of art, not of holy men, is the better figure of divine goodness.

*   *   *

The techniques for total manipulation of the human soul were in existence in 1932, when *Brave New World* first appeared. Ivan Petrovich Pavlov had four years more to live, he had done his work, and had been able to see something of the possibilities of its social application. Like his fellow-countryman Bakunin,[2] Pavlov was the product of a great phase of intellectual optimism which could not be held back by Czarist repression—indeed, censorship and obscurantism were a positive stimulus to the revolution of thought. Bakunin believed that men were already good; Pavlov believed that men could be made good. A materialist of the true nineteenth-century brand, he saw the human brain as an organ, in Wundt's words, secreting thought as the liver secretes bile, and no more of a mystery to the scientific investigator than any other organ of the body. The brain,

2. Mikhail Bakunin (1814–1876), émigré Russian anarchist and socialist.

seat of thought and emotion, instigator of action, could be probed, cut about, radically altered, but it must always be altered in the direction of a more efficient mechanism, a machine dedicated to the improvement of its owner's functioning as a human organism. This was the ultimate Pelagianism. The perfectibility of man should be not merely a pious aspiration but a scientific programme. He worked on dogs and discovered that their reflexes could be conditioned: ring a bell when bringing food and the dog will salivate; ring a bell without bringing food and the dog will still salivate. The potentialities of this discovery were enormous, and Huxley saw them clearly. In *Brave New World*, infants of the lowest social group must be made to hate the consumer goods they can never afford to buy. Children are encouraged to crawl towards highly coloured toys with gurgles of delight; as they start to touch them, electric bells shrill, sirens hoot, electric shocks are given off by the toys themselves. A few sessions of such conditioning, and the children will hate toys. In the same way, in maturity, they can be made to loathe champagne and caviar-surrogate. This is negative conditioning, conditioning employed in the service of rejection, but positive conditioning is used too. Make sweet scents and lovely music arise out of dustbins and the child is ready to be a lifelong refuse operative.

The Soviet State wished to remake man and, if one knows Russians, one can sympathize. Pavlov deplored the wild-eyed, sloppy, romantic, undisciplined, inefficient, anarchic texture of the Russian soul, at the same time admiring the cool reasonableness of Anglo-Saxons. Lenin deplored it too, but it still exists. Faced with the sloth of the waiters in Soviet restaurants (sometimes three hours between taking the order and fulfilling it), the manic depression of Soviet taxi-drivers, the sobs and howls of Soviet drunks, one can sometimes believe that without Communism this people could not have survived. But one baulks, with a shudder, at the Leninist proposal to rebuild, with Pavlov's assistance, the entire Russian character, thus making the works of Chekhov and Dostoevsky unintelligible to readers of the far future.

Lenin gave orders that Pavlov and his family should be lodged in capitalist luxury, fed with special rations, and that every possible technical facility should be granted the master, so that he could devise ways of manufacturing Soviet Man. Pavlov went on working with his dogs ("How like a dog is man," as Shakespeare, if he had read B. F. Skinner, might have said), looking for the seeds of life in the cerebral cortex, afflicting the creatures with diseases of the nervous system in order that he might, with the utmost tenderness (for nobody loved dogs as Pavlov did), cure them. Meanwhile the Soviet police followed up hints about the induction of neuroses, the driving of the Russian soul to breaking point. And the ancient point was being made about nothing in itself being good or bad, only the way in which fallible human beings use it. Certainly, humanism was being given the lie: man can be changed; the criminal can be turned into a reasonable citizen; the dissident can become orthodox; the obdurate rebel can be broken. But Soviet Man was not made.

We hear less of Pavlovianism these days than of Skinnerism. B. F. Skinner,[3] a practising behavioural psychologist, teaches, and has written in his book *Beyond Freedom and Dignity*, about the conditions under which human society can alone survive, and these involve changing man through a battery of positive reinforcements. It is never enough to demonstrate to man, on the assumption that he is a rational creature, the rational advantages of losing his aggressive tendencies and developing a social conscience. Only by associating a particular mode of behaviour with pleasure can it be made to seem desirable. The other, negative, way, whereby people associate an opposed mode of behaviour with pain, is inhumane. But there is something in all of us that is unconcerned with the manner in which circus animals are trained—whether with sugar lumps or the whip; it is the training itself that disturbs us. We make a distinction between schooling and conditioning. If a child plays truant or shuts his ears or throws spitballs at his teacher, this at least is evidence of free will. There is something in all of us that warms to the recalcitrant pupil. But to consider hypnopaedia, or sleep-teaching (which also features in *Brave New World*), cradle conditioning, adolescent reflex bending, and the rest of the behaviourist armory, is to be appalled at the loss, even if rewarded with sugar lumps, of individual liberty. Skinner's title appals in itself. Beyond truth, beyond beauty, beyond goodness, beyond God, beyond life. Big Brother does not go so far.

*   *   *

It was the sense of this division between well us and sick them that led me to write, in 1960, a short novel called *A Clockwork Orange*. It is not, in my view, a very good novel—too didactic, too linguistically exhibitionist—but it sincerely presented my abhorrence of the view that some people were criminal and others not. A denial of the universal inheritance of original sin is characteristic of Pelagian societies like that of Britain, and it was in Britain, about 1960, that

---

3. B. F. Skinner (1904–1990), American psychologist. Skinner was an exponent of a hard version of behaviorism, the school of psychology that treats mental states such as feelings as behavior, not as aspects of a privileged consciousness.

respectable people began to murmur about the growth of juvenile delinquency and suggest, having read certain sensational articles in certain newspapers, that the young criminals who abounded—or such exuberant groups as the Mods and Rockers, more playfully aggressive than truly criminal—were a somehow inhuman breed and required inhuman treatment. Prison was for mature criminals, and juvenile detention centres did little good. There were irresponsible people who spoke of aversion therapy, the burning out of the criminal impulse at source. If young delinquents could be, with the aid of electric shocks, drugs, or pure Pavlovian conditioning, rendered incapable of performing antisocial acts, then our streets would once more be safe at night. Society, as ever, was put first. The delinquents were, of course, not quite human beings: they were minors, and they had no vote; they were very much them as opposed to us, who represented society.

Sexual aggression had already been drastically burnt out of certain rapists, who first had to fulfill the condition of free choice, which meant presumably signing a vague paper. Before the days of so-called Gay Liberation, certain homosexuals had voluntarily submitted to a mixture of negative and positive conditioning, so that a cinema screen showed naked boys and girls alternately and at the same time electric shocks were administered or else a soothing sensation of genital massage was contrived, according to the picture shown. I imagined an experimental institution in which a generic young delinquent, guilty of every crime from rape to murder, was given aversion therapy and rendered incapable of contemplating, let alone perpetrating, an antisocial act without a sensation of profound nausea.

The book was called *A Clockwork Orange* for various reasons. I had always loved the Cockney phrase "queer as a clockwork orange," that being the queerest thing imaginable, and I had saved up the expression for years, hoping some day to use it as a title. When I began to write the book, I saw that this title would be appropriate for a story about the application of Pavlovian, or mechanical, laws to an organism which, like a fruit, was capable of colour and sweetness. But I had also served in Malaya, where the word for a human being is *orang*. The name of the antihero is Alex, short for Alexander, which means "defender of men." *Alex* has other connotations— a lex: a law (unto himself); a lex(is): a vocabulary (of his own); a (Greek) lex; without a law. Novelists tend to give close attention to the names they attach to their characters. *Alex* is a rich and noble name, and I intended its possessor to be sympathetic, pitiable, and insidiously identifiable with us, as opposed to them. But, in a manner, I digress.

Alex is not only deprived of the capacity to choose to commit evil. A lover of music, he has responded to the music, used as a heightener of emotion, which has accompanied the violent films he has been made to see. A chemical substance injected into his blood induces nausea while he is watching the films, but the nausea is also associated with the music. It was not the intention of his State manipulators to induce this bonus or malus: it is purely an accident that, from now on, he will automatically react to Mozart or Beethoven as he will to rape or murder. The State has succeeded in its primary aim: to deny Alex free moral choice, which, to the State, means choice of evil. But it has added an unforeseen punishment: the gates of heaven are closed to the boy, since music is a figure of celestial bliss. The State has committed a double sin: it has destroyed a human being, since humanity is defined by freedom of moral choice; it has also destroyed an angel.

The novel has not been well understood. Readers, and viewers of the film made from the book, have assumed that I, a most unviolent man, am in love with violence. I am not, but I am committed to freedom of choice, which means that if I cannot choose to do evil neither can I choose to do good. It is better to have our streets infested with murderous young hoodlums than to deny individual freedom of choice. This is a hard thing to say, but the saying of it was imposed on me by the moral tradition which, as a member of Western civilization, I inherit. Whatever the conditions needful for the sustention of society, the basic human endowment must not be denied. The evil, or merely wrong, products of free will may be punished or held off with deterrents, but the faculty itself may not be removed. The unintended destruction of Alex's capacity for enjoying music symbolizes the State's imperfect understanding (or volitional ignorance) of the whole nature of man, and of the consequences of its own decisions. We may not be able to trust man—meaning ourselves—very far, but we must trust the State far less.

It is disturbing to note that it is in the democracies, founded on the premise of the inviolability of free will, that the principle of the manipulation of the mind may come to be generally accepted. It is consistent with the principles of Ingsoc that the individual mind should be free, meaning free to be tormented. There seem to be no drugs in use in Airstrip One, except temporarily mind-dulling cheap and nasty gin. A strong centralized State, with powerful techniques of terrorization, can keep the streets free from muggers and killers. (Queen Elizabeth I's England hanged rioting apprentices on the site of the riot.) Our own democratic societies are growing weak. There is a great readiness to be affected, in the direction of the loss of authority, by pressure groups of all kinds, including street gangs as much as aggressive students. The lack of a philosophy at the centre (which neither Ingsoc nor Communism lacks) is matched by indecisiveness in dealing with crime. This is human; we leave draconian deterrents and punishments to the totalitarian States. But the eventual democratic response to crime may well be what could be represented as the most human, or humane, or compassionate approach of all: to regard man's mad division, which renders him both gloriously creative and bestially destructive, as a genuine disease, to treat his schizophrenia with drugs or shocks or Skinnerian conditioning. Juvenile delinquents destroy the State's peace; mature delinquents threaten to destroy the human race. The principle is the same for both: burn out the disease.

We must, say both Koestler and Skinner, accept the necessity of change. A new race, *Homo sapientior*, must be created. But, I say again, how far can we trust the therapists, who are as imperfect as ourselves? Whose blueprint of the new man must we follow? We want to be as we are, whatever the consequences. I recognize that the desire to cherish man's unregenerate nature, to deny the possibility of progress and reject the engines of enforced improvement, is very reactionary, but, in the absence of a new philosophy of man, I must cling to whatever I already have. What I have in general is a view of man which I may call Hebreo-Helleno-Christian-humanist. It is the view which the Savage in *Brave New World*, who has been reared in the wilds on a volume of William Shakespeare, brings to the stable utopia of AF 632: "I don't want comfort. I want God, I want poetry, I want real danger, I want freedom, I want goodness. I want sin." The World Controller, Mustapha Mond, sums it up for him: "In fact, you're claiming the right to be unhappy." Or the right, perhaps, not to find life dull. Perhaps the kind of humanity that can produce *Hamlet*, *Don Giovanni*, the Choral Symphony, the Theory of Relativity, Gaudí, Schoenberg and Picasso must,[4] as a necessary corollary, also be able to scare hell out of itself with nuclear weapons.

[U.K. versus U.S. Editions][†]

Sir,—In your issue of December 14 (Letters), William Baker seems to be complaining about certain differences between the new Penguin edition of *A Clockwork Orange* (a fruit of my early middle age not now by me much regarded, though Mr Baker is kind enough to

---

4. Burgess represents human creativity with classical, romantic, and modernist examples: a tragedy by Shakespeare, an opera by Mozart, Beethoven's last symphony, Einstein's revision of the Newtonian universe, the architecture of the Catalan Antoni Gaudi (1852–1926), the music of the Austrian modernist composer Arnold Schoenberg, and the art of Pablo Picasso.

† Letter to the editor, *Times Literary Supplement*, January 11, 1980, 38. Reprinted by permisssion of the Estate of Anthony Burgess, in care of the International Anthony Burgess Foundation.

consider it "superb") and the previous editions. The new edition now follows exactly the original hardcover edition put out by Heinemann in 1962, and still in print.

When, in 1961, the typescript of the novel was offered to Messrs W. W. Norton in New York, the managing editor was unwilling to publish without the excision of the final chapter. This, which presents my thug protagonist growing up and rejecting violence as a way of life, was considered to be a let down. I was told that American readers would prefer unregenerability and thuggishness stretching to the crack of the doom. I weakly agreed to the excision, and the book appeared in the United States with its arithmology impaired (two sections of seven chapters each, one of six). It appeared also with a glossary which was none of my work and was a defiance of my intention. The book is so structured that the reader learns the Nadsat, or teen, language as he goes along, without need of consultation of a glossary. If he does, in fact, find he needs this, then my long experience as a teacher of foreign languages has been wasted.

Stanley Kubrick read this American edition and made a film out of it. He discovered the existence of the final chapter, still in the old Pan edition as well as the Heinemann, only when he had finished the film. Whether an earlier discovery would have modified his adaptation is something we will never know. The popularity of the film led to a new paperback edition put out by Penguin Books which slavishly followed the American edition, glossary and all. I read this edition only recently and was shocked. Hence a new edition which is no more than a restoration of the text as originally written. I have "dropped" nothing except what was added by another hand. I have added what was originally there. I hope I have answered Mr Baker's questions.

Anthony Burgess
44 rue Grimaldi, Monte Carlo, Monaco

A Clockwork Orange Resucked†

I first published the novella *A Clockwork Orange* in 1962, which ought to be far enough in the past for it to be erased from the world's literary memory. It refuses to be erased, however, and for this the film version of the book made by Stanley Kubrick may be held chiefly responsible. I should myself be glad to disown it for various reasons, but this is not permitted. I receive mail from students who try to write theses about it, or requests from Japanese dramaturges to turn it into a sort of Noh play. It seems likely to survive, while other works of mine that I value more bite the dust. This is not an unusual experience for an artist. Rachmaninoff used to groan because he was known mainly for a Prelude in C Sharp Minor which he wrote as a boy, while the works of his maturity never got into the programmes. Kids cut their pianistic teeth on a Minuet in G which Beethoven composed only so that he could detest it. I have to go on living with *A Clockwork Orange*, and this means I have a sort of authorial duty to it. I have a very special duty to it in the United States, and I had better now explain what this duty is.

Let me put the situation baldly. *A Clockwork Orange* has never been published entire in America. The book I wrote is divided into three sections of seven chapters each. Take out your pocket calculator and you will find that these add up to a total of twenty-one chapters. Twenty-one is the symbol of human maturity, or used to be, since at 21 you got the vote and assumed adult responsibility. Whatever its symbology, the number 21 was the number I started out with. Novelists of my stamp are interested in what is called arithmology, meaning that number has to mean something in human terms when they handle it. The number of chapters is never entirely arbitrary. Just as a musical composer starts off with a vague image

† "A Clockwork Orange Resucked" in Burgess, *A Clockwork Orange*, v–xi. Copyright © 1986 by Anthony Burgess from *A Clockwork Orange* by Anthony Burgess. Used by permission of W. W. Norton & Company, Inc., and the Estate of Anthony Burgess, in care of the International Anthony Burgess Foundation. Burgess's reflections on *A Clockwork Orange*, published in the Norton reprint of the novel with the addition of the twenty-first chapter, is included for its author's speculations on how political contexts influenced preferences for the two versions of his novel.

　　Eric Swenson, Burgess's editor at Norton, presented a different account of how the U.S. edition took the form it did, in "Publisher's Note": "This new, American edition of *A Clockwork Orange*, as the author so forcefully puts it in his Introduction, is longer by one chapter—the last. This chapter was included in the original, British edition, but dropped from the American edition and therefore from Stanley Kubrick's film version. The author and his American publisher—who is delighted to give this fascinating book a new and larger life—differ in their memories as to whether or not the dropping of the last chapter, which changed the book's impact dramatically, was a condition of publishing or merely a suggestion made for conceptual reasons. Whichever is true, the larger truth is that *A Clockwork Orange* is a modern classic which must, indeed, be made available to Anthony Burgess's American readers precisely in the form he wishes it to be. It is so done."

of bulk and duration, so a novelist begins with an image of length, and this image is expressed in the number of sections and the number of chapters into which the work will be disposed. Those twenty-one chapters were important to me.

But they were not important to my New York publisher. The book he brought out had only twenty chapters. He insisted on cutting out the twenty-first. I could, of course, have demurred at this and taken my book elsewhere, but it was considered that he was being charitable in accepting the work at all, and that all other New York, or Boston, publishers would kick out the manuscript on its dog-ear. I needed money back in 1961, even the pittance I was being offered as an advance, and if the condition of the book's acceptance was also its truncation—well, so be it. So there is a profound difference between *A Clockwork Orange* as Great Britain knows it and the somewhat slimmer volume that bears the same name in the United States of America.

Let us go further. The rest of the world was sold the book out of Great Britain, and so most versions—certainly the French, Italian, Spanish, Catalan, Russian, Hebrew, Rumanian, and German translations—have the original twenty-one chapters. Now when Stanley Kubrick made his film—though he made it in England—he followed the American version and, so it seemed to his audiences outside America, ended the story somewhat prematurely. Audiences did not exactly clamour for their money back, but they wondered why Kubrick left out the dénouement. People wrote to me about this—indeed much of my later life has been expended on Xeroxing statements of intention and the frustration of intention—while both Kubrick and my New York publisher coolly bask in the rewards of their misdemeanour. Life is, of course, terrible.

What happens in that twenty-first chapter? You now have the chance to find out. Briefly, my young thuggish protagonist grows up. He grows bored with violence and recognises that human energy is better expended on creation than destruction. Senseless violence is a prerogative of youth, which has much energy but little talent for the constructive. Its dynamism has to find an outlet in smashing telephone kiosks, derailing trains, stealing cars and smashing them and, of course, in the much more satisfactory activity of destroying human beings. There comes a time, however, when violence is seen as juvenile and boring. It is the repartee of the stupid and ignorant. My young hoodlum comes to the revelation of the need to get something done in life—to marry, to beget children, to keep the orange of the world turning in the rookers of Bog, or hands of God, and perhaps even create something—music, say. After all, Mozart and Mendelssohn were composing deathless music in their teens or nadsats, and all my hero was doing was razrezzing and giving the old in-out. It is with a kind of shame that this growing youth looks back on his devastating past. He wants a different kind of future.

There is no hint of this change of intention in the twentieth chapter. The boy is conditioned, then deconditioned, and he foresees with glee a resumption of the operation of free and violent will. 'I was cured all right,' he says, and so the American book ends. So the film ends too. The twenty-first chapter gives the novel the quality of genuine fiction, an art founded on the principle that human beings change. There is, in fact, not much point in writing a novel unless you can show the possibility of moral transformation, or an increase in wisdom, operating in your chief character or characters. Even trashy bestsellers show people changing. When a fictional work fails to show change, when it merely indicates that human character is set, stony, unregenerable, then you are out of the field of the novel and into that of the fable or the allegory. The American or Kubrickian *Orange* is a fable; the British or world one is a novel.

But my New York publisher believed that my twenty-first chapter was a sellout. It was veddy veddy British, don't you know. It was bland and it showed a Pelagian unwillingness to accept that a human being could be a model of unregenerable evil. The Americans, he said in effect, were tougher than the British and could face up to reality. Soon they would be facing up to it in Vietnam. My book was Kennedyan and accepted the notion of moral progress. What was really wanted was a Nixonian book with no shred of optimism in it. Let us have evil prancing on the page and, up to the very last line, sneering in the face of all the inherited beliefs, Jewish, Christian, Muslim and Holy Roller, about people being able to make themselves better. Such a book would be sensational, and so it is. But I do not think it is a fair picture of human life.

I do not think so because, by definition, a human being is endowed with free will. He can use this to choose between good and evil. If he can only perform good or only perform evil, then he is a clockwork orange—meaning that he has the appearance of an organism lovely with colour and juice but is in fact only a clockwork toy to be wound up by God or the Devil or (since this is increasingly replacing both) the Almighty State. It is as inhuman to be totally good as it is to be totally evil. The important thing is moral choice. Evil has to exist along with good, in order that moral choice may operate. Life is sustained by the grinding opposition of moral entities. This is what the television news is all about. Unfortunately there is so much original sin in us all that we find evil rather attractive. To devastate is easier and more spectacular than to create. We like to have the pants scared off us by visions of cosmic destruction. To sit down in a dull room and compose the *Missa Solemnis* or *The Anatomy of Melan-*

choly[1] does not make headlines or news flashes. Unfortunately my little squib of a book was found attractive to many because it was as odorous as a crateful of bad eggs with the miasma of original sin.

It seems priggish or pollyannaish to deny that my intention in writing the work was to titillate the nastier propensities of my readers. My own healthy inheritance of original sin comes out in the book and I enjoyed raping and ripping by proxy. It is the novelist's innate cowardice that makes him depute to imaginary personalities the sins that he is too cautious to commit for himself. But the book does also have a moral lesson, and it is the weary traditional one of the fundamental importance of moral choice. It is because this lesson sticks out like a sore thumb that I tend to disparage *A Clockwork Orange* as a work too didactic to be artistic. It is not the novelist's job to preach; it is his duty to show. I have shown enough, though the curtain of an invented lingo gets in the way—another aspect of my cowardice. Nadsat, a Russified version of English, was meant to muffle the raw response we expect from pornography. It turns the book into a linguistic adventure. People preferred the film because they are scared, rightly, of language.

I don't think I have to remind readers what the title means. Clockwork oranges don't exist, except in the speech of old Londoners. The image was a bizarre one, always used for a bizarre thing. "He's as queer as a clockwork orange" meant he was queer to the limit of queerness. It did not primarily denote homosexuality, though a queer, before restrictive legislation came in, was the term used for a member of the inverted fraternity. Europeans who translated the title as *Arancia a Orologeria* or *Orange Mécanique* could not understand its Cockney resonance and they assumed that it meant a hand grenade, a cheaper kind of explosive pineapple. I mean it to stand for the application of a mechanistic morality to a living organism oozing with juice and sweetness.

Readers of the twenty-first chapter must decide for themselves whether it enhances the book they presumably know or is really a discardable limb. I meant the book to end in this way, but my aesthetic judgement may have been faulty. Writers are rarely their own best critics, nor are critics. "*Quod scripsi scripsi*" said Pontius Pilate when he made Jesus Christ the King of the Jews. "What I have written I have written." We can destroy what we have written but we cannot unwrite it. I leave what I wrote with what Dr. Johnson called frigid indifference to the judgement of that .00000001 of the

---

1. The *Missa Solemnis* (1824) is a setting of the mass (the Eucharist liturgy in Latin) by Beethoven; *The Anatomy of Melancholy* (1621) by the English churchman and scholar Robert Burton (1577–1640) is an encyclopedic work exploring the record in human culture of the condition we now term depression.

American population which cares about such things. Eat this sweet-ish segment or spit it out. You are free.

[Origins and Adaptations][†]

The novel, properly novella, entitled *A Clockwork Orange* first appeared in the spring of 1962. I had written its first version in late 1960, when I was coming to the end of what the neurological specialists had assured my late wife would be my terminal year. My late wife broke the secret in time for me to work hard at providing some posthumous royalties for her. In the period in which I was supposed to be dying from an inoperable cerebral tumour, I produced the novels entitled *The Doctor Is Sick, Inside Mr Enderby, The Worm and the Ring* (a reworking of an earlier draft), *One Hand Clapping, The Eve of Saint Venus* (an expansion in novella form of a discarded opera libretto) and *A Clockwork Orange* in a much less fantastic version than the one that was eventually published. This first version presented the world of adolescent violence and governmental retribution in the slang that was current at the time among the hooligan groups known as the Teddyboys and the Mods and Rockers. I had the sense to realise that, by the time the book came to be out, that slang would already be outdated, but I did not see clearly how to solve the problem of an appropriate idiolect for the narration. When, in early 1961, it seemed to me likely that I was not going to die just yet, I thought hard about the book and decided that its story properly belonged to the future, in which it was conceivable that even the easy-going British state might employ aversion therapy to cure the growing disease of youthful aggression. My late wife and I spent part of the summer of 1961 in Soviet Russia, where it was evident that the authorities had problems with turbulent youth not much different from our own. The stilyagi, or style-boys, were smashing faces and windows, and the police, apparently obsessed with ideological and fiscal crimes, seemed powerless to keep them under. It struck me that it might be a good idea to create a kind of young hooligan who bestrode the iron curtain and spoke an argot compounded of the two most powerful political languages in the world—Anglo-American and Russian. The irony of the style would lie in the hero-narrator's being totally unpolitical.

There was what must seem, to us who are living in a more permissive age, an unaccountable delay in getting the work accepted for publication. My literary agent was even dubious about submitting

† From *A Clockwork Orange: A Play with Music* (Hutchinson, 1987), v–vi; vii–x. Reprinted by permission of the Estate of Anthony Burgess, in care of the International Anthony Burgess Foundation.

it to a publisher, alleging that its pornography of violence would be certain to make it unacceptable. I, or rather my late wife, whose Welsh blood forced her into postures of aggression on her husband's behalf, reminded the agent that it was his primary job not to make social or literary judgements on the work he handled but to sell it. So the novella was sold to William Heinemann Ltd in London. In New York it was sold to W. W. Norton Inc, though with the last chapter missing. To lop the final section of the story, in which the protagonist gives up his youthful violence in order to become a man with a man's responsibilities, seemed to me to be very harmful: it reduced the work from a genuine novel (whose main characteristic must always be a demonstration of the capacity of human nature to change) to a mere fable. Moreover, though this was perhaps a minor point, it ruined the arithmology of the book. The book was written in twenty-one chapters (21 being the symbol of human maturity) divided into three sections of exactly equal size. The American reduction looks lopsided. But the American publisher's argument for truncation was based on a conviction that the original version, showing as it does a capacity for regeneration in even the most depraved soul, was a kind of capitulation to the British Pelagian spirit, whereas the Augustinian Americans were tough enough to accept an image of unregenerable man. I was in no position to protest, except feebly and in the expectation of being overborne: I needed the couple of hundred dollars that comprised the advance on the work.

*   *   *

But the nasty little shocker was gaining an audience, especially among the American young. Rock groups called 'Clockwork Orange' began to spring up in New York and Los Angeles. These juveniles were primarily intrigued by the language of the book, which became a genuine teenage argot, and they liked the title. They did not realise that it was an old Cockney expression used to describe anything queer, not necessarily sexually so, and they hit on the secondary meaning of an organic entity, full of juice and sweetness and agreeable odour, being turned into an automaton. The youth of Malaysia, where I had lived for nearly six years, saw that *orange* contained *orang*, meaning in Malay, a human being. In Italy, where the book became *Arancia all'Orologeria*, it was assumed that the title referred to a grenade, an alternative to the ticking pineapple. The small fame of the novella did not noticeably enrich me, but it led to a proposal that it be filmed. It was in, I think, 1965, that the rock group known as the Rolling Stones expressed an interest in the buying of the property and an acting participation in a film version which I myself should write. There was not much money in the project, because the permissive age in which crude sex and cruder violence could be frankly presented had not yet begun. If the film was to be made at all, it would have to be in a cheap underground version leased out to clubs. But it was not made. Not yet.

It was the dawn of the age of candid pornography that enabled Stanley Kubrick to exploit, to a serious artistic end, those elements in the story which were meant to shock morally rather than merely titillate. These elements are, to some extent, hidden from the reader by the language used: to *tolchock* a *chelloveck* in the *kishkas* does not sound so bad as booting a man in the guts, and the *old in-out in-out*, even if it reduces the sexual act to a mechanical action, does not sicken quite so much as a Harold Robbins description of cold rape. But in a film little can be implied; everything has to be shown. Language ceases to be an opaque protection against being appalled and takes a very secondary place. I was bound to have misgivings about the film, and one of the banes of my later life has been the public assumption that I had something to do with it. I did not. I wrote a script, like nearly everybody else in the script-writing world, but nobody's script was used. The book itself, as in a literary seminar, was taken on to the film set, discussed, sectionally dramatised with much free improvisation, and then, as film, stowed in the can. All that I provided was a book, but I had provided it ten years previously. The British state had ignored it, but it was not so ready to ignore the film. It was considered to be an open invitation to the violent young, and inevitably I was regarded as an antisocial writer. The imputation that I had something to do with the punk cult, whose stepfather I was deemed to be by *Time* magazine, has more to do with the gorgeous technicolor of Kubrick's film than with my own subfusc literary experiment.

I am disclosing a certain gloom about visual adaptation of my little book, and the reader has now the right to ask why I have contrived a stage version of it. The answer is very simple: it is to stem the flow of amateur adaptations that I have heard about though never seen. It is to provide a definitive actable version which has auctorial authority. And, moreover, it is a version which, unlike Kubrick's cinema adaptation, draws on the entirety of the book, presenting at the end a hooligan hero who is now growing up, falling in love, proposing a decent bourgeois life with a wife and family, and consoling us with the doctrine that aggression is an aspect of adolescence which maturity rejects. This is not, of course, altogether true: our football assassins are presumably grown men, but there is something about football which restores the mindlessness of adolescence: grown men should have something better to do than watch a ball being kicked around. This view will make me unpopular with intellectual fans like Sir Freddie Ayer, but I sincerely hold it. Alex the hero speaks for me when he says in effect that destruction is a substitute for creation, and that the energy of youth has to be expressed through aggression because it has not yet been able to subdue itself through creation. Alex's aggressive instincts have been stimulated by classical music, but the music has been forewarning him of what he must some day become: a man who recognises the Dionysiac in, say, Beethoven but appreciates the Apollonian as well.

*   *   *

Cultural Settings

PAUL ROCK AND STANLEY COHEN

The Teddy Boy[†]

The Teddy Boy is as deserving of a place in a discussion of the fifties as any of his more respectable contemporaries. He was the most visibly 'difficult' of the problems that had become associated with post-war youth. In a stable society, one generation's experience has meaning for its successors. When a society undergoes rapid social change, however, less and less of the traditional wisdom is useful to those who are expected to learn from their elders. When Britain emerged from the war there appeared to be a tendency for the generations to grow apart—for the young to seek guidance from their fellow young. This tendency was increased by the relative economic emancipation of working-class adolescents in the fifties and the establishment of a commercial market reinforcing and creating specifically adolescent desires in consumer goods and services. Colin MacInnes's somewhat stylised 'teenager' personified this new tendency: he says of his elder brother Vernon: 'He's one of the generations that grew up before teenagers existed . . . in poor Vernon's era . . . there just weren't any: can you believe it? . . . In those days, it seems, you were just an overgrown boy, or an undergrown man, life didn't seem to cater for anything else between.'[1]

By no means all adolescents were affluent enough to take on the new glossy teenage image, by no means all were delinquent or even in slight conflict with their elders, but these differences tend to be ignored by the older generation. There was a tendency to perceive all adolescents as members of a problem group. This tendency is not peculiarly British. Friedenberg comments on the American situation:

---

† From Vernon Bogdanor and Robert Skidelsky, eds., *The Age of Affluence, 1951–1964* (London: Macmillan, 1970), 288–320. Reprinted by permission.
1. Colin MacInnes, *Absolute Beginners* (London: Allison & Busby, 1959).

Only as a customer and, occasionally, as an athlete are adolescents favourably received. Otherwise they are treated as a problem and, potentially, a threatening one. No other social groups
except convicted criminals and certified lunatics are subjected
to as much restriction. . . . Willing as they are to trade with
him [American adults] have no doubt that the 'teen-ager' is an
enemy. . . . Hostility does not come this easily to the middle
class, which prefers to define any nuisance that it wishes to
abate, or social situation that it finds threatening or embarrassing, as a problem. Our youth problem is a notable accomplishment. We have made it ourselves, out of little. . . . Many adults
seem to use the terms 'teenager' and 'juvenile delinquent' as if
they were synonyms.[2]

The trends in Britain, although lagging slightly behind, are parallel. We have had our Beats, Mods and Rockers, and Hippies—all
in their turn inevitably labelled problems. The first and greatest of
this sequence was the Ted. He seems to stalk like some atavistic
monster through much of the otherwise prosaic newspaper reporting of the fifties.

The Teddy Boy emerged without much warning. There was little
preparation for his appearance as a fully fledged deviant, i.e. a person defined as a social problem. He had curious parents; one was
the upper-class Edwardian dandy, the other the older delinquent
subculture of South London. His 'Edwardian' clothes were originally worn by the middle and upper classes, but this was for only a
short period after the war. Indeed, the style was worn throughout
the 1950s, but its meaning changed dramatically over the decade.
Dress is lent significance by its wearers and by its audiences. When
the long jackets and the tight trousers covered the middle class, the
fashion was proclaimed a pleasing innovation, but it was rapidly
reappraised when it spread to young working-class males in 1953. It
seems that these new 'Edwardians' were the lumpenproletarian
'creepers', not the 'respectable' working class. Fyvel says that 'the
Edwardian style in its full bloom had utterly unexpectedly trans-
ported itself across the Thames to working-class South London. . . .
From all accounts, the first Teds who introduced the fashion south
of Waterloo and Vauxhall were a pretty rough lot . . . they still had
links with the older cloth-capped gangs which in earlier years had
dominated areas like the Elephant.'[3]

As a result, the middle class felt that it could no longer share the
style with its new adherents. 'It means,' explained a disconsolate

---

2. Edgar Friedenberg, 'Adolescence as a Social Problem', in Howard S. Becker, ed. *Social Problems: A Modern Approach* (New York: Wiley, 1966) 37–38.
3. T. R. Fyvel, *The Insecure Offenders: Rebellious Youth in the Welfare State* (London: Chatto, 1961), 49–50.

young ex-Guardee over a champagne cocktail, 'that absolutely the whole of one's wardrobe IMMEDIATELY becomes UNWEARABLE.'[4] Those who now wore Edwardian dress were described in a vocabulary which derived from former modes of delinquency. Unfavourable social types were summoned forth to define them. They were 'zoot-suiters',[5] 'hooligans'[6] and 'spivs'. The newspapers did not hesitate to award them an unambiguous identity. The clothing was unchanged but its wearers had translated it into a stigma:

> The cosh boys have killed all hopes of men's fashions that *really* are different. For years men have been accused of not being venturesome enough in their appearance, of being content with the same old drabness. Then came a change. The Edwardian look came along. . . . But it's all over now. The cosh boys have moved in. Take the Edwardian look. Three years ago Savile-row tailors got together to push it. They pushed it on the young Mayfair bloods, they pushed it on the Guardees, they pushed it on the Business men. They pushed it so successfully that it became the uniform of the dance hall creepers. Now, very quickly, Savile-row has stopped pushing the Edwardian look, it's out.'[7]

The newspapers deplored the fact that the diffusion of Edwardian dress had denied it to the middle class. But they did not attach any other significance to this phenomenon. The new wearers were not at first recognised as a new phenomenon. A person who dressed in Edwardiana was 'really' a familiar actor in an unfamiliar guise. He was an old deviant in new clothes, merely a spiv or a cosh-boy who had taken up a once middle-class fashion.

The Edwardian had not developed a distinctive personality by 1953. In July, for example, a group of Edwardians were involved in the stabbing of a youth near Clapham Common. Although some newspapers mentioned the dress of Michael Davies, the person convicted of the murder, it was not shown to have any symbolic importance. The *Daily Mirror* merely stressed that the convicted man was concerned about his appearance. It did not even specify that he had worn an Edwardian suit:

> Michael Davies, the Clapham Common thug sentenced to die for murder at the Old Bailey yesterday, was crazy about girls. . . . Ever since he was a boy he was out to impress the girls. He took great pains to look like a dandy. Like most of his companions, nearly all his money went on flashy clothes, and just before the murder, he borrowed twelve pounds from his uncle to buy a

4. *Daily Mirror*, 17 November 1953.
5. *Daily Sketch*, 14 November 1953.
6. *Daily Herald*, 14 November 1953.
7. *Daily Sketch*, 9 December 1953.

suit. . . . This man was a born coward beneath his bravado and his 'gay dog' clothes.[8]

Davies was labelled a 'thug' who fortuitously happened to be a dandy. Nevertheless, the link between Edwardian clothes and deviance was to grow. It eventually became so strong that, three years later, the Mayor of Harrogate was unable to determine which was cause and which effect. He stated that 'there would appear to be a very real connection between the action of individuals and the type of dress they wear, and this is nowhere more marked at the present time than in the so-called Edwardian style which is worn by so many of the young hooligans of our country. Is it the outfitter who provides the style, or the hooligans who make the demand on the outfitter?'

In 1953 this link was only gradually becoming established. It was known that the clothes were worn by many disreputable people, but it was assumed that these people would be disreputable with or without Edwardian dress. Tony Parker, who documented the Clapham Common murder, observed of the Edwardians at the time of the stabbing that 'by those who thought they were better-class they were laughed at, derided, called "Teddy boys". But not with much more than mild amusement, not with hostility in those days, or contempt or fear. That was to come later. After this night particularly, after this night first, and then after other things.'[9] An association between appearance and a delinquent self requires reinforcement by a number of notorious incidents and, in many cases, a dramatic event. The incidents occurred in 1953 and early 1954. The dramatic event took place a little later.

The way in which these incidents were reported itself signified that the style was beginning to symbolise a social problem. Communication about its wearers was to be used to clarify the nature of the problem. In February 1954, for example, the *Sunday Chronicle* stated that the Edwardian suit 'was mortally wounded . . . when one of its wearers, described as an Edwardian dandy, attacked a young woman in a suburban train. . . . And clothes dealers say that more and more of these suits are being sold to them for give-away prices because they have become the emblem of the spiv and the cosh-boy.'[1] The delinquencies committed were few, but their perpetrators were conspicuous and eminently 'newsworthy'. Unpleasantness caused by Edwardians was eagerly recorded. Four months before this attack, the *Tailor and Cutter* felt constrained to protest that

> By a series of vicious coincidences, apparently all the old ladies who have been beaten up lately, all the modest young men who

8. *Daily Mirror*, 23 October 1953.
9. Tony Parker, *The PloughBoy* (London: Hutchinson, 1965) 20–21.
1. *Sunday Chronicle*, 28 February 1954.

have had their faces slashed and all the poor little pussy cats who have had tin cans attached to their tails have been beset by wicked young dandies in Edwardian clothes.

What a hullabaloo would stir among the nationals if the *Tailor and Cutter* headlined every social transgression with the significant headlines: 'Killer wears tan boots with blue suit', or 'Crepe shoes only worn by footpads'.

Observations published in early 1954 were more interesting as prophecies than as social commentary. As self-fulfilling predictions they may well have precipitated what was to happen later. This was the phase in the natural history of the Teddy Boy when 'society' defined and refined its relation to the new group. Erikson has argued that 'an enormous amount of modern "news" is devoted to reports about deviant behaviour and its punishment . . . these items . . . constitute our main source of information about the normative contours of society. In a figurative sense, at least, morality and immorality meet at the public scaffold, and it is during this meeting that the community declares where the line should be drawn.'[2] The Edwardian had to be weighed up and assessed. Later on, when he was at his most notorious, the newspapers devoted almost no space to describing him. He was then established as a known outsider.

The basis for this social placement was laid in 1954. Public pronouncements showed what sort of creature an Edwardian was. They construed sartorial uniformity as social uniformity. They imputed a solidarity and an organisation to the Edwardians. The Chairman of the Dartford Juvenile Court proclaimed to some offenders that 'You lads have set yourselves on a path of crime. You have turned yourselves into that very undesirable, horrible type of youth which likes to call itself Edwardian. It is a lot of rubbish. There has never been anything more rubbishy than this Edwardian cult. It will lead to prison or something worse.'[3] Society heard these pronouncements as well as the Edwardians. The reactions of others are of crucial importance in the creation of an identity. Through this ritual denunciation, not only did 'society' resolve an attitude towards the Edwardians, the Edwardians resolved an attitude towards themselves.

This dramatisation of the social implications of dress was likely to have engendered those very traits which were deplored. It seems plausible to suppose that the early Edwardians experienced pressures to become either more 'thuggish' or less 'Edwardian' in appearance. The marginal Edwardian would have been drawn closer to the despised group, or would have left it entirely.

2. Kai T. Erikson, 'Notes on the Sociology of Deviance', in Howard S. Becker, ed., *The Other Side: Perspectives on Deviance* (Glencoe, Ill.: Free Press, 1964) 14.
3. *Evening Standard*, 24 February 1954.

Not only was the Edwardian given an identity, he was also given a new name. This renaming of a phenomenon is immensely significant because it announces that a change has taken place in 'society's' attitude towards the phenomenon. 'The direction of activity depends on the particular ways that objects are classified. . . . The renaming of any object, then, amounts to a reassessment of your relationship to it, and *ipso facto* your behaviour becomes changed along the lines of your reassessment.'[4] 'Teddy Boy' was first displayed in print in March 1954. It seems that the Edwardian could no longer be regarded simply as the old spiv or the old cosh-boy. The old categories or response were inappropriate. New categories had to be invented. The first national newspaper which referred to 'Teddy Boys' provided its readers with an orientation towards them. It described them as 'Teddy boys—young thugs who dress in Edwardian-style clothes. . . .'[5] The Edwardian was renamed because his acts had acquired a dramatic quality which could not be conveniently dealt with in the old terminology. In March, for example, a Camberwell youth centre was wrecked by 'cosh-boys' in Edwardian suits who were armed with razors and knuckledusters. There had been assaults at dances and uproars in cinemas. The Edwardian had to be appreciated as a new type of person.

It may be seen, however, that although the Teddy Boy was now an entity in his own right, he was firmly placed in a galaxy of similar social types—thugs, spivs and so on. His nature was clearly established. In time, like these other social types, he would become a model to be held up before society so that right-thinking people could avoid his behaviour. Just as the first Edwardians had been called cosh-boys and hooligans, so would later anti-social behaviour be labelled 'Teddy Boy'. An eligible person would not have to wear Edwardian clothes. In 1955, for example, the middle class were ironically again associated with Edwardianism. 'University students were warned yesterday: "Stop this Teddy Boy touch attitude". . . . The reason: hooliganism by university students who run the city's [Birmingham's] annual carnival.'[6]

Spivs and cosh-boys who change their style of dress but remain spivs and cosh-boys have not necessarily become more frightening. A change which is seen to entail a complete metempsychosis *can* be frightening. This was disturbing, but there were other reasons for concern as well. The Teddy Boys were multiplying. They had emerged in South London in 1953. By April 1954 they had spread to the provinces. A child psychiatrist argued that 'the fact that these

4. Anselm Strauss, *Mirrors and Masks: The Search for Identity* (Glencoe, Ill.: Free Press, 1959) 21–22.
5. *Daily Sketch*, 22 March 1954.
6. *Daily Express*, 17 November 1955.

Edwardian "creepers" are appearing in small country towns should surely convince us it is time to take this phenomenon seriously'. It was now fitting to write of them in terms associated with pathology and epidemiology. Dr Lowenfeld called their proliferation 'an emotional chicken-pox'.

*   *   *

B. F. SKINNER
[Behavior Modification][†]

*   *   *

"I shall have to be technical," said Frazier. "But only for a moment. It's what the science of behavior calls 'reinforcement theory.' The things that can happen to us fall into three classes. To some things we are indifferent. Other things we like—we want them to happen, and we take steps to make them happen again. Still other things we don't like—we don't want them to happen and we take steps to get rid of them or keep them from happening again.

"*Now*," Frazier continued earnestly, "if it's in our power to create any of the situations which a person likes or to remove any situation he doesn't like, we can control his behavior. When he behaves as we want him to behave, we simply create a situation he likes, or remove one he doesn't like. As a result, the probability that he will behave that way again goes up, which is what we want. Technically it's called 'positive reinforcement.'

"The old school made the amazing mistake of supposing that the reverse was true, that by removing a situation a person likes or setting up one he doesn't like—in other words by punishing him—it was possible to *reduce* the probability that he would behave in a given way again. That simply doesn't hold. It has been established beyond question. What is emerging at this critical stage in the evolution of society is a behavioral and cultural technology based on positive reinforcement alone. We are gradually discovering—at an untold cost in human suffering—that in the long run punishment doesn't reduce the probability that an act will occur. We have been so preoccupied with the contrary that we always take 'force' to mean

---

† From *Walden Two* (1948; rpt. Indianapolis: Hackett, 2005), 243–47. Reprinted by permission of Hackett Publishing Company, Inc. All rights reserved. *Walden Two* is a work of fiction by B. F. Skinner that describes a community called Walden Two (alluding to Henry David Thoreau's social experiment in *Walden; or, Life in the Woods* [1854]). In the dialogue extracted here, Frazier, one of the founders, debates the nature of the community with Professor Castle, who has been invited to visit Walden Two ten years on from its foundation.

punishment. We don't say we're using force when we send shiploads of food into a starving country, though we're displaying quite as much *power* as if we were sending troops and guns."

"I'm certainly not an advocate of force," said Castle. "But I can't agree that it's not effective."

"It's *temporarily* effective, that's the worst of it. That explains several thousand years of bloodshed. Even nature has been fooled. We 'instinctively' punish a person who doesn't behave as we like—we spank him if he's a child or strike him if he's a man. A nice distinction! The immediate effect of the blow teaches us to strike again. Retribution and revenge are the most natural things on earth. But in the long run the man we strike is no less likely to repeat his act."

"But he won't repeat it if we hit him hard enough," said Castle.

"He'll still *tend* to repeat it. He'll *want* to repeat it. We haven't really altered his potential behavior at all. That's the pity of it. If he doesn't repeat it in our presence, he will in the presence of someone else. Or it will be repeated in the disguise of a neurotic symptom. If we hit hard enough, we clear a little place for ourselves in the wilderness of civilization, but we make the rest of the wilderness still more terrible.

"Now, early forms of government are naturally based on punishment. It's the obvious technique when the physically strong control the weak. But we're in the throes of a great change to positive reinforcement—from a competitive society in which one man's reward is another man's punishment, to a cooperative society in which no one gains at the expense of anyone else.

"The change is slow and painful because the immediate, temporary effect of punishment overshadows the eventual advantage of positive reinforcement. We've all seen countless instances of the temporary effect of force, but clear evidence of the effect of not using force is rare. That's why I insist that Jesus, who was apparently the first to discover the power of refusing to punish, must have hit upon the principle by accident. He certainly had none of the experimental evidence which is available to us today, and I can't conceive that it was possible, no matter what the man's genius, to have discovered the principle from casual observation."

"A touch of revelation, perhaps?" said Castle.

"No, accident. Jesus discovered one principle because it had immediate consequences, and he got another thrown in for good measure."

I began to see light.

"You mean the principle of 'love your enemies'?" I said.

"Exactly! To 'do good to those who despitefully use you' has two unrelated consequences. You gain the peace of mind we talked about the other day. Let the stronger man push you around—at least you avoid the torture of your own rage. *That's* the immediate consequence. What an astonishing discovery it must have been to find that in the long run you could *control the stronger man* in the same way!"

"It's generous of you to give so much credit to your early colleague," said Castle, "but why are we still in the throes of so much misery? Twenty centuries should have been enough for one piece of behavioral engineering."

"The conditions which made the principle difficult to discover made it difficult to teach. The history of the Christian Church doesn't reveal many cases of doing good to one's enemies. To inoffensive heathens, perhaps, but not enemies. One must look outside the field of organized religion to find the principle in practice at all. Church governments are devotees of *power*, both temporal and bogus."

"But what has all this got to do with freedom?" I said hastily.

Frazier took time to reorganize his behavior. He looked steadily toward the window, against which the rain was beating heavily.

"Now that we *know* how positive reinforcement works and why negative doesn't," he said at last, "we can be more deliberate, and hence more successful, in our cultural design. We can achieve a sort of control under which the controlled, though they are following a code much more scrupulously than was ever the case under the old system, nevertheless *feel free*. They are doing what they want to do, not what they are forced to do. That's the source of the tremendous power of positive reinforcement—there's no restraint and no revolt. By a careful cultural design, we control not the final behavior, but the *inclination* to behave—the motives, the desires, the wishes.

"The curious thing is that in that case the *question of freedom never arises*." * * *

* * *

JOHN R. PLATT

[Against "Autonomous Man"]†

Beyond Freedom and Dignity[1] is Skinner's first attempt to develop a full-scale coherent philosophy. The "freedom" and "dignity" of the title are ironic and again should be put in quotation marks. But the

† From "The Skinnerian Revolution" in Harvey Wheeler, ed., *Beyond the Punitive Society: Operant Conditioning: Social and Political Aspects* (San Francisco: W. H. Freeman, 1973), 40–41. Reprinted by permission.
1. B. F. Skinner's *Beyond Freedom and Dignity* (New York: Knopf, 1971) argued that the prospect of increasing the collective good through the application of scientific techniques (the modification of individual behavior) was hindered by belief in free will.

key word is "beyond," for he goes past his critics and his debates with conventional psychology and tries to relate his organism—environmental behavioral formulations to family and social practices, evolution and death, ethics and values and cultural survival, and the design of the future. From the point of view of its scope and its coherent restatement of the relation between man and society—based, for the first time, on experiment rather than on introspection or philosophy—it is a masterpiece. It will have to be taken into account by all future social philosophers, and it may be the capstone of his life's work.

The "freedom" and "dignity" of the title are not attacked, in this case, because they are mentalistic "states," but because they have been key concepts in his opponents' attack on his work and his philosophy. Skinner sees them as cardboard verbal concepts expressing a fuzzy-minded and false view of man, a view that is blocking a clear understanding of the relations between man and society, a view that must be demolished if we are to understand how to make an improved society.

He sees "freedom" as having been a useful watchword against tyranny and against elites who tried to control others by negative reinforcement and punishment. To proclaim that men are not inherently slaves or subjects was a justification of escape or retaliation, and a valuable aid in countercontrol. But, of course, it was also used by the punishers and the moralist elites to justify punishment: if a man was "free," then his acts had no outside causes, and society could apply its controls nowhere but to his own body.

Skinner says this is false, that there is no such "free" or "autonomous man," that the experiments show that all of man's behavior is shaped deterministically by the reinforcements from his environment from the time he is born. Modern social work and criminology come close to this view, and regard most, if not all, of delinquency and crime as being due to genetics, brain damage, sickness, or a poor environment, for which the delinquent was not responsible.

Conversely, Skinner sees "dignity" as society's way of praising "autonomous man" for "uncaused" acts of generosity, self-sacrifice, courage, or defiance under pressure or punishment. But if we had had a search for the roots of this behavior as careful as our search for the roots of crime and delinquency, we might find the environmental shaping to be just as determining in this case.

Skinner concludes that "freedom" and "dignity" are myths that are preventing us from seeing how continually and subtly we are being shaped by our environment. They keep us using gross methods of

---

Platt's outline and contextualization of Skinner's position helps us to see that Burgess and Skinner bear the same relationship as Augustine and Pelagius. [Editor's note.]

praise and punishment that are ineffective in preventing each others'
delinquencies and malfunctions and do not help us shape the good
behaviors that we might achieve.

*   *   *

JOOST A. M. MEERLOO

["Menticide"]†

This book attempts to depict the strange transformation of the free
human mind into an automatically responding machine—a transformation which can be brought about by some of the cultural
undercurrents in our present-day society as well as by deliberate
experiments in the service of a political ideology.

The seduction of the mind and stealthy mental coercion are
among the oldest crimes of mankind. They probably began back in
prehistoric days when man first discovered that he could exploit
human qualities of empathy and understanding in order to exert
power over his fellow men.

The modern words 'brainwashing', 'thought control', and 'menticide' serve to provide some indication of the actual methods by
which man's integrity can be violated. When a concept is given its
right name, it can be more easily recognized—and it is with this
recognition that the opportunity for systematic correction begins.

In this book the reader will find a discussion of some of the
imminent dangers which threaten free cultural interplay. It emphasizes the tremendous cultural implication of the subject of enforced
mental intrusion. Not only the artificial techniques of coercion are
important but even more the unobtrusive intrusion into our feeling
and thinking. The danger of destruction of the spirit may be compared to the threat of total physical destruction through atomic
warfare. Indeed, the two are related and intertwined.

*   *   *

† From *Mental Seduction and Menticide: The Psychology of Thought Control and Brain-
Washing* (1956: London: Jonathan Cape, 1958), Preface. Reprinted by permission.

WILLIAM SARGANT

[Brain-Washing]†

Politicians, priests and psychiatrists often face the same problem: how to find the most rapid and permanent means of changing a man's beliefs. When, towards the end of World War II, I first became interested in the similarity of the methods which have, from time to time, been used by the political, religious and psychiatric disciplines, I failed to foresee the enormous importance now attaching to the problem—because of an ideological struggle that seems fated to decide the course of civilization for centuries to come. The problem of the doctor and his nervously ill patient, and that of the religious leader who sets out to gain and hold new converts, has now become the problem of whole groups of nations, who wish not only to con-firm certain political beliefs within their boundaries, but to prosely-tize the outside world.[1]

Great Britain and the U.S.A. therefore find themselves at last obliged to study seriously those specialized forms of neurophysio-logical research which have been cultivated with such intensity by the Russians since the Revolution, and have helped them to perfect the methods now popularly known as 'brain-washing' or 'thought control.' In August, 1954, the United States Secretary of Defence announced the appointment of a special committee to study how prisoners of war could be trained to resist brain-washing. He admitted the desirability of reviewing the existing laws, government agree-ments, and policies of military departments, with regard to prison-ers captured by nations in the Soviet orbit. This committee reported back to the President in August, 1955.[2]

In Great Britain, too, the necessity for more vigorous research into the techniques of rapid political conversion has also been widely recognized. Several years ago, for instance, Mrs. Charlotte Haldane pleaded that research should be undertaken into the psy-chological mechanism of the process by which she, the wife of a famous British scientist, had been converted to a belief in the offi-cial Russian interpretations of Marxian dialectics; and into that of her sudden reconversion to the Western point of view, after failing to detect the falsity of the Russian system for so many years. Koestler

† From *Battle for the Mind: A Physiology of Conversion and Brain-Washing* (London: Heinemann, 1957), xv–xvi. Reprinted by permission.
1. Sargant, 'The Mechanism of Conversion. *British Medical Journal*, II.311, 1951.
2. P.O.W.—*The Fight Continues After the Battle*. Report of the Secretary of Defence's Advisory Committee on Prisoners of War (Washington: U.S. Government Printing Office, 1955).

and many others have described very much the same experience in their own lives.[3]

Many people are also bewildered at the spectacle of an intelligent and hitherto mentally stable person who has been brought up for trial behind the Iron Curtain, and prevailed upon not only to believe but to proclaim sincerely that all his past actions and ideas were criminally wrong. 'How is it done?' they ask.

* * *

GEORGE STEINER

[Art and Morality][†]

We know now that a man can read Goethe or Rilke in the evening, that he can play Bach and Schubert, and go to his day's work at Auschwitz in the morning. To say that he has read them without understanding or that his ear is gross, is cant. In what way does this knowledge bear on literature and society, on the hope, grown almost axiomatic from the time of Plato to that of Matthew Arnold, that culture is a humanizing force, that the energies of spirit are transferrable to those of conduct? Moreover, it is not only the case that the established media of civilization—the universities, the arts, the book world—failed to offer adequate resistance to political bestiality, they often rose to welcome it and to give it ceremony and apologia. Why? What are the links, as yet scarcely understood, between the mental, psychological habits of high literacy and the temptations of the inhuman. Does some great boredom and surfeit of abstraction grow up inside literate civilization preparing it for the release of barbarism? * * * We come *after*, and that is the nerve of our condition. After the unprecedented ruin of humane values and hopes by the political bestiality of our age.

That ruin is the starting-point of any serious thought about literature and the place of literature in society. Literature deals essentially and continually with the image of man, with the shape and motive of human conduct. We cannot act now, be it as critics or merely as rational beings, as if nothing of vital relevance had happened to our sense of the human possibility, as if the extermination by hunger or violence of some 70 million men, women and children in Europe

---

3. A. Koestler, "The God that Failed," in *Six Studies in Communism* (London: Hamish Hamilton, 1950).
† From *Language and Silence: Essays 1958–1966* (London: Faber, 1967), 15–16, 23–25. Copyright © 1958, 1960, 1961, 1962, 1963, 1964, 1965, 1966, 1967 by George Steiner. Reprinted by permission of Georges Borchardt, Inc., on behalf of the author, and Faber and Faber, Ltd.

and Russia between 1914 and 1945 had not altered, profoundly, the quality of our awareness. We cannot pretend that Belsen is irrelevant to the responsible life of the imagination. What man has inflicted on man, in very recent time, has affected the writer's primary material—the sum and potential of human behaviour—and it presses on the brain with a new darkness.

Moreover, it puts in question the primary concepts of a literary, humanistic culture. The ultimate of political barbarism grew from the core of Europe. Two centuries after Voltaire had proclaimed its end, torture again became a normal process of political action. Not only did the general dissemination of literary, cultural values prove no barrier to totalitarianism; but in notable instances the high places of humanistic learning and art actually welcomed and aided the new terror. Barbarism prevailed on the very ground of Christian humanism, of Renaissance culture and classic rationalism. We know that some of the men who devised and administered Auschwitz had been trained to read Shakespeare or Goethe, and continued to do so.

This is of obvious and appalling relevance to the study or teaching of literature. It compels us to ask whether knowledge of the best that has been thought and said does, as Matthew Arnold asserted, broaden and refine the resources of the human spirit. If forces us to wonder whether what Dr. Leavis has called 'the central humanity' does, in fact, educate towards humane action, or whether there is not between the tenor of moral intelligence developed in the study of literature and that required in social and political choice, a wide gap or contrariety. The latter possibility is particularly disturbing. There is some evidence that a trained, persistent commitment to the life of the printed word, a capacity to identify deeply and critically with imaginary personages or sentiments, diminishes the immediacy, the hard edge of actual circumstance. We come to respond more acutely to the literary sorrow than to the misery next door. Here also recent times give harsh evidence. Men who wept at Werther or Chopin moved, unrealizing, through literal hell.

This means that whoever teaches or interprets literature—and both are exercises seeking to build for the writer a body of living, discerning response—must ask of himself what he is about (to tutor, to guide someone through *Lear* or the *Oresteia* is to take into one's hand the springs of his being). Assumptions regarding the value of literate culture to the moral perception of the individual and society were self-evident to Johnson, Coleridge and Arnold. They are now in doubt. We must countenance the possibility that the study and transmission of literature may be of only marginal significance, a passionate luxury like the preservation of the antique. Or, at worst, that it may detract from more urgent and responsible uses of time and energy of spirit. I do not believe either to be true. But the question must be asked and explored without cant. Nothing is more worrying regarding the present state of English studies in the universities than the fact that such inquiry should be deemed bizarre or subversive. It is of the essence.

This is where the claim of the natural sciences derives its force. Pointing to their criteria of empirical verification and to their tradition of collaborative achievement (in contrast to the apparent idiosyncrasy and egotism of literary argument), scientists have been tempted to assert that their own methods and vision are now at the centre of civilization, that the ancient primacy of poetic statement and metaphysical image is over. And though the evidence is uncertain, it does seem likely that of the aggregate of available talent, many, and many of the best, have turned to the sciences. In the *quattrocento* one would have wished to know the painters; today, the sense of inspired joy, of the mind in free, unshadowed play, is with the physicists, the biochemists and the mathematicians.

But we must not be deceived. The sciences will enrich language and the resources of feeling (as Thomas Mann showed in *Felix Krull*, it is from astrophysics and microbiology that we may reap our future myths, the terms of our metaphors). The sciences will recast our surroundings and the context of leisure or subsistence in which culture is viable. But though they are of inexhaustible fascination and frequent beauty, the natural and mathematical sciences are only rarely of ultimate interest. I mean that they have added little to our knowledge or governance of human possibility, that there is demonstrably more of insight into the matter of man in Homer, Shakespeare or Dostoevsky than in the entirety of neurology or statistics. No discovery of genetics impairs or surpasses what Proust knew of the spell or burden of lineage; each time Othello reminds us of the rust of dew on the bright blade we experience more of the sensual, transient reality in which our lives must pass than it is the business or ambition of physics to impart. No sociometry of political motive or tactics weighs against Stendhal.

And it is precisely the 'objectivity', the moral neutrality in which the sciences rejoice and attain their brilliant community of effort, that bar them from final relevance. Science may have given tools and insane pretences of rationality to those who devised mass murder. It tells us scarcely anything of their motives, a topic on which Aeschylus or Dante would be worth hearing. Nor, to judge by the naïve political statements put forward by our present alchemists, can it do much to make the future less vulnerable to the inhuman. What light we possess on our essential, inward condition is still gathered by the poet.

But, undeniably, many parts of the mirror are today cracked or blurred. The dominant characteristic of the present literary scene is the excellence of 'non-fiction'—of reportage, history, philosophic argument, biography, the critical essay—over traditional imaginative forms. Most of the novels, poems and plays produced in the past two decades are simply not as well written, not as strongly felt, as are modes of writing in which the imagination obeys the impulse of fact. Madame de Beauvoir's memoirs are what her novels should have been, marvels of physical and psychological immediacy; Edmund Wilson writes the best prose in America; none of the numerous novels or poems that have taken on the dread theme of the concentration camps rivals the truth, the controlled poetic mercy of Bruno Bettelheim's factual analysis, *The Informed Heart*. It is as if the complication, pace, and political enormity of our age had bewildered and driven back the confident master-builder's imagination of classic literature and the nineteenth-century novel. A novel by Butor and *Naked Lunch* are both escapes. The avoidance of the major human note, or the derision of that note through erotic and sadistic fantasy, points to the same failure of creation. Monsieur Beckett is moving, with unflinching Irish logic, towards a form of drama in which a character, his feet trapped in concrete and his mouth gagged, will stare at the audience and say nothing. The imagination has supped its fill of horrors and of the unceremonious trivia through which modern horror is often expressed. As rarely before, poetry is tempted by silence.

*   *   *

CRITICISM

On Burgess's Novel

ROBERT TAUBMAN

Review[†]

'Yarbles, bolshy great yarblockos to thee and thine' is the language of
A Clockwork Orange—Jacobean English mixed with 'nadsat-talk', the
teen slang of the near future. It is a great strain to read. Anthony
Burgess follows up acutely and savagely the divergent tendencies of
our time: with satellites in orbit and men landing on the moon, the
few decent scarecrows who survive from the past are being beaten
up in the streets by gangs of delinquents. Little Alex, the delinquent
narrator, suffers a spell of corrective treatment in prison, on traditional lines—'Goodness comes from within, 6655321'—and since this
fails, undergoes a mental operation that reverses his responses,
though not for long. There's not much fantasy here; Mr Burgess
works by keeping close to the way things are now, and the novel can
be read, for instance, as straight satire on the indulgence of a good
many current writers to their teenage heroes. Little Alex looks for
a moment like sharing at least one of the well-known redeeming
virtues, love of music—Bach and Mozart send him, all right, only
the trances they induce are if anything more hideous than his ordinary life.

*　*　*

ANONYMOUS

Review[‡]

"A viscous verbiage . . . which is the swag-bellied offspring of
decay . . . English is being slowly killed by her practitioners." Lord

† From the *New Statesman* 63.1627, May 18, 1962, 718. Reprinted by permission.
‡ Originally published in the *Times Literary Supplement (TLS)*, May 25, 1962, 377.
Reprinted by permission.

Hailsham's lament might be applied to *A Clockwork Orange*, except that here the killing seems intentional. Mr. Burgess is an accomplished writer, who has set out, in the peculiar slang of "nadsat", the autobiography of a teenager from fifteen to eighteen.

"The holy bearded veck all nagoy hanging on a cross" is an example of the author's language and questionable taste. The publishers promise "an easily digested feast of picaresque villainy and social satire". But satire implies hatred, and of any such viewpoint this book appears to be sadly lacking. "What sort of a world is it at all? Men on the moon and men spinning round the earth . . ." is a question legitimately asked of our times, but it gets no clear answer here. The author seems content to use a serious social challenge for frivolous purposes, but himself to stay neutral.

JULIAN MITCHELL

Horrorshow on Amis Avenue[†]

Anthony Burgess must have garnered some excellent reviews in his short, busy writing career (*A Clockwork Orange* is his eighth novel since 1956). No one can match his skill at anguished farce about the end of empire. His characters seem to be trapped in a tent whose pole has just been sawn in two by an overenthusiastic administrator doing his part in a campaign to save wood. It is hilarious to watch their frantic heaving and humping beneath the spoiled canvas, to hear their absurd multilingual pidgin groans. But as we wipe away our tears of laughter, we notice that someone has just thrown petrol over the collapsed and writhing tent: frozen with horror, we see him strike a match.

If Mr. Burgess is, in some ways, a pupil of Mr. Waugh, he yet has an originality of manner and subject which place him, to my mind, among the best writers in England. Yet he has never received the critical attention granted to Angus Wilson and Kingsley Amis, with whom at least he deserves to rank. Certainly his prose is more attractive than either's, and he is prepared to take risks which they are not. And if his novels seem rather hollow and heartless at times, from a tendency to move his characters about to illustrate his points instead of letting the characters find their own way to making them, the points are major ones about our times.

A Clockwork Orange is set in the future, in an England where the streets are called things like Amis Avenue. It is narrated by Alex, a

† "Horrorshow on Amis Avenue," *The Spectator*, May 18, 1962, 661–62. Reprinted by permission.

beguiling adolescent gang-leader with ultra-violent tendencies and a passion for classical music, in a teenage slang which takes a few pages to grasp. A splendid slang it is, though, full of stuff like 'yarbles' and 'profound shooms of lip-music brrrrr' and 'droog.' The key praise-word is 'horrorshow,' for Alex's world is horrible and sadistic, and he is one of the toughest juvenile delinquents one could hope to meet. Very properly gaoled for killing a cat-loving old lady, Alex is subjected to a new cure for criminals, similar to that for alcoholics: he becomes sick and faint at the thought of violence or the sound of classic music (connected by him with violence). Released, he finds himself the victim of the entire world, at the mercy of policemen, old professors and politicians. His responses are no longer his own.

Mixing horror with farce in his inimitable manner, Mr. Burgess develops his theme brilliantly, though there is a certain arbitrariness about the plot which is slightly irritating and I find it difficult to accept the contention that being young is like being a clockwork toy—you walk into things all the time. But the language is an extraordinary technical feat and the whole conception vigorously exhibits Mr. Burgess's great imaginative gifts. No doubt ignorant and anonymous reviewers will criticise him for 'experimenting' (as John Wain was recently and absurdly criticised): they will be merely exhibiting their ignorance and anonymity. Mr. Burgess is far too good and important a writer not to go in any direction he chooses.

* * *

DIANA JOSSELSON
Review[†]

Reading the book before the blurb, I thought *A Clockwork Orange* was a first novel. Actually, as I suppose everyone else knows, it is Anthony Burgess' eighth, his seventh being a British Book Society choice; and the blurb in the English edition assures us "he is now incontrovertibly established as a novelist of prime stature." Well.

The story is about juvenile delinquents in that nearish future English novelists often choose to write about, when the world is apparently under an American-Russian condominium and is an extremely disagreeable place to live in.

The book is written in "nadsat," the local slang of the delinquents, since it is supposed to be the autobiography of Alex, the j.d. described in both the English and American blurbs as "genial." Readers with

---

† From the *Kenyon Review* 25.3 (Summer 1963), 559–60. Reprinted by permission of the *Kenyon Review*.

a smattering of Russian will find minor philological enjoyment in recognizing "horrorshow," "droog," "the old moloko," "devotchkas," "rot," "slovo," etc. "Horrorshow," which means wonderful, is the most successful invention in "nadsat"; most of the others are straight transliterations without bilingual punning. Other elements of the invented language are scientific-futuristic or simply valueless substitutes in the manner of much real slang, e.g. "viddy" with "glazzies"—to see with eyes. "Cancers" for cigarettes is rather good. The English blurb suggests that "it will take the reader no more than fifteen pages to master and revel in the expressive language of 'nadsat.'" Since, beginning even on page two, the author cheats, as it were, by providing a glossary as he goes along—"rooker (a hand, that is) . . . litso (face, that is)"—instead of forcing the meaning by context as the game would seem to call for, mastery may be said to be simultaneous with exposure.

Comparison can be made with William Golding's *The Inheritors*, where the reader is also thrust into an unknown world and a new language. But when a Golding Neanderthaler says, "I have a picture," there is excitement for the reader, and revelation. How much one cares for these hairy creatures, how much one hates their successor, Man.

(Closer comparison should perhaps be made with science fiction.)

One also hates Man's descendant, Burgess' genial hero Alex, and his language and way of thinking. No effort is made to explain Alex or explain juvenile delinquency. Presumably it is the natural result of the political system and the disruptions through which civilization has gone, resulting in a breakdown of law and order and a state of culture symbolized by "Jonny Zhivago, a Russky koshka, singing 'Only Every Other Day.'" Most of the book is taken up by descriptions of the various crimes perpetrated by Alex and his gang. Each one is horrible—chaining glazzies out is a favorite—and each unmotivated. The gang unloads its large quantity of pocket money at the beginning of an evening in order to have "more of an incentive like for some shopcrasting," and it takes various drugs in milk to help get in the mood. The end of an evening for Alex is to listen in bed to Mozart and Bach full-blast on his stereo, reliving and imagining violence until he reaches orgasm: "And so the lovely music glided to its glowing close."

Eventually, Alex is imprisoned and finally subjected to a new two-week reform treatment, in which the criminal reflex is "killed." Alex leaves prison "good," having been conditioned to feel nausea at the beginning of each criminal impulse—and at the sound of Mozart. In the horrible world he goes into from prison, he becomes everyone's victim, including the politicians', and finally attempts suicide. During the resultant hospitalization the authorities, for political reasons, undo the previous therapy and our Alex is restored to horrorshow ugliness.

Credibility of a sort has been maintained up to this point, but the last chapter lets the reader down so badly that he must reconsider the value of the whole. Alex, it appears, *outgrows* his delinquency, as do the other delinquents when they reach eighteen or so. Alex thinks sentimentally about having a son, foresees his son's juvenile delinquency, and his son's son's. "And so it would itty on to like the end of the world, round and round and round."

But Alex isn't Penrod. Beatings, blindings, rapes, murders are not adolescent awkwardnesses to be grown out of. Surely there is something here akin to what Stephen Spender calls the fallacy of "false symmetries," such as implying McCarthy was as bad as Stalin. There is some sort of cheat involved in making the reader suffer all those painful pages of terrible violence, only to have the perpetrators put away their chains and knives and knuckles as childish things, and live as solid citizens ever after. So false a note is struck by this ending that the whole book in retrospect seems false—a clockwork orange put together with mild ingenuity but to no purpose and with no real vitamins.

ROBERT GORHAM DAVIS
Review†

* * *

Very relevant is the English novel, *A Clockwork Orange*, experimental in a double sense. The teen-age narrator Alex is a murderous Holden Caulfield, ingenious and witty in a horrid way, who lives in a controlled, badly controlled, society of the very near future. Alex and his pals and most of the young people around him are totally alienated. They devote themselves to sex, violence, drugs and—significantly—music of all kinds, Beethoven as well as rock-and-roll. Nearly every night, like the rather more aristocratic Mohawks in eighteenth century London, they go out stealing, raping, smashing up homes and shops, just for the sport of it, and fighting other gangs with knives and chains.

---

† "The Perilous Balance," review of William Burroughs, *The Ticket that Exploded*; Anthony Burgess, *A Clockwork Orange*; Leslie Fiedler, *The Second Stone*; Cecil Hemley, *Young Crankshaw*; John Bowen, *The Birdcage*; J. D. Salinger, *Raise High the Roofbeam, Carpenters* and *Seymour*; Ruth Prawer Jhabvala, *Ready for Battle*; and Raja Rao, *The Serpent and the Rope*. *Hudson Review* 16.2 (Summer 1963), 280–89 (283–84; 289). Reprinted by permission.

All this is described in detail and with relish. The author, Anthony Burgess, maintains distance by using a strange argot, partly slang but mostly made of what seem to be Russian words, "tashtook," "ptitsas," "litsos," "britva," "devotchka," "slovos," "goloss." There are two or three to a sentence often, and the reader has gradually to learn them from context. Russian words are chosen because Russia suggests a brutal statism. The novelty of the terms and the slight effort required to find and remember their meanings keeps from being too monotonously gory the chronicle of meaningless brutalities boastfully described by their perpetrator.

Alex is finally sent to prison for the murder of an old lady. Clever and eager for release, he gets himself chosen as the first subject of a new experiment in treating delinquents. He is given an improved form of the drug used to cure alcohol and tobacco addiction. While this drug is sickeningly at work throughout his body, Alex, with eyes propped open, is forced to watch Nazi horror films. At last he is so thoroughly conditioned that seeing or reading about or even thinking of violence makes him sick. It is the calculated reversal of those situations in art and life in which cruelty or particular perversions get reinforced because doing them or having them described by others is associated with immediate pleasure. What makes Alex indignant—and his capacity for indignation is one of his most convincing qualities—is the fact that Beethoven is used during the experiment by an insensitive psychologist who thinks of music simply "as a useful emotion-heightener."

As a result, Alex is tossed back defenseless into the world, without even the solace of music. In a series of coincidental meetings that make the novel pure parable, he encounters former associates and victims who, one and all, to an extent which is a libel on humanity, seize upon his helplessness as a chance to get back at him. This makes Alex even more righteously indignant, an indignation which the author shares. Using Sartre's argument in *Saint Genet, Comédien et Martyr*, he turns Alex into an articulate apostle of existential or even Christian freedom. The state committed a far worse crime than anything which Alex had done, when it took away his interior freedom to be himself. The state is afraid of selves that can freely choose. It doesn't matter that they may choose evil. In earlier novels from *Great Expectations* to *An American Tragedy*, social conditions or false social values were made responsible for forcing the individual into crime. Society should be in the dock, we were told, instead of the accused. But *A Clockwork Orange* insists, not very convincingly, that Alex chooses evil freely because he enjoys it. This choice must be respected, even if the destructions and rapes and maimings totally violate the practical, if not metaphysical, freedom of other people. By a perverse logic, images of violence are put at the service of a dreadful, dead-end concept of freedom. At the conclusion of the novel, Alex, for complicated political reasons, has been deconditioned and lies in bed, a junior Caligula, listening to the scherzo of Beethoven's Ninth Symphony and imagining himself cutting up the bloody face of the whole world with his "britva."

*　*　*

Many writers now want an end to compromise. To them most works of art seem, as dreams were to Freud, compromise formations. For them society, any society, is something outside the individual, imposed upon him, unimaginable as an act of choice. They want to strike through the mask, to rewrite past literature in terms of an unmasked reality. But this reality is, as Raja Rao would say, an illusion, the impossible product of human beings trying to shock humanity. The stories of Poe would collapse completely if they were reduced to the primalities that Marie Bonaparte quite correctly sees buried in them. Even the infantile family romance would have to disappear, because it is a social relation. All that could remain would be bodies in various positions, bodies without sharable minds or imaginations. In this final physical solipsism, the individual is totally free. But such isolation is actually intolerable. So inescapable is the need for society, for sharing, for a response from others, that if only bodies are left, then those bodies must be entered by every conceivable means, as Burroughs so endlessly fantasies; or, since they cannot answer in any other way, cut up with *A Clockwork Orange*'s britvas to make them scream.

ANDREW BISWELL

[Composition]†

As Burgess and Lynne sailed back to London, he was already making notes towards *Honey for the Bears*, and contemplating the hard task of finishing *A Clockwork Orange*. The ending of the novel was an area of particular difficulty. He was still revising and reworking it more than thirty years later. Critics agree that the ending represents a large area of contention. Briefly stated, the problem is that the earliest published editions, the UK Heinemann edition of 1962 and the US Norton edition of 1963, have different endings. Subsequent paperback editions compound the problem: depending on their place of publication, they follow either the Heinemann text (twenty-one chapters) or the Norton text (twenty chapters).

Although Burgess believed that the presence or absence of this twenty-first chapter made a significant difference to the meaning of

† From *The Real Life of Anthony Burgess* (London: Picador, 2005), 246–58. Copyright © Andrew Biswell 2005. Reprinted by permission of the author.

the novel, it is evident from his writings on the subject that he held different opinions at different times as to which ending was 'correct'. The difference in emphasis between the two versions is best explained with reference to the theological contention that underpins so much of Burgess's thinking: between Augustinianism and Pelagianism, as first expressed in *A Vision of Battlements*.

The Norton text of *A Clockwork Orange* ends at part three, chapter 6 (the twentieth chapter) and shows us Alex recovering in hospital from his suicide attempt, now apparently unbrainwashed or deprogrammed. He is given a series of psychological tests, and his responses are evidently those of an unconditioned thug. Towards the end of this chapter, he proposes to return to his former ultraviolent ways: 'I could viddy myself very clear running and running on like very light and mysterious nogas, carving the whole litso of the creeching world with my cut-throat britva [. . .] I was cured all right.' He has been restored to the unrepentant criminal Alex whom we encounter at the beginning of the novel. There is an artful and uncompromising circularity about this ending, and an emphatic rejection of the notion that novels should concern themselves with the moral progress of their protagonists. By emphasizing the unreformed sinfulness of Alex, the twentieth chapter reveals itself to be an Augustinian conclusion. Alex has been 'cured', but not saved.

The Heinemann text ends at part three, chapter 7 (the twenty-first chapter), and admits the possibility of regeneration. Alex, who has recovered from the Ludovico conditioning, returns to the streets and forms another gang of droogs—Len, Rick and Bully. The opening paragraph refers us back to the novel's opening page by repeating the sentence 'We were sitting in the Korova Milkbar making up our rassoodocks what to do with the evening, a flip dark chill winter bastard, though dry.' But the echo is not sustained, and there are indications that Alex, now aged eighteen ('not a young age'), is maturing. He is now listening to lieder as well as symphonic music, 'just a goloss and a piano, very quiet and like yearny', and we learn that he has begun to think about mortality:

> I got a sudden like picture of me sitting before a bolshy fire in an armchair peeting away at this chai, and what was very funny and very very strange was that I seemed to have turned into a very starry chelloveck, about seventy years old.

Deciding not to take part in a proposed evening of ultra-violence, he goes alone to a café where he meets Pete, one of his former droogs, who is now married and has settled down to a life of 'harmless' bourgeois domesticity, 'little parties, [. . .] wine-cup and word-games'. Alex begins to think in terms of finding a wife and having a child. As he contemplates a future that is likely to involve fatherhood, his narrative ends with a clearly stated farewell to teenage outrages:

> Yes yes yes, there it was. Youth must go, ah yes. But youth is only being in a way like it might be an animal. No, it is not like being an animal so much as being like one of those malenky toys you viddy being sold in the streets, like little chellovecks made of tin and with a spring inside and then a winding handle on the outside and you wind it up grrr grrr grrr and off it itties, like walking, O my brothers. But it itties in a straight line and bangs straight into things bang bang and it cannot help what it is doing. Being young is like being like one of these malenky machines.

This turning away from ultra-violence may be interpreted as Pelagian, in the sense that Alex acknowledges his potential for goodness autonomously, without the direct intervention of divine grace. At no point does he express remorse for his former wickedness, yet the position he articulates here is a willed and reasoned turning away from his former criminality. For this reason, the twenty-first chapter is a Pelagian conclusion. These theological resonances are everywhere present, though nowhere stated, in the novel's two possible endings.

The margins of the typescript record one half of a long conversation between Burgess and his editor at Heinemann, James Michie. The overwhelming majority of the marginal comments relate to Burgess's hesitations about Nadsat. He writes next to certain words 'Don't like this' (with reference to the verb 'filly' on page 207) or 'Don't like this much' (referring to 'lubbilubbing' on page 211). He seems to have marked up the first seven chapters of the typescript for his editor, indicating areas of uncertainty and possible revision. There are fewer alterations after Alex's incarceration at the end of part one. According to James Michie, Burgess sent the first section of the book to Heinemann and proceeded with the rest of the book after receiving editorial advice.[1]

A few examples from the typescript illustrate how the novel took shape over the course of the four months when Burgess was composing and revising it, between April and August 1961. In the margin of page twenty, next to the word 'zheena' (meaning 'wife'), Burgess asks whether there might be a 'better word'. Later he circles the word 'droog' and writes in the margin, 'Should [it] be drook?' He writes that he is 'Not too happy' about the word 'drencrom', which is

---

1. James Michie to author, 15 November 2000. Michie states: 'The only thing I remember is giving some advice about the rate at which the reader is expected to learn the new language. I was saying, "Make it gently *accelerando*. You can't throw too much of it at them too quickly because otherwise the dumber ones among them will think this is too difficult." I think that's one of the great successes of the book: you can read it and you learn a new vocabulary without pain.'

one of the drugs sold with the old moloko plus at the Korova Milk-bar. Elsewhere he alters 'smeeking' (meaning 'laughing') to 'smeck-ing'. These hesitations and revisions suggest that Nadsat, rather than being an argot that was carefully planned out in advance, acquired its real shape as the novel was being written and revised. Burgess also frequently uses the left-hand margin to provide Cyrillic trans-literations of Nadsat words. The general tendency of these revi-sions seems to be towards a thickening or enriching of Nadsat at the expense of Standard English. When Alex is about to seduce the two ptitsas from the disc-bootick, Burgess alters the line, 'Aha, I know what you want, I think', to rakish mock-Elizabethan: 'Aha, I know what thou wantest, I thinkest'. A Clockwork Orange reveals itself to be a text which became steadily more complex, from a lin-guistic point of view, during the process of revision. Indicating one possible cut ('Now they would take sleep-pills. Perhaps, knowing the joy I had in my night music, they had already taken them'), Burgess writes in the margin that these words are 'Too ordinary'.

One comment on the typescript raises a point about cultural his-tory. When Alex and his gang put on their 'maskies' or disguises, one of the masks shows the face of Elvis Presley. Next to the words 'Elvis Presley', Burgess writes, 'Will this name be known when [the] book appears?' Burgess worried that Elvis was a passing fashion, unlike the upmarket literary writers whose names became street-names in the novel: 'Amis Avenue', 'Priestley Place', 'Marghanita Boulevard'. The typescript also contains four bars of music, which accompany the prisoners' hymn ('Weak tea are we new brewed / But stirring make all strong. / We eat no angel's food, / Our times of trial are long') in part two, chapter 1. Burgess's music is in the key of G minor, and it is approximately in the style of one of J. S. Bach's Chorales. The likely reason for the absence of music in the Heinemann edition is that the printing cost of inserting these four bars would have been prohibitive. The 1962 edition was published a couple of years before cheap offset lithography became widely available.

The other significant feature of the typescript is the presence of illustrations. Burgess provides a series of seven line-drawings, very similar in style to his character sketches for The Eve of Saint Venus.[2] One of the 'millicents' or policemen who arrests Alex is depicted as an ill-shaven, ape-like thug, and throughout the text we find other images of exploding clockwork oranges, disgorging their cogs. The most inter-esting drawing is the one which shows our friend and narrator Alex. Burgess sketches him dressed in what he would call 'the heighth of fashion', with a dangling quiff of hair, large padded shoulders and

---

2. The Eve of Saint Venus sketches are in a notebook in the archive of the Anthony Bur-gess Center at the University of Angers.

an extravagant cravat. These pictures are slapdash pen-and-ink affairs drawn at high speed: it may be that Burgess was at one time thinking of *A Clockwork Orange* as an illustrated novel; it is also possible that the drawings were included merely for the sake of whimsical decoration, perhaps as a private joke between the author and his editor.

Finally, the most revealing annotation on the typescript is a handwritten query referring to the disputed twenty-first chapter. At the end of part three, chapter 6, there is a note in Burgess's hand: 'Should we end here? An optional "epilogue" follows.' The implication of this question is that Burgess genuinely did not know how the novel should conclude when it left his typewriter in August 1961; and it is obvious from the published texts that his editors, James Michie at Heinemann and Eric Swenson at Norton, arrived at very different answers.

*   *   *

The account of the novel's history that Burgess gave to Cullinan was repeated in a letter to the editor of the *Times Literary Supplement*, published on 11 January 1980.[3] * * * According to this letter, the dropping of the twenty-first chapter, to which the author 'weakly agreed', was a pre-condition of publication in the United States. Burgess fails to mention that he already had doubts about it himself. On reading Burgess's letter, the Vice Chairman and Executive Editor at Norton, Eric Swenson, disagreed with the statements it contained about the editorial process, and he wrote a letter of his own to the *TLS*:

> Anthony Burgess's letter to you of January 11 has come to my attention. I am the editor of the American edition of CLOCK-WORK ORANGE to which he refers. His claim that we refused to publish unless the last (up-beat) chapter of the published, British edition were dropped is hereby denied. We did tell him that the Polyanna ending left us unconvinced; he replied that he agreed, that he had added it only to mollify his *British* publisher, and that he would be pleased if we dropped it. As I have written him, we seem to have diametrically opposed memories of the matter. I, however, claim to have supporting documents and witnesses.[4]

Burgess sold the annotated typescript of *A Clockwork Orange* to McMaster University in Ontario in 1967. By the time he recorded his conversation with Cullinan in 1972, he was no longer able to refer to the marginal notes he had made during the process of

---

3. See p. 164 of this Norton Critical Edition. [*Editor's note.*]
4. Eric Swenson, letter to the editor, *Times Literary Supplement*, 20 February 1980 (Norton archive).

composition. Like much of Burgess's journalistic and autobiograph-
ical writing, this interview shows an author who is at some level
engaged in creatively reimagining the history of his own work.

Burgess's most detailed statement on the editing of the American
Clockwork Orange is in 'A Clockwork Orange Resucked', his introduction to the revised 1987 Norton edition.[5] * * * This implies,
contrary to Swenson's account, that there was no discussion between
author and editor of which ending was more satisfactory from a
moral or aesthetic point of view. * * * The particular criticism he
makes in the preface is that the novel's sermon on free will is spelt
out too plainly by the prison chaplain, rather than being implied or
dramatized in a less direct way.

Eric Swenson, once again dismayed by the imputation that he had
acted in a draconian fashion when editing the novel, wrote a short
essay in reply to Burgess, which he proposed to include, along with
Burgess's introduction, in the 1987 Norton edition. This unpublished document gives a valuable second perspective on the editorial
process:

> What I remember is that he responded to my comments by tell-
> ing me that I was right, that he had added the twenty-first,
> upbeat chapter because his British publisher wanted a happy
> ending. My memory also claims that he urged me to publish an
> American edition without that last chapter, which was, again
> as I remember it, how he had originally ended the novel. We
> did just that. It may or may not prove anything that the trun-
> cated American edition has been far more successful than the
> British version. Be that as it may, the dropping of chapter
> twenty-one was never a condition of publication.[6]

A letter of 7 July 1986 from Swenson to Burgess explains the
circumstances in which Swenson's essay was suppressed:

> I gather [. . .] that you do not want my contribution to the
> debate in the new edition of CLOCKWORK ORANGE—which I
> understand and more than half expected. My only wistful wish
> is that somewhere in your Introduction you might introduce
> the thought that your publisher has a different memory of
> events [. . .] One of the principles of my editorial life is that
> the author is indeed the author [. . .] We would never have
> excised the last chapter over your objections.[7]

In the light of these documents from the Norton archive, it seems
likely that Burgess's memory of events is at fault. But the original

---

5. See p. 165 of this Norton Critical Edition. [*Editor's note.*]
6. Eric Swenson, 'A *Clockwork Orange*, Rewound'. Unpublished typescript.
7. Eric Swenson, letter to Burgess, 7 July 1986 (Norton archive).

exchange of letters between Burgess and Swenson from the early 1960s, which would settle the issue decisively, is missing from the files.

Burgess has a good deal to say about the composition of *A Clockwork Orange* in his private letters. The earliest references to the novel occur in a series of twenty-seven letters and postcards that he sent to his friends Diana and Meir Gillon between April 1961 and February 1962. He began his correspondence with the Gillons after he had reviewed their collaboratively written novel, *The Unsleep*, for the *Yorkshire Post*.[8] These letters provide a detailed account of his anxieties and hesitations about the novel while he was in the process of composing it. In the first surviving letter, written in April 1961, Burgess writes:

> I'm in the early stages of a novel about juvenile delinquents in the future (I'm fabricating with difficulty a teenage dialect compounded equally of American and Russian roots). There's a lot, I think, to be done in this field.[9]

The futuristic element noted here is clearly visible in the novel. The references to satellite television 'worldcasts' and to 1960 as a distant historical date are two indications that the events of the book take place at some point late in the twentieth century or early in the twenty-first. However, while his Nadsat language was originally planned as a fusion of Russian and American (rather than British) English, the American element seems to have been dropped at some point before he completed the 1961 typescript, which shows little evidence of Americanisms.[1] The one exception is Alex's American-sounding use of 'like' as a syntactical filler, as in 'We had four of these lomticks of like Prison Religion this morning.'

Other letters from the Gillon correspondence reveal Burgess's uncertainty about how readers of the novel will respond to Nadsat, and he voices a particular anxiety (both in the letters and in the margins of the typescript) about the difficulty of his invented argot from the reader's point of view. He quotes a sample passage from the novel-in-progress for the attention of the Gillons' son, who was learning Russian in 1961:

> To revert to this question of inventing a slang to be used by juvenile delinquents in the future. I wonder if your son could make anything of this? (From my tentatively titled *A Clockwork Orange*)—'. . . He was creeching out loud and waving his

---

8. See Burgess, 'Another Brave New World', *Yorkshire Post*, 6 April 1961, 4.
9. Burgess, letter to Diana and Meir Gillon. Quoted in *Books, Maps, Photographs and Manuscripts*, Phillips auction catalogue, 104.
1. Later, in the 1987 Norton introduction, Burgess refers to Nadsat as 'a Russified version of English'.

rookers and making real horrorshow with the slovos, only the
odd blurp blurp coming from his keeshkas, like some very rude
sort of interrupting sort of a moodge making a shoom . . .' I
also have malchicks smecking away and lewdies getting razdraz
and dratsing with nozhes and britvas and a length of the old
oozy from round the tally. I wonder if this sort of thing will
work. One can read the reviews before one's started writing,
but it doesn't help, does it? One does what one has to do.[2]

A *Clockwork Orange* is unique among Burgess's works in that he
sought editorial advice, both from his editor at Heinemann and from
the Gillons, while the book was underway. None of his other type-
scripts are marked up with possible cuts to a comparable extent. Nor
are there any letters relating to other novels which speak of similar
doubts as to whether 'this sort of thing will work'.

In a later letter, it is the novel's violence that concerns him. Burgess writes that he has been 'pushing on desperately' with *A Clockwork Orange*, 'which nears its climax and quick denouement', but
adds that 'because of its language and boring violence people may
hate it (violence is meant to be boring, but some critics won't see
that)'. The tone of anxious pessimism comes through again as he
approaches the novel's conclusion:

> I just plod on and this week hope to bring *A Clockwork Orange*
> to its bitter end—about 70,000 words only or even less; I don't
> think readers will be able to take all that much of it. I'm not at
> all satisfied, but I obviously can't scrap it now.

*   *   *

PHILIP E. RAY

[Structure and Human Growth]†

Most interpreters of Anthony Burgess' *A Clockwork Orange* have
tended to follow the lead of such early commentators as Bernard
Bergonzi, A. A. DeVitis, Carol M. Dix, and Robert K. Morris in
defining the theme of the novel as the conflict between the natural
and untainted Individual and the artificial and corrupt State. Bergonzi's observation that "in its emphasis on the nature of human
freedom in a totalitarian society the book has philosophical as well

---

2. Burgess, letter to Diana and Meir Gillon. Quoted in *Books, Maps, Photographs and
Manuscripts*, 105.
† From "Alex Before and After: A New Approach to Burgess' *A Clockwork Orange*," *Mod-
ern Fiction Studies* 27.3 (Autumn 1981), 479–87. Reprinted by permission.

as literary importance"[1] is typical of the thinking that shaped the framework in which subsequent critical discussion has taken place. And this tendency has recently achieved a fitting culmination in the account of the novel that Burgess himself has published, an account which concludes with this dictum: "we may not be able to trust man—meaning ourselves—very far, but we must trust the State far less."[2]

This essay attempts to present a different approach to both the content and the form of *A Clockwork Orange*, an approach which complements rather than contradicts the other. This essay will, however, focus on the relations of Alex, Burgess' hero and narrator, with characters frequently neglected or overlooked by the critics: the owner of the cottage named "HOME" (16; his wife; and the unnamed and unborn male child whom Alex mentions only in the final chapter. In other words, characters who are the willing or unwilling agents of the State—for example, the prison chaplain, the prison governor, Dr. Brodsky, the Minister of the Interior—will receive less attention than they sometimes do. The specific thesis that this essay will argue for is twofold: that Burgess has the owner of HOME represent the person Alex will become, his future self, and the boy who does not yet exist represent the person he has already been, his past self, in order to express the view that human growth is inevitable; and that the tripartite structure of the novel directly mirrors this chronological sequence of Alex's identities.

The three parts of *A Clockwork Orange* are of equal length, each having seven chapters, but they otherwise fall into an ABA pattern.[3] Parts One and Three are set in the city streets and country lanes of a future England so paralyzed by violent crime that it has surrendered them to the very teenagers who commit the crimes. Part Two is set in a prison—"Staja (State Jail, that is) Number 84F" (51—where the government is attempting to regain the upper hand by checking within the mind of the particular criminal the impulse toward violence. Alex, who has his own gang despite his mere fifteen years, is sent to jail for murder at the close of Part One; in Part Two he successfully undergoes the State's experimental Reclamation Treatment only to reenter, in Part Three, a world that is unchanged. Thus Burgess has Alex's adventures in Part Three—especially his return to his parents' flat, his encounters with "the crystal veck" and with Dim

1. Bernard Bergonzi, *The Situation of the Novel* (Pittsburgh, PA: U of Pittsburgh P, 1970), 185.
2. *1985* (Boston: Little, Brown, 1978), 96.
3. To some readers, ABA may seem to be an abbreviation for "Anthony Burgess Author." Others, who are more familiar with Burgess' rapidly increasing canon, will recall the fact that the title of his 1977 novel *ABBA ABBA* refers to the rhyme scheme of the octave of the Petrarchan sonnet. But, as I will attempt to demonstrate below, the primary significance lies elsewhere.

and Billyboy, and his visit to the cottage named HOME—duplicate or parallel those in Part One with this significant difference: whereas he earlier victimized others in committing robbery, burglary, assault, rape, and even murder, he himself is now the victim. With his natural instincts and drives artificially blocked, Alex is the "clockwork orange" of the title. One part of the moral that Burgess wishes the reader to draw here is that, in attempting to transform the violent tough into the peaceful citizen, the State has succeeded in rendering Alex incapable of self-defense.

The other part of the moral is that the State has also rendered Alex incapable of enjoying the music of his adored "Ludwig van." * * * But consider for a moment the notion that in figurative terms music is "celestial bliss" and Alex an angel. If this is so, then it is certainly logical to regard all of his utterances, the entire narrative related by him to the reader, as musical: if Alex is, in some sense, an angel, his story is, in that same sense, a song. And the question of what sort of song redirects our discussion to the matter of the novel's structure, for the ABA pattern in music is universally recognized as the distinguishing characteristic of the *da capo aria* in eighteenth-century Italian opera, a kind of aria which "consists of two sections followed by a repetition of the first, resulting in a tripartite structure ABA."[4] And it is perhaps no accident, then, that at one point in the story Alex listens with powerful emotion to what Burgess makes quite clear is an operatic aria (21). One wishes that Burgess had provided more information about his imaginary composer of operas: when he lived, what kinds of operas he wrote, and so on. But he does provide enough so that certain parallels can be drawn later between Alex and the wretched heroine whose aria he now hears.

To return to the actual workings of the ABA pattern in the novel. Burgess reinforces the reader's sense of the pattern by opening each of the three parts with the question "'What's it going to be then, eh?'" (3, 51, 85) and by having Alex ask it in Parts One and Three and the prison chaplain ask it in Part Two. Thus, in the A Parts Alex is free to pose the question for himself, whereas in Part B someone else, significantly an employee of the State, must pose it for him. Similarly, the hero's name, which (as one would expect) remains constant in Parts One and Three, is replaced by a prison identification number in Part Two: "6655321". In the A Parts Alex can call himself by whatever name he chooses (it is surely important that he never once uses his surname); in Part B he is called by a number, not even a name, chosen by the State. As Alex describes the change, "I was 6655321 and not your little droog Alex not no longer" (51).

Alex's name is significant in another, even more essential way because it provides the chief clue to the thematic function of the owner of the cottage called HOME. When in Part One Alex and his "droogs" break into the cottage, they not only vandalize it but also beat the owner and rape his wife, who later dies as a result. When in Part Three Alex returns, he does so alone and, having just been beaten himself, stands utterly defenseless before the man he has wronged. The latter fails, however, to recognize Alex (primarily because he was wearing a mask on the night of the break-in) and provides him with aid and shelter instead of punishment or revenge. The owner of HOME even manages, in thinking aloud about his dead wife, to identify Alex with her when he says to Alex, "'Poor poor boy, you must have had a terrible time. A victim of the modern age, just as she was. Poor poor poor girl'" (101). Alex, of course, does recognize the owner and, wishing to learn his name, searches for a copy of the book that he was writing, and that Alex read from, on that fateful night:

> It struck me that I ought to get to know the name of this kind protecting and like motherly veck, so I had a pad round in my nagoy nogas looking for *A Clockwork Orange*, which would be bound to have his eemya in, he being the author. . . . on the back of the book, like on the spine, was the author's eemya— F. Alexander. Good Bog, I thought, He is another Alex. (101)

Having just been let out of prison, Alex has now ceased to be 6655321. He finds, however, that not only is he Alex again (with the addition of the "clockwork") but that someone else is Alex, too. He has somehow managed to encounter a second version of himself.

What, then, do Alex and F. Alexander have in common besides their names? Both, oddly enough, are authors of books entitled *A Clockwork Orange*. (Burgess keeps the reader aware of Alex's authorial role by having him frequently address his audience by means of the curious formula "O my brothers" and refer to himself as "Your Humble Narrator.") One important difference between the two authors is, of course, that, while F. Alexander is writing his book on the night of Alex's first visit to HOME and has a bound copy of it on his shelves during the second visit, Alex has not yet begun to write his. In the reader's eternal present, Alex is writing it now. But, precisely because he has already done what Alex will someday do, F. Alexander is being defined here as a future version of Alex's self.

At this point in the story, the second visit to HOME, Burgess hints at the theme of the inevitability of human growth, to which he returns in the final chapter. There he sounds it loudly by having Alex answer the oft-repeated question "'What's it going to be then, eh?'" with the idea of getting married and having a son. As Alex himself puts it, "there was this veshch of finding some devotchka or other who would be a mother to this son. . . . That's what it's going to be then, brothers, as I come to the like end of this tale" (121). Once he has found and wed his "devotchka," Alex will, of course, have come to resemble F. Alexander in his role as a married man. But here it is not yet apparent whether growth, which will be inevitable for everyone else, will be so for him. Having "clockwork" in his heart and brain may mean that Alex will be the same forever.

There is, however, one other obstacle in the way of Alex's growing up to possess a future, and that obstacle is, ironically enough, F. Alexander himself. When he learns that Alex is one of those responsible for the death of his wife, he tries to force Alex to commit suicide. The attempt fails when Alex, having thrown himself out of an upper-story window, receives medical care that not only saves his life but also reverses the effects of the Reclamation Treatment. Thus Burgess underscores his irony by having F. Alexander insure that Alex will possess a future through the former's effort to deny the latter a present. Trying to murder Alex has the indirect result of bringing him back to human life, for F. Alexander manages to kill only the "clockwork" inside his head.

F. Alexander is clearly, in some sense, a father to Alex, albeit a murderous one. Before the attempt on his life, Alex sees F. Alexander as treating him in a parental manner, although he gets the gender wrong: he calls his host and comforter "this kind protecting and like motherly veck" (101). And perhaps, when he discovered the name on the back of the book, he ought to have considered the first initial as carefully as the surname. If, as seems almost certain, it stands for "Father," then Burgess has arranged this reunion as one between Son Alex and Father Alexander.

There is further evidence for this view of F. Alexander in the facts that he is the owner of HOME (that significantly named dwelling) to which Alex as a latter-day Prodigal Son returns and is not punished but rather welcomed and feasted; that, unlike Alex's actual father (whom Alex would never think of striking and to whom he always refers contemptuously as "pee"), F. Alexander arouses powerful feelings in Alex; and that he is married to the most important woman in the story and in Alex's life so far. Burgess follows here the Freudian model of family relations by placing the father and the son in competition for the mother and by having the son's path to manhood lead directly through the father's defeat or death. Alex the son succeeds not only in possessing the mother but also in taking her away from the father, an event which intensifies the latter's natural desire to triumph over his rival into a rage for murder and revenge. But, of course, that act of violence brings about the more rapid displacement of the father by the son when

Alex finds that his suicidal leap has resulted in the removal of the "clockwork" and in no permanent injury to himself.

The actual fate of F. Alexander, Burgess leaves obscure until Alex's conversation with the Minister of the Interior in the novel's penultimate chapter. Visiting Alex in the hospital to assure him that all is now well and to exploit the favorable political publicity, the Minister informs him that

> "There is a man . . . called F. Alexander, a writer of subversive literature, who has been howling for your blood. He has been mad with desire to stick a knife in you. But you're safe from him now. We put him away." (113)

The State now regards F. Alexander as it once regarded Alex. Certain phrases used by the Minister—"howling for your blood," "mad with desire"—would appear to be more appropriate if applied to a person both more animallike and more physically violent than F. Alexander. But, in any case, he has been declared "a menace" (113) just as though he were roaming the streets at night with a band of "droogs." Therefore F. Alexander gets, at the end of Part Three, precisely what Alex got at the end of Part One: imprisonment in a State Jail. This fate also makes sense, because he is Alex's double as well as his symbolic or mythic father: thus the career of F. Alexander not only anticipates but also repeats the career of Alex.

But this relationship also contributes to the working out of the ABA structure. In the first A section Alex is simply Alex; in the B section he becomes both 6655321 and the "clockwork" man; and in the second A section he resumes his public identity as Alex but is not truly or fully Alex because he still has the "clockwork" within him. When, however, he meets again the owner of HOME, he encounters a father figure, an older and wiser Alex, a future version of the self, who unwittingly assists him in the task of removing the "clockwork" and becoming himself once more. The ill effects of his prison stay cannot, in other words, be overcome until our hero wrestles with and defeats his own image invested with Age and Authority, until the son replaces the father. What could provide a more striking illustration of the process of human growth?

If the vision of his future granted him in the final chapter holds true, Alex will accomplish something in life that F. Alexander did not: the begetting and raising of a son. He describes his prophetic moment in the following passage:

> I kept viddying like visions, like these cartoons in the gazettas. There was Your Humble Narrator Alex coming home from work to a good hot plate of dinner, and there was this ptitsa all welcoming and greeting like loving. . . . I had this sudden very strong idea that if I walked into the room next to this room

> where the fire was burning away and my hot dinner laid on the
> table, there I should find what I really wanted. . . . For in that
> other room in a cot was laying gurgling goo goo goo my son.
> Yes yes yes, brothers, my son. (120)

The place Alex describes is obviously an idealized version of home,
which means that he has just paid, although in "vision," his third and
final visit to HOME. The fire and the dinner are the comforts that Alex
destroyed on his first visit but will soon require for himself; the "ptitsa
all welcoming and greeting like loving" is the mother transformed
into a wife who will in no way resist his advances; and the father, who
earlier attempted to block his path, is now absent. To complete the
circle, however, there is the baby boy, who, like F. Alexander, will be
"another Alex" and bear Alex's other name, whatever that may be.
This son will be F. Alexander's opposite in that he will represent
Alex's past, whereas F. Alexander represented Alex's future. Alex perceives this even now, as he concedes in advance that he will be unable
to prevent his son from making the very same mistakes that he made:

> My son, my son. When I had my son I would explain all that to
> him when he was starry enough to like understand. But then
> I knew he would not understand or would not want to under-
> stand at all and would do all the veshches I had done . . . and
> I would not be able to really stop him. (121)

Knowing the "veshches" or things his son will do, Alex also knows
that he will be unable to prevent him from doing them, both the
good and the evil. As his son grows up, Alex will behold his past
being repeated, just as F. Alexander beheld his. Everything human
is inevitable, Burgess seems to say, both the good and the evil.

But Alex's tale is still a story of liberation: he has escaped from
not only the literal prison of Staja 84F but also the figurative prisons of adolescent boyhood and "clockwork" humanity. And the
reader who recalls that "music is a figure of celestial bliss" will want
to translate "liberation" as "salvation." But it is the individual capable of growth—the "'creature of growth and capable of sweetness'"
(17), as F. Alexander puts it in his typescript—that has been liberated or saved, not the group, the tribe, or the species. When he is
born, Alex's son will not be free or blissful. He will be doomed,
rather, to live through the error of his father's ways. Here, then, is
that final flowering of the logic of the novel's structure: after A, B;
after B, A again. After the freedom of the mature Alex, the imprisonment of his son. Could Alex somehow liberate his son, the structure of A Clockwork Orange would surely have to be ABC, which
would signify progress without repetition.

The da capo aria itself, if the reader chooses to think of either
Alex or the heroine of Das Bettzeug as performing this sort of aria,

represents the same lack of freedom: having sung A and B, the performer must sing A again. And it is precisely here that the meaning of this imaginary opera comes into clear focus. The surname of the composer, "Gitterfenster" (21), is a German word best translated as "barred window," that is, the window of a prison. The heroine has sought presumably to escape this prison, whether literal or figurative, but, realizing that she can succeed only through suicide, has now taken that step: hence Alex's description, "it was the bit where she's snuffing it with her throat cut, and the slovos are 'Better like this maybe'" (21). She is, therefore, in the very same situation as Alex when F. Alexander's friends leave him in their locked flat with the music turned on: "I viddied what I had to do . . . and that was to do myself in, to snuff it" (107). The window in this prison is not barred, however, because F. Alexander and his friends want Alex to jump: "the window in the room where I laid down was open" (107). And they have even left behind a helpful hint in the form of a "malenky booklet which had an open window on the cover," proclaiming: "'Open the window to fresh air, fresh ideas, a new way of living'" (107). So Alex, saying in effect what the heroine said, goes to the window and jumps. And he succeeds, just as she may have, in achieving personal liberation—not through death, but rather through the return to life, or, to put the matter somewhat more accurately, by the return to normal life after the nonhuman existence of a "clockwork" man, which is merely another formulation of the sequence "freedom"-"imprisonment"-"freedom"; that is, ABA.

RUBIN RABINOVITZ

[Dualism, Not Progress][†]

In his most famous novel, *A Clockwork Orange*, Anthony Burgess explores a number of interesting issues such as free will, the meaning of violence, and a cyclical theory of history. Resolving these issues, however, is complicated by an extraneous factor: the American editions of the novel lack Burgess' original conclusion and end with what is the penultimate chapter of the first English edition.

*   *   *

If Alex remains violent, as he does in the American version, the reader's attitude towards him is mainly one of condemnation; but Burgess' inquiry into the origins of violence requires a hero who

† From "Mechanism vs. Organism: Anthony Burgess' *A Clockwork Orange*," *Modern Fiction Studies* 24.4 (Winter 1978–79), 538–41. Reprinted by permission.

cannot be so easily condemned and dismissed. The original version
in a sense provides the less sentimental ending if Alex is transformed from a monster into an ordinary human being with whom
the reader can identify. Obdurate Alex is a threat to safety; Alex
reformed threatens moral complacency, by suggesting that a love of
violence is universal.

Regardless of which ending one prefers, Burgess wrote his novel
assuming that it would appear intact, and it deserves to be considered in the complete version. As it turns out, many of his ideas are
clarified when the last chapter is restored. An example is Burgess'
treatment of the theme of freedom and determinism. Burgess
appears in *A Clockwork Orange* to disapprove of the Ludovico technique (a scientific process for forcing criminals to reform); the loss of
free will seems to be too great a price to pay. But if this is true, and if
Burgess shares the point of view of the Chaplain and F. Alexander
who oppose the Ludovico technique for similar reasons, it is unclear
why Burgess portrays these characters in a sardonic fashion.

The novel's final statement about free will comes in the deleted
chapter, when Alex says that in his youth he had not been free but
determined. In his violent phase, he says, he had been

> like one of these malenky toys you viddy being sold in the
> streets, like little chellovecks made out of tin and with a spring
> inside and then a winding handle on the outside and you wind
> it up grrr grrr grrr and off it itties, like walking, O my brothers.
> But it itties in a straight line and bangs straight into things
> bang bang and it cannot help what it is doing. Being young is
> like being like one of these malenky machines.

The young are like clockwork men; their proclivity towards violence
is built into them. His son, Alex says, will also go through a violent
phase, and Alex "would not be able to really stop him. And nor would
he be able to stop his own son, brothers."

Alex concludes that there is a cycle of recurring phases in which
each young man undergoes a period of existence as a violent, mechanical man; then he matures, gets greater freedom of choice, and his
violence subsides. The cycle, says Alex, will go on forever: "and so
it would itty on to like the end of the world, round and round and
round. . . ." The circularity of the repeating pattern leads Alex to
compare the progress of generations to an image of God turning a
dirty, smelly orange in his hands, "old Bog Himself (by courtesy of
Korova Milkbar) turning and turning and turning a vonny grahzny
orange in his gigantic rookers." The determined progress of the
clockwork man, who must move in a straight line, is thus contrasted
with the circular shape and movement of God's orange, symbol of
life and organic growth. The "vonny grahzny" orange is also like the

world, which on the same page is called "grahzny vonny." For Alex, life has aspects both of determinism and free will, line and circle, clockwork and orange.

Burgess used similar line-circle imagery in *The Wanting Seed*, which was published in the same year as *A Clockwork Orange*. In both novels, determinism and mechanical progress are associated with lines, while freedom and organic growth are associated with circles. Reality for Burgess often emerges from the interaction of contrary principles like these; in *A Clockwork Orange* Alex's linear, determined youth is contrasted with his freedom in maturity when he decides to marry, have a child, and give up his violence. But the cycle continues, and paradoxically Alex's freedom will lead him to have a child who once more will be subjected to the deterministic phase of the process.

By the end of the novel, Alex is mature enough to deal with this paradox. Troubled as he is by the idea that his son will be violent, he remains resolute in his desire to have children. The growth of Burgess' heroes is often indicated by their willingness to accept life and the mixed bag of contradictory values it offers.

The sense that Alex has accepted life is enforced when he finally answers the question which introduces each part of the novel and which is repeated eleven times: "What's it going to be then, eh?" Initially the question seems only to be about what sort of drink to order, but as it recurs it acquires existential overtones. The answer finally comes towards the end of the deleted chapter:

> But first of all, brothers, there was this vesch of finding some devotchka or other who would be a mother to this son. I would have to start on that tomorrow, I kept thinking. That was something like new to do. That was something I would have to get started on, a new like chapter beginning.
> That's what it's going to be then, brothers. . . .

The question is answered just after Alex sees himself as a participant in the historical cycle and his life as a microcosmic version of the cycle. He has understood that history grows out of the struggle of opposing forces and has accepted a similar clash of contradictory urges in his own personality.

Alex's ideas suggest that Burgess has been influenced by Hegel's theory of history; and some of the characters in his other novels (like the history teacher who is the protagonist of *The Long Day Wanes*) actually discuss Hegel's theory. Burgess' system, however, differs in a number of respects from Hegel's. In the Hegelian dialectic, the opposition of thesis and antithesis produces a synthesis which resembles the stages that preceded it, but which is also different in some ways from these stages. The new element in the synthesis leads to the idea—very important in Hegelian thought—that progress comes with the dialectical historical cycle.

Burgess' theory denies this idea of progress. His system posits two antithetical, alternating stages; the third stage is actually only a repetition of the first. In this system, innovations are never permanent; the changes in one era are undone by a regressive process in the next, so there can be no true historical progress.

The idea that history repeats itself and the pessimistic outlook which it engenders may come from Toynbee or Spengler,[1] whose cyclical theories of history were in vogue when Burgess was a student. Vico, whom Burgess mentions in his Joyce criticism, may also be a source. Burgess calls himself a Manichean,[2] and he often takes a dualistic Manichean view of contending moral forces.

*   *   *

Burgess feels that it is his work as an artist to portray conflicting elements which eventually blend into a single confluent entity. In *Urgent Copy*, a collection of reviews and essays, he gives an example: impressed by the juxtaposition of Spanish and British cultures in Gibralter, he composed a symphony in which disparate themes relating to these cultures clash initially but ultimately harmonize.[3] The symphony was written before any of his novels, and this process of juxtaposing conflicting values provided him with a method he later used in his writing. * * *

Burgess, then, follows the yin-yang principles in understanding change as a clash and interaction of opposed values which can lead either to chaos or to harmony. In the concluding essay of *Urgent Copy*, he explains that, though one would like to live by a single set of values, reality is most often apprehended in sets of opposing values like good and evil, white and black, rich and poor. Politicians and theologians, who claim they can find unity in merging these values, actually offer either promises (a classless society, for example) or intangibles (God, metaphysical ideas). Only a work of art, says Burgess, can achieve a synthesis of opposites which presents an immediate vision of unity.[4] Obviously, *A Clockwork Orange* is meant to serve as an example of the sort of work that can truly reconcile opposing values.

1. Arnold Toynbee (1889–1975) and Oswald Spengler (1880–1936): historians of civilization, noted for their theories of historical cycles in, respectively, *A Study of History*, 12 vols. (1934–61) and *The Decline of the West* (1917). [Editor's note.]
2. Giambattista Vico (1668–1744), Neapolitan who founded the philosophy of history with *The New Science* (1725). Manichaeism was a gnostic religion flourishing in the first millennium. Its cosmology centred on the universal struggle between good and evil. [Editor's note.]
3. "Epilogue: Conflict and Confluence," *Urgent Copy* (New York: Norton, 1968), 269.
4. *Urgent Copy*, 265–66.

DAVID LODGE

[U.S. Audiences]†

* * *

Most of the great modern novels end in the same sort of way, 'with the sense of life going on': *Ulysses, Women in Love, Mrs Dalloway, A Passage to India* and many others. With the increasing acceptance of the open rather than the closed ending, the issue of whether or not to conclude a story with a happy union of lovers scarcely arises for the modern novelist as it did so frequently for the Victorians. But I can think of two modern instances comparable to the case of *Great Expectations*, i.e. where we can compare two different endings to the same story. The first is Evelyn Waugh's *A Handful of Dust* (1934). In the standard text, the disillusioned hero, Tony Last, who has gone abroad after being deceived by his wife, meets a gruesome living death in the Brazilian jungle, condemned to read aloud the works of Dickens to a mad, homicidal settler. The American magazine that published the novel in serial form, however, found the last chapter too macabre, and asked for a less disturbing conclusion. With a readiness more characteristic of a Victorian than of a modern novelist, Waugh obliged, and even reprinted the alternative ending later in a volume of his own short stories. In this version, Tony Last returns from an uneventful visit to Brazil, is reconciled to his now penitent wife, and quietly plots to deceive her as she deceived him. Not exactly a happy ending, but one that has more old-fashioned poetic justice about it than the original, in which Tony Last seems to suffer out of all proportion to his sins.

In the 1930s, it would appear, the American reading public was rather more squeamish than the British (*A Handful of Dust* was serialised in the British *Vogue* with the original ending). But times have changed, as the case of Anthony Burgess's *A Clockwork Orange* illustrates. *A Clockwork Orange* is a futuristic fantasy narrated by a teenage hoodlum called Alex who is guilty of appalling acts of violence. When he is convicted and sent to prison, he is offered his freedom on condition that he accepts Pavlovian aversion therapy. This cures him of his violent urges, but it also dehumanises him. By an accident, the effects of his therapy are lost, and he reverts to his evil but vital character. Burgess seems to be offering us a stark choice between accepting the evil consequences of

† From *Working with Structuralism: Essays and Reviews on Nineteenth and Twentieth Century Literature* (Boston: Routledge & K. Paul, 1981), 152–53. Reprinted by permission of Curtis Brown Group Ltd., London, on behalf of David Lodge. Copyright © David Lodge, 1981.

freedom or the tyranny of a totalitarian law-and-order state. In the form in which most readers know the novel, there does not seem much to choose between them in terms of human happiness. But in the first edition of the novel there was a final chapter which ended the story more hopefully, with a hint of real regeneration for Alex. Burgess explained in an interview:

> When I wrote it, originally, I put in a chapter at the end where Alex was maturing. He was growing up and seeing violence as part of adolescence. He wanted to be a married man and have children. He sees the world going round and round like an orange. But when they were going to publish it in America, they said, 'We're tougher over here,' and thought the ending too soft for their readers. If it was me, now, faced with the decision, I'd say no. I still believe in my ending.[1]

It is surprising, in view of this latter statement, that the British paperback edition of A Clockwork Orange, published by Penguin, follows the American hardback edition, as does the celebrated film of the novel made by Stanley Kubrick. The vast majority of the audience for A Clockwork Orange know it, therefore, in a far more pessimistic form than its author intended.[2]

WILLIAM HUTCHINGS

[Revisions of the "Myth"][†]

* * *

Anthony Burgess has long been dissatisfied with the truncated text of A Clockwork Orange that was published in the United States, which omitted the novel's final chapter and added an unauthorized and unnecessary glossary; the untruncated text remained unavailable in the United States until 1987. Stanley Kubrick's much-acclaimed 1971 film (with which Burgess was also highly displeased) was based on the American edition of the novel; Burgess did not write the screenplay, which was also separately published in 1971.

---

1. Interview in *Penthouse* (undated). My attention was first drawn to this case by Peter Handley.
2. A new Penguin edition of the novel, with the original ending restored, was published in 1979. In a letter to the *Times Literary Supplement* (11 January 1980), Anthony Burgess explained that he had only recently discovered that the first Penguin edition omitted the final chapter which he had 'weakly agreed' to excise from the American edition. He also records that Stanley Kubrick was unaware of the existence of the original ending when he made his film of A Clockwork Orange.
† From "'What's It Going To Be Then, Eh?': The Stage Odyssey of Anthony Burgess's A Clockwork Orange," *Modern Drama* 34.1 (March 1991): 35–48 (35–37; 38–41; 43–44). Reprinted by permission of University of Toronto Press Incorporated.

                              *   *   *

The first known stage adaptation of *A Clockwork Orange* was created by John Godber, produced at the Edinburgh Festival in 1980,
and revived in "pub theatre" productions in 1982 and 1984; since
Godber's unauthorized version has not been published, however,
details of his adaptation must be gleaned from reviews. His most
startling innovation is the use of a wheelchair-bound narrator,
identified as Alex II, who observes the action from atop a black-box
set of walls and raked floors, while another actor, playing Alex I,
reenacts events from his earlier, violent life. * * *

   In order to "stem the flow of amateur adaptations that [he had]
heard about but never seen,"[1] Burgess completely reworked the
novel into his own "authorized" dramatization, first published in
1987 as *A Clockwork Orange: A Play with Music*. While retaining
many of the book's now-famous scenes and its invented "nadsat"
teenage slang. Burgess's adaptation is surely no less controversial
than Kubrick's own, since it not only restores the novel's "original"
ending but adds a surprising final confrontation between Alex and
a character resembling Kubrick himself. Designed as "a little play
which any group may perform," Burgess's stage version requires
only minimal props and offers few specifics about costume design;
"this is not grand opera," he wryly remarked in its preface.[2]

   In February 1990, a *second*, greatly expanded, and radically different "authorized" adaptation, known as *A Clockwork Orange
2004*, was produced by the Royal Shakespeare Company at the
Barbican Theatre in London; although Burgess is credited as the
sole author in the published version, in a prefatory note he acknowledges that the play's director, Ron Daniels, gave "invaluable help
with the adaptation"[3] and may be presumed to have been responsible for many of the changes made between the two versions.
With music provided by Bono and the Edge, *A Clockwork Orange*
became—if not "grand opera"—at least what reviewer John Heilpern
termed "a crypto-musical designed as a commercial blockbuster,"[4]
as the English-language adaptation of *Les Misérables* had become
since its production by the Royal Shakespeare Company in 1985. It
was, however, far less enthusiastically received.

                              *   *   *

The portrayal of the book's more violent scenes has long been a central issue in all adaptations of *A Clockwork Orange*, since an on-stage

---

1. See p. 171 of this Norton Critical Edition.
2. Anthony Burgess, *A Clockwork Orange: A Play with Music* (Hutchinson, 1987).
3. *A Clockwork Orange 2004* (London: Arrow, 1990).
4. John Heilpern, "The Fate of British Theatre?" review of *A Clockwork Orange 2004*),
   Vogue, June 1990, p. 132.

or on-screen enactment of a beating, murder, or rape is inherently different from its novelistic description in language, particularly Alex's "nadsat" slang which provides a certain distancing (and often comic) effect in the book. Stung by criticism that the book's violence is excessive and might incite such behavior among impressionable readers—fears that were even more widely (and loudly) voiced after the release of Kubrick's film—Burgess sought to minimalize the violence in his initial stage adaptation, wherein stage directions are reduced to a minimum. Thus, for example, in the confrontation between Alex's droogs and the rival gang headed by Billyboy, the stage direction indicates only that

> The knives and bicycle chains come out. . . . There is now a fight, very exactly choreographed to music. DIM is the most vigorous but least stylish of the four droogs. The gang of BILLYBOY limps off, slashed, bloody. (*Play*, 2–3)

With appropriate choreography, such a scene could easily become as balletic as that between the Sharks and the Jets in *West Side Story* (1957), on which it may in fact have been modeled; although much is left to the director's discretion, the scene's stylization and the presence of the music (as in the film) mitigate its realism. In the 1990 version, however, the music is removed, the stage directions are more specific, and the violence is more graphic:

> The knives and bicycle chains come out. . . . There is now a fight. . . . DIM is the most vigorous but least stylish of the four droogs. Dancing about with his razor, ALEX slashes. Blood pours down either side of BILLYBOY's face, while LEO, his number one, blinded by DIM's chain, howls and crawls about like an animal. Police sirens are heard. The droogs scatter. (*2004*, 12)

Even when portrayed this directly, however, such violence seems tame in comparison to that in other contemporary plays (e.g., those of Edward Bond) or in modern productions of *Macbeth* or *Titus Andronicus* (among many others), and in countless films that have been marketed primarily on the basis of their state-of-the-art special effects and ever-more-graphic mayhem, cruelty, mutilation, and gore.

Whereas such depictions of violence have long since surpassed anything in any version of *A Clockwork Orange*, the film's notorious scene in which the writer F. Alexander is accosted, beaten, bound, and forced to watch while his wife is raped has retained its notoriety as a landmark in cinematic sadism; in the film, notoriously, the scene is choreographed to the tune of "Singin' in the Rain." Each of the three stage adaptations adopts a different strategy in depicting this crucial scene, however. In Godber's work, presumably, it was among the incidents from Alex's past that were (however unconvincingly) mimed; in Burgess's 1987 version, the scene was moved off-stage entirely, and the initial assault occurred in the street rather than in their home (where it takes place in the novel, the film, and the subsequently revised version). With surprising coyness, Burgess demurs even at using the word "rape" in his stage directions in his 1987 text and intends to have the action conveyed solely through music: after "having their mouths stuffed by the balled-up manuscript . . . the man is left for near-dead on the ground while the wife is, God help her, prepared for—" [sic], an act so unspeakable that its name is unspoken even in the playwright's stage directions. The "preparation" (the nature of which is also unspecified) is to be accompanied by "the melody of the second movement of Beethoven's Sonata Pathétique" as the droogs sing about loving "the old in-out"; as "the lights dim as they take the struggling girl off," the music becomes more "manic" before it post-coitally "dies away" (Play, 5). Yet, however much Kubrick's rendition of the scene exploits its violence and prurience (particularly in its use of close-ups as Alex cuts to shreds the woman's red jumpsuit before the rape itself occurs), Burgess's 1987 version seems too drastic in its remedy, undercutting the incident's inherent horror by reducing it to an unseen act in an unspecified off-stage elsewhere. Although ample precedents for off-stage violence abound from classical times onward, and although musical alarums can denote scenes of struggle of whatever kind, the omission of such scenes from A Clockwork Orange would seem inevitably to mitigate a work to which violence is literally (and physically) integral.

Accordingly, in the 1990 version, the rape scene was returned both to the stage and to the home of F. Alexander, where it occurred in the novel. Wearing a Disraeli mask (while his droogs sport masks of P.B. Shelley, Elvis Presley, and Henry VIII), Alex orders Dim to "grab hold of this veck here [F. Alexander] so that he can viddy all"; then, following a gratuitous "Bog [God] help us all," Alex/Disraeli "untrusses and plunges" as F. Alexander "howls in rage." However, the stage directions then specify that, "suddenly unmasking," Alex resumes his role as on-stage narrator, directly addressing the audience:

> Then after me it was right old Dim should have his turn, then Pete and Georgie had theirs. Then there was like quiet, and we were full of like hate, so we smashed what there was left to be smashed. The writer veck and his zheena were not really there, bloody and torn and making noises. But they'd live. (2004, 14)

In "suddenly" removing the mask and resuming his role as narrator (surely a unique redefinition of coitus interruptus), Alex in effect distances himself from the action by mediating it through language, reliably but briefly reporting events that remain unseen, though their nature has been unmistakably demonstrated on stage. In so doing, he maintains the distinction between the minacious, antisocial

Alex-who-acts (Alex I in Godber's version) and the forthright, confiding, post-reformation Alex-who-narrates (Godber's Alex II).

The fact that Alex's narrative voice pervades the novel provides an inevitable problem for all of the various adapters of *A Clockwork Orange*—and one that they have attempted to resolve in a variety of ways. Because it is immediately recognizable with its pervasive nadsat slang, it is perhaps the most distinctive "voice-print" in modern literature—the unique and idiosyncratic product of his particular sensibility, cunning but confiding, minacious but oddly meliorative, inherently asking the reader to understand if not condone; he addresses the reader repeatedly as "brother," with the fervor and insidiously affective intent of a reformed sinner at a religious revival meeting, while remaining wholly and sincerely unrepentant. Paradoxically, it creates within the novel a sort of "alienation effect," distancing the reader from even his most horrific exploits, rendering them less "alienating" than a realistic (i.e., ostensibly objective) third-person description of the same events would be. Most importantly, however, it is both adolescent and postadolescent at the same time. Alex's bravado and *brio* epitomize the hormone-charged sensibility of many fifteen-year-old males: aggressive, heedless, headstrong, and combative but occasionally physically awkward in the presence of his elders (slipping and sliding in saucers of milk while assaulting the cat-owning elderly lady), unconcerned about the consequences and implications of his rash but immediately gratifying actions, and insensitive to whatever discomfort he causes others, whether inadvertently or by design. Yet, notwithstanding its narrative immediacy, Alex's *apologia pro vita sua* is in fact a retrospective account of events; it is recounted by a postcorrective, reconditioned and deconditioned Alex who uses the past tense throughout in describing his former self (or, more precisely, selves). In the twenty-first chapter, he has not only assumed all the postadolescent respectability that lawfully gained income from a worthwhile job can convey, but he also looks forward to assuming the domestic (and ostensibly domesticating) responsibilities of a home, a wife, and a child. The dual narrative perspective of adolescent and postadolescent sensibilities, both of which are integral to the novel, has been notoriously difficult for the various adapters to sustain.

Whereas Godber presented Alex-who-acts and Alex-who-narrates as two separate characters, with the latter being inexplicably wheelchair-bound, and whereas Kubrick utilized a voiceover in the film, Burgess attempted to dispense with Alex's narrative function almost entirely in the 1987 version of the play. Apart from a song in which the phrase "my brothers" may be addressed either to the audience or his droogs (*Play*, 8), Alex speaks directly to the audience only twice in this adaptation: immediately before jumping out the window in his suicide attempt ("Goodbye. May Bog forgive you for a ruined jeezny" [*Play*, 40]) and at the very end of the play, in a speech that is taken from the novel's final paragraph. The remainder of Alex's lines are skillfully reworked into dialogue with other characters, though this version of the play reduces the novel to a too-small number of vignettes. The number of scenes from the novel has been greatly increased in the 1990 version, however, and Alex's narrative function has been restored, beginning with the play's opening lines. Whereas Burgess's previous adaptation had begun with a droogs' aria "freely adapting the Scherzo of Beethoven's Ninth Symphony" (*Play*, 1), the later stage version omits the novel's famous opening line, "'What's it going to be then, eh?'" and begins instead with the book's second sentence, "That ['There' in the novel] was me, that is Alex, and my three droogs, that is Pete, Georgie and Dim . . ." (2004, 1). While the 1990 version is thus the most faithful to the book in sustaining Alex's narrative tone and function, its retention led the critic for *Sight and Sound* to charge that the book had been "incompletely dramatised."[5] * * * As his American editors contended from the outset, Burgess's still vigorously defended preference for an ending showing "the capacity of regeneration in even the most depraved soul" (*Play*, vi) does indeed seem to undermine the effectiveness of the work, particularly by undercutting its theological complexity. Though Burgess cites an intended epigraph from *The Winter's Tale* in which the shepherd remarks that "I would there were no age between ten and three-and-twenty, or that youth would sleep out the rest; for there is nothing in the between but getting wenches with child, wronging the ancientry, stealing, fighting,"[6] the necessity of the *choice* between good and evil is *not* simply to be outgrown with adolescence, as the author's preferred final scene and chapter so strongly contend. In effect, such a facile solution—like the astonishingly trite verse that expresses it—reduces the complex moral issues of free choice and personal responsibility to the uncomplicated moral strictures of James Russell Lowell's "The Present Crisis" of 1844 (whose cadence makes it no less suitable than Burgess's banal lyric to be sung to the "Ode to Joy"): "Once to every man and nation, comes the moment to decide / In the strife of Truth with Falsehood, for the good or evil side."[7] In the modern (or postmodern) world, however, the choice of Truth and "the good . . . side" is infinitely more complex, far more ambiguous, and much less certain

5. Philip French, "A Clockwork Orange," *Sight and Sound: International Film Quarterly.* 59 (Spring 1990), 87.
6. Shakespeare, *The Winter's Tale*, in *The Riverside Shakespeare*, ed. G. Blakemore Evans (Boston, 1974), 3.3. 59–63.
7. James Russell Lowell, "The Present Crisis," in *The Complete Poetical Works of James Russell Lowell* (Boston, 1925), ll. 21–22.

than Lowell would so reassuringly have us believe: the "decision" seldom if ever comes but "once," clearly drawn in black-and-white absolutes—and it is certainly not to be "outgrown" with adolescence.

During an interview with Samuel Coale in 1981, Burgess remarked that it had become "a damn nuisance" to have become associated so much with only *A Clockwork Orange*, and he added that

> I'm not particularly proud of *A Clockwork Orange*, because it has all the faults which I rail against in fiction. It's didactic. It tends toward pornography. It's tricky. It's gimmicky. . . . The damn book . . . is not all that interesting or important. It's had a mythical impact of some kind.[8]

Yet, in providing still more versions of the story, Burgess has assured the continuation of both the controversy and the choice that have surrounded the novel since its appearance over a quarter of a century ago; indeed, on the opening night of the Royal Shakespeare Company's production, he reportedly denounced the play's rock score as "Neo-wallpaper";[9] it replaced unpublished music that Burgess himself had composed for the 1987 version (subtitled *A Play with Music*), so yet another controversy has begun. In effect, those who want to see and/or read *A Clockwork Orange* now have more choices than ever before: two different versions of the novel (one with twenty chapters, one with twenty-one), Kubrick's film, his published screenplay, and two Burgess stage adaptations are now available, with no two versions being the same. The story of Alex and his droogs has, in fact, taken on an essential mythic quality, as Joseph Campbell defined it— the ability to be transformed variously through time, while retaining much of its underlying, valuable, and original content.

ESTHER PETIX

[Nadsat, Empathy, and Distance][†]

* * *

The novel's tempo, and its overwhelming linguistic accomplishment is to a great degree based upon the language Nadsat, coined for the book: the language of the droogs and of the night. It is the jargon

---

8. Samuel Coale, "An Interview with Anthony Burgess," *Modern Fiction Studies*, 27 (Autumn 1981), 488.
9. Heilpern, p. 132.
† From "Linguistics, Mechanics, and Metaphysics: Anthony Burgess's *A Clockwork Orange* (1962)," in Robert K. Morris, *Old Lines, New Forces: Essays on the Contemporary British Novel, 1960–1970* (Rutherford, NJ: Fairleigh Dickinson UP, 1976), 38–52 (42–44). Reprinted by permission of The Associated University Presses.

of rape, plunder, and murder veiled in unfamiliarity, and as such it works highly successfully. Anthony De Vitis asserts that Nadsat may be an anagram for Satan'd,[1] but Burgess insists on the literal Russian translation of the word for "teen." The novel makes a fleeting reference to the origins of the language. "Odd bits of old rhyming slang . . . a bit of gipsy talk, too. But most of the roots are Slav. Propaganda. Subliminal penetration (75)."

Close examination of the language reveals a variety of neologisms applied in countless ways. First, there is the overwhelming impact of a Russianate vocabulary that is concurrently soothing and unnerving to the reader. It most certainly softens the atrocities of the book. It is far simpler, for example, to read about a "krovvy-covered plot" or "tolchocking an old veck" than it is to settle into two hundred pages of "blood-covered bodies" or "beatings of old men."[2] The author keeps his audience absorbed in the prolonged violence through the screen of another language. But the Russian has a cruelty of its own; and there are disquieting political undercurrents in Burgess's imposition of Slavic upon English, at least for the tutored ear.

Nadsat, like all of Burgess's conventional writing, harbors a number of skillful puns. People are referred to as "lewdies"; the "charlie/charles" is a chaplain; "cancers" are cigarettes, and the "sinny" is the cinema. There is, to be sure, little room for laughter in a novel as sobering as this, and Burgess's usual authorial grin is only suggested in this very bitter glimpse of tomorrow. Still, there is no absence of satire. In many ways Alex is still a youth, and the reader is repeatedly shocked by a profusion of infantilisms starkly juxtaposed with violence. Burgess flecks his dialogue of evil with endearing traces of childhood in words like "appy polly loggies," "skolliwoll," "purplewurple," "baddiwad," or "eggiwegg" for "apologies," "school," "purple," "bad," and "egg." It is necessary for Burgess to achieve an empathic response to Alex, and these infantilisms within Nadsat are reminiscent of Dickensian innocence—serving well as buffer zones (or are they iron curtains?) between the "good" reader and the "evil" protagonist.

Other clues to this grim future world are Burgess's truncated and mechanized synechdoches: The "sarky guff" is a "sarcastic guffaw." "Pee and em" are Alex's parents; the "old in-out-in-out" is sexual intercourse (generally rape!); a "twenty-to-one" (the number is scarcely fortuitous) is a gang beating; "6655321" is Alex's prison name, and "StaJa 84" (State Jail 84) is his prison address.

---

1. Anthony De Vitis, *Anthony Burgess* (New York: Twayne Publishers, 1972), p. 56.
2. Translations are taken from Stanley Edgar Hyman's glossary of Nadsat appended to more recent editions of *A Clockwork Orange*.

Closely linked with the mechanical hybrids used in Nadsat are certain words conspicuous by their absence. There are no words, for example, that give positive feelings of warmth or caring or love. When Alex wants to refer to goodness he has to do so by opting out of Nadsat and for English, or by calling evil "the other shop."

Yet the total effect of Nadsat is greater than the sum of its various parts. Alex, in the capacity of "Your Humble Narrator," uses the language to extrapolate a future both vague and too familiar. He sings of a time when all adults work, when very few read, and when society is middle class, middle-aged, and middle-bound. We are told only that 1960 is already history and that men are on the moon. The reader is offered no other assurances. And as the linguistic impact of Nadsat becomes more comprehensible, one is left to wonder if the world of clockwork oranges is so safely distant after all.

When one has truly and carefully followed the linguistic threads of Burgess's novel, the Minotaur guide can be heard arguing a matter deeply tragic in implications. By definition language, like its human author, man, has an essential right to reflect the fits and starts of a time-honed, familiar friend. There ought to be an ordered sense of choice, a spirit of chorus and harmony and solo. Jabberwocky is for fun; Nadsat is a very different construct and far more fearful. Though at times it can be beautiful, there is the lonely wail of tomorrow wrenched from the desperate sighs of today. In Nadsat one finds the Platonic form of mechanism: the cadence of a metronome and the ticking-tocking ramifications of humanity without its essence.

*   *   *

JULIE CARSON

[Linguistic Invention]†

What discussion there has been of the language of A Clockwork Orange has dealt mainly with the gypsy talk of Alex, "nadsat," a hybrid of Russian and onomatopoetic words. Virtually no critic, however, has investigated a linguistic technique certainly as obvious as the nadsat lexicon: Alex's system of pronominalization. It is with the thou/you pronoun distinction, and not the nadsat vocabulary, that Burgess indicates the significant changes in the central character in the novel.

† From "Pronominalization in A Clockwork Orange" in Papers on Language and Literature 12.2 (Spring 1976), 200–205. Reprinted by permission.

In "The Pronouns of Power and Solidarity," Roger Brown and Albert Gilman propose a "connection between social structure, group ideology, and the semantics of the pronoun." They base their conclusions on data from sixteen countries, whose native languages make distinction between familiar and formal pronouns.[1] Their findings are especially applicable to A *Clockwork Orange*, for Alex is the only character who deviates from the standard pronoun system. Burgess sets him off in two ways: from general society by giving him the nadsat vocabulary, and from his own group, with the pronoun distinction. The use of an argot to set a group apart is common enough. But a deviation from, yet within, an argot carries greater implications, revealing Alex's position of power relative to both society and to his droogs.* * *

Alex uses the formal "thou" in situations in which he is clearly in control, as in his dialogue with Dim, the least competent of his droogs: "'Come, gloopy bastard as thou art. Think not on them'" (15). Later when his droogs are in rebellion, Alex draws a fine line in his respect among his droogs; Dim he continues to address "thou," but to the other two droogs he uses the conventional pronoun: "'Oh now, don't, both of you malchicks. Droogs, aren't we?'" (22). His droogs are not mollified, despite Alex's addressing them as "you," his equals, and they press their revolt. Alex then gets "more razdraz inside," frightened by the impending violence, and capitulates his position of power. After he agrees to go "bedways," in his acquiescent stance, Alex addresses Dim, the former object of physical abuse, as an equal: "'You understand about that tolchock on the rot, Dim. It was the music see'" (22).

There are three other important examples of the thou/you distinction early in the novel. One occurs when Alex and his droogs break into F. Alexander's HOME. As the bizarre scene begins to unfold, in the only line which calls for pronoun usage, Alex uses "thou"; "'Never fear. If fear thou hast in thy heart, O brother, pray banish it forthwith'" (17). In the entire episode of destruction and rape, Alex dominates the situation. By telling Alexander not to fear, he clearly mocks Alexander, who indeed has a great deal to fear. Later in the novel, Alex uses "thou" when he deceives his father and asserts his ability to control situations: "'Never worry about thine only son and heir, O my father,' I said. 'Fear not. He canst taketh care of himself, verily'" (35). The third significant use of "thou" occurs when Alex is verbally and then physically assaulting Billyboy: "'Well, if it isn't fat stinking billygoat Billyboy in poison. How art thou, thou globby bottle of cheap stinking chip-oil? Come and get one in the yarbles, if you have any yarbles, you eunuch jelly, thou'" (13). In the last example

1. *Style in Language*, ed. Thomas A. Sebeok, (Cambridge, MA: MIT Press, 1960), 253–57.

what appears to be ambivalence (the use of both pronoun forms) might be explained in either of two ways: first, the power relationship between Alex and Billyboy is not clear. They are rivals and peers. But in this scene, Alex is on the attack, not to Dim or to Alexander or to his father, whom he considers his subordinates-victims, but to a person he must hold in derision, yet whose power he respects. Billyboy is not so weak an adversary that he can be dismissed with the "thou" form; in fact, Alex does not win the encounter. It is broken up by police sirens. Interestingly, as the sirens wail, and the threat of a higher authority looms, Alex reverts to conventional usage: "'Get you soon, fear not,' I called, 'stinking billygoat. I'll have your yarbles off lovely'" (14). * * *

When Alex and his droogs break into Alexander's HOME, the power relationship is clear: Alex is plainly in control. But in the next major crime they commit, a curious thing happens: although Alex seems to be dominating the situation (he has, after all, only an old woman as his adversary) he uses the conventional pronoun form: "'Hi hi hi. At last we meet. Our brief govoreet through the letter-hole was not, shall we say, satisfactory, yes? Let us admit not, oh verily not, you stinking starry old sharp'" (42). In no comparable situation had Alex lapsed into the conventional form "you"; Burgess offers here a linguistic clue to the imminent power change. Alex of course, is caught in this crime and imprisoned. Perhaps most interesting of all is that from this episode until he is "cured" of the Ludovico technique, with one exception, Alex never says "thou" to anyone, no matter what his estimation of them. Clearly Burgess exploited the rare and subtle use of "thou" to indicate Alex's power position, thus affirming Brown and Gilman's observation that "a man's consistent pronoun style gives away his class status" (254).

Alex perceives each of his relationships correctly: he knows, in other words, when he may use the "thou" form. As Brown and Gilman explain, "The general meaning of an unexpected pronoun choice is simply that the speaker, for the moment, views the relationship that calls for the pronoun used" (274). Likewise, Alex knows when to use "you," as when the police brutally interrogate him and Deltoid spits in his face. Alex replies: "'Thank you, sir, thank you very much, sir, that was very kind of you sir, thank you'" (48). With one exception Alex never uses any other second person pronominal form during his arrest, imprisonment, or hospitalization.

The Ludovico technique evokes a number of reactions in Alex: he becomes nonaggressive, nonviolent, and respectful to established societal codes. Accordingly, he also ceases to use "thou" in his dialogues. Perhaps the most significant example of the change effected in him occurs shortly after his release from the hospital. When he meets Dim, his pronominal style has altered considerably, revealing his apprehension of his new role in the power structure: "'Read to you,' I said, a malenky bit nasty. 'You still too dim to read for yourself, O brother'" (97). After the beating that Dim and Billyboy inflict on him, Alex ironically seeks help at Alexander's HOME, where he has earlier used the "thou" pronominal code. When he returns to seek help from Alexander (admittedly a subordinate position) he uses conventional pronouns, but later in the conversation after reading an attack on the government Alexander had written in his name, Alex comments: "'Very good. . . . Real horrorshow. Written well thou hast, O sir.' And then he looked at me very narrow and said: 'What?' It was like he had not slooshied me before. 'Oh that,' I said, 'is what we call nadsat talk. All the teens use that, sir'" (104). Alexander's sudden close attention to Alex's speech could not have been evoked only by the obvious lexical deviance, "horrorshow." Earlier in their conversation Alex had defined "ptitsa" (100) and "the charlie" (100) for Alexander, or had used nadsat words which Alexander let pass by without questioning: "polly" (103), "slooshy" and "jeezny" (103). But after Alex revealed himself with the use of "thou" Alexander's suspicions about his identity were aroused.

There is some ambivalence in Alex's pronominal code in this episode at HOME. But it reflects Alex's uncertainty of his role there. The use of "thou" is an obvious slip on Alex's part. But later, when he asserts himself "I did not like that crack about zombyish, brothers, and so I said: 'What goes on, bratties? What dost thou in mind for thy little droog have?'" (104). Alex allows himself to slip into the total nadsat argot of lexicon, syntax, and morphology because of his great fear. He is suddenly aware that Alexander and his group are acting in their own interests and not in his. He assesses the situation quickly and adopts nearly the proper linguistic posture for his power position, but he cannot restrain himself entirely; his language, after all, has been his greatest means of self-identification and self-assertion. Alexander's final torture of Alex consists of playing Beethoven, inducing him to commit suicide. As Alex prepares to jump to his death, he cries: "'Goodbye, goodbye, may Bog forgive you for a ruined life'" (107–8). Again, in what appears to be his final role as victim, Alex uses the pronoun "you" appropriate to the situation, rather than the inappropriate power semantic "thou." Alex's suicide attempt is of course abortive, and his fall causes much of the Ludovico technique to be ineffective. Although Alex does not linguistically revert to his former self, as the story line might suggest, if one interprets only the action of the story during Alex's final hospitalization, it appears that he is indeed his former self. He relies heavily on the nadsat vocabulary; he exhibits his former usual extraordinary lust; he treats his parents with great disdain; he threatens physical violence to those who contradict him; and he insults the most overt symbol of the established order, the Minister of the Interior. But he does all these things with pronominal ambivalence. He addresses the nurse: "'What gives, O my little sister? Come thou and have a nice lay-down with your malenky droog in this bed'"; his parents: "'Well well well well well, what gives? What makes you think you are like welcome?'"; the Minister of the Interior: "'Bolshy great yarblockos to thee and thine'" (108, 110, 112). To three of the four persons he speaks to in his final hospitalization, after he has been apparently cured of the Ludovico technique, he readopts his special pronominal code. He has reasserted himself to everyone but his parents for their leaving him was on a tentative basis: "'You'll have to make up your mind,' I said, 'who's to be boss'" (111). In Alex's final confrontation with the Minister of the Interior, he uses "thou" exclusively—"'Bolshy great yarblockos to thee and thine'" (112)—for he consistently interprets the Minister as inferior: "And in he came, and of course it was none other than the Minister of the Interior or Inferior . . ." (112). Other epithets he uses to refer to the Minister explicitly call attention to the inferior role he attributes to him: "int Inf Min" and "intinfmin" (113).

Anthony Burgess thus draws subtle distinctions by developing a pronominal code within the nadsat argot which, in turn, gives explicit linguistic clues to the power structures in *A Clockwork Orange*. He reflects current findings of linguistic research which suggests that there is a power semantic which is clearly revealed in nonreciprocal power relationships. He has developed a linguistic technique both subtle and sophisticated and one that enhances the brilliance of *A Clockwork Orange*.

ROGER FOWLER

[Anti-Language]†

* * *

The social situation of Alex and his associates is a paradigm case for the formation of an anti-language. They constantly assert their opposition and contempt for all that is, in their own words, bourgeois, middle-aged, middle-class. They attack the representatives of these values by violent assaults on property and people. Since their actions are illegal, they are also at war with the state and its law enforcement agencies. Their speech is an invented argot (invented

† From "Anti-Language in Fiction," in *Literature as Social Discourse: The Practice of Linguistic Criticism* (Bloomington: Indiana UP, 1981), 142–61 (150–55, and 157–58). Reprinted by permission.

by Burgess) very much on the principles of classic criminal slang, and contrasted with the speech of members of the norm society. * * * The main feature of the teenage gang speech is a special vocabulary, mostly Russian in origin, with some rhyming slang—'hound and horny', 'twenty-to-one'—the latter presumably designed to connect the anti-language with that of the modern London underworld. * * * Here's a brief and typical sample:

> So off we went our several ways, me belching arrrgh on the cold coke I'd peeted. I had my cut-throat britva handy in case any of Billyboy's droogs should be around near the flat-block waiting, or for that matter any of the other bandas or gruppas or shaikas that from time to time were at war with one.

Here we have both relexicalization and overlexicalization. *Peet*, *britva*, and *droog* are simply arbitrary relexicalizations, for 'drink', 'razor' and 'friend'. Other relexicalizations display the semantic inversions noted elsewhere. The best example is the word *horror-show*, meaning 'good', derived from the Russian word *xorosho* which means 'good'. Alex consistently applies it to acts of violence, that is, acts which are positive in his system of values but negative for the culture generally. The double-valued semantic of the word is signalled in its English spelling: the English transliteration produces a word which is overtly bad in meaning for, for example, Alex's parents, but implicitly good in meaning for Alex: horror plus show.

Overlexicalization is illustrated by 'bandas or gruppas or shaikas': three words all referring to marauding teenage gangs. It is not clear whether these words have three distinct meanings—which is possible if they reflect a diversified, special knowledge in the sub-culture—or all mean the same, in which case the phrase is an hyperbole. Interestingly, the same problem is presented by other anti-languages: in Elizabethan rogues' slang, for instance, there are numerous words for 'woman' and it is not possible to tell whether they have different meanings. Perhaps, on the analogy of the well-known Eskimo over-lexicalization for 'snow', the sub-culture possesses a highly differentiated sexual world-view; on the other hand, they may be boastfully playing with words.

The element of verbal play links anti-language with the special rhymes and sayings of children's culture (cf. the Opies' work) and with the ritual insults and flytings which have been much studied in BEV and in other societies.[1] Alex's language is permeated with puns and phonetic games, to a large extent but not exclusively playing on

1. I. and P. Opie, *The Lore and Language of School Children* ([1959] Frogmore, St. Albans: Paladin, 1977); T. Kochman, ed., *Rappin' and Stylin' Out* (Urbana: University of Illinois Press, 1972); A. Dundes, J.W. Leach and Bora Özkök, 'The Strategy of Turkish Boys' Verbal Dueling Rhymes,' in Gumperz and Hymes, *op. cit.*, pp. 130–60.

the invented lexicon: 'The stripy shest'. 'the old cold moloko. Hohoho, the old moloko', 'slooshying the sluice'. Or his friend Dim: 'Bedways is rightways now, so best we go homeways. Right?'. Or a pun, very self-conscious: 'the fuel needle had like collapsed, like our own hahaha needles had'. Alliteration, onomatopoeia, rhyme, chiasmus, hyperbole, parallelism—all are plentiful in the speech of Alex and his friends. Presumably, these devices are meant to signify energy, confidence, creativity: to emphasise their freedom from the patterns of the language and so their freedom from the norms of the society.

Alex's stance towards his implied readers suggests intimacy: 'O my brothers'; When he speaks contemptuously of the bourgeoisie, the middle-aged, it is as if they are alien to the reader as well as to himself. Yet, Alex's implicit addressee *is* the book-reading class, assumed to be mature, curious and sympathetic. The narrative is certainly not addressed to his peer-group. The special words are often glossed: 'a rooker (a hand, that is)', 'litso (face, that is)', 'nagoy (bare, that is)' or the anti-language word is added as an after-thought to the normal word: 'very big built up shoulders ("pletchoes" we called them)'. A helpful, mediating, rather than resistant strategy. As we shall see, the glosses in *Naked Lunch* have a very different effect.

Overall, the impression is given that speech antitheses can be mediated: the implicit dialogue is cooperative rather than antagonistic. In fact, beneath the provocative surface of the vocabulary, Alex's own language is thoroughly middle-class. Burgess gives Alex none of the conventional signs of non-standard speech: no regional dialect, no ungrammaticality, no restricted code in Bernstein's sense (Alex once produces a comic illiteracy: see p. 17). In this Alex is distinguished from his aptly named friend 'Dim', who is linguistically coded as socially and mentally deficient. Alex's language characterizes him as an anti-social deviant, a violent thug, but one who possesses the faculties of discrimination and evaluation usually assumed to be the prerogative of the middle-class intelligentsia. From this point of view, pp. 24–25 are revealing. Returning from a night of violence and murder, Alex masturbates to the accompaniment of some *recherché* contemporary serious music, after which he settles down to Mozart and Bach. An equation of two experiences is being implied. Burgess wants us to see Alex's delinquency as producing experiences which are, for him, as aesthetically satisfying as the Jupiter and the Brandenburgs are for us. This is crude; and it prepares for the later judgement, that the aversion conditioning was immoral because, although it 'cured' Alex of his destructive anti-social behaviour, it deprived him of the power to express himself in his own way.

The rapprochement of norm and deviation is done in the language of the extract. Alex's speech, always elaborate in syntax, is especially so here. The sentence structure is varied; sometimes elaborately hypotactic, sometimes appropriately paratactic, as in the mimetic last sentence of the penultimate paragraph taking the narrative to a climax. There is parallelism, repetition with variation ('embellished and decorated'), syntactic chiasmus ('the trombones crunched red-gold under my bed, and behind my gulliver trumpets three-wise silverflamed'). Most nouns are subject to complex pre-modification and post-modification. There are nominalizations and thematizations. Phonetic devices such as alliteration mount to Jakobsonian density. Metaphor is endemic and extravagant. The invented words are absorbed in a context which transforms them from deviations to poeticisms: the context is no longer that of urban delinquency and violence, but one of high literariness, with strong associations of Hopkins and Joyce. If Burgess is trying to argue the authenticity of the values of the anti-society, he does so by assimilating the anti-language to an extreme form of the high language, the language of literary modernism. The verbal play, which I suggested above might signify freedom and creativity, in effect signifies the reverse: socialization into the aesthetic norms of the (for the reader) dominant society. Burgess has closed the dialogic gap, neutralized the antithesis. Instead of allowing us to experience Alex's world-view as that of an alien but authentic subject, he translates that world-view into mediating terms which draw on our own, habitualized, norm-ideology.

*   *   *

I'd like to end with some general comments and questions about anti-language in fiction. Can any general aesthetic function be proposed for it? On first sight, if we consider anti-languages as class codes or social dialects, then anti-language as a technique in fiction seems to be a technique of representation. If you have speakers from deviant groups in your novels, then you get their speech code right. However, I have argued that anti-language is a process rather than a code. In social reality, the process is a negotiation of status, identity and ideology between an official establishment and a group which diverges from its norms. In fiction, the negotiation becomes one between the groups of protagonists within the fiction: between the author, his characters, and the reader. From a compositional point of view, the process comes under the heading of techniques of defamiliarization. Technically, it impedes perception in just the way that Shklovsky's theory requires. It allows the writer to thicken the texture of his prose, not only by the Jakobsonian phonetics of rhyming slang and the like, but also by the lexical and semantic devices which I have illustrated. There are also, very frequently, syntactic indicators of the class affiliations of speakers. These peculiarities—peculiarities, that is to say, from the point of view of the bourgeois reader—are not *just* poetic in the Jakobsonian sense, i.e. unmotivated verbal play. Nor do these linguistic processes simply identify a social group. Their motivation is to reveal to the bourgeois reader the life-experience, or world-view, of the deviant group, to give access to an alternative reality. The revelation of an alien mode of experience from an outside world and an underworld is valuable enough within a literary genre which assumes *possession* of language as an object, in the form of novels possessed as books on the shelf; which assumes that language is closed and monolithic; and which assumes privatization, enclosure, of experience and ideas. At the very least, the reading of a novel of deviancy does something to enlarge the experience of middle class readers by *showing* alternative life-styles and modes of speech. And it does much more if these are presented as a troubling challenge to the norms encoded in middle class language.

But the justification of anti-language in relation to fiction is not just that it allows the middle class reader a vicarious experience of an illegitimate life-style. It is the *logic*, not the *content*, of anti-language which offers to be interesting for the study of fiction. Neither the violence and criminality of the cases I have discussed, nor the manifest unconventionality of their language, defines the essence of anti-language. The essential feature is the antithetical logic of the relationship between an official and an unofficial voice: an unresolved, unmediated, antithesis which preserves a critical, dialogic openness in the novel's examination of its central ethical or social or psychological (or whatever) concerns.

* * *

ZINOVY ZINIK

[Burgess and Russian]†

* * *

The name of Anthony Burgess is inevitably associated in the public mind with this outrage of a novel [*A Clockwork Orange*], the shocking book whose punk characters, outcasts, the scum of the phantasmagorical English future, communicate in an artificial Anglo-Russian slang. But this black utopia has a preamble in the shape of another, not so famous novel of the same period by Burgess, *Honey for the Bears*.[1] Only ten or so years ago the book would have read as

† From "Dublin Dragomans," *Times Literary Supplement (TLS)*, June 25, 2004, 12–13. Reprinted by permission of the author.
1. *Honey for the Bears* (London: Heinemann, 1963).

an outdated satirical Cold War document of a bygone epoch. It tells the story of an English businessman, Paul Hussey (or Gussey, as the russified version of the name goes), and his wife Belinda visiting Leningrad. As is clear from the beginning, the trip has a dubious underside to it. It is not charity work that drags Belinda and Paul to Russia; nor is it tourism. Feeling imprisoned in the England of self-hatred, these people are trying to escape their own selves. Russian chaos, anarchy, corruption and violence are freedom to them. Or rather, an alternative freedom, as opposed to the one that transformed them into slaves of their own suppressed desires. Russia for them is a session of psychoanalysis, a purgatory, a sort of emotional incitement. After all, it was Burgess who called Russia the subconscious of the West.

The novel has recently been brought up to date by the revolutionary changes in Russia, that have once again made that country a honey pot for the type of bears described by Burgess. It was not until I met Burgess in person and later read his autobiography that I appreciated the documentary nature of his novel, the graphic accuracy with which events in his life, such as his own trip to Soviet Russia with his alcoholic first wife, were pictured. Unlike polyglot Burgess, his wife could hardly make out Cyrillic. To help her with elementary Russian, Burgess plastered the walls of their London flat with bits of paper, with words on them written out in chunky Cyrillic letters. They were words that had a similar look and pronunciation in both Russian and English (*tualet* and the like), those "hieroglyphs which were imposed on the old capitalist buildings . . . with the strangeness of the future or of the other planets, the symbols of a monstrous unacceptable mystique", as he later put it in *Honey for the Bears*. He was working on *A Clockwork Orange* at the time.

"It flashed upon me", Burgess writes in his autobiography,

> that I had found a solution to the stylistic problem of *A Clockwork Orange*. The vocabulary of my space-age hooligans could be a mixture of Russian and demotic English. . . . The Russian suffix for -teen was *nadsat*, and that would be the name of the teenage dialect, spoken by *drugi* or droogs or friends in violence. . . . As the book was about brainwashing, it was appropriate that the text itself should be a brainwashing device. The reader would be brainwashed into learning minimal Russian.

The Russia Burgess knew embodied for him a nightmare fantasy of a future authoritarian England. Burgess told me of his disappointment with the Russian translators of *A Clockwork Orange*, who couldn't be bothered to think of an equivalent for the foreign slang, a pseudo-English Russian of some sort. That's what actually happened, though: on the collapse of the Soviet regime the whole of

Russia, propped up by big bucks, switched to Volapuk, embracing its *marketink*, *kholdink* and *body-bildink* as part of modern Russian vocabulary. That transgression, the illicit crossing of language borders, is an extremely catchy business. There were times when I used to entertain myself by making up Russian phrases with a Latin-based typewriter, utilizing the Latin letters that, like c and m, resemble Cyrillic. MOCKBA (Moscow), PECTOPAH (restaurant) or CAMO-BAP (samovar), to mention just a few, would sound hideous to a native English speaker. * * *

The search for a universal language which does not eliminate the individuality of your own voice is a secret passion and the holy grail of every novelist. Once in Europe, Burgess was quite serious about reviving Latin, the last universal language. "My advocacy of Latin was taken for what it was: homesickness for the Christendom of thirteenth-century Europe", he writes in his autobiography. Following in Dostoevsky's footsteps, he considered himself a European because he could have been defined by his nostalgia for the lost European past, actual Europeans having long become a multilingual, motley crew. In Burgess's mind this personal version of Latin is identified with his spiritual origin, his native home. And vice versa: the sensation of the mother tongue as foreign is one of the most precious gifts of self-consciousness, the prerogative of years and years of exile.

* * *

PAUL PHILLIPS

[Burgess and Music]†

* * *

A *Clockwork Orange* overturns the proposition that great music possesses intrinsic "goodness". Listening to Western civilization's most admired and beloved classical masterpieces inflames the novel's "Humble Narrator" to commit acts ranging from masturbation to physical assault, rape, and murder. His broad knowledge of opera, sacred vocal music, symphonic works, concertos, and chamber music distinguishes him as a singularly bright young man, setting him apart from nearly all of the novel's other characters, be they adults or teen-age droogs, while showing that his zest for evil has nothing to do with lack of intelligence. Indeed, Alex's appeal as a character is largely

† From *A Clockwork Counterpoint: The Music and Literature of Anthony Burgess* (Manchester UP, 2010). Reprinted by permission.

attributable to his passion for serious music, which subconsciously dissuades the reader from concluding that he is "all bad", for how can anyone who loves Beethoven's Ninth, for however pernicious a purpose, be wholly evil?

Musical allusion in *A Clockwork Orange* is comparable to Nadsat in its combination of fact and fabrication. Actual musical works cited in the novel include the "Jupiter" Symphony and Brandenburg Concerto No. 6 (25); sacred music by Bach and Handel (53), with specific mention of Cantata No. 140, *Wachet auf, ruft uns die Stimme* (56); and the "Prague" (No. 38) and G minor (No. 40) symphonies of Mozart (90). The association of clockwork with counterpoint is articulated through mention of the Brandenburg Concerto, as Alex reflects upon his assault of F. Alexander earlier that evening, the title of the writer's manuscript, and the polyphonic music of "the starry German master": "The name was about a clockwork orange. Listening to the J. S. Bach, I began to pony better what that meant now" (25). Claude Debussy's Quartet in G minor, op. 10, is encoded as "a very nice malenky string quartet, my brothers, by Claudius Bird-man" (30), a reference to the Dutch biologist Louis Philibert le Cos-quino de Bussy (1879–1943), a noted "birdman", who, after many years spent in Sumatra, donated a large collection of avian creatures to the University of Amsterdam's Zoological Museum.

An international array of fictitious composers, compositions, and performers depict Alex's musical tastes as unusually sophisticated. *Das Bettzeug* ("The Bedding" or "The Bedclothes") by Friedrich Git-terfenster ("Barred-Window") exemplifies obscure German opera, while Otto Skadelig, whose surname means "harmful" in Danish, represents Scandinavian culture. Alex orders a recording of Beethoven's Ninth "by the Esh Sham Sinfonia under L. Muhaiwir", which utilizes Arabic geographic terms: *Esh Sham*, meaning "Syria" (literally, "the left"), and *Muhaiwir*, an archaeological site in Iraq (30). The recording of the American concerto that Alex plays on his stereo to cap off an evening of mayhem invokes the names of two writers of antiquity—the Greek poet Choerilos of Samos (fl. 5th century B.C.) and Roman dramatist Plautus (ca. 254–ca. 184 B.C.):

> Now what I fancied first tonight was this new violin concerto by the American Geoffrey Plautus, played by Odysseus Cho-erilos with the Macon (Georgia) Philharmonic, so I slid it from where it was neatly filed and switched on and waited (24).

The name Adrian Schweigselber, whose Symphony No. 2 is cho-sen and played by Alex as a recessional in the prison chapel, evokes another, better known fictional composer: Adrian Leverkühn, the protagonist of *Doktor Faustus*, a book whose narrative use of music and emphasis on the theme of good versus evil resonate powerfully with the themes of *A Clockwork Orange*. Burgess greatly admired *Doktor Faustus*, calling it, in *The Novel Now*, "the finest novel ever written about a creative artist".[1] His use of the syllable "schweig" (from the verb *schweigen*, meaning "to be silent") in the name Schweigselber echoes Thomas Mann's obsessive repetition of that word throughout the critical central chapter (XXV) of *Doktor Faustus*, which recounts the Faustian bargain between Leverkühn and the Devil; moreover, "schweig" alludes to the Schweigestill family in Pfeiffering, where Leverkühn eventually settles. Pronouncements such as "Freedom is the freedom to sin" and "Evil contributed to the perfect wholeness of the universe, and without the former the latter would never have been whole, which was why God permitted evil"[2] by Leverkühn's one-time theology instructor Eberhard Schleppfuss are virtually interchangeable with lines in *A Clockwork Orange* and Burgess's explanations of its philosophical basis.

The fictional compositions of Gitterfenster and Plautus arouse Alex physically and sexually. Hearing the "devotchka" in the Korova Milkbar sing a short passage from *Das Bettzeug*, Alex feels "all the little malenky hairs on my plott standing endwise and the shivers crawling up like slow malenky lizards and then down again" (21). The Violin Concerto sends him into synesthetic rapture, the description of Alex's reaction to Plautus's music recalling Burgess's account of the bliss he felt upon discovering Debussy's *Prelude to "The Afternoon of a Faun."*

> The trombones crunched redgold under my bed, and behind my gulliver the trumpets three-wise silverflamed, and there by the door the timps rolling through my guts and out again crunched like candy thunder. Oh, it was wonder of wonders. (24)

Through musical and sexual use of language, Burgess accelerates the "tempo" of his writing by progressively shortening phrases, increasing the "speed" of the prose until it reaches verbal "orgasm". Emulating Bloom's experience on Sandymount Beach as fireworks erupt in the sky, Alex ejaculates at the moment that Plautus's Violin Concerto reaches its climax:

> . . . there were devotchkas ripped and creeching against walls and I plunging like a shlaga into them, and indeed when the music, which was one movement only, rose to the top of its big highest tower, then, lying there on my bed with glazzies tight

---

1. *The Novel Now: A Student's Guide to Contemporary Fiction* (New York: Norton, 1967), 35.
2. Thomas Mann, *Doctor Faustus*, trans. by John E. Woods (New York: Vintage International, 1999), 111–12. See also "From Mann to modernity: Anthony Burgess and the intersection of music and literature" by Christine Lee Gengaro in *Anthony Burgess and Modernity*, 95–108.

shut and rookers behind my gulliver, I broke and spattered and cried aaaaaaah with the bliss of it. And so the lovely music glided to its glowing close (25).

But it is the music of Ludwig van Beethoven that animates Alex above all, providing the mental "soundtrack" of well-known works that becomes one of the book's most disturbing features. By associating Beethoven with Alex's heinous acts of violence, Burgess implicitly poses the question of whether great art contains intrinsic moral value, implying that there is no equivalence between the two. Whereas most other compositions cited in the novel lead Alex only to imagine assault and rape, Beethoven's possess the power to impel him to actually carry out acts of violence. In the record shop, Alex picks up two "ten-year-young devotchkas" whom he brings home, plies with Scotch, and rapes to the accompaniment of his new recording of the Ninth. Hearing the finale of Beethoven's Violin Concerto on a passing car's radio impels Alex to whip out his knife and slash Georgie and Dim to assert his authority. Alex assaults the cat-loving "starry ptitsa" in full view of her bust of Beethoven, whose stone face "witnesses" the attack. After his arrest and incarceration in a crowded prison cell, Alex experiences a hallucinatory dream of Debussy's faun meshing surreally with Beethoven and a distorted version of the "Ode to Joy":

> Boy, thou uproarious shark of heaven,
> > Slaughter of Elysium,
> Hearts on fire, aroused, enraptured,
> > We will tolchock you on the rot and kick your grahzny vonny bum (49).

With the Ode still replaying in his mind, Alex is awakened by the police, who inform him that the old woman has died of her injuries, meaning that he is now a murderer.

After Alex's incarceration, Beethoven continues to influence both his subconscious and conscious existence. His murder of a fellow prisoner spawns a grotesque autoerotic-musical fantasy in which he imagines himself a musician in a giant orchestra led by a conductor ("a like mixture of Ludwig van and G. F. Handel") who can neither hear nor see (59–60). Playing the phallic "white pinky bassoon" protruding from his abdomen, Alex laughs so hard from the tickling sensation that his guffaws disturb even the deaf-blind maestro. That killing leads to Alex's selection for the notorious Ludovico Technique, a form of pharmaceutically enhanced aversion therapy that eliminates the recipient's free will and ability to choose between good and evil. Since Ludovico is the Italian form of Ludwig, Burgess surreptitiously implies Beethoven's connection to the treatment, especially when the Fifth Symphony is played during the drugged, forced viewing of films depicting acts of extreme physical and sexual brutality. The unintended consequence of the procedure—that Alex sickens upon hearing Beethoven's music—is of no concern to Dr Brodsky, the Ludovico Technique's chief proponent and practitioner. Alex's protestations ("Using Ludwig van like that. He did no harm to anyone. Beethoven just wrote music".) fall on the tone-deaf ears of the doctor, who regards the matter as immaterial: "So you're keen on music. I know nothing about it myself. It's a useful emotional heightener, that's all I know" (74). Ironically, Brodsky is right. Music *is* an emotional heightener for Alex—at least for most of the novel's first twenty chapters. Alex is fully aware of the myth that appreciation of great art is supposed to calm down youths like him, but knows it to be false, since he is acutely aware of how much it excites him instead:

> Music always sort of sharpened me up, O my brothers, and made me like feel like old Bog himself, ready to make with the old donner and blitzen and have vecks and ptitsas creeching away in my ha ha power (30).

Once released back into society, Alex discovers that listening to any classical music, not just Beethoven's Fifth, produces the same sickened reaction. He returns to the shop where he had bought his recording of Beethoven's Ninth and asks for a recording of Mozart's Symphony No. 40 in G minor. The clerk puts on the "Prague" Symphony instead, but it makes no difference. As soon as the music comes on, Alex becomes nauseous, flees the listening booth, and inadvertently winds up in the custody of F. Alexander. Alex's former victim tortures him by forcing him to listen to the "harmful" music of Otto Skadelig, but the plan backfires when Alex's suicide attempt and subsequent medical treatment reverse the effect of the Ludovico Technique, as he discovers in his hospital bed.

Back to his old self, it is only a matter of time before Alex's broken bones heal and he returns to his former ways. To exploit him for political purposes, the Minister of the Interior pays him a visit and bribes him with music in the form of a new stereo and a collection of shiny new records. Asked what he'd like to hear—" 'Mozart? Beethoven? Schoenberg? Carl Orff?' "—Alex responds, " 'The Ninth . . . The glorious Ninth.' "

> Oh, it was gorgeosity and yumyumyum. When it came to the Scherzo I could viddy myself very clear running and running on like very light and mysterious nogas, carving the whole litso of the creeching world with my cut-throat britva. And there was the slow movement and the lovely last singing movement still to come. I was cured all right (114).

Alex's maturity and newfound identity in the twenty-first chapter as a responsible member of society is reflected in his altered relationship to music, which has become the basis of his profession. Indicating that he has grown up, Alex develops a preference for "malenky romantic songs, what they call *Lieder*" over the bombastic music of "bolshy orchestras (118)". As an employee of the National Gramodisc Archives, he comprehends music more intellectually, appreciating the remarkable achievements of Mozart, Mendelssohn, and Benjamin Britten, whose early works include *Les Illuminations,* a nine-movement setting of poems by Arthur Rimbaud for soprano or tenor and string orchestra, composed in 1939 at the age of 26.

> Eighteen was not a young age. At eighteen old Wolfgang Amadeus had written concertos and symphonies and operas and oratorios and all that cal, no, not cal, heavenly music. . . . And there was this like French poet set by old Benjy Britt, who had done all his best poetry by the age of fifteen, O my brothers. Arthur, his first name. Eighteen was not all that young an age, then (120).

The novel ends with its protagonist determined to retain his job, save his earnings, marry, and have a family: "Alex like groweth up, oh yes".

When speaking with musicians, as when interviewed by Oscar Peterson on BBC television in 1977, Burgess emphasized the novel's musical nature:

> It is about music, because the hero of the book is a young thug called Alex who adores music . . . He becomes violent, joyously violent, when he hears the scherzo of the Ninth Symphony or the finale. But when he is cured, when the State takes him over and gives him the special injections which make him feel sick when he contemplates violence, he feels sick also when he contemplates music . . . The important thing was that the State, modern science, with all these techniques, could take over a boy's brain and so change it that whenever he listened to music in the future it wasn't heaven, it was hell, and that's what it was about.[3]

The idea that musical structure could be applied successfully to fiction had intrigued Burgess from his earliest years as an author. In an essay published the same month as the first edition of *A Clockwork Orange*, he proposed the application of specific musical forms to fiction:

3. *Oscar Peterson Invites*, 8 March 1977 broadcast.

> I still think that the novelist has much to learn from musical
> form: novels in sonata-form, rondo-form, fugue-form are per-
> fectly feasible. There is much to be learnt also from mood-
> contrasts, tempo-contrasts in music: the novelist can have his
> slow movements and his scherzi. Music can also teach him
> how to modulate, how to recapitulate; the time for formal pre-
> sentation of his themes, the time for the free fantasia.[4]

The tripartite structure of *A Clockwork Orange* represents a literary version of sonata form, a structure in which principal themes are
presented in the *exposition*, freely manipulated in the *development*,
and reestablished in the *recapitulation*, with a *coda* reinforcing the
final sense of stability. The three parts of the novel correspond to
exposition, development, and recapitulation, respectively, with the
last chapter of Part Three forming the coda. The novel opens with
the recurring motif "What's it going to be then, eh?", consistently
identified with Alex, followed by the presentation of a series of principal "themes" in the "exposition". Most of these return, in various
degrees of transformation, in the "development" and virtually all
recur in the "recapitulation", often in inverted relation to the original appearance. The book's "themes" include violence; sexual acts;
dreams; establishing dominance through physical confrontation;
protest against the subversion of free choice, as represented by
F. Alexander and the text of the book; societal authority; and music,
principally (though not exclusively) Beethoven's. The final chapter
of Part One, in which Alex is removed from his gang and taken into
police custody, corresponds to the *closing section* of the exposition,
in which the presentation of new themes comes to an end in preparation for inventive manipulation of some (but often not all) of these
themes in the development.

In sonata form, the development frequently begins in the minor
mode of the tonic when tonic is a major key. Alex's announcement at
the start of II/1, just after restatement of the main motif, that "this
is the real weepy and like tragic part of the story" represents a literary version of mode change from major to minor (51). The murder of
the new inmate in II/2 takes up the theme of violence introduced in
the opening chapters of Part One, while the sexual acts in I/2–4 are
transmuted into the phallic imagery of the "white pinky bassoon" in
Alex's dream in II/2 and the public demonstration of the "cure" of
his sexual desire in II/7. Alex's nightmare in II/5 mirrors his dream
about "droog Georgie" in I/4. The theme of protest against the loss
of free will passes from F. Alexander in Part One to the prison chaplain in Part Two, while the theme of societal authority, represented
by the truant officer P. R. Deltoid and the police in the "exposition",

4. "The Writer and Music", *The Listener* 67:1727 (3 May 1962), 761–62.

is taken over by various officials (Dr Brodsky, the Prison Warden, the Governor, and the Minister of the Interior) in the "development". The final part of a musical development section is the "retransition", in which the return of the tonic key in the recapitulation is signaled by the arrival of that key's dominant chord. In *A Clockwork Orange,* the last chapter of Part Two serves this function, demonstrating Alex's post-Ludovican readiness to retransition back into society.

Part Three comprises transformation and inversion of the themes presented in Part One consistent with the musical procedure of modulation and restatement typical of sonata-form recapitulation. Whereas in I/1 Alex drank moloko, consorted with his three pals, and prowled city streets by foot, in III/1 he drinks chai, rides the autobus through the city, and attempts (unsuccessfully) to reunite with his family, now consisting of three—dad, mum, and Joe, who has become "like a son to them"—to equal the number of droogs in the opening chapter. Victims of Alex's violence in the "exposition" become his victimizers in the "recapitulation"—the "starry schoolmaster" (I/1, III/2), Billyboy and Dim (I/1–2, III/3), and F. Alexander (I/2, III/5). As Burgess once summed it up, "The place where Alex and his mirror-image F. Alexander are most guilty of hate and violence is called HOME, and it is here, we are told, that charity ought to begin".[5] Following a series of analogous correspondences throughout the rest of the "recapitulation" comes the "closing section" (III/6), which finds Alex in a position parallel to those at the conclusion of the "exposition" and "development": at the culmination of one structural period in his life and ready to enter another.

The final chapter (III/7) comprises the "coda", bringing what Burgess considered a sense of resolution to the novel, although many (most notably Stanley Kubrick, who left it out of the film) have found it disappointingly anticlimactic.[6] The common musical practice of restating the opening of the exposition in the coda is imitated here through literary parody, with Alex back in the Korova Milkbar with a new trio of droogs. The mock-equivalence of this scene to the opening brings closure to the literary structure, allowing Alex to choose a mature, constructive path of responsible behavior over the destructive, evil acts of his youth.

The motif "What's it going to be then, eh?" demarcates the novel's sonata form in a manner comparable to the repetitions of the

5. "Clockwork Marmalade", *The Listener,* 87: 2238 (17 February 1972), 198.
6. To Edward Forman, the final chapter is "as much a betrayal as a maturing: a betrayal of creativity and above all a betrayal of Beethoven, whose angel trumpets and devil trombones have been silenced by Alex's new taste for 'very quiet and like yearny' music". Forman, "Violence, Sex and Music—Equivalent Addictions? Music in *A Clockwork Orange*" in *Portraits of the Artist in* A Clockwork Orange (Angers: Presses de l'Université d'Angers, 2003), 139.

familiar four-note motif from the start of Beethoven's Fifth Symphony at structurally significant points throughout the first movement. This line occurs twelve times in the novel—four times in the exposition (I/1), three in the development (II/1), three in the recapitulation (III/1), and two in the coda (III/7)—set apart each time as a separate, complete paragraph.[7] Its final appearances in III/7 provide compelling evidence that Burgess considered the twenty-first chapter as essential to the novel's structure as a coda in sonata form. With his fondness for applying what he termed "arithmology" to the structure of his novels, he carefully constructed A Clockwork Orange in three parts of seven chapters each to produce a total of twenty-one chapters, symbolizing the traditional age of maturity:

> 21 is the symbol of human maturity, or used to be, since at 21 you got the vote and assumed adult responsibility . . . The number of chapters is never entirely arbitrary. Just as a musical composer starts off with a vague image of bulk and duration, so a novelist begins with an image of length, and this image is expressed in the number of sections and the number of chapters into which the work will be disposed. Those twenty-one chapters were important to me.[8]

(Why Alex matures at eighteen instead of twenty-one is one of the novel's chief inconsistencies.)

The twelve appearances of "What's it going to be then, eh?" are as obligatory as the novel's twenty-one chapters, and it is hardly a coincidence that 12 is the retrograde of 21. Without the "coda", there would be just ten occurrences of the motif, a number irreconcilable with the novel's arithmological structure. The number 12 equals the number of different musical pitches, points in the circle of fifths, and markers on a clock, all potent symbols in a book "about music" with "clock" in its title. Like hands spinning about a clock face or themes returning in a sonata form recapitulation, the principal themes and characters return in Part Three of A Clockwork Orange to bring the story full circle.

Burgess's commitment to the novel's musical structure may offer the strongest explanation for the marked change of tone in Chapter 21. In sonata form, the coda's function is to bring the composition to rest, achieving resolution by offsetting the drama built up in earlier sections, especially the development. In a Beethovenian coda, such as the unprecedentedly long one that concludes the Eroica Sym-

---

7. The appearances of the motif within a paragraph in II/1 (51) and in variant form ("That's what it's going to be then, brothers") near the end of III/7 (121) are structurally insignificant.
8. Anthony Burgess, "A Clockwork Orange Resucked", in this Norton Critical Edition, pp. 165–68.

phony's first movement, resolution is achieved by repeating motifs, previously used in highly dramatic ways, within a new context that eliminates the prior sense of urgency. This is exactly what Burgess does in Chapter 21, turning the bellicose fifteen-year-old Alex of the exposition into the pacific eighteen-year-old of the coda while converting the Korova Milkbar from a location of incipient violence into a scene of quasi-autumnal calm.

* * *

TODD F. DAVIS AND KENNETH WOMACK

[The Family]†

* * *

In spite of what appear to be Alex's obvious attempts to establish and participate in various family structures throughout the novel—indeed, to search for some form of "HOME"—critics continue to ignore the role of the family as a substantial narrative force in Burgess's text. An interdisciplinary reading of *A Clockwork Orange* using recent insights in ethical criticism and family systems psychotherapy demonstrates not only the necessity of the twenty-first chapter as the fruition of Burgess's moral vision, but also the centrality of family structures as catalysts for interpersonal development and as ethical foundations for individual change. * * * In addition to functioning as a self-reflexive means for critics to explain the contradictory emotions and problematic moral stances that often mask literary characters, ethical criticism provides its practitioners with the capacity for positing socially relevant interpretations by celebrating the Aristotelian qualities of living well and flourishing. * * * In addition to its obvious therapeutic applications, family systems psychotherapy's clinical vocabulary affords literary scholars with a critical mode for investigating, in fictional narratives, the role of the family both as an agent of change and as a mechanism for maintaining stasis. In contrast with Freudian and psychoanalytic approaches to literary study, family systems psychotherapy maintains that the family presupposes the individual as the matrix of identity. * * * Merging the terminology of family systems psychotherapy with the moral philosophy inherent in contemporary ethical criticism allows us to recognize the vital intersections in the novel between Burgess's

† From "'O my brothers': Reading the Anti-Ethics of the Pseudo-Family in Anthony Burgess's *A Clockwork Orange*," *College Literature: A Journal of Scholarly Criticism and Pedagogy* 29.2 (Spring 2002): 19–36. Reprinted by permission of *College Literature*.

satirical anti-ethics and the problematic familial structures that Alex encounters throughout the narrative.

In *A Clockwork Orange*, Burgess depicts numerous incarnations of what for the purposes of this essay we will refer to as the "pseudo-family," the dysfunctional interpersonal unit that problematizes Alex's various efforts to establish selfhood and to transcend the violent landscapes of his youth. In contrast with the family, which by its very definition attempts to provide its members with secure states of being in which to develop and thrive as differentiated selves, the pseudo-family offers only the illusion of genuine community. Lying beneath the facade of the pseudo-family is the interpersonal violence of self-indulgence that leads inevitably to betrayal and the creation of pseudo-selves, or those individuals, according to Barnard and Corrales, who remain unable to maintain any real stasis between their inner feelings and their outward behavior.[1] Alex's destructive encounters with the pseudo-family in the novel force him to persist in various states of homeostatic equilibrium, rendering him unable to effect the process of morphogenesis that might provide him with the means for finally glimpsing a mature, fully realized sense of self.

While the first twenty chapters of Burgess's novel offer various representations of the pseudo-family—from Alex's ultra-violent gang of "droogs" and his self-serving Post-Corrective Adviser, P. R. Deltoid, to his ineffectual parents and the sadistic practitioners of Ludovico's Technique—*A Clockwork Orange*'s restored twenty-first chapter depicts Alex's single creative act: his hopeful vision of a healthy, functional family. * * * In order for Burgess to attempt moral satire, he must trust that his audience will perceive his portrayal of a world filled with surreal violence, sadistic sexuality, and uncontrollable drug abuse as one that calls for some moral equivalent, some sense of implicit humanity. Alex's anti-ethics—his refusal to engage in ethical deliberation, his pursuit of destructive action, his disregard for any other life—ultimately ends in exhaustion, and his ensuing vision of a potentially healthy family structure suggests the possibility for individual change rooted in a community of nurture.

Alex's lack of any functional family system in which he can interact with mature and fully realized adult selves manifests itself in his own hyper-exaggerated sense of pseudo-self, the persona that he invents in order to fulfill his desires to belong to and be accepted by the various spurious family structures that Burgess depicts in the novel. While he clearly creates a work of dystopian satire in *A Clockwork Orange*, Burgess nevertheless avails himself of genuine teen

1. Barnard, Charles P., and Ramon Garrido Corrales, *The Theory and Technique of Family Therapy* (Springfield: Thomas, 1979), 85-7.

angst in his characterization of Alex, a fifteen-year-old at the beginning of the novel, who, like many his age, finds his sense of self
precariously lost in a state of flux and moments of beguiling awk-
wardness. Alex responds to these feelings of uncertainty and change
by trying on different costumes, behavioral modes, and verbal man-
nerisms in an effort to establish what he perceives to be a stable
sense of identity. * * * Alex conjoins his inner and outer worlds
through his adroit use of the neo-Slavic Nadsat language, the linguistic signifier of his pseudo-self. Language, which represents the
internal life of the mind through external expression, provides Alex
with a means for interacting with his peers, as well as for delivering
violence to the unfortunate bystanders who cross his path. * * *
While the Nadsat language offers numerous phrases for describing
acts of violence and an entire lexicon of misogynistic tropes—
including several different epithets for deriding women—it lacks
noticeably any words for denoting love, compassion, or the kind of
interrelationship that one might experience in a functional family
system. Essentially a pseudo-language constructed upon a series of
playful phrases, puns, and uncertain connotations, Nadsat, despite
its braggadocio, succeeds rather ironically in demonstrating Alex's
tremendous feelings of insecurity, his lack of sophistication, and his
naivete. Alex's indeterminate usage of the word "like," for example,
exemplifies the manner in which his application of the Nadsat language parallels the pseudo-experiences that he undergoes in the
skewed reality of his life. Often used as a means for reconciling his
inner emotions with the outer world from which he feels so utterly
disconnected, Alex's constant use of "like" connotes his social dislo-
cation and his emotional separation from the world beyond the self.
In one instance, after he and his droogs terrorize yet another hap-
less victim, he remarks that "there was like quiet and we were full of
like hate" (19), revealing his inability to comment with any certainty
about the validity of either the quality of his environment or his
degree of emotional response, respectively. Yet this linguistic phenomenon does not simply relate to the description of negative emotional reactions, as Alex demonstrates in his confusion about the
full range of emotional responses during his late encounter with love:
"And he like gave this Georgina of his a like loving look" (120), Alex
observes, unable to identify with any precision the passionate import
of a romantic gesture.

In addition to its inherent uncertainty about the nature of emotional responses, the Nadsat language lacks any signifiers that allude
to the future and all that it might entail. Alex's uncertainty about the
future elicits his repeated refrain: "What's it going to be then,
eh?". While Alex frequently avails himself of Nadsat's neo-Slavic
vocabulary, his efforts at communicating about the future force

him to revert to English for any discussion about his fate, rather than employing the Russian sud'ba as the potentially appropriate phrase for referring to this future state of being. For Alex, the notion of fate simply remains yet another confusing and unfamiliar concept—an idea that he can only fathom by invoking the distancing mechanism provided by the Nadsat articulation of "like": "It all seemed right and proper and like Fate," he remarks in one instance (52). Alex and other progenitors of the teen language of Nadsat simply cannot imagine a future, fated or otherwise, because they devote all of their energies to sustaining the facade of the pseudo-selves that they must maintain to survive in the present. When he finally refers to the darker possibilities of his own fate while undergoing the controversial Ludovico's Technique, Alex lacks any concrete signifier for describing his future: "I viddied that there would be no escaping from any of all this," he says, stunned into a linguistic stupor (73). Alex's inability to express his feelings about the future is only matched, rather ironically, by his unparalleled capacity for registering insolence and disrespect. His irreverent appropriation of a mock-Elizabethan discourse constitutes the single fullest and most unrestrained expression of his pseudo-self in *A Clockwork Orange*. As his personal idiom for expressing vitriol and contempt for his elders, Alex's mock-Elizabethan prattle imbues him with the means for verbally lampooning his victims even as he prepares to assault them with his steely "britva": "Never fear," Alex proclaims; "if fear thou hast in thy heart, O brother, pray banish it forthwith" (17). * * *

During his metaphorical search for "HOME," Alex comes into contact with a variety of pseudo-families that might usefully be considered in terms of traditional sociological categories, including nuclear, extended, and institutional families—common support systems that all individuals seek out in order to fulfill the realization of the self. Rather than affording him with the opportunity to alter his dysfunctional patterns, each of these pseudo-families allows him to sustain the homeostasis of his vacuous existence. Alex encounters nuclear families in the form of his parents and his droogs. Despite their significant role as his family-of-origin, Alex's parents offer little more than a physical presence in his life. While he and his parents live together at Municipal Flatblock 18A, their concern for him manifests itself only in the dream world, as opposed to the reality of their daily existence. In one instance, Alex's father complains about a vivid dream in which he sees Alex lying on the street in a pool of his own blood after being severely beaten by street thugs like his son. Rather than attempting to placate his father's fears, Alex instead gives his father money with which to buy Scotch, a gesture that suddenly allays his father's concerns and leaves his parents "with loving smiles all round" (35). Later, after returning "home" from prison, Alex's parents fail him once again by replacing him with a stranger whom they treat as their de facto son. Again, the father's paternal loyalty seems to be motivated by the possibility of financial gain: "Well, you see, son," Alex's father tells him, "Joe's paid next month's rent already. I mean, whatever we do in the future we can't say to Joe to get out, can we?" (89).

Alex's metaphorical "droog" brothers—the remaining members of his nuclear family—also falter as participants in his implicit support system. Rather than enjoying genuine feelings of compassion and fraternity, Alex and his droogs share nothing more than a brotherhood of violence and depravity. Ironically described by Alex as "a very smiling and polite square" (6), his droog brethren offer no loyalty to Alex beyond what his leadership and their sheer numbers allow them to achieve during their nightly rampages. As with any group of small children, Alex and his droogs vie for position and manipulate each other to satisfy their selfish desires. Their relationship even functions upon a hierarchy of sorts, with Alex asserting himself as patriarch while the others protest about democracy: "There has to be a leader," Alex argues. "Discipline there has to be. Right?" (22). Dim, the slow-witted brute, Georgie, Alex's traitorous subordinate, and Pete, the quartet's smooth-talking diplomat, round out the membership of Alex's gang. A self-assured and self-deluded leader, Alex foolishly considers his droogs to be mere "sheep" under his control. In a robbery gone awry, Alex's droogs shock his sense of fraternal propriety after they betray him by knocking him unconscious and abandoning him to the police: "Where are my stinking traitorous droogs?" (45). Alex laments, only to effect a double betrayal later when he implicates Dim, Georgie, and Pete by name for their role in the crime. As with his parents, Alex's droog brothers function as his support system only as long as he serves to further their selfish ends. The same pseudo-self that allows Alex to be betrayed by his droogs deludes him into believing in their absolute loyalty and in his own unparalleled authority.

* * *

Alex completes the initial stages of his ethical transition during a chance meeting with his old droog Pete, now married and selling insurance. By witnessing Pete's radical transformation from droog to husband, Alex undergoes a conversion of his own. * * * [T]he future suddenly exists; no longer trapped in the endless cycle of gang violence, he finally usurps his pseudo-self and imagines the creation of his own family: "Tomorrow is all like sweet flowers and the turning vonny earth and the stars and the old Luna up there and your old droog Alex all on his oddy knocky seeking like a mate" (121). While this moment marks the beginning of Alex's transformation, it should not be misconstrued as some naive happy ending, shot in Technicolor and accompanied by the joyous song of a bluebird. As suggested before, Alex's use of the word "like" alludes to his inability to truly understand the range of emotional experience. Because Alex has never been part of (nor truly known) a fully functioning, healthy family, he cannot abandon, even in this moment of catalepsis, the linguistic qualifiers of his past life. While he is able to transcend the parameters of the Nadsat language in order to speak about his hope for the future, he continues to reveal his insecurity about what being and having an adult, romantic companion may entail when he says that he is "seeking *like* a mate" (emphasis added). Yet, given the nihilistic brutality of his past life and the absence of any person who has demonstrated care or love toward him, Alex's yearning for a mate and child, his very capacity to conceive of such a community, suggests a far more hopeful turn than the novel's first twenty chapters would ever have allowed us to expect.

Without the twenty-first chapter, then, A *Clockwork Orange*'s narrative omits Alex's ethical transformation and Burgess's own redaction of the pseudo-families that plague his narrator's youth. The novel's twentieth chapter closes with Alex's sarcastic conclusion to his hospital stay: "I was cured all right" (114). Yet A *Clockwork Orange*, published in its entirety, not only allows us to witness the inception of a genuine "cure," but also enables us to recognize the pseudo-self in all of its absurd proportions. Robbed of Alex's dream of a functional family system, the novel would languish in Alex's protracted condition of homeostasis. Alex's morphogenesis occurs both because of his cataleptic impression and because of his understanding that, as Burgess reasons in his introduction to the novel, "to devastate is easier and more spectacular than to create" (167). Finally grown up and fully prepared to accept the difficult challenges of selfhood, Alex no longer chooses the easier road to ultraviolence, opting instead to embark upon a lifetime of familial commitment and human renewal.

GEOFFREY SHARPLESS

[Education, Masculinity, and Violence]†

Critics conventionally position Burgess's *A Clockwork Orange* within the sub-genre of futuristic dystopias without considering its nostalgia for a version of masculinity best understood as typical of the Arnoldian public school. This misprision is natural, since the Russianized argot and Dionysian "ultra-violence" of Alex the droog do not immediately evoke *Tom Brown's School-days*[1]—or any other portrait of the public school boy. Nonetheless, juxtaposing these narratives, which are separated by more than a hundred years, throws important illumination on *A Clockwork Orange*, and redirects critical attention to the persistence of Arnoldian masculinity in twentieth-century British literature.

* * *

Burgess's critics might have been more alert to Alex's matriculation in an Arnoldian program had they considered more carefully *Time for a Tiger*[2], the first piece of Burgess's Malayan trilogy. This novel, about the difficulty of exporting Rugby-like schools to the minions in Britain's empire, depicts an educator who abandons the Arnoldian ideal, and is absorbed by the exotic country he goes to convert. This might itself have been sufficient to establish that Burgess had an overt interest in public school pedagogy. The hero of *A Clockwork Orange*, however, is an unequivocal practitioner; even his resistance is characteristic. Indeed, Alex's remarkable fraternity with the Arnoldian product suggests a complete triumph for the latter's pedagogy. This similarity holds even for the most optimistic and influential version of the public schoolboy, Tom Brown,[3] whose story "made the modern public school."[4]

This pairing of Tom and Alex would be unusual if only because Alex seems to be one of the most evil representations of boyhood ever forwarded popularly and Tom—for another era—one of the most virtuous. As Coleridge observed, however, opposites are but farthest apart of the same kind—and, rather than incommensurate, prove

---

† From "Clockwork Education: The Persistence of the Arnoldian Ideal," *Postmodern Culture* 4.3, May 1994. Reprinted by permission of the author.
1. Hughes, Thomas, *Tom Brown's School-days* (New York: St. Martin's Press, 1967).
2. *Time for a Tiger* (London: Heinemann, 1956).
3. *Tom Brown's School-days* (1857), novel by Thomas Hughes, who attended Rugby School, the setting for the novel, during the era of the reforming headmaster Thomas Arnold. (Thomas Arnold was the father of the English poet and literary critic Matthew Arnold, author of *Culture and Anarchy* [1867–68]). [Editor's note.]
4. Mack, Edward C., and W. G. Armytage, *Thomas Hughes* (London: Ernest Benn Ltd., 1952).

to be the two sides of the same coin. Reading Alex and Tom as twins, it does not take long to discover even in Hughes's happy fantasy of Rugby that his Arnoldian telos of self-control, heterosexual love, moderation, and upright morality is interpenetrated with perversity, pederasty, a fetishization of style, Machiavellian management training, an interest in hand-to-hand combat and blood-letting, and, ultimately, a conviction that adult heterosexual manliness smacks of death.

*   *   *

Burgess's inability to decide whether the novel is anarchistic or moralistic has appeared not only in his un-Joycean interventions in the novel's exegesis, but in the publication of different versions of the text. As first issued, the novel had twenty chapters; conceived and written, the novel had twenty-one chapters, that number standing, in what Burgess called his "arithmology," for the age of adulthood. In most readings the excluded twenty-first chapter is taken to address precisely the question of the story's final moral position, as expressed in an acceptance of adulthood.

*   *   *

While a critical claim can be heard that there is, or at least should be, a consensus that the shorter version is more interesting, each ending poses a conundrum. In neither ending is evil punished, nor is Alex shown to repent or regret his atrocities. Neither ending answers whether the conscious conditioning by the state is any more or less moral than the unconscious conditioning by family, economy, etc. Neither ending reveals if conditioning is better or worse that makes us peaceable or allows us to be violent, or if we can ever be more than merely clockwork. Both endings are thoroughly and equally ambivalent about the point Burgess claims the novel makes entirely too obvious—about moral choice. Similarly, the point that Burgess himself can be heard prefering the shorter ending, and that we should credit this *obiter*, is also dubious. Burgess calls the shorter version "sensational" but "not a fair picture of human life," and then, undoubtedly savoring the irony, defends the longer version via Pontius Pilate's "Quod scripsi scripsi" (168).

That Burgess himself does not know whether he wants this text to end by celebrating the perverse pleasures of boyhood or the muted satisfactions of adult masculinity reflects the very contradiction that mobilizes Tom Brown. Suspended between an Arnoldian disdain for boys' "wickedness," and Hughes's hopeful fantasy about the utopia of boyish pleasure, both *A Clockwork Orange* and *Tom Brown's School-days* relate the importance of resisting adulthood, and retaining the pleasures of remaining in a timeless, childish perversity. Both versions of *ACO* and *TBS* are significantly structured by their concern, as Matthew Arnold put it, that "faith in machinery is . . . our besetting danger."[5] Both texts are deeply—almost furiously—nostalgic for a moment of health and wholeness that never existed. Thus, when Alex is implicated in the Arnoldian tradition of schoolboy Eros, this does not return the narrative to a lost simplicity, because that tradition is itself subject to the contradictions that animate A Clockwork Orange. Alex's brutal conditioning, his strange language and dress, his savage sexuality, his wickedness, cruelty, and sadism, his devious sensitivity to the ebb and flow of group power, were in fact essential to Arnold's Rugby School, and helped catapult it into international prominence as an unsurpassed institution of man-making.

The Arnoldian pedagogy engages and activates the Victorian concern with the male body as a locus of political power. The nineteenth-century British schoolboy doctrine that athletic contests like rugby and football formed the character of the man derives significantly from Tom Brown. * * * Moral health, Arnoldian Victorians like Hughes believed, was profoundly implicated in physical achievement. The notion of moral health came to include physical courage: unless one was willing to assume physical risk, one could not hope to achieve moral salvation.

*   *   *

The modern public school, as invented through Tom Brown's School-days, manifested the Victorian obsession with the physical body's perfectability and corruptibility. While Hughes repeatedly praises Thomas Arnold in the text, he also unconsciously reveals that the headmaster, in his treatment of the bodies of his students, enacted his morbid identification with Christ's physical suffering. Hughes wishes to portray school rituals like boxing, football—and even fagging and bullying—as expressing the unalloyed joys of youthful play. Yet School-days also reveals Dr. Arnold's abhorrence of the liminal and transgressive body of youth. The book's textual and graphic representation of the body illustrate Arnold's theory that to educate boys is to turn them from beasts into Christians—to re-enact the moral development of human society: moral ontogeny recapitulating moral phylogeny.

Where Hughes differs from Arnold is in his attitude towards boyhood. Arnold sees boyhood solely as a condition to be mortified and overcome; Hughes agrees that in the end it must be left behind, but relishes the opportunity it offers for maximizing the pleasures of the body. Without reference to any moralizing process, he concludes his paean to rugby with a remarkable claim about the proportionate value of sport to everyday life:

5. Arnold, Matthew. Culture and Anarchy (New York: Chelsea House, 1983).

This is worth living for; the whole sum of school-boy existence gathered up into one straining, struggling half-hour, a half-hour worth a year of common life. (*TBS*, 106)

＊ ＊ ＊

＊ ＊ ＊ Though Hughes periodically reminds us that violent play is good for the state, Tom Brown loves it for its own sake. Alex's passion for "the old ultra-violence," while notched higher in damage inflicted, reflects the same celebration of the pleasures of the incoherent body that characterize Tom Brown's matches in the mud and blood of the close. Alex never tires of detailing the propensity of adult vecks to turn into porous gore and blood when beaten. The droogs describe blood as "our dear old droog"; "red-red vino on tap and in all the same places, like it's put out by the same big firm" (18); "Then out comes the blood, my brothers, real beautiful" (7); "A fair tap with a crowbar . . . brought the red out like an old friend" (10); and "then it was blood, not song nor vomit, that came out of his filthy rot. Then we went on our way" (12).

These separate confirmations that bodies are never discrete entities, but oozing, porous and liminal, precede a gang-fight that culminates in a glorious extrusion of blood. Having enhanced the ecstasy of this bloodletting by taking "milk with knives" to "sharpen" his sensations, Alex's success in piercing the body of the other droog makes him rhapsodic:

> [Billyboy] was a malenky bit too slow and heavy in his movements to vred anyone really bad. And, my brothers, it was real satisfaction to me to waltz—left two three, right two three— and carve left cheeky and right cheeky, so that like two curtains of blood seemed to pour out at the same time, one on either side of his fat filthy oily snout in the winter starlight (14).

Reversing the direction of our analysis about the culture of Rugby School and the managed violence of the playing-field, we can locate the culture at work in this scene of droogish anarchy: we can not only find the violence in the gentleman; we can find the gentleman in the violence. The "curtains of blood" in the above passage do not herald the apocalypse, but evoke a sportsman's appreciation for the results of good technique that borders on the aesthetic. We hear Alex's pride in his team—the captain's sense of the players' movements around him. He details with pleasure his own movements, and the violence softens into a gentleman's dance, with the expert's assessment of the opponent's weaknesses, and of proper footwork.

＊ ＊ ＊

The emphasis on style—even in the middle of marked danger—would seem to sharpen the subversive point of Alex's pleasure in flouting the conformity expected of the Arnoldian male body. Like Oscar Wilde's dandy—another response to the certitudes of public school masculinity—Alex uses style as a declaration of independence. Thus, when Alex recalls his fight scene with Billyboy, he remembers that his droogs looked marvelous; Alex proudly observes that his droogs were "dressed in the heighth of fashion" (3). For Alex, his clothes assert that he controls his own body, and he uses the image he presents to the public as a "semiotic guerrilla warfare," in Eco's phrase.

* * *

Alex's personal style of dress seems at first to indicate his resistance to power. But when Alex appropriates fashion as a means of asserting his identity he is building a new temple on the site of the old. Instead of forwarding himself as a new man, his preoccupation with style and taste above all else renders his portrait as an "old boy" strikingly clear: Alex disdains those who do not follow his idea of fashion.

That Alex, in insisting on irony and rebellion, is merely recreating a conformist world in microcosm, appears most readily in his confrontation with Dim. For example, "Poor old Dim" does not know or care that Alex's ostensible punkishness engages a high-culture seriousness toward aesthetics yoked to his own political ambition. Alex approves of the genital designs of his droogs Pete, who has a hand, and Georgie, a flower, on his groin, but finds himself in a perplexing spot for an anarchist when he finds Dim's choice of a clown's face in bad taste—evidently too close to naming "the clown he was" (7). Such an overt image lacks the tension and irony Alex requires to see himself and his droogs as beings of superior taste. Alex feels demeaned by his association and fellowship with such a philistine as Dim. This conflict is the first suggestion that Alex's idiosyncratic style, which at first seems to be a marker of his resistance to British culture, has roots in the traditional mechanisms of class. * * *

[Reading Alex as an Arnoldian schoolboy] helps to correct the interpretive error that Nadsat signifies postmodern chaos and anarchy: in fact, the words always have a direct and obvious referent. * * * He does not speak Nadsat because the modern youth of the day don't know any better. His use of Nadsat is a cultural achievement in the same sense that his fashion statements are: both enhance his own authority. He does not just narrate the story, but authors himself as the subject who knows. The reader, by contrast, becomes the cultural exile. If you cannot figure out what Alex means, your existence—at least as a reader—is marginal.

Recognizing the power of language, Alex has learned to talk very well indeed. He is a student of different dialects of his society, and notices when words are alien; he remembers the words of an older prisoner's slang he cannot fathom, and makes sure to point out that this superannuation has made the speaker powerless. He hears two younger girls in a record shop "who had their own way of govoreeting" (31), and immediately gets the idea to seduce them. He comments on this encounter, which consists primarily of Alex's sadistic sexual attacks, that "they must still have their education. And education they had had" (33). His familiarity with the allusive patterns that determine appropriate speech can become quite humorous; here, in an ironic improvisation, he speaks a Shakespearean language of the duel: "How art thou, thou globby bottle of cheap stinking chip-oil? Come and get one in the yarbles, if you have any yarbles, you eunuch jelly, thou" (13). He also believes that he can shift his shape through the proper words, and, when trying to get out of prison, he imitates a sycophantic "gentleman": " 'Sir, I have done my best, have I not?' I always used my very polite gentleman's goloss govoreeting with those at the top.' 'I've tried, sir, haven't I" (55). Even the lyrical idioms of traditional Eros are accessible when he needs to escape the nausea he is programmed to feel when experiencing violent impulses towards women

> O most beautiful and beauteous of devotchkas, I throw like my heart at your feet for you to like trample all over. If I had a rose I would give it to you. If it was all rainy and cally now on the ground you could have my platties to walk on so as not to cover your dainty nogas with filth and cal (84).

To celebrate Nadsat as verging on a perverse interior gibberish misses that Alex demands that language be meaningful enough to free him from an inner exile. Nadsat represents a rupture with "normal" teleologies only if you ignore its conventional referentiality. Similarly, even the intermittent triumphs of Alex's perversity, whether linguistic or physical, do not manage to forestall his inevitable graduation into an Arnoldian version of adult health—at least in the longer version of the book.

* * *

The irony of Burgess's ambition to replace the droog with the Arnoldian schoolboy is that they have always been thoroughly integrated; Alex's wickedness and cruelty are as much the stuff of empire-building as is the Arnoldian gentleman's phantasy of morality. In effect, though Rugby's classrooms are now called Correctional Schools, State Jails, and conditioning laboratories, and the playing fields have become the London streets, Alex's education terminates in the same phantasized ideal of adult masculinity that

Tom's does. Burgess has not overturned a public school idea of proper masculine development, but fulfilled Thomas Arnold's ambition to write his pedagogy across the face of the world.

SHIRLEY CHEW

[Circularity]†

It may be that soon there will be little room for enlightened and old-fashioned people like Woolton.[1] Certainly none in the achieved technological future of *A Clockwork Orange* (1962). This rebarbative world is overrun by hoodlums and policemen, and presided over by sinister scientists with the power to wind a person's very instincts contrariwise. Advanced knowledge has merely confirmed the belief that man is depraved, yet, fortunately, little more than a mechanical toy, a clockwork orange. The only form of individualism left resides in someone like Alex and finds expression in slick brutality. In concentrating here on the flair of the young for physical and sexual violence, Burgess provides an answer to the charge of corrupting their morals which the teachers of the earlier novels were faced with.

In his dual role of villain and victim, Alex resembles Milton's Satan. The structure of the plot is circular and the Alex of the second half of the novel, reclaimed by clever doctors so efficiently from violence that the very thought of hurting anyone even in self-defence nauseates him, is punished in sequence by each of his former victims. Finally, for political reasons and by the process of hypnopaedia, he is returned to his original nature. In this manner, his crimes are offset by evidences of the same strong sadistic tendencies in other people. His teen-age friends and enemies have been from the first soulless brutes, as apt hoodlums as policemen. The experts in behavioural transformation are more sophisticated in their enjoyment of vicarious violence. The so-called idealists who oppose the existing government are quite ready to destroy Alex to further their cause. And in a fantastical scene, maundering nonagenarians in the public library turn wild and attack Alex in vindication of old age. This episode lines up with the scene earlier in the same novel when Alex is set on by savage cats while robbing a house, with the war of the sexes in *The Wanting Seed* (1962), and the imperturbability of Vythilingam before Crabbe's drowning in *Beds in the East*, as an instance when Burgess' macabre imagination working sheer and intense reaches a breathtaking weirdness.

---

† From "Mr. Livedog's Day: The Novels of Anthony Burgess," *Encounter* 38 (June 1972), 57–64 (59–60). Reprinted by permission.
1. Woolton is the humanistic headmaster in Burgess's novel *The Worm and the Ring* (London: Heinemann, 1961). [Editor's note.]

Alex is a hoodlum with a difference. He cannot bear dirt, or drunkenness. He is devoted to serious music though characteristically its beauty and passion only move him to glorious visions of violence. He has a proper contempt for the impersonality of institutions, and the language he uses reflects his dauntlessness, his intelligence, his exuberance, as well as his limitations. It is an ingenious invention, onomatopoeic, concrete, and vigorous, swelling every now and then to the orotund flourishes of religious preachers. In case the reader fails to make sense of it, Burgess allows Dr Branom of the reclamation centre to describe the origins of this language: "Odd bits of old rhyming slang. . . . A bit of gipsy talk, too. But most of the roots are Slav." Moreover the context is so carefully created that the meaning of Alex's words becomes evident even if one has no knowledge of Russian—a method of instruction familiar to language teachers.

> Mother Slouse, the wife, was sort of froze behind the counter. We could tell she would creech murder given one chance, so I was round that counter very skorry and had a hold of her, and a horrorshow big lump she was too, all nuking of scent and with flipflop big bobbing groodies on her. I'd got my rooker round her rot to stop her belting out death and destruction to the four winds of heaven, but this lady doggie gave me a large foul big bite on it and it was me that did the creeching, and then she opened up beautiful with a flip yell for the millicents.

The idiosyncratic language, the neat structure, the absence of any character with whom we can readily identify—these make the closed world of Alex convincing and vivid. They persuade us that it is a fable we are reading although we recognise in it trends in normal society which have been pushed to the extreme. So that when at the end, for a very naturalistic reason (the fact of growing up), Alex tires of his hoodlum ways and begins to hanker for a sedate domestic life with wife and baby, the novel loses its integrity and falls into the sentimental. Realism has impinged awkwardly upon fantasy. Alex's ways in *A Clockwork Orange* have been so deliberately narrow and consistent in their perversity that they belong to the world of allegory. We need only compare him with those heroes of Burgess upon whom sufferings have been imposed in excess of their follies to realise that his punishments are ritualistic rather than in measure. The conclusion of the novel invokes therefore new criteria for judging Alex's conduct which make the preceding savagery seem gratuitous and something of an exercise in the brutal on the part of the author.

*   *   *

259

BERTHOLD SCHOENE

[Fashion and Masculinity]†

* * *

* * * Burgess's dystopian mode has encouraged humanist critics to read *A Clockwork Orange* both ahistorically and generically as a case study of man's free choice between vice and virtue. A gender-specific analysis of the novel's almost exclusively male cast, all of which are subject to severe patriarchal conditioning, has so far been neglected. Forty years after its original conception, the novel fails to shock or convince as an ominous allegorical prophecy concerning the future fate of human civilisation. However, it remains intriguing as the excessive and hyperbolic climax of a specifically male tradition in post-war British literature, namely the Angry Young Men movement of the 1950s and early 1960s.

* * * Alex hides behind a mask, fashioning himself and his entourage of 'droogs' after the ideal of a highly stylised hypermasculinity. Symptomatically, 'nadsat'—Alex and his droogs' arcane sociolect—operates not only as a rebellious, anarchic counter-code but also as an elaborate adaptation of the neologistic diction favoured by comic-book superheroes. The more eloquent Alex's command of nadsat, the more successfully can he detach himself from the compromising emotionality of his boyish self. Nadsat forms a crucial, . . . constitutive part of the droogs' manly masquerade, merging them into a uniform elitist group and thereby perfecting the artifice of their fearless and seemingly invulnerable warrior masculinity. Alex's extreme style consciousness signals that he lives his life in camouflage. In fact, he performs an almost grotesque drag act of masculinity, impersonating a phantasmatic superhero whose glamorous costume and exaggerated bodily contours he is eager to copy, yet of course hopelessly unable ever to match perfectly:

> The four of us were dressed in the heighth of fashion, which in those days was a pair of black very tight tights with the old jelly mould, as we called it, fitting on the crotch underneath the tights . . . Then we wore waisty jackets without lapels but with these very big built-up shoulders ('pletchoes' we called them) which were a kind of a mockery of having real shoulders like that (3–4).

† From "Anthony Burgess's *A Clockwork Orange*," in *Writing Men: Literary Masculinities from* Frankenstein *to the New Man* (Edinburgh: Edinburgh UP, 2000), 66–76. Reprinted by permission of Edinburgh University Press.

The droogs' identity is a strenuous, adopted pose. Notably, the boys' incongruous outfit is not of their own making but fastidiously tailored after the fashion of the day which, in turn, reflects the hegemonic gender dictates of the totalitarian patriarchy in which they live. In Alex's world, masculine superiority manifests and expresses itself by dint of a hierarchically motivated dress code that accentuates a man's public rank and persona at the same time as it elides the uniqueness of his individual self. Instead of rebelling against such insidious ideological impositions, Alex internalises them, as his awe on meeting 'the Minister of the Interior or Inferior' demonstrates. According to Alex, 'you could viddy who was the real important veck right away, very tall and with blue glazzies and with real horrorshow platties on him, the most lovely suit, brothers, I had ever viddied, absolutely in the heighth of fashion' (61). Although Alex takes great pains at presenting himself as a free, anarchic individualist, he remains highly susceptible to the impact of patriarchal imperatives whose most coercive implications appear entirely to elude him. Instead of striving to break out of totalitarianism's densely woven network of behavioural norms and rules, and create himself proprioceptively in opposition to the system he perceives as oppressive, [Alex] readily dons the straitjacketing gender role of an essentially anti-individualistic, self-annihilating masculinity. As yet another boy keen to live up to the superheroic ideal, his desires and behaviour become predictable, rendering him extremely vulnerable to strategic manipulation as an instrument in the political plots and schemes of various patriarchal functionaries.

*   *   *

The droogs' ultraviolence, meted out with little apparent discrimination as they roam the streets, is never gratuitous but serves to assert the boys' manliness which seems constantly at risk of domestic etiolation. Alex and his droogs are typical representatives of the in-vogue fantasy of young male rebellion against conformity, cherished in the 1950s by a whole generation of disenchanted men and most enduringly inscribed in mainstream culture by Hollywood movies celebrating the impetuous individualism of iconic vanguard figures like, for example, James Dean and Marlon Brando. Unlike the United States, however, post-war Britain was devoid of any such indelible national myths as the American Dream. Deprived of its erstwhile imperial opportunities for exotic self-expansion and self-aggrandisement, the nation was caught up in a gradual, if steady process of decline. The ideals of patriarchal masculinity seemed on the wane for lack of adequately heroic causes. Significantly, the central complaint of British literature's most renowned Angry Young Man, Jimmy Porter in John Osborne's play *Look Back in Anger*, is that 'there aren't any good, brave causes left'.[1] Jimmy's sentiment noisily reverberates in Alex's 'disappointment at things as they were those days. Nothing to fight against really. Everything as easy as kiss-my-sharries' (11).

The violence perpetrated by Alex and his droogs is perhaps best explained as a desperate attempt at young, male self-assertion, escalating out of control due to the stagnancy and ideological immobility of the political system into which it unleashes itself. In the 1950s, British society found itself at a loss for viable means and strategies to accommodate the young male energies its own glamorisation of a certain kind of heroic masculinity had fostered. Conscriptive army service turned out to be a hopelessly inadequate substitute for the loss of real-life challenges like the war effort or the adventures opened up by the imperial enterprise. At the same time, attempts at domesticating the male by redefining the masculine role as that of a breadwinner, considerate partner in marriage, responsible father and DIY expert only resulted in the Angry Young Man backlash[2], of which Alex and his droogs are symptomatic, if extremist representatives. Alex and his droogs appropriate the patriarchal ideal of heroism-cum-servitude, claiming the heroism for themselves while associating servitude of any kind with the emasculating sphere of feminine domesticity. In *A Clockwork Orange* militant heroism becomes its own anarchic cause and, freed of its employment in patriarchally sanctioned schemes, it soon reveals its fundamentally barbaric, droogish complexion. *A Clockwork Orange* holds the message that patriarchy is always at risk of producing masculinity as a violent, destructive force which—in case it cannot be appropriately contained—may turn against the system and attack it by dint of its own devices.

[Alex] would no doubt make an excellent soldier if only his surplus energies could be reclaimed and applied to an authorised common cause. Significantly, one of the droogs (Dim) as well as the leader of another gang (Billyboy) reappear later in the novel as policemen, displaying the same old violent behaviour, only now it is authorised and perpetrated 'in the State's name' (96). Subscribing to the proverbial wisdom that 'boys will be boys, as always was' (96), Burgess presents adolescent male violence as inevitable. To him, the most crucial question seems to be if and how a system manages to tame and employ the raw aggressiveness of young men. After all, the difference between an anarchic terrorist and a good soldier or dutiful policeman, between what is commonly regarded as good or evil, is frequently determined by little more than the colour and design of their respective uniforms. Alan Sinfield has pertinently

---

1. John Osborne, *Look Back in Anger and Other Plays* (London: Faber and Faber, 1993), 83.
2. Lynn Segal, *Slow Motion: Changing Masculinities, Changing Men* (London: Virago, 1990), 1–25.

differentiated between 'violence which the state considers legitimate and that which it does not', concluding that 'violence is good . . . when it is in the service of the prevailing dispositions of power; when it disrupts them it is evil'[3] [. . .]

Even before Alex is subjected to the Reclamation Treatment of Ludovico's Technique, designed to make him a good person and valuable citizen, his behaviour is conditioned by the proprieties of conduct that structured and determined masculine gender performances in imperial Britain. Public-school pedagogy, which aims at rei(g)ning angry young male violence by codifying it, is so pervasive that it has left its mark even on working-class Alex, who lives in a towerblock and is on one occasion described as a 'wretched little slummy bedbug, breaking into *real* people's houses' (43). Like Jack's in *Lord of the Flies*, Alex's savagery is far from wild or out of control; on the contrary, it follows the normative script of what finds societal approval as appropriate masculine behaviour and what does not. Keen to live up to the ideals of upper-class masculinity, Alex is a puppet on invisible strings long before he delivers himself into the hands of experimenting behavioural scientists. A substantial part of the delight and satisfaction Alex derives from lashing out against others comes from his expertise at implementing gentlemanly rules and techniques of combat. * * *

* * *

[Alex] must first and foremost be regarded as a deprived working-class youth reaching out for the power of the privileged upper-class male. Categorically excluded from the power benefits of hegemonic manliness, he overcompensates for his social inferiority by casting himself in the role of a superheroic leader, all the time copying, and thus perpetuating, the legitimate, 'educational' violence of his public-school oppressors.

The droogs' first victim in *A Clockwork Orange* is a frail, old schoolmaster on his way back from the library. By beating him up to teach him—as so many others who are to follow—'a lesson' (7), Alex testifies to his difficult love/hate relationship with the totalitarian system. He quashes schoolmasterliness only in order to establish his own equally schoolmasterly authority. As in *Lord of the Flies*, the supra-individual power principle with its network of compelling symbols proves invariably more resilient than any of its flesh-and-blood representatives. Patriarchal masculinity is a force that feeds on its practitioners who find themselves at constant risk of becoming casualties in masculinity's ceaseless and essentially arbitrary struggle for

3. Alan Sinfield, "*Macbeth*: History, Ideology and Intellectuals," in Wilson and Dutton, eds, *New Historicism and Renaissance Drama* (London: Longman, 1992).

self-assertive dominance over whatever it chooses to perceive as its other(s). * * * Burgess fails to unravel and effectively criticise the oppressive dynamics determining the dystopian condition he envisions in *A Clockwork Orange*. His didactic approach is in itself characteristic of a patriarchal humanism which unselfconsciously tends to universalise any historically or culturally specific problem. Only sporadically does Burgess allude to the social conditioning of Alex's identity; most of the time, he stresses his protagonist's indeterminacy as an exceptional and wildly anarchic individualist. * * * Burgess's total indifference to the gender-specificity of Alex's condition shows itself perhaps most revealingly in his boy hero's ethical manifesto in which Alex outlines the reasons for his passionate commitment to the pleasures of droogery:

> But, brothers, this biting of their toe-nails over what is the CAUSE of badness is what turns me into a fine laughing malchick. They don't go into the cause of GOODNESS, so why the other shop? If lewdies are good that's because they like it, and I wouldn't interfere with their pleasures, and so of the other shop. And I was patronizing the other shop. More, badness is of the self, the one, the you or me on our oddy knockies, and that self is made by old Bog or God and is his great pride and radosty. But the not-self cannot have the bad, meaning they of the government and the judges and the schools cannot allow the bad because they cannot allow the self. And is not our modern history, my brothers, the story of brave malenky selves fighting these big machines? I am serious with you, brothers, over this. But what I do I do because I like to do (29).

Addressing an exclusively male audience and clearly expecting sympathy and understanding, Alex refers to his ultraviolent badness as an inalienable constituent of his individuality. To deprive him of the freedom to act upon his bad impulses would not only represent a violation of his most basic human rights; ultimately, it would effect a total extirpation of the self. According to Alex's reasoning, patriarchal totalitarianism cannot tolerate his badness because it cannot tolerate the expression or manifestation of any kind of outstanding difference. As a result, Alex's badness becomes a morally good cause worth fighting for. His droogery, ultimately practised in defense of itself, becomes justified as a heroic means of resistance against systemic oppression.

The simplistic logic informing Alex's ethical argument can easily be dismantled. What is more interesting is that Alex chooses to portray his ultraviolent badness as natural, as innate to his self, although it clearly represents something socially acquired. * * * Alex derives his heroic self-image from meticulously moulding himself after a certain masculine ideal. His gender masquerade is motivated by a deeply paranoid insecurity about his masculinity. In fact, Alex's violence and droogish self-fashioning seem designed to distract from his 'queerness' as a working-class boy who listens to Beethoven and is fond of displaying a sophisticated manner that borders on aristocratic snobbery. His conspicuous difference and striking lack of typically boyish, working-class interests make him potentially very vulnerable to ostracism and abuse by his peers. He strategically protects himself from being 'othered' and discursively feminised—as a boy not quite boyish enough—by taking the lead role of chief bully, a position which he defends with great ferocity and cunning. Rather than 'fighting these big machines', Alex appropriates the communal dynamics that ensure their continuing operation. What he describes as his self is little more than a by-product of skilful gender mimicry, a protective shell against ubiquitous threats of emasculation. Alex is a loose, if undoubtedly fitting, cog ready to be inserted into the patriarchal clockwork, a system that forces males to conceal the intrinsic complexity of their human disposition behind the imposing artifice of a self-oppressive, mask-like masculinity.

* * * One cannot quite suppress a genuine wonderment at the great naivety and implausibility of Burgess's depiction of Alex's sudden maturation. Instead of signalling a triumphant liberation from the wicked impulses of irrational boyhood or the ideological clutches of totalitarianist coercion, Alex's growing up in fact adds the last finishing touch to a process of consistent patriarchal conditioning, a process so powerful and pervasive that even a self-professed individualist like Alex cannot escape it.

* * *

As an ethical treatise on 'good' and 'evil', Burgess's novel is substantially flawed due to its total disregard for the wider systemic dynamics of class, gender and power. Alex is no free, unpredictable subject fighting for the survival of his spiritual self. The individuality he displays prior to his scientific conditioning is as scripted and acquired as the role he feels compelled to adopt at the end of the novel. Both are determined by political expediency. Had Burgess genuinely intended to portray the oppression of individual freedom by state power, he ought to have created his protagonist as an outsider for whom to follow the various scripts of patriarchal masculinity would have been an impossible act. * * * Anger and violence are no deviations from the norm and hence pose no insurmountable threat to the order of patriarchy. On the contrary, they represent constitutive, easily manipulable elements of the masculine standard, subject to systemic expediency and the vicissitudes of political fashion.

PATRICK PARRINDER

[Dystopias]†

CACOTOPIA. nonce-wd. *A place where all is evil; opp. by Bentham to Utopia "nowhere", taken as Eutopia "a place where all is well."*

Not content with rescuing the word from oblivion, Anthony Burgess has made three contributions to the genre of the cacotopian vision. *1985*[1] is no more a novel of direct prophecy than were its predecessors, *A Clockwork Orange* and *The Wanting Seed*, both published in 1962. The composite structure of Burgess's most recent future fantasy, a mixture of fiction, essay, dialogue and "interview", should suffice as a reminder that the "parallel worlds" of fiction in no sense foretell the actual shape of things to come. *1985* updates Orwell less in the sense of advancing his *annus fatalis* by one, than of presenting the Worst of All Imaginary Worlds as seen by a representative conservative English writer a generation after Orwell wrote. And if the novella at the centre of the book must be judged a let down by Burgess's best standards, *1985* deserves attention for its wide-ranging political and social discussions, for the Orwellian pastiche of its note on "Worker's English", and, above all, for its reassessment of that most powerful of modern cacotopias, *Nineteen Eighty-Four*.

* * *

* * * There is an inordinate amount or flesh-creeping in *Nineteen Eighty-Four*, but very little in Burgess's fictive "sequel", which never for one moment persuades us that it is tragedy rather than farce. Not even *A Clockwork Orange*, despite the reputation of Kubrick's film, haunts us in the way that Orwell's nightmare does. There are, of course, manifest differences of talent and temperament (and arguably Orwell's book is not really as funny as Burgess makes out). Yet Burgess's inability or unwillingness to profoundly disturb our sensibilities also points to the literary and ideological differences between the two writers.

There is, in Burgess's view, something deficient in Orwell's understanding of the nature of freedom. *Nineteen Eighty-Four* is an "allegory of the eternal conflict between any individual and any collective", but it misstates that conflict, since Orwell "could see the possibility of evil only in the State. Evil was not for the individual: original

† From "Updating Utopia? Burgess's Future Fiction," *Encounter* 56.1 (January 1981), 45–53 (45–46, 50–53). Reprinted by permission.
1. Anthony Burgess, *1985* (Hutchinson, 1978; Arrow Books, 1980).

sin was a doctrine to be derided." Against Orwell's secular, liberal-humanist view of man, Burgess sets his own conservative and Christian position based on a synthesis of the Pelagian doctrine of free will and the Augustinian doctrine of original sin. Readers will recognise this position from his previous works: in *The Wanting Seed*, for example, the cacotopian bureaucracy oscillates between extremes of liberal paternalism ("Pelphase") and martial repression ("Gusphase"). The agony of *Nineteen Eighty-Four* results, in his view, from Orwell's dilemma as an "inveterate proponent of free will" and thus of human perfectibility. It is, in fact, proportionate to the depth of its author's commitment to socialism.

At this level the opposition between Orwell and Burgess is that of the radical liable to shattering disillusionment and the conservative immune to political hopes; and these positions are familiar enough. One can answer Burgess by saying that the renunciation of any vision of political progress and change is a genuine impoverishment. Burgess counters the generalisations of socialism by preaching the virtue of individual Christian love. He does not say how we can love our neighbours without wishing to help those of them who are victims of injustice. He suggests Orwell's Pelagianism was a comforting illusion, but it is no less comforting for Burgess to regard this Old Etonian who sought to join the proletariat as a thwarted human being, who would eventually find himself trapped by "a personal despair of being able to love." However, I wish to get beyond the *impasse* of this kind of debate by arguing that Burgess's reading of the text of *Nineteen Eighty-Four* has not been close enough. He has manifestly overlooked some of the sources of its universality and power.

*   *   *

Beside Winston Smith, the heroes of Anthony Burgess's cacotopias are much more straightforward specimens of Bourgeois Man. Tristram Foxe in *The Wanting Seed* and Bev Jones in *1985* are both ex-history teachers whose refusal to conform lands them in a series of picaresque adventures. There is something desultory about their wanderings, so that they strike us more as fictive devices to enable Burgess to unfold their respective societies than as genuine or would-be free spirits. Neither has much life of his own. Since everything they do is "in character", their function is to propagandise for the free individual without ever forcing us to consider what such freedom might mean. Their gestures of independence satisfy the formal demands of the narrative without deeply engaging the reader's imagination.

It is different with Alex, the teenage gang-leader and narrator of *A Clockwork Orange*, who at first glance would appear to represent anything but Bourgeois Man. Yet, though Burgess now looks back on this most celebrated of his novels with some slight embarass-ment, the lesson of *A Clockwork Orange* is still central for him:

> It is better to have our streets infested with murderous young hoodlums than to deny individual freedom of choice. . . . The evil, or merely wrong, products of free will may be punished or held off with deterrents, but the faculty itself may not be removed.

Alex, it will be remembered, is imprisoned for manslaughter and then lured into undergoing an experimental Reclamation Treatment by the prospect of an early release. The Treatment consists of aver-sion therapy which destroys his enjoyment of thuggery, and, as an unforeseen side-effect, of music, literature, and sex. He makes an unsuccessful suicide attempt, after which the effects of the therapy wear off. Subsequently Alex, who has become the leader of another gang, gives up violence of his own accord; he has turned eighteen, nature has taken its course and he is ready to "go straight."[2]

"*Alex* is a rich and noble name, and I intended its possessor to be sympathetic, pitiable, and insidiously identifiable with us", Burgess writes in *1985*. One of its meanings is *a lex*: without a law. Alex is, of necessity, a literary creation, a transformation of the teenage hood-lum into "your little droog", "your Humble [and highly articulate] Narrator." Among Burgess's battery of devices for making him sym-pathetic are his linguistic command, his love of classical music, and his sense of belonging in the same league of precocious youths as Mozart and Rimbaud. He is one of "Bakunin's Children", the spokes-men of intergenerational warfare to whom Burgess devotes a surpris-ingly sympathetic chapter in *1985*. In addition, *A Clockwork Orange* suggests its kinship with such novels as J. D. Salinger's *A Catcher in the Rye* and Colin MacInnes's *Absolute Beginners*. Like Salinger's and MacInnes's teenage heroes, Alex has seen it all before he should even have begun. "That was everything. I'd done the lot, now. And me still only fifteen", he reflects in prison. Burgess's characteristic lin-guistic virtuosity is here deployed in the creation of *nadsat*, a teenage argot based on Russian vocabulary with some added bits of Romany. (The Russian is said to have entered their heads by "subliminal penetration.") Another significant trait, which contributes to our sense that we have here a romanticisation of the bandit or ruffian no

---

2. Curiously enough, the final chapter in which this happens has been omitted from at least two editions of the book, including that on which Kubrick's film was based. For Burgess's account of how he "weakly agreed" to this excision, see his letter in the *Times Literary Supplement*, 11 January 1980 (164).

less blatant than the left-wing romanticisation of the urban guerrilla, is Alex's obvious attraction towards the bookish types whom he delights in mugging. He has no difficulty in grasping the meanings of the title of the book one of them is writing—*A Clockwork Orange*. After this, it is no surprise that he is able to expound Burgess's own theory of original sin:

> badness is of the self, the one, the you or me on our oddy knock-ies, and that self is made by old Bog or God and is his great pride and radosty. But the not-self cannot have the bad, meaning they of the government and the judges and the schools cannot allow the bad because they cannot allow the self. And is not our modern history, my brothers, the story of brave malenky selves fighting these big machines? I am serious with you, brothers, over this.

Scratch the most unlikely of Burgess's heroes and he is liable to turn into a history teacher. One can see why its author now describes *A Clockwork Orange* as "too didactic, too linguistically exhibitionist."

Alex's counterparts in *1985* are the still more improbable "kumina youths", bands of Robin Hood–style Blacks who have started an Underground University—staffed by unemployed history teachers!—to keep alive the outlawed traditional culture. They are philosophers of violence, taking their cue from Shakespeare ("Literature teaches revenge") among others. They talk and chant in Latin while engaging in multiple pederastic rape. These amateurs of the *vie de bohème*, late 20th-century style, do not have to be taken seriously; but Alex, who uses Beethoven and Mozart as background music for his private theatre of pornographic violence, evidently does. ("I am serious with you, brothers.") How is it that Alex can indulge his sadistic fantasies to the accompaniment, not of the "hideous, grinding" sounds of Orwell's Two Minutes' Hate, but of the Ode to Joy in Beethoven's Ninth, without internal conflict? Should not such a response to Beethoven be regarded, not merely as startling and brutal, but as psychopathic and perverse? This would seem to be the real problem with *A Clockwork Orange*, though it is one that Burgess would dismiss, apparently, as of no more than secondary interest.

"Oh bliss, bliss and heaven", Alex exclaims, listening to a violin concerto and imagining an orgy of indiscriminate violence against men, women and girls. When he loses his enjoyment of music as a result of the Treatment, the reader is moved to indignation at this destruction of his personality. Yet what Burgess is portraying here is surely a type of mental derangement. It is a bit tame to suggest that this is something Alex will simply grow out of. (Possibly the only thing he can grow up into is a novelist!) At issue here is the idea of the moral neutrality of art, which Burgess asserts in a passage in *1985* where he discusses George Steiner's example of the camp commandant in Nazi Germany, who, having supervised the killing of a thousand Jews, went home to hear his daughter play a Schubert sonata and cried with "holy joy." Burgess argues that there is no real mystery in this:

> The answer is that the good of music has nothing to do with ethics. Art does not elevate us into beneficence. It is morally neutral, like the taste of an apple.

This is scarcely convincing. The camp commandant's achievement, perhaps, was to show how efficient a machine the human brain can be when it is determined, at all costs, to play out a particular role. His impressions are kept in rigidly separate compartments. Art, unlike apples, is man-made and we are right to recognise something perverse in this. Alex's achievement, by contrast, is one of yoking heterogeneous impressions violently together. His is a much more difficult, unlikely, and (it might be argued) insane feat than the camp commandant's, since the latter does not find that his holy joy at Schubert's sonata consists in fantasies of killing Jews. If this is correct, we can only consider it a gross sentimentality when, in the chapter he has restored to the most recent (1979) reprint, Burgess shows Alex growing up into "normality."

Our little droog, it turns out, has unconsciously, as it were, cut out a newspaper photograph of a baby and put it in his pocket! Boys will be boys—with, alas, a little of the old ultra-violence—but one day they grow up, and you can tell by the fact that they start dreaming of a son. The truth is that Alex's path to normality can only be miraculous or fraudulent (he is, let it be remembered, a first-person narrator). The suggestion that nature, by an unexplained miracle, could do the job bungled by therapy seems confused, and perhaps even dishonest; this is not the sort of ambiguity that enriches a novelist's portrayal of character.

* * *

GEOFFREY AGGELER

[Pelagianism and Augustinianism][†]

A desire to ascertain the 'liberalism' or 'conservatism' of writers who have provided us with significant commentaries on human experience is frequently an efficient cause of much of the critical

† From "Pelagius and Augustine in the Novels of Anthony Burgess," *English Studies* 55 (1974); 43–55 (43–47; 51–55). Reprinted by permission.

exegesis of their works. * * * So it is with Anthony Burgess. The temptation to label him in these terms is especially strong because so many of the conflicts in his novels are between 'Pelagian liberals' and 'Augustinian conservatives'. By his use of these terms, Burgess intends to remind us of the ultimate origins of much of the 'liberalism' and 'conservatism' in western thinking. In Burgess's view, the liberal's optimism, his belief in the fundamental goodness and perfectability of man, derives from an ancient heresy—the Pelagian denial of Original Sin. And not surprisingly, he feels that the doctrinal bases of much of the pessimism pervading western conservative thinking can be traced to Augustine's well known refutations of Pelagian doctrine. In view of the frequency of clashes between 'Augustinians' and 'Pelagians' in Burgess's fiction, it may be worthwhile to review briefly the seminal debate.

Pelagius, a British monk who resided in Rome, Africa, and Palestine during the early decades of the fourth century, set forth doctrines concerning human potentiality which virtually denied the necessity of Divine Grace and made the Redemption a superfluous gesture.[1] Such an assault on basic Christian doctrine does not, however, seem to have been part of his original design. What he sought to promote initially was an awakening of Christians from the sinful indolence into which they had fallen largely, he felt, as a result of underestimating their spiritual potentialities as human beings. He believed that even as the Roman ideal of preeminent heroic virtue, embodied in the term *virtus,* was attainable by any Roman who applied himself, so the Christian ideal was attainable by any Christian through his own efforts utilizing only his natural gifts. If this were not the case, then how could we account for the virtuous, self-denying lives of the pagan philosophers? And what about the Patriarchs? What about Job? The fact that they were able to please God without the explicit guidance of the Torah is indisputable evidence of the natural goodness of humanity. It cannot be denied, of course, that the evidence of man's innate goodness became less plentiful after the time of the Patriarchs, but this, in Pelagius's view, would explain the necessity of the explicit revelation of God's Law. The Law was revealed to guide men back to the path of righteousness which their forefathers had followed by natural inclination.

It is not surprising that Grace, in its most widely accepted orthodox Christian sense, as an infusion of the Holy Spirit, did not occupy a very prominent place in his scheme of salvation. He likened it to

---

1. Quotations from the writings of Pelagius are taken from *Documents of the Christian Church,* ed. Henry Bettenson (Oxford, 1967). In summarizing Pelagian doctrine, I am heavily indebted to the analyses by W. J. Sparrow-Simpson in *The Letters of St. Augustine* (New York: Macmillan, 1919) and John Burnaby in *Augustine: Later Works* (London: Library of Christian Classics VIII, 1955).

a sail attached to a rowboat in which the only essential instruments of locomotion are the oars. The oars he likened to the human will, and while the sail may make rowing easier, the boat could move without it: 'Velo facilius, remo difficilius; tamen et remo itur'[2] His cavalier treatment of divine grace is a concomitant of his total rejection of orthodox doctrines concerning Original Sin: 'Everything good and everything evil, in respect of which we are either worthy of praise or of blame, is *done by us, not born with us*'.[3] Adam's sin has no effect on new-born infants, who are in the same spiritual condition he was before the Fall. And since they are in a state of prelapsarian innocence, they may attain eternal life even without baptism. Moreover, even as it was not through Adam's sin that men became mortal, so it is not through Christ's resurrection that they may have life beyond the grave. The fact that men had led sinless lives before Christ's coming indicated that the Law, as well as the Gospel, could lead men to God's kingdom.[4]

Augustine was horrified by these teachings, and, recognizing them as essentially an abandonment of Christianity itself, he devoted fully as much energy to discrediting them as he had previously devoted to refuting the Manichees. In mounting his attack, he relied heavily upon Scripture, especially the Epistles of St. Paul, but his fervor and the intensity of his insistence on the helplessness and fundamental wickedness of man without divine grace cannot be accounted for simply in terms of his objective appreciation of the soundness of Pauline doctrine. Clearly, he was also moved by the memory of his own early slavery to sin which he describes so vividly in the *Confessions*. It is in the *Confessions* that he utters a prayer which outraged Pelagius: 'I have no hope at all but in thy great mercy. Grant what thou commandest and command what thou wilt'.[5] In Augustine's view, human nature had been vitiated and corrupted as a result of Adam's sin, and all of Adam's descendants are in a 'penal' condition wherein they are effectively prevented from choosing the path of righteousness by ignorance and the irresistible urgings of the flesh. Men may overcome this condition and lead virtuous lives only if they have been granted God's free gift of grace: ' "For it is God", says the apostle, "who worketh in you both to will and to do, according to his good will" '[6]

While Augustine stresses that grace is a 'free' gift granted only to the Elect, that man is utterly unable to gain it by his own efforts, he is always careful to point out that man does indeed have freedom of

2. Quoted by Sparrow-Simpson from a sermon, *Letters of St. Augustine*, p. 131.
3. *Documents*, ed. Bettenson, p. 53.
4. *Ibid.*, pp. 53–4.
5. *Confessions* X, 40 (trans. Edward P. Pusey, Modern Library, 1949, p. 29).
6. *The Spirit and the Letter*, trans. John Burnaby, *Augustine: Later Works*, p. 196.

choice. While he may not be able to choose the path of righteousness without divine aid, his sins are completely voluntary. The path of sin was freely chosen by Adam, and it is freely chosen by his descendants. In this connection, it should be noted that his view of the nature of sin itself differs radically from that of Pelagius. Whereas Pelagius had thought of sin as merely action, which had no permanent effect upon the sinner, Augustine saw sin as 'an abiding condition or state'. All men are spiritually enfeebled by Original Sin, but an actively sinful man increasingly paralyzes his moral nature by his deeds.[7]

* * *

When the debate is viewed in broader terms, the nature of man himself emerges as the pivotal issue, and one can see that the diametrically opposed assumptions of Augustine and Pelagius could be taken as premises of diametrically opposed political philosophies as well as attitudes toward social progress as far removed as hope and despair. The Pelagian view of humanity justifies optimism and a Rousseauvian trust in *la volonté générale*. Indeed, if one could accept Pelagius's sanguine estimates of human potentiality, one might hope to see Heaven on earth. For surely, if men can achieve spiritual perfection and merit eternal salvation solely through the use of their natural gifts, then the solutions to all problems of relations within earthly society must be well within their grasp. They need only to be enlightened properly, and their fundamental goodness will inevitably incline them toward morally desirable social goals. The realization of a universally acceptable utopia would not depend upon the imposition of any particular social structure. Rather, humanity, if properly enlightened, could be trusted to impose upon itself a utopian social scheme.

To say the least, there is a good deal less hope implied in Augustine's doctrines. One can readily see that his fundamentally pessimistic view of human potentiality, his basic distrust of human nature, could be taken as the basis of policies of rigorous enforcement in human affairs. A utopia organized upon Augustinian premises must necessarily be a police state and in this connection, it is certainly no accident that the human community most closely approximating such a utopia was Geneva in the time of Calvin. Calvin, like Luther, relied very heavily upon Augustine in the formulation and support of his doctrines, and it would appear that the enormous importance he attached to the enforcement of discipline within the Christian community derived largely from his fundamental agreement with the Augustinian view of human nature.[8]

7. *On Free Will,* trans. John H. S. Burleigh, *Augustine: Earlier Works* (London: Library of Christian Classics VI, 1953), p. 201.
8. As R. H. Tawney observes, 'Having overthrown monasticism, its [Calvinism's] aim was to turn the secular world into a gigantic monastery, and at Geneva, for a short time, it almost succeeded . . . Manners and morals were regulated, because it is through the

As I have indicated, Burgess's view of the debate encompasses its broadest implications, and some awareness of these implications, especially within social and political spheres of western thinking, is essential to an appreciation of his social satire. * * *

*   *   *

Initially, Alex is not directly involved in the political upheavals disturbing the state. His only concern is the pursuit of sensual enjoyment, which he finds in various activities, including thievery, street fighting, rape, and the sounds of classical music. When he adds murder to his list of atrocities, he finds himself in prison, and it is here that he first feels the effects of governmental policy. The usual 'DISAPPOINTMENT' occurs as a result of the failure of liberal methods of government, and a more 'Augustinian' governing body is elected by a terrorized populace caring little about 'the tradition of liberty' and in fact quite willing to 'sell liberty for a quieter life'. Unlike the Augustinian government in *The Wanting Seed*, this body does not resort to mass murder in maintaining order. Instead, it relies upon the genius of modern behavioral technology, specifically that branch of it which aims at a total destruction of the human will. Alex, who has brought attention to himself by murdering a fellow inmate, is selected as 'a trail-blazer' to be 'transformed out of all recognition'.

The essential feature of Alex's transformation is the complete elimination of his ability to choose socially deleterious courses of action. Psychological engineers, using selected stimuli, force upon him what B. F. Skinner might call the 'inclination to behave'.[9] He is led to associate all violence with unbearable nausea and headaches. Only charity and humility can save him from these extreme physical discomforts. Even his beloved classical music, since it is associated in his mind with socially deleterious desires, must become a source

---

minutiae of conduct that the enemy of mankind finds his way to the soul; the traitors to the Kingdom might be revealed by pointed shoes or golden ear-rings, as in 1793 those guilty of another kind of *incivisme* were betrayed by their knee-breeches. Regulation meant legislation, and, still more, administration. The word in which both were summarized was Discipline. Discipline Calvin himself described as the nerves of religion, and the common observation that he assigned to it the same primacy as Luther had given to faith is just.' (*Religion and the Rise of Capitalism*, New York: Mentor Books, 1958, pp. 101–2).

9. *A Clockwork Orange* can in fact be read as a refutation of Skinner's *Walden Two*, a novel which is simply a blueprint for a utopia in which most human problems could be solved by a scientific technology of human behavior. The principles of this behavioral technology rest heavily upon the assumption that man is not free. As Frazier, Skinner's mouthpiece, expresses it, 'You can't have a science about a subject matter which hops capriciously about. Perhaps we can never *prove* that man isn't free; it's an assumption. But the increasing success of a science of behavior makes it more and more plausible'. This would mean of course that most of the ills of society could be eliminated eventually through the efforts of benevolent behavioral psychologists, applying various stimuli and utilizing 'the tremendous power of positive reinforcement'. The citizenry of Skinner's utopia would '*feel free*' and be totally unaware of any restraint or compulsion. They would, however, be anything but free: 'By a careful cultural design, we control not the final behavior, but the *inclination* to behave—the motives, the desires, the wishes.' (*Walden Two*, New York, 1962, pp. 257–62).

of nausea. When his 'rehabilitation' is complete, he is free to enter society again, if not a useful citizen at least a harmless one.

He is not only harmless but helpless as well, and shortly after his release, he is unfortunate enough to fall into the hands of another bulwark of Augustinian government, the police. Police forces maintained during an Augustinian reaction differ greatly from those of a Pelagian era both in their composition and their numbers. There are of course many more of them available to deal with unregenerate human nature, but they are not necessarily recruited from the ranks of the Elect. In fact, as Alex finds, the government has issued uniforms, weapons and authority to former hoodlums, apparently on the theory that their criminal desires can be expressed usefully in the maintenance of order on the streets. Alex, who is unable to summon enough aggression even to defend himself against an assault by one of his former victims, is 'rescued' by officers whom he recognizes as former comrades. After these worthies renew their acquaintanceship by administering 'a bit of the old summary', Alex is left to drag his battered body through a pouring rain to the threshold of a little cottage where he is welcomed and pitied by another 'victim of the modern age'.

The occupant of the cottage is a writer and revolutionary whose political ideals incline toward Pelagian liberalism. In spite of a number of terribly disillusioning experiences, he maintains a belief in the fundamental goodness and perfectability of man, 'a creature of growth and capable of sweetness'. He and his fellow revolutionaries see Alex as an excellent propaganda device to be used in the overthrow of the Augustinian government, an example of what its 'debilitating and will-sapping techniques of conditioning' can accomplish. They do not, however, have any real sense of him as anything but a propaganda device. Like Swift's political 'projectors', they are so full of abstract ideals and visionary schemes that they have little concern for practical human realities.[1] They are full of moral outrage but have no clear moral sense. To them, Alex is not an unfortunate human being to be assisted but 'an unfortunate victim' who can embarrass the government by his very existence. His moral nature has been destroyed, and the only way to make him an even greater embarrassment is to have him destroyed altogether by the government. So it happens that these Pelagian liberals, dedicated to the preservation of liberty and the dignity of man, find themselves utilizing the responses implanted in Alex by the Augustinian psychologists to drive him to suicide.

The scheme very nearly succeeds, and while Alex is recovering in the hospital from a death dive, a power struggle rages. The govern-

---

1. cf. *Gulliver's Travels*, III, Ch. VI.

ment receives ample amounts of embarrassing publicity concerning the attempted suicide, but somehow they weather it, and one day Alex awakens to find himself fully as vicious as before his treatment. More psychologists, using 'deep hypnopaedia or some such slovo', have restored his moral nature, his 'self', and his concomitant appetites for Beethoven and throat-cutting. As he listens to the 'glorious Ninth of Ludwig van', he exults,

> Oh, it was gorgeosity and yumyumyum. When it came to the Scherzo I could viddy myself very clear running and running on like very mysterious nogas, carving the whole litso of the creeching world with my out-throat britva. And there was the slow and the lovely last singing movement still to come. I was cured all right.

The Augustinians are delighted. In this 'depraved' condition he cannot embarrass them further.

* * *

In Burgess's view, then, the Pelagian-Augustinian debate, which manifests itself historically as a 'waltz', is symptomatic of western man's acceptance of a faulty dilemma. Presumably, sanity and vision could lead men to a rejection of both 'Pelagianism' and 'Augustinianism' and a creation of society based upon a realistic assessment of individual human potentiality. But since sanity and vision are lacking, and since the individual 'self' is viewed as a threat to social stability by both Pelagians and Augustinians, then man is left with the two bleak alternatives presented in *The Wanting Seed*. If he isn't, in one sense or another, 'eaten' by a military-industrial complex, he will be persuaded to castrate himself, in one way or another, for the sake of social stability.

SAMUEL McCRACKEN

[Free Will and Ludovico's Technique]†

Although *A Clockwork Orange* had a respectable little reputation before its visual enshrinement by Stanley Kubrick, it was not upon its publication widely or intensely reviewed. One of its champions, the late Stanley Edgar Hyman [. . .], saw the work as a tract about free will, showing the unacceptable nature of the method by which the thug-hero Alex is turned from a free agent, however vicious still capable of salvation, into a state-produced "clockwork orange," how-

† From "Novel into Film; Novelist into Critic: *A Clockwork Orange* . . . Again." Copyright © 1973 by the Antioch Review, Inc. First appeared in the *Antioch Review*, Volume 32, No. 13. Reprinted by permission of the Editors.

ever incapable of evil incapable also of good. Anthony Burgess himself, responding to recent criticism of both the novel and the film,* has now told us that this is indeed what he (and Kubrick) had in mind. While this interpretation is plausible enough as a schema for the film, for the novel it simply will not do.

Life in a post-intentional fallacy universe ought to have prepared us for a novelist who is a deficient critic of his own work; but since a careful reading of the novel leads to an interpretation very nearly opposite to that which he now provides, Burgess seems unusually unsure of what he was about. * * * Dropping the suggestion that the novel may be a bit of a potboiler, he proceeds to call it a tract, or sermon, the text of which is presumably somewhere in the Epistle to the Galatians. There is no chance of salvation without the choice of sin, and the brutal State, by brainwashing (Burgess' own word) Alex has deprived him of the choice and hence the chance. This is itself a serious sin, indeed: "The wish to diminish free will is, I should think, the sin against the Holy Ghost."

The belief that Alex has indeed been brainwashed and deprived of free will is possible only with the help of a careless reading of the crucial passage, during which he is subjected to what the State is pleased to call Reclamation Treatment; that this treatment is the sin against the Holy Ghost can be believed only by taking at face value the opinions of two characters, the writer F. Alexander (along with his late wife, one of Alex's principal victims), and the prison chaplain, the charlie, who has been trying his own more orthodox version of Reclamation Treatment. But as a careful reading of the novel will make quite clear, Alex is not deprived of free will and F. Alexander and the charlie are in any event consistently undercut as defenders of the view that he should not be deprived of what he has been, free choice.

Thus. The Treatment consists of no more than an unusually efficacious form of aversion therapy: Alex is exposed to films of great violence and violent sex, to a background of the Beethoven which is his only love, while being kept in a state of extreme nausea. As a result, he can no longer wreak violence, experience sex, or hear Beethoven's Ninth, without getting very sick to his stomach. His new condition is demonstrated to an audience of those his regenerators wish to convince of his regeneration: taunted and knocked about by a bully, he falls to his knees and licks the bully's boots; confronted with a luscious girl, he can do no more than impotently worship her in the accents of *amour-courtois*. During this demonstration, an argument breaks out between Dr. Brodsky and the charlie.

This characterization of what is done to Alex—common, so it seems, to F. Alexander, the charlie, and Burgess the critic, but not

---

* *The Listener,* February 17, 1972. [See pp. 139–42 of this Norton Critical Edition.]

shared by Brodsky—is grotesquely inaccurate. First of all, it is not brainwashing as the term is commonly used. In life, the experience of certain Korean War prisoners shows what the process entails: they were provided with a new set of opinions and values by a relentless program of indoctrination masquerading as political education. One of the most famous fictional victims of the process, Raymond in *The Manchurian Candidate*, is turned into a puppet-gunman through processes he no longer remembers, becoming finally no more than an intermediate linkage between the finger of his masters and the trigger of the gun they have provided him.

Alex, in contrast, is not provided with new values. At no time after his conditioning, when he is offered an occasion of sin, is his reaction other than what it had been. During the demonstration, his first thought is that of the convict who tries to knife a cellmate before the guard can intervene: Alex wants to get his knife into his tormentor before the nausea can overwhelm him. What he *is* provided with, in supplement to his old drives, is a sort of internal injunction, the nausea which is always quicker than the knife. This resident injunctive power, far from depriving him of choice, merely offers him one: between eschewing violence and getting sick. And given the choice, he opts for the former. It is noteworthy that it is, as it were, a power of injunction and not of arrest. The latter could easily have been arranged by a technique which would paralyze him whenever the murderous rages well up. *Scene*: Alex, wired to the nausea-inducer, but free to move about; enter a tormenter; as long as Alex is absolutely motionless, neither nausea nor torment; as soon as he does, both. One might have thought that a novelist as inventive as Burgess should have had no difficulty in devising incidents thus more appropriate to his sermon.

Nor is Alex the victim of subliminal, even subtle, conditioning. He freely signs a release in order to undergo treatment, he is entirely conscious during the conditioning process, his memories of it are acute, and the mechanism itself, once installed, is entirely perceptible. In contrast, his restoration to his earlier state is accomplished through hypnopedia while he recovers from his suicide attempt; it is only those who wish him free to pursue the violent tenor of his ways who are willing, behind his back, to play about thus with his mind.

When the charlie early on warned Alex that he would never again have any desire to be bad, he was in error as to the fact, for Alex continues to have such desires. And when, later on, the charlie changes his tune, and argues the insincerity of the conversion, saying that Alex has no "real" choice, driven as he is by self-interest, he is in error as to the theory, for he equates freedom of choice with freedom *simpliciter*, believing that if society says Boo, it is repressive and fascist. One is almost embarrassed to draw so hackneyed a distinction, but the charlie has confused freedom and license. One can almost hear him saying: "But the law against murder, with its horrid penalties, deprives him of freedom. The insincerity of his not murdering is obvious, motivated by self-interest. He has no *real* choice." Real choice = absolute license.

The charlie is not the only commentator to be mistaken on this head. Burgess himself, it will be remembered, has described the State's treatment of Alex as having diminished his free will, an action he thinks to be no less than the sin against the Holy Ghost. However, he may see the matter these days, when he wrote the novel he made it abundantly clear that the Treatment left intact Alex's will towards the dreadful. What has been diminished is that which he enjoyed at the start of the narrative, uninhibited freedom for carrying out his will. Now, the State perennially tries to interfere with such freedom; the fact that it failed to do so with Alex is a serious reproach of its competence. But it normally tries to bias the choice between behavior tolerable and that intolerable by entailing the latter with undesirable consequence. The charlie himself is part of a system of control which restricted Alex's choices, in the form of scope for action, far more narrowly than the Treatment. But neither the Treatment nor the prison diminish free will; this can be done only by a brainwashing which makes the having of certain desires either impossible or compulsory, a process to which Alex patently is not subjected. But free *choice* is diminished for everyone, by everyone; it is diminished whenever the State makes a law; whenever one man says No to another; whenever one man's desires outrun his own competence. None of which has anything to do with free will or salvation. If it did, the inhabitants of totalitarian societies, their capacity for evil made smaller by their limited opportunity to break the law (totalitarian law forbids much that is desirable to forbid, as well as much that is not) would attain an easier salvation than others. Burgess can hardly believe this, any more than he can believe that Alex is any less sinful because of the chains in which Brodsky binds him. The testimony of the novel is that Burgess once understood this all very well, for what he now says is the argument of the novel is presented there by two highly dubious spokesmen. The writer F. Alexander, himself the author of a flatulent treatise called *A Clockwork Orange* ("to attempt to impose upon man, a creature capable of growth and capable of sweetness . . . to attempt to impose, I say, laws and conditions appropriate to a mechanical creation, against this I raise my sword-pen. . . .") has enough sophistication to regard the reclaimed Alex, from the likes of whom he has suffered, as a pitiful victim. But when he finally realizes that he has suffered from Alex himself, his benevolence collapses into primitive feelings of revenge, and he must be put away in order to make the streets safe for Alex. For he will allow Alex free choice only on the condition that Alex foreswear the option of beating F. Alexander and raping his wife.

The charlie is never exposed to such a test of his benevolence. Living as he does in a fortress full of guards, one of the few places in the world he can live with Alex in safety, he can afford to luxuriate, arguing free choice. His Christianity (which Alex aptly calls 'Prison Religion') is protected by its maximum security environment, blurred by a continuous haze of alcohol. He is as much deluded by his safety and his drink as F. Alexander is by his prose and Alex by his slang.

* * *

In this connection, commentators hitherto have been so dazzled by the cleverness of the language with which Burgess equips Alex that they have hardly wondered why he has done so. Burgess has recently provided an explanation which is more than a little difficult to take seriously: when the reader has finished the novel, he will have penetrated the vocabulary of the Russian-based Nadsat, and hence will have gotten, willy-nilly, a basic Russian lexicon. He will thus understand a little of what it means to be brainwashed. Although the process as Burgess describes it is perhaps more akin to brainwashing than anything which happens to Alex before his final "cure," it is so much like programmed instruction as to leave us in doubt just how seriously Burgess has violated our integrity. If we believe that this be the sin against the Holy Ghost, we will believe anything.

The more obvious effect of the Nadsat Burgess himself has pointed out: the reader, seeing the violence by means of a language he is yet learning, is insulated from it, and it becomes, as Burgess observes, largely symbolic. Symbolic certainly for the reader, but for Alex? Burgess describes his relation to language as a paradox: his name might be taken to mean *wordless*, yet he has plenty of words, and that he uses language is one of the criteria which mark him as a human being. But he uses it in a curious way. It seems clear that he *thinks* in Nadsat, and consequently he organizes reality by means of what is his second language. Whether or not he does this through choice (there are dark hints of subliminal penetration from the East) is beside the point. When describing the horrors which fill up his existence, he does so in something other than his mother tongue, in a jargon of limited, and (compared to English) syllabose, vocabulary. As we all know, for the practice of calling nasty things by other than their right names there is a perfectly good term. Whether or not we end up considering Alex's use of Nadsat as euphemistic, we must recognize that between reality and his perception of it he draws the veil of jargon. One is tempted to parody Orwell's famous metaphor: "the soft Slav roots fall upon the images like snow, gently blurring the outlines."

Thus the self-deluded members of the Free-Choice Party. In contrast is the cool, bureaucratic professionalism of its principal opponent. Although Brodsky carelessly and redundantly conditions Alex against sex, when a proper aversion to violence would have kept him from all rape but the statutory, and callously deprives him of his music, these are errors of technique, not of principle. What he does not do, as the charlie charges, is to try to make him good. Not only are all of Alex's bad intentions left untouched, but the extent of the areas in which he is enjoined from action is fairly modest. He is not provided with an aversion for theft, for bad language, for laying about idly, or any number of other behaviors which any sensible social engineer would wish to modify. *Scene:* Alex hooked up to the orgasm-inducer; on the screen, a time-clock; with every punch. . . . No, all that he desires to do is to keep Alex from committing a limited inventory of viciously antisocial acts by the simple expedient of a little deterrent in the form of nausea. It is no more than that will-o'-the wisp of law enforcement, the *certain* deterrent, levelled against the desire to act, rather than the act itself. No one would consider a law which prescribed thirty minutes' vomiting as the punishment for a life of murder and rape to have much deterrent effect. But when such a consequence is made absolutely certain, Brodsky shows us, that is all it takes.

Although Burgess seems to have the easy contempt for the State so familiar these days ("towards that mechanism, the State, which, first, is concerned with self-perpetuation, and second, is happiest when human beings are predictable and controllable, we have no duty at all, certainly no duty of charity") Brodsky and the Minister of the Inferior, understanding that the State after all is responsible for maintaining society, realize that Alex, a creature who inflicts insensate violence on anything which gets in his way, cannot be allowed to run loose. The alternatives, life imprisonment or death, are restrictions on free choice far more severe than the Reclamation Treatment. Given the Alexes, who appear to be very numerous, perhaps all the teen-age males in England, and given the desire to maintain something a little better than the Hobbesian state of nature, the Treatment is the procedure of choice. The State's choice, and Alex's. Although Burgess the critic says that "such evil as Alex enacts must be checked and punished," in the novel this position is maintained only by the Prison Governor, who puts it in terms discordant with the Christianity which is supposed to inform the work: "An eye for an eye, I say. If someone hits you, you hit back, do you not? Why then should not the State, very severely hit by you brutal hooligans, not hit back also?" But Brodsky and the State, Alex concurring, reject the doctrine of punishment and opt for a combination of crude rehabilitation and deterrence.

F. Alexander and the charlie reject the positions of the Governor and the State alike, making a fatal substitution of theology for politics, quite as if Alex's free choice could never be exercised to the detriment of another's. Indeed, as the novel ends, the government, under pressure from the opposition party for which F. Alexander is a propagandist, coolly relieves Alex of his aversions and is about to turn him loose, a media-hero with a sinecure into the bargain. As the charlie said, God help us all. This appalling turn of events, most immediately the result of political expediency, has for its ideological justification thinking which confuses sin and crime so thoroughly as to treat all crimes as sins and leave their punishment to God, omitting any interest in preventing them as crimes; Brodsky, at least, does not make the symmetrical error of taking crimes for sins and punishing them, arrogating thus the function of God. He is entirely willing to concern himself, in his measured way, with a few of Alex's least permissible works, and to leave his faith to the charlies of the world; like Elizabeth I, he will not make windows into men's souls, willing as he may be to follow them about with an eternal process-server.

Now as it happens, I find social control by such a process-server nearly as repugnant as does Burgess the critic, if not for the same reasons. For one thing, Brodsky's real-life equivalents would never be so restrained. *Scene:* a group of six-year-olds attached to the nausea-inducer; on the screen, an angry mob chants "Down with the government!" And ever after, the slightest desire to criticize the State will put them into a state they will be at great pains to avoid. And the Reclamation Treatment has certain affinities with that regeneration through chemistry preached by the Learies and the Reiches, who tell us that certain drugs destroy the will to certain evils. But the Treatment is repellent most of all because it symbolizes the bankruptcy of a society which having bred an Alex cannot, try as it may, come up with any better solution to his problem than chaining him thus. But given the world of the novel, the State has pretty clearly opted for the best choice open to it; such is the most reasonable interpretation, and if I am to avoid instructing Burgess as to what his intentions were, I must accept his statement of them but reply that he has so spectacularly betrayed them as to have ended up on the side of his demons.

* * *

TREVOR J. SAUNDERS

[Punishment]†

* * *

One can well imagine how strongly Socrates and his pupil Plato would have disapproved of the cinema, and what strenuous efforts they would have made to exclude it from their ideal state as morally subversive like much other artistic activity. Yet there is one film, or perhaps just part of it, which Plato, who was after all quite prepared to exploit the arts when it suited him, could well have felt tempted to make compulsory viewing for the legislators of his utopia: Stanley Kubrick's *A Clockwork Orange*. This film, of Anthony Burgess's book of the same name (London 1962), has been widely denounced precisely for its allegedly corrupting influences, notably its scenes of violence and its portrayal of the central character, Alex, an exquisitely vicious young man with an innocent expression and a winning smile, whose major pastimes are drug-taking, rape, and committing various forms of advanced hooliganism on defenceless persons. How then, could Plato ever have supposed that his legislators might have something to learn from such a film?

One of the most important characters in the story is an energetic politician known as the Minister of the Interior, a member of a future British government which has adopted a tough line on the issue of law and order. Part of his policy is to try to break away from 'outmoded penological theories' (61), which rely on harsh and retributive—and ineffective—punishments, and to experiment instead with a technique of *curing* criminals. This sounds enlightened, and perhaps in a sense it is; but it proves to be anything but gentle. The Minister of the Interior and his colleagues are interested in results, and results alone. Their sole aim is to *stop* the criminal from committing another crime. Questions of moral choice, freedom, responsibility, justice, guilt or sin simply do not interest them. As a certain Dr. Brodsky put it (82), 'We are not concerned with motive, with the higher ethics. We are concerned only with cutting down crime'. The Minister engages a team of scientists, headed by Dr. Brodsky, to subject a specimen criminal to 'Ludovico's Technique'. Alex, who has just spent 2 years in prison under a brutal and retributive regime, volunteers and is accepted. The treatment turns out to consist of enforced and prolonged viewing, with eyes forcibly kept open, of films depicting extreme brutality. This overdose of vicarious violence, accompanied by drug-induced nausea, which

---

† From "Plato's Clockwork Orange," in *The Durham University Journal* 68.2 (June 1976), 113–17. Reprinted by permission.

encourages the *association* of nausea and violence, leaves Alex with a conditioned response, a nausea and revulsion from violence, so that he is utterly incapable of committing it further, however much he may actually want to: whenever he attempts violence he finds that non-violence is more pleasurable, or perhaps one should say less unpleasant; and so he desists, for to change to an attitude of benevolence or submission is the only way to get rid of the nausea. When he leaves custody, not only is he incapable of committing violent crime on his own initiative, but even when, under extreme provocation, he tries to meet violence with violence, he is overcome by nausea and is quite unable to resist.

This hard-headed and ruthless pragmatism of the Minister of the Interior strikes us as essentially modern. The devices he is prepared to employ seem akin to brainwashing, or even to brain-surgery with a view to altering the personality. Now doubtless the technical *methods* of the Minister are indeed modern; but in his general approach to the problems of crime and punishment he is—startled though he would be to know it—in fundamental agreement with Plato. * * * His views are a startling anticipation of certain modern reformative theories of punishment:

> When anyone commits an act of injustice, serious or trivial, the law will combine instruction and constraint, so that in the future either the criminal will never again dare to commit such a crime voluntarily, or he will do it a very great deal less often; and in addition, he will pay compensation for the damage he has done. This is something we can achieve only by laws of the highest quality. We may take action, or simply talk to the criminal; we may grant him pleasures, or make him suffer; we may honour him, we may disgrace him; we can fine him, or give him gifts. We may use absolutely *any* means to make him hate injustice and embrace true justice—or at any rate not hate it.[1]

* * *

[What] Plato and the Minister have in common is an impatience with the assessment of moral responsibility and guilt, which leads to punishments that look back to the offence. The whole emphasis is on results, on the production of people who do not commit crime. But there is a crucial difference. Plato's aim is to reform the criminal in the sense of curing him of his *desire* to commit crime: when cured, he will 'hate' injustice and 'embrace', or at any rate not hate, true justice (862d). The Minister, on the other hand, is indifferent to what the criminal may desire, provided that, if he desires crime, he will be prevented from committing it by Dr. Brodsky's aversion-therapy. And so we see in the film that although Alex, when let

1. Plato, *The Laws*, trans T. J. Saunders (Harmondsworth: Penguin, 1970).

out into the world after his course of treatment, *wants* to resist when attacked by his former victims, he simply cannot—and consequently becomes as helpless and defenceless as a child. The prison chaplain, who exclaims in horror that Alex has been robbed of choice (82–83), is wide of the mark: it is not choice that has been taken from him, but the ability to put into effect one particular choice—of violence. Dr. Brodsky leaves the character and personality intact, and in an odd way it is heartening to know it—to know at the end of the story that an attempt to treat a human being as mere machinery has failed, and that before long Alex will be back committing violence 'real horrorshow' (to use his own teenage argot). Much of the weight of Plato's policy, by contrast, falls on the reform of personality, and to that extent he is *more* radical than Dr. Brodsky and the Minister, who are at first sight as radical as one can be.

Why then do I think Plato could have learned something from *A Clockwork Orange*? It seems to me the film would have made it clear to him that radical, advanced penology will inevitably fail if it is out of step with the views and expectations of society at large. Dr. Brodsky's treatment left Alex quite unfitted to hold his own in a society that is not only competitive and combative but intensely conservative in its views about crime and punishment. When he is released, he finds that society is not at all impressed by the fact that he is now harmless, and to that extent 'cured'. His former victims want their pound of flesh; they want him to suffer because they think he 'deserves' to, and they set about seeing to it that he shall. They insist, in fact, in reimporting all those primitive retributivist notions which the Minister thought he had made irrelevant. The effect on Alex is of course traumatic: in a lengthy and pathetic scene (one of the few in which we feel sorry for him), he returns after his 'cure' to his family and receives an embarrassed and chilly welcome.

* * *

* * * The merit of *A Clockwork Orange* is that it highlights a central difficulty of legislation, that of operating reformative penology as a sort of closed system. That is why I am suggesting that Plato might have been very willing to allow his legislators to view, in some suitable Platonic cave, a performance of *A Clockwork Orange*.

SAM JOHNSON

[Rebellion and Accommodation]†

In her study *The Origins of Totalitarianism*, written in 1963, Hannah Arendt asserts:

> It is the appearance of some radical evil, previously unknown to us, that puts an end to the notion of developments or transformations of qualities. Here, there are neither political nor historical, nor simply moral standards but, at most, the realization that something seems to be involved in modern politics that actually should never be involved in politics as we used to understand it, namely, all or nothing . . . (443)[1]

It is this configuration of 'radical evil' which I shall be endeavouring to trace amongst the multiple underworlds of Anthony Burgess's novel *A Clockwork Orange*, a fictional realm in which boundaries insidiously blur between the perpetrators and the castigators of crime and where 'all or nothing' would seem to be the dictum of lawbreakers and law-keepers alike. * * *

* * *

As both the chief perpetrator and chief eye-witness of felonious crime within the text, the initial phase of Alex's testimony offers us an outrageous but nevertheless compelling rendition of counterculture rebellion. The multiple signs and effects of sub-cultural deviation from normative behaviours and ethics are written large by Burgess, and the text affords us forceful insight into the potency of the spectacle and the allure of the deviant 'other'. The excess and hyperbole of this representation of the disaffected subject, however, only thinly disguises what I perceive to be one of the central concerns of the novel; namely the upsurgence of adolescent identity and resistance as a cultural phenomenon in post-Fifties Western society. Significantly, Alex is not 'merely' a criminal, a rapist, a murderer—he is an adolescent, a teenage 'delinquent' who ostentatiously flaunts his deviance and laughingly flouts the exigencies of adult law. So to undertake any examination of the 'threat' which he poses to the established order, we should perhaps initially consider some sociological and psychoanalytic configurations of adolescence which go

† From "Deciphering Adolescent Violence and Adult Corruption in Anthony Burgess's *A Clockwork Orange*," in Emmanuel Vernadakis and Graham Woodroffe, eds., *Portraits of the Artist in* A Clockwork Orange (Angers: Presses de l'Université d'Angers, 2003), 27–39 (27–31; 34–39). Reprinted by permission.
1. Hannah Arendt, *The Origins of Totalitarianism,* 2d ed. (New York: Meridian Books, 1958).

some way towards defining why the adolescent subject (and, more markedly, the adolescent criminal) provokes such a radical response from 'progressivist' reformers within the narrative. And in doing so we may also clarify why the adolescent underworld has acquired such a privileged position amongst other late twentieth century discourses and fashionings of militancy and dissent.

The threshold condition of adolescence is one characterised by a dichotomous crisis of physiology and identity as the subject undergoes manifold disruptions and destabilisations of bodily, circumstantial and inter-personal contexts. Posited within the border state of separation and individuation following childhood yet preceding the achievement of adult autonomy and agency, the adolescent figure is set the task of reconstituting his/her identity beyond the parameters of those holding environments (school, family, childhood friendships) which effectively sustained the sense of self throughout pre-adolescence. And running parallel to this reconstitution of identity, we can also witness the individual adolescent subject confronted with the pressing necessity of assuming or renegotiating role or societal function and the tensions which arise from the mis- or non-alignment of the one with the other. Compounding the fragility which we now identify as a chief characteristic of the post-modern psyche, adolescent subjectivity is thus both provisional and precarious. And whilst this engenders an exciting quality of un-formedness, of risk and possibility which emanates from the adolescent figure it also renders the in-between subject acutely vulnerable to the projections and displacements of adult desire and adult will.

Two theoretical models which are particularly useful in pinpointing the cultural and ideological significance of the adolescent within the macro-picture are those of Habermas (most particularly in relation to 'communicative action', citizenship and emancipation) and Julia Kristeva's liberating reworking of adolescence in her essay 'The Adolescent Novel'. Habermas focuses our attention upon the socialisation process and the systematic incorporation of the subject into the public domain. In employing the terms of social theory, we may hypothetically situate the adolescent figure on the cusp between one paradigm of social integration (namely, that involving the interactive collaboration of the subsystems of family, kinship, the educational institution and other cultural determinants such as religion) and another; namely that of the social collocation of the subject in economic, technological and political systems of meaning and production. A central concern for Habermas seems to spring from the apparently inevitable modification of the subject as a site of ethical and moral consciousness as s/he is accommodated into, and compromised by, state, bureaucratic and capitalist mechanisms. He voices his concern that in order to achieve this 'accommodation' an interactive process of *agreement* must be set in motion (that of communicative action) so as to minimise the alienation and desensitisation of the nascent self. This contract of citizenship then allows that 'fitting in' and conceding 'anti-social' individual interests can also grant a form of emancipation into the realm of personal agency backed by legitimate power structures.

But an inevitable (and in the instance of *A Clockwork Orange* horrific) clash of interests thus arises if the adolescent subject resists or rejects 'accommodation', preferring to remain unfixed and metaphorically 'unhoused' within the dominant culture—refusing the hegemonic consensus of 'adult' interests and investing in alternative strategies of self-actualisation and self-determination. According to a Kristevan formula, adolescence can be defined as a realm of ambiguity, narcissism and disguise all of which serve to mask or protect the psychic re-organisation of the subject-in-process. This psychoanalytic model locates the transformative adolescent subject within the arena of role-play, a gradual process of elimination whereby the 'I' tests and discards versions of 'me' in a quest to coalesce some kind of entity out of irreconcilable or chaotic fragments of past and possible future selves. In the miniature, then, the adolescent must seize agency in order to define his own needs and boundaries. This process is thus by definition antithetical to the 'closure' and alignment of the subject as 'citizen' desired by a society predicated upon order and homogenisation of desire, and so creates the potential for a chasm or cleft in social and ideological structures and systems of meaning.

The 'underworld' of uninhibited and uncurtailed desire which Alex champions at the opening of the novel is one of adolescent experimentation drawn to pathological proportions. Sociologically, Alex himself is in many ways 'typically' (if not stereotypically) adolescent (disavowing family, yet dependent upon them for shelter; denuded of his rights as a child but not yet enfranchised as an adult; a voracious consumer but not yet a producer of either goods or income). Gang warfare, petty theft and the use of what we might now deem as designer drugs lend him a sensationalist 'difference'— but it is not in these elements of his criminal behaviour that Alex is exceptional. He and his gang inhabit a twilight world, in which adults instill neither fear nor respect as they remain cocooned within their well-barricaded homes, ghettoised by the threat of adolescent anarchy without. Doffing school uniforms to reinvent themselves as 'droogs' by night, Alex and his compatriots respect no boundaries (of property, of bodies) but, again, it would seem that this is not unusual in the dystopic landscape which Burgess pens. This is a reign of terror which, like any other, is sustained through purchasable complicity and silence and is perpetuated through the non-interventionist policies of self-interested parties. But what is distinctive about Alex's decadent and elaborate brand of criminality is the 'signature' left upon his deeds, the baroque style of his methods, and, of course, of his narrative delivery.

*　*　*

So, in Alex's campaign of violence we observe the taboo fantasies, power-trips and lingo of 'pulp' which are intended for private, voyeuristic consumption made public, powerfully physicalised and brutally enacted upon the 'authentic' landscape which he and his gang terrorise. The brand of escapism enjoyed by this coterie is not so much one characterised by 'suspension of disbelief' as one which renders 'belief' in either social or divine justice archaic and futile. This disparity between the fictionalised possibilities of pulp (where there are no consequences, no real effects), and the irreparable damage inflicted by the thrill-addicted adolescents marks the dangerous incongruity of the 'uncivilised' imagination of the youths and the civilising forces which encompass them. And it is this glaring disjunction which catalyses the ostensible forces of civilisation into a programme of reformist terrorism which equals and outweighs that of the initial instigators of violence. For all of these elements signal that despite his very self-conscious parade of physical and sexual brutalities, Alex's intelligence and imagination are far from brutalised or inhibited, and thus his subversive (as opposed to his criminal) potential is very much intact and untapped and thus must be colonised and/or castrated.

In Part Two of *A Clockwork Orange*, we observe a significant refocalisation of the text as our critical energies are directed towards those contextual determinants which would contain or redefine Alex's ambivalent 'potential' in accordance with the exigencies of the body politic. The institutional apparatuses which underpin Burgess's novel proliferate in number and in influence as the text progresses and we see an army of corrupt and corrupting representatives of legitimate power set in motion to ostensibly 'reclaim' Alex from the condition of moral turpitude into which he has fallen. However, we increasingly discover that the socially endorsed reformation and rehabilitation of Alex entails sinister disciplining and retributive mechanisms and that scientific 'experimentation' upon the disempowered adolescent comes to constitute a terrifying assault upon the subjectivity of the central protagonist in their bid to 'cleanse' his identity of 'evil'. We are thus implicated within two of the most sensitive of the many universal debates which this challenging novel raises. Firstly, the probity, or otherwise, or implementing unjust methods of correction in the name of Justice. And secondly, the viability, or otherwise, of individual sovereignty in the face of legal,

Biblical or technological discourses [. . .] reinforcing hegemonic rule. * * *

Alex's encounters with mechanisms of state or institutional power can be sub-divided into three distinct categories; namely those of observation, discipline and [. . .] torture. In the first section of the novel, dominated by the adolescent figure acting upon his environment, we can identify models of surveillance in place, but ironically, it is the very fact that they are visible that renders them redundant. The endeavours of 'corrective schools', social workers and the police (or 'millicents') to cooperate with Alex and thus curtail his riotous escapades fail to impact upon his transgressive behaviour and in perpetuating his resistance to the overtures of what is presented as 'reason', we can observe the liberal tolerance of 'carers' gradually being eroded. However, although he presents himself as 'spectacle' and actively invites the attention of an audience, paradoxically, Alex cannot estimate the extent to which he is watched by what he perceives as fundamentally benign institutions. * * *

So the public spectators of Alex's sensationalist theatre are displaced by the covert gaze of disciplining institutional bodies and it is from this element of invisibility, suggestively antithetical to Alex's ostentatious displays of power, that the underworld of state control derives its ultimate authority.

The initial phase of Alex's 'recovery' is predicated upon isolating the fifteen-year old anti-hero from those pre-established frames of reference which provide him with the means of self-confirmation. Plucked from his own 'underworld' context of adolescent gangland and deprived of the linguistic currency of Nadsat he is repositioned within the dehumanising confines of the adult prison, where he is allocated the numeric title of '6655321' becoming '. . . not your little droog Alex not no longer' (51). The hierarchisation and corruption of the penal system are clearly flagged up within the text as Alex becomes an informer on behalf of the Prison Chaplain. Burgess underlines the abusive exploitation of Alex within this disciplinary network, yet simultaneously we see the cute adolescent ironically capitalising upon the ethically vulnerable figure, the 'man of God', in order to further what he perceives to be his own ends. In this black market which traffics both illicit goods and, more importantly, illicit information, we find, everyone is a commodity and thus everyone is purchasable, regardless of status as either 'supervised' or 'supervisee'. Effectively, Alex's precociousness enables him to manipulate and maximise upon every aspect of the world which he knows; his vulnerability lies in the 'secret' which lies at the heart of the rehabilitation programme and it is in withholding this knowledge that the adult realm succeeds in rendering him a docile and selfless body.

*   *   *

The sadistic voyeurism of Dr Branom and Dr Brodsky and the political self-aggrandizement of the 'Minister of the Inferior' prompt and 'legalise' their utilisation of technologies of state violence. Masked behind a camouflage of liberalism their illiberal measures constitute frightening acts of cruelty upon the 'unformed' adolescent subject. Sedated by drugs and injected with a chemical cocktail designed to attack the neurological system, Alex is repeatedly physically and psychologically tortured, the victimiser radically rewritten as the victim. Coupled with this, the ironic deployment of media images of violence and unreleased video-tape footage of Alex's criminal violations as a means of attacking the ostensible 'root' of their patient's malady, escalates to obscene proportions, evidently foregrounding the retributive quality of their actions.

Each stage of the narrator's re-conditioning thus entails a further infringement of his autonomy as he is systematically deprived of his civil, physical and psychological liberties. In this nightmarish encounter between the state and the subversive subject, Alex is located at the ideological inter-section of institutional power and individual agency and consequently, the text throws us into the discursive territory of human rights. With an utter disregard for Alex's humanity, this state-condoned underworld of official reformers implement totalitarian or fascistic violences upon the body and mind of the teenage reprobate. The wholly unethical, dehumanising treatment of Alex's case corresponds with what Habermas has termed as a 'technocratic consciousness which reflects not the sundering of particular ethical situations but the repression of ethics as a category of life' (*Towards a Rational Society* 1971, 112–3).[2] For these methods do not endeavour to 'educate' or 'guide' the adolescent towards an ethical consciousness of the implications and thus the undesirability of his own actions—that is they do not enhance his subjective right to do right; rather they displace an ethical faculty with a psychosomatic trigger of repulsion and physical nausea. Thus, the 'underworld' of the technocrats, financed by the publicity machines of politicians, abrogate all laws established in defence of civil and human rights, clinically de-subjectivising Alex and rendering him a mere simulacrum of his previous self. Without question, it is in *this* underworld that we identify the 'radical evil' of Arendt's opening quotation, and what is yet more disquietening is that whilst the sub-culture of the adolescent is reconstituted as an integral and thus governable aspect of mainstream existence, the underworld of surveillance and regulation remains camouflaged, inviolable, ominously intact.

2. Jürgen Habermas, *Towards a Rational Society: Student Protest, Science and Politics* (London: Heinemann, 1971).

ROBBIE B. H. GOH

[Language and Social Control]†

* * *

The novel's vision of social control is thus encoded in the different kinds of linguistic performances on the part of Alex, the Everyman of this dystopian world. Alex's "infantile" experiments with language—with small morphemic units and the possibilities of transplanting them to create new words, with sounds and their iconic and phonemic qualities—constitutes a sort of micro-politics of the individual. Set against this is the repetitive, deceptive and dehumanising language which Alex attributes to the adult figures of power in his society, but which also threatens to take over his discourse. Nowhere is the novel's dystopian vision more trenchantly articulated than in the narrative's code of intratextual influences and repetitions, in its intrusive numerical patterns and forms, associated with social power and corruption.

* * *

In this foregrounding of language as political arena, it is Alex's concern with iconicity and onomatopoea in particular which embodies the novel's narrative hopefulness. Iconicity, in Charles Sanders Peirce's seminal terms, is a relationship of "similarity" or "resemblance" between the formal or material aspects of the sign, and its signified. For Peirce, the icon refers to its referent "merely by virtue of characters of its own" (which characters are said to "resemble" or be "similar" to the referent object), whereas a "symbol" signifies "by virtue of a law, usually an association of general ideas." Thus it is possible to distinguish between the non-mimetic, abstract and conventional signification of symbolic signs on the one hand, and iconic signs on the other hand, where the formal properties of the sign mime the signified.

* * *

* * * Much of Alex's linguistic playfulness in *A Clockwork Orange* reveals a similar mimologic desire, as when he describes a toothless victim (whose dentures he and his gang have just destroyed) as making "chumbling shooms—'wuf waf wof'" (7). "Chumbling" clearly borrows from the morpho-semantic structure of existing words like "mumbling," "rumbling" and "grumbling," which carry similar

† From "'Clockwork' Language Reconsidered: Iconicity and Narrative in Anthony Burgess's *A Clockwork Orange*," in *Journal of Narrative Theory* 30.2 (Summer 2000):263–80. Reprinted by permission.

connotations of indistinct, low sounds. The voiced labial sound /m/ in the middle of these words which closes off the first syllable, together with the predominantly low vowels, contribute to this sense of indistinctness, corroborated by words like "stumbling," "bumbling" and even "rambling," with their sense of slow, difficult or obstructed movement. Since the novel uses orthographic experimentation rather than standard phonetic renditions of sounds, it is not possible to determine exactly how the toothless victim enunciates these words. It may be that the victim makes "chumbling shooms" because the sudden loss of his dentures causes him to create fricative sounds in the unaccustomed gap created in his mouth.

It is possible to quarrel over the exact phonetic reproduction of the victim's "chumbling shooms" (whether fricative or plosive, alveolar or velar, and so on), although that is not the novel's main point. Rather, the novel compels the reader to speculate on the likely or possible production of these "chumbling" sounds, in the light of the speaker's lack of teeth. The focus is not the actual sound made by the victim, but rather the abrupt change in speech pattern and sound production (compared to his earlier righteous indignation and high moral tone) as a result of the change in the conditions governing that production. Alex's act of brutality forces the victim (and, vicariously, the reader) to discover or at least dwell on the ineluctably physical basis of words, a basis which Alex's narrative then recreates and lingers on with evident fascination. The link between bodily posture and language is recalled later in the novel, when Alex's father (in response to his son's aggression) is described as speaking "like humble mumble chumble" (34). We are not told that Alex's father wears dentures, but "chumble" recalls the earlier victim of Alex's violence, the "umble" syllables yoking the sense of impeded or difficult progress evident in the earlier instance with a sense of pronounced caution or cringing withdrawal in the later episode. So just as the first victim's "chumbling" suggests a sudden change in his mouth's physical production of sounds, the father's "chumbling" likewise depicts (from the point of view of Alex's delighted interest) a shift in speech production which marks a physical recoiling from the implicit threat of violence in Alex's discourse. Indeed, Alex's neologistic link between the two victims has some physiological basis: when Alex is more explicitly violent with his parents, one of his threats is to "kick your zoobies [i.e. teeth] in" (110), which (their unsurprised and resigned response suggests) is not a new threat. The father's "humble mumble chumble" is thus, from Alex's imaginative point of view, almost a physical reflex to a well-known and specific threat of mutilation.

*   *   *

Not surprisingly, many of these nonlexical iconic elements stem from bodily experience: not just the labial sensation of making "lip-music," but also the inchoate verbal outcries accompanying sexual orgasm ("aaaaaaah," 25), tiredness ("yawwwww," 20), battle-rage ("Aaaaaaarhgh," 37) and pain or shock ("hauwwww hauwww hauwww," 38). Alex's "aaaaaaah" of orgasm in this instance serves to distinguish this episode, to a certain extent, from his many other sexual experiences. The latter are registered in chillingly impersonal terms: as the athletic metaphor of "plunging" (18), the transient mechanical action of "the old in-out" (68), or the coldly abstract phrase "doing the ultra-violent" (73). Again, there is an iconic and bodily logic to this differentiation: the latter expressions are used when Alex is in his (as it were) public or social role, as the leader of his gang's gang rapes, or otherwise fulfilling the persona of the young delinquent. In contrast, his onomatopoeic expression of sexual pleasure is auto-erotic and private, as he lies listening to his beloved Beethoven's Ninth in his own room. His "aaaaaaah" of pleasure not only schematically conveys something of the extra length and duration of his climax, as well as the throaty back-vowel sounds he makes in the intensity of his pleasure; by standing out from the other representations of sex, it also marks the place of the private, personal Alex. The iconic moment suggests, if not exactly a redeeming view of Alex, then at least an alternative self to the language and perspective of his public or group behaviour.

This attention to iconic detail is not confined to organic bodies, however, and Alex's narrative also delights in what happens to inanimate objects: their movement, impact, texture, contact, and so on. Thus, a chain whirled during a fight is rendered, not with the expected "whoosh," "whirl" or "whirr" (all of which are in the O.E.D.), but rather "whisssssshhhhhhhhhh" (14), where the pronounced hissing sound heightens the sense of the sheer velocity of the movement. The same chain, swung by the same agent Dim, is later turned treacherously on Alex, but the sound is represented differently, as "whishhhhh" (44). The differences in the two representations reinforce the concrete distinctiveness of these two experiences, as perceived by Alex: on the first occasion, there is a fight in the open between two gangs, a confused melee in which Dim's chain reaches out at greater speed and force across a greater distance to hit Alex's opponent; on the second occasion, in contrast, Alex is standing in a doorway, and Dim's unexpected blow is delivered "gently and artistic like" at a close, specific target. This departure from more common lexical onomatopoeia like "whirl," this violation of notions of orthographic regularity and economy, thus allows the novel to register distinct and different experiences of objects, in this case rendering different experiences of the momentum, sound and impact of the weapon.

Similarly, a car pushed into a muddy canal submerges with a "splussshhhh and glolp" (19) which conveys not only Alex's close and delighted interest in the process, but also a rich suggestion of textures and physical properties: the thickness of the filthy water and the slight resistance this offers the sinking car, the sudden escape of an air bubble, perhaps the hissing of the still-warm engine, and so on. A disc (of an organ hymn) played on the prison chapel's turntable comes on with a "growwwwowwwwowwww" (54), suggesting the sonorous blare of the pipe organ, the wobbly rotation of the turntable, and the hollow and reverberating accoustics of the chapel all at once. It is not that these iconic or onomatopoeic items somehow signify the material object or its surrounding environment in any naively immediate or objective way. Rather, they entice the reader's participation in an alternative semiotics in which the sign refers, not to conventional and abstract meanings, but via its own palpability to corresponding qualities in the physical consistency, properties, and kinetics of things. The fact that this semiotic process is suggestive but cannot be conclusive in any scientific or empirical way, only emphasizes Alex's (and the reader's) interpretative activity—which, in the novel's view, is preferable to the passive acceptance of conventional meanings.

✵   ✵   ✵

A *Clockwork Orange*'s vision of the politics of language emerges out of the reader's sensitivity to linguistic violence which is fostered by Alex's peculiar narrative. It allows the reader to become aware of linguistic regularity and repetition disguised as idiosyncracy, which is associated with the treacherous adult advisors and acquaintances of Alex's world, its power brokers and institutional figures. Thus, for example, when the political subversive who wants to exploit Alex, Z. Dolin (omega to Alex's alpha), is introduced to us as "coughing kashl kashl kashl" (104), several orthographic and morphemic aspects come to the fore. Regularity is marked not only by the thrice-repeated word (a microcosm of the tripartite structure of the novel, its "trinity" which determines shape and meaning), but also by the near- or quasi-lexical aspects. It certainly suggests "cash" (which is what both Dolin and his enemies in government implicitly offer Alex, as a bribe to induce him to co-operate with their political machinations), but also "catch" (both in Joseph Heller's sense of a preventive legalism, and the physical arrest and incarceration always threatened in a police state), "casual" (which is the manner and attitude of the state throughout its horrendous treatment of Alex), as well as "casualty" (what Alex becomes within all these power processes). More distantly (but possible, depending on how the vowels in "kashl" were to be pronounced) it could also invoke "causal," suggesting the entire social determinism of Alex's world. These morphemic resemblances and overtones, a function of the relative regularity of the syntactic structure of "kashl," prime the reader to note other aspects of linguistic and social constraints operative in the novel.

It is hardly surprising to notice, then, that Dolin's cough is not distinctive or idiosyncratic, but exactly echoes the sounds of Alex's exhausted car earlier in the novel ("coughing kashl kashl kashl," 19). The order in which these identical sounds are presented is also iconically important: Dolin's cough imitates the car, the human performance reproduces the mechanical, in the narrative's schematisation. Another such damning imitation of the mechanical occurs with Alex's mother, whose seemingly spontaneous and genuine expression of grief at Alex's sentencing is rendered "owwwww owwwww owwwww" (51). This initially has some of the features (redundancy, length, violation of expected consonant-vowel combinations) of Alex's inventive neologisms. However, the human spontaneity of her performance is spoilt, somewhat, by her repetition of this performance when Alex is in hospital: "Owwwww," and "Owwwwwww" (110–1). The repetitive nature of these outbursts overwhelms the little variation that exists (between five or six "w"s, suggesting a slight variation in duration of the sound, and between the lower case and upper case "o," suggesting differences in emphases).

* * *

Alex's linguistic violence—the iconic and bodily gestures he forces language to perform, in violation of conventional rules—is more significant even than his physical acts of violence: curiously, while he is willing to gratify his various lusts at the expense of others, he is particular about taking life. The deaths of the old woman with the cats and of his cellmate are unintended, and Alex in both cases may be said to have some provocation in their offensive behaviour to him. His violence does not preclude a certain careful awareness of the extent of the harm he is inflicting: he sums up his assault on the old bibliophile in chapter one with "We hadn't done much, I know" (8), and similarly at the end of the assault on the occupants of "HOME" scrupulously opines that "they'd live" (19), although as it turns out he is partly wrong. More significantly, his physical actions also function at times as an interruption of greater evil (even if this is not the intended result): thus his fight with Billyboy's gang allows their intended rape victim to run away (13), and his criminal career and violent "rehabilitation" by the state brings a halt to the use of Ludovico's Technique as a state tool. In the same way, his iconic neologisms and experimentations are a linguistic violence that interrupts the greater evil of society's hypocritical moralising, and self-serving politics.

* * *

To remain "unregenerably" stuck in a certain condition is mechanical, while to change is moral and human; one can see the logic of

Burgess's argument, and its relevance to the novel. However, it is also a sweeping view which seems curiously detached from the particulars of the novel's language and structure. Alex's turn towards a "conventional" life at the end of the novel also sees him turning away from what is vitally inventive and interesting in his use of language, and embracing a borrowed and stilted discourse. Significantly, his vision of a "grown up" life is also derivative and repetitive, taken from the unpalatable and pretentious life presented to him by Pete and his new wife Georgina (whose name marks her as a repetition of and surrogate for Pete's old gang friend, Georgie, in Pete's present life). It is a life of "smallness" ("small flat," "very small money"), name-dropping ("you wouldn't know Greg"), and triviality ("wine-cup and word-games"). The most that can be said for it is that it is "harmless" (119–120), although as the rest of the novel shows, passive conformity to society's discourse and values is its own evil.

In the uncertainty and loneliness ("But what was I going to do?") provoked by Pete's smug vision, Alex's narrative voice and language also change significantly, as he adopts the terms and values approved by society. He frames this vision of marital bliss and parenthood in terms of public, stock images: the newspaper cutting of a baby which he keeps, the domestic scene "like these cartoons in the gazettas" (120). The final paragraph is particularly telling: while some traces of Nadsat remain, it is also clear that Alex's language mutates into the inherited language and mechanical repetitions associated earlier in the novel with politicians, adults in bad faith, and social powers. Thus the repetition in quick succession of the vague phrase "all that cal," a sign that Alex (for perhaps the first time in his narrative) cannot find inventive language equal to the situation before him. Even his nonlexical, iconic language lacks conviction: his "lipmusic" is now "brrrrrr," far less phonemically complex or striking than his earlier performances, and it is also a near-repetition of the prison buzzer (60), and an exact repetition of the doorbell of one of Alex's victims we encounter earlier in the novel (40).

Burgess's dystopian critique of society offers no simplistic social curative, no modernist faith in social regeneration. Even in its less contrived and symmetrical 20-chapter form, the novel's vision of the micropolitics of the individual is far from rosy: if the individual finds moments of authenticity and resistance in a form of linguistic violence, this is so closely affiliated with a chilling physical violence which is, however, the only means of interrupting society's linear determinisms. In the 21-chapter form that Burgess intended, the triumph of society's language-as-power is even more pronounced, with Alex's final assimilation. If any hopefulness remains, it lies in the praxis of linguistic inventiveness in search of new meaning, which the novel's narrative creates for the reader.

On Stanley Kubrick's Film

PETER HUGHES JACHIMIAK

[Subcultural Appropriations]†

This chapter aims to consider *A Clockwork Orange* within both modernity, as it entered its late modern phase, and youth culture. In doing so, it will conceptualise *A Clockwork Orange*, both Anthony Burgess's novella (1962) and Stanley Kubrick's screen adaptation (1971), as an intertwined artistic entity which has been filtered through popular culture, appropriated by multifarious subcultural youth amid this modernity-into-late-modernity transition. [. . .] Under scrutiny here is the way in which the content and iconography of both texts have been turned into a unique stylistic resource with which subcultural youth have helped position themselves within a turbulent and troublesome late modernity.

* * *

Since Kubrick's self-imposed ban, a perpetual mythologisation of both the book and the film has taken place: a mythologising of the latter as it was now unavailable; a mythologising of the former as it remained the only available format in which *A Clockwork Orange* could be consumed. Yet, come the video age, the film did resurface—albeit in pirated form—and 'so began the copying of a copy of a copy'.[1] Thus, throughout the next three decades it became the property of, what has been termed, 'dis/connected' youth.[2] Of course, all of this only served to maintain awareness of Burgess's legacy amid underground youth culture; for, significantly, while Kubrick's version languished in pirated VHS semi-obscurity, more and more ill-educated youths struggled with reading Burgess's original. This, of

† From "'Putting the Boot In': *A Clockwork Orange*, Post-'69 Youth Culture and the Onset of Late Modernity," in Alan R. Roughley, ed., *Anthony Burgess and Modernity*. New York: Manchester UP, 2008), 147–64. Reprinted by permission.
1. George Marshall, *Spirit of '69—A Skinhead Bible* (1991) (Lockerbie: S. T. Publishing, 1994), 65.
2. Nick Barham, *Dis/connected—Why Our Kids Are Turning Their Backs on Everything We Thought We Knew* (London: Ebury Press, 2004).

course, is all now historical half-myth itself as, following Kubrick's death in 1999, it was celebrated that 'now, for the first time in 27 years, *A Clockwork Orange* is back on British cinema screens'.[3]

*   *   *

The skinhead subculture, evolving out of what Stanley Cohen (1972)[4] termed the 'hard mods', seemed to simply appear, en masse, on the streets of inner-city Britain at the end of the 1960s, as flower-power began to wilt, and the Enoch Powell 1970s began to rear their ugly shaven head. Chris Welch, in a *Melody Maker* article in early 1969—the year in which the media discovered this violence-orientated youth subculture—made explicit their menace: 'The sight of cropped heads and the sound of heavy boots entering the midnight Wimpy bar or dancehall is the real cause for sinking feel-ings in the pit of the stomach . . . the maniacal, humourless laugh-ter, the black staring eyes seeking a victim.'[5] As if Welch is describing a scene from *A Clockwork Orange*, skinheads, then, were potentially just as deadly as the on-screen Droogs. For Knight (1982) lists the offensive weapons regularly carried by skinheads: sharpened metal combs, Kung Fu stars, darts, and '[t]he Millwall brick . . . a newspa-per folded again and again and squashed together to form a cosh'.[6] According to Hebdige (1979), skinheads are a 'somewhat mythically conceived image of the traditional working-class community with its classic focal concerns, its acute sense of territory, its tough exteri-ors, its dour "machismo" '.[7] Paul Du Noyer (1981) paid close atten-tion to the external signifiers of the skinheads, insisting that 'these new mutants were aggressively working class, taking traditional styles (big boots, braces, short hair) up to the point of parody'.[8] The skinheads' attraction to *A Clockwork Orange* was that, as well as paying homage to their aggressive style, it updated their look and provided it with some sort of futuristic whiteness, thus suggesting longevity for skinheads and associated violent masculinity. To skin-heads, *A Clockwork Orange* promised both a pat on the back and recognition of their place in British subcultural history.

*   *   *

3. Peter Bradshaw, 'The old ultra-violence', 'Friday Review', *Guardian* (3 March 2000), 2.
4. Stanley Cohen, *Folk Devils and Moral Panics: The Creation of the Mods and Rockers* (1972; London: Routledge, 2004).
5. Chris Welch, 'Now it's a mod, mod, mod, mod world', in *NME Originals—1960s Swing-ing London* (8 February 1969, reprinted December 2003), 1:11.
6. Nick Knight, *Skinhead* (London: Omnibus Press, 1982), 17.
7. Dick Hebdige, *Subculture—The Meaning of Style* (1997) (London: Routledge, 1997), 55.
8. Paul Du Noyer, 'The seventies—rebellion, revival and survival', in Tony Stewart (ed.), *Cool Cats—25 Years of Rock 'n' Roll Style* (London: Eel Pie Publishing, 1981), 102–31, 104.

The early 1970s saw skinheads transform into several mutant varieties—bootboy, smoothie, suedehead—all drawing, stylistically, from the recently released cinematic adaptation of Burgess's novel; thus, readily appropriating *A Clockwork Orange* style, mixing both the city and the street. As Martin Roach (1999) makes note, this all amounted to a macabre cocktail 'of city gent style and bootboy intimidation'.[9] In particular, suedeheads went as far as wearing bowler hats and accessorising themselves with umbrellas that included 'sharpened metal points to aid and abet a few rounds of fisticuffs'.[1] It is worth bearing in mind that, according to Robinson (1993), the bowler hat—as worn by both McDowell in *A Clockwork Orange* and by the sharp, streetwise suedeheads—very much epitomises the totality of modernity. Due to its association with bureaucrats and bureaucracy, Robinson insists that we should understand 'the bowler as a sign of the modern, of the energetic ongoing, no matter in what dark direction', that it 'allude[s] to the past while floating into the future'.[2] As soon as Alex dons the bowler—the symbol of modernity—it is transformed into a sinister subcultural accessory of late modern youth.

It has to be noted, however, that *A Clockwork Orange* also allowed members of the otherwise hypermasculine and homophobic skinhead subculture to dip the toes of their Doc Martens into the sequinned water of the far more feminised glam rock style. For it was Alex's strikingly Biba-esque right eye that allowed the ultramasculine boot to be topped off by the femininely absurd, over-made-up eye. Indeed, 'as 1972 shaded into '73 . . . *Cabaret* and *A Clockwork Orange* filled the screens with cinematic decadence'.[3] It was on Arsenal's Highbury terraces that this skin/glam mongrel, who wore Doc Martens in various dayglo colours with clear evidence of make-up, was first spotted: 'Put together it was both threatening and alluring.'[4] In this 1970s wasteland, rather than be found in any make-believe milk-bar, Droog lookalikes, then, could be found in pubs and clubs and on the terraces—a bizarre parody, the result of the incongruous fusion of two seemingly oppositional dominant youth fashions of the time: glam rock, the preserve of heterosexual 'brickies in mascara', and skinhead, the bald-headed prol. In short, '[i]f Alex's false eyelash looked like a nod to Glam, his uniform was out and out Skins'.[5]

9. Martin Roach, *Dr. Martens Air-Wair with Bouncing Souls* (Wollaston: Air-Wair, 1999).
1. Marshall, *Spirit of '69*, 55.
2. Fred Miller Robinson, *The Man in the Bowler Hat—His History and Iconography* (Chapel Hill: U of North Carolina P, 1993), 167.
3. Robert Elms, *The Way We Wore—A Life in Threads* (London: Picador, 2005), 93.
4. Ibid., 98.
5. Ali Catterall and Simon Wells, *Your Face Here: British Cult Movies Since the Sixties* (London: Fourth Estate, 2001), 114.

*   *   *

Both Burgess's novelistic warning from modernity and Kubrick's late modern stylised adaptation are very much still with us. Almost totally devoid of shock value, which is the result of being subdued by on- and off-screen violence that has surpassed anything that even the author and the director could fathom up, *A Clockwork Orange* is now a retro-futuristic artefact that finds itself reproduced time and time again amid a youth culture 'supermarket of style'.[6] More often than not, this is in reference towards the global triumph of Britain's subcultural heritage, as *A Clockwork Orange* has now been subsumed within today's nostalgia-obsessed popular culture. For example, Richard Jobson's bleak semi-biographical cinematic portrayal of the three stages of a young man's life—*16 Years of Alcohol* (2003)[7]— makes explicit the centrality of violence during the protagonist's teenage years, as he leads a Skinhead gang in Edinburgh during the late 1960s and early 1970s. Significantly, the cover of the *A Clockwork Orange* soundtrack LP is momentarily visible in the scene set in a record shop, and the film's opening sequence—showing the drunken, dancing group of four skinheads (harshly lit silhouettes that dominate the opening to some paved, inner-city subway)—is not only an acknowledgement of the centrality of the film to the Skinheads' subcultural identity but a blatant homage to Kubrick's infamous set piece. Furthermore, in May 2005 *Scootering* magazine placed on its cover the bright orange 'Clockwork Cutdown', a customised scooter completely covered in murals depicting Alex in stills from Kubrick's adaptation of *A Clockwork Orange*.[8] Likewise, in July of the same year Detour Records (essentially an on-line record shop selling 'music for the scooter scene') released the Pop Stars seven-inch single by the Pork Dukes with a sleeve that echoed the original promotional film poster for *A Clockwork Orange*, substituting the blade-wielding McDowell for a similar 'tooled-up', bowler-wearing pig.[9] In August 2005 the beer producer Stella Artois ran a double-page advertisement in many monthly magazines that consisted of familiar filmic scenes. Essentially set within an overcast 'middle-England' town, just opposite the local pub and red phone box, the ad depicts a gang of Droogs drinking milk outside a sleepy Korova milk bar. Such a contemporaneous neutering of *A Clockwork Orange* to the commonplace, to the banal of the everyday, only serves to emphasise that the shock of the novel and the schlock of

---

6. Ted Polhemus, *Street Style—From Sidewalk to Catwalk* (New York: Thames & Hudson, 1994), 130–35.
7. Significantly, the Region 1 DVD release of this film has the tagline '*Trainspotting* meets *A Clockwork Orange*' on its cover.
8. Anon., *Scootering* (May 2005), Edition 227.
9. Anon., Detour Records, mail order catalogue (July 2005), No. 46.

the film have now been stirred into a kitsch slurry following their repeated appropriation within late modern youth culture. Its boot-boy kick reduced to that of lame parody, A *Clockwork Orange* no longer scares, now it just sells.

* * *

In this way, A *Clockwork Orange* is no longer a prophecy of society's decline: instead, due to its permeation of youth subcultures and, more generally, popular culture, it is now a text that encourages cohesion at a time of social fragmentation. Chris Jenks (2005), questioning the generally held assumption that we now exist in a terminally fragmented society, stresses that '[t]he idea of a subcul-ture can be understood simultaneously as part of this problem and also as a rearguard attempt to establish islands of social stability'.[1] I would insist, then, that A *Clockwork Orange* should be under-stood as 'a text that binds'. Once disparate bands of youths—in drawing aesthetic and stylistic inspiration from both the book and the film—have proven that commonalities exist between what at first appear to be diametrically opposed subcultures and youth groupings. Yet, through their appropriation of A *Clockwork Orange*, these so-called dis/connected youths of late modernity, such as skinheads and punks, are more connected than often thought. * * * Thus, A *Clockwork Orange*, as a modernist dystopian text, serves to provide inspirational cohesion to globally dis/connected youth in a late modernist world.

---

1. Chris Jenks, *Subculture—The Fragmentation of the Social* (London: Sage, 2005), 136.

STEVEN M. CAHN

[Freedom]†

A Clockwork Orange has been the subject of much critical interpretation. Two views of the movie have become predominant. One states that director Stanley Kubrick is condemning the violence in our society, while the other states that he is glorifying it. To my mind, however, neither interpretation is correct, for *A Clockwork Orange* is not a film of social commentary but instead one of philosophical speculation. In attempting to raise philosophical issues about the human condition, Kubrick has simply used violence as an example of a human phenomenon. He has also used sex, and he has also used music. Those critics who concentrate on the brutal aspects of the film are simply criticizing Kubrick's example, ignoring or perhaps missing the fact that it is just that, an example. Kubrick has focused on violence because it is powerful and universal. Just why it is universal is not his concern in this film. What is his concern is the nature of all human action, whether attractive or not.

When we originally meet the movie's central character Alex, he is, although strangely charming, both vicious and brutal, and clearly not to be admired. But it is equally clear that his later state of conditioned non-violence is portrayed as more undesirable. He may be a "true Christian", who will be allowed to go "free", as the government minister insists, but, as the prison chaplain claims, Alex is obviously not free, because he has not accepted "Christian" values through choice. Thus the implication of the film at first seems to be that a free human being, no matter how destructive, is preferable to a pacified individual, completely conditioned and unable to act freely.

But is Alex, who says at the end of the film, "I was cured", truly as free as he believes? Is he really unconditioned? Or has he not exchanged a more obvious, more efficient conditioning for a less obvious, less efficient form? Has the world that brought him up not at the same time conditioned him? Do not Alex's parents and friends condition him to brutality by responding only when he bullies them? Does not society in general condition him by reinforcing his sexual fantasies with erotic art? And what about the prison chaplain who pleads for Alex's freedom of choice? Does he not attempt to condition Alex and other listeners by trying to impose a fear of

---

† "*A Clockwork Orange* Is Not About Violence," in *Metaphilosophy* 5.2 (April 1974): 155–57. Reprinted by permission.

suffering in an afterlife? Perhaps, then, the film is condemning modern society by presenting a member who has responded fully to certain aspects of the conditioning process.

But there is an irony running throughout the film that undercuts any social commentary. For instance, the brutal and shocking scenes of the film, and there are many, are all intruded upon humorously by such devices as incongruous background music, altered camera speeds, or an almost choreographed direction. Somehow the violence is made meaningless, as though the actions are neither good nor evil, but simply unreasoned, animalistic responses. Indeed, upon reflection, it becomes apparent that almost all human actions in this film are depicted as cold, reflex behavior. Qualities such as sensitivity and sympathy, *human* qualities, are notably absent.

By presenting human action in such an inhuman light, by dwelling so heavily on the conditioning process, and by his emphasis on the meaning of the word "free", Kubrick indicates that what he is offering is a dramatization of behaviorism. The film is a portrait of human life as a series of learned, automatic responses to the stimuli of the environment. Like the famed Pavlov dogs, Alex learns responses that satisfy his needs, and he performs them again and again. For instance, when he is with his parents, he reacts as their conditioning has taught him to react, by bullying and lying. They are among the thousands of stimuli in his environment, which includes his friends, rival gangs, women, Beethoven's music, and the prison chaplain. Toward each Alex reacts as he has been conditioned, and the conditioned reaction replaces thinking and free choice. Kubrick implies that the Ludovico conditioning technique is merely a concentrated version of what goes on every minute of every human being's life. Alex's abhorence of violence at the end of two weeks is not reasoned, but simply a reflex, just like his attitude toward his parents. This new reaction is sharper only because it has been more efficiently conditioned. Just as Alex is not free when he leaves the Ludovico Institute, so, Kubrick is suggesting, no human being is free at any time in his life. The implication is that conditioning, whether good or evil, prevents us from being free, and yet conditioning is inescapable. This is the same view that B. F. Skinner has promulgated in a highly sophisticated version, most recently in *Beyond Freedom and Dignity*.[1] Naturally we recoil when we ponder the possibility that our society is conditioning violence. But perhaps it is more frightening to consider the possibility that no matter what values our society conditions, human beings can never be free agents.

1. B. F. Skinner, *Beyond Freedom and Dignity* (New York: Knopf, 1971).

This theory of hard determinism is of course highly controversial, and it is important also to consider what role individual biology has in determining each person's reactions to environmental stimuli. In any case further philosophical investigation is beyond the scope of this paper. What I am arguing, however, is that *A Clockwork Orange* is not essentially a vision of a new world of the future, nor is it a commentary on muggings in the subway, the violence of pro football, or the horrors of Viet Nam. Rather, the movie is a dramatization of the view that no human being is right when he calls himself "free".

VINCENT CANBY

Review[†]

Stanley Kubrick's ninth film, *A Clockwork Orange*, which has just won the New York Film Critics Award as the best film of 1971, is a brilliant and dangerous work, but it is dangerous in a way that brilliant things sometimes are.

I'd hardly put it in the same category with nuclear energy, "A Declaration of Independence" and *The Interpretation of Dreams*, but it is a movie of such manifold, contradictory effects that it can easily be seen in many ways and may well be wrongly used by a number of people who see it. It is an almost perfect example of the kind of New Movie that is all the more disorienting—and thus, apparently, dangerous—because it seems to remain aloof from, and uninvolved with, the matters it's about.

Somewhere during the second third of the film, Alex (Malcolm McDowell), a vicious teenage London hood who has the cheeriness of a ratty Candide, is subjected to the Ludovico Technique, a type of aversion therapy that effectively neutralizes Alex's passions for both ultra-violence and the music of lovely lovely Ludwig Van, by making him physically ill whenever these passions arise.

After some plot permutations that I need not go into, Alex is suddenly returned to his old self. While he is recovering in the hospital, he is visited by the Minister of the Interior (whom Alex calls Fred), who presents Alex with a new stereo. As the Fourth Movement from Beethoven's Ninth Symphony fills the soundtrack, Alex's eyeballs, like those of some idiot doll, roll upward in their sockets and momentarily we share another one of Alex's sado-masochistic

---

† "Disorienting but Human Comedy," in *The New York Times*, section II, January 9, 1972, 1, 7. Reprinted by permission.

sex fantasies: he is thrashing around in the turf at Ascot, forcibly putting the old in-out to another helpless, faceless woman, while the handsomely dressed ladies and gentlemen applaud in silence and boredom. The music stops abruptly and Alex announces triumphantly: "I was cured!"

In a movie of more conventional emotional structure, where identification with the central character has been easy and complete, we might, I suppose, share something of Alex's triumph. However, we've spent the last two hours or so being alternately amused, horrified, sickened and moved by Alex who has, among other things, beaten up an old bum; bludgeoned to death a nutty health farm lady (with a giant porno art sculpture of a penis and testicles); and then has himself been turned into a helpless vegetable by the Ludovico Treatment.

Alex's return is a return to a kind of crafty viciousness that most of us know only in the darkest corners of our souls. In other words, we can't—or shouldn't—share Alex's triumph. I am saddened—and a bit confused—for although THE END flashes on the screen, that is not really the end of *A Clockwork Orange*. As we walk out of the theater, and as the final credits are flashing on the screen, the theater is filled with the sound of Gene Kelly singing "Singin' in The Rain," backed by one of those fulsome old M-G-M orchestrations from the 1952 movie. The effect is that of the Ludovico Treatment gone slightly awry. Our reactions are both blissful (the recollection of the great Stanley Donen–Gene Kelly film) and, more immediately, terrifying (the memory of a scene in *A Clockwork Orange* in which Alex, doing a passable soft-shoe, kicks into semi-unconsciousness a man whose wife he is about to rape, all the while singing "Singin' in The Rain.")

A friend of mine has suggested that Kubrick was pulling a fast one by running the old Kelly recording over the end credits of the film, thereby hoping to wipe away or, at least, to diminish the frigid effect of the movie. It seems to me, however, that the point of the Arthur Freed–Nacio Herb Brown number is much more interesting—and typical of Kubrick's method throughout *A Clockwork Orange*.

Although the film, like Anthony Burgess's novel from which it is adapted, is cast as futurist fiction, it is much more a satire on contemporary society (especially on British society of the late 1950s and 1960s) than are most futurist works, all of which, if they are worth anything, are meaningful only in terms of the society that bred them. It may even be a mistake to describe the movie *A Clockwork Orange* as futurist in any respect, since its made-up teenage language (Nadsat), its décor, its civil idiocies, its social chaos, or their equivalents, are already at hand, although it's still possible for most of the people who file in and out of the Cinema I on Third Avenue to ignore a lot of them.

A *Clockwork Orange* is about the rise and fall and rise of Alex in a world that is only slightly less dreadful than he is—parents, policemen, doctors and politicians are all either evil, opportunistic or simpleminded. Yet Kubrick has chosen to fashion this as the most elegantly stylized, most classically balanced movie he has ever made—and not, I think, by accident. It isn't just that the narrative comes full circle, that characters, as in something by Dickens, met early, show up by chance later on, that the final resolution returns us to the beginning to make the ending just that much more bleak.

It's also because every moment of unspeakable horror is wrapped in cool beauty, either through Kubrick's camera eye, or by music on the soundtrack. When Alex and his droogs come upon the rival Billyboy's gang, preparing to rape a helpless devotchka in (Alex tells us on the soundtrack) "the old derelict casino," we begin the scene with a close-up of a lovely faded rococo fresco at the top of the proscenium of the casino stage (music by Rossini), before we pan down to the mayhem below. There is even beauty in this voice-over narration, in the words of Nadsat and in the Elizabethan syntax occasionally affected by Alex and his friends.

It seems to me that by describing horror with such elegance and beauty, Kubrick has created a very disorienting but human comedy, not warm and lovable, but a terrible sum-up of where the world is at. With all of man's potential for divinity through love, through his art and his music, this is what it has somehow boiled down to: a civil population terrorized by hoodlums, disconnected porno art, quick solutions to social problems, with the only "hope" for the future in the vicious Alex.

It is hardly a cheery thought, which is why the sound of Gene Kelly singing "Singin' in The Rain" as we leave the theater is so disconcerting. It's really a banana peel for the emotions.

A *Clockwork Orange* might correctly be called dangerous only if one doesn't respond to anything else in the film except the violence. One critic has suggested that Kubrick has attempted to estrange us from any identification with Alex's victims so that we can enjoy the rapes and the beatings. All I can say is that I did not feel any such enjoyment. I was shocked and sickened and moved by a stylized representation that never, for a minute, did I mistake for a literal representation of the real thing.

Everything about A *Clockwork Orange* is carefully designed to make this difference apparent, at least to the adult viewer, but there may be a very real problem when even such stylized representations are seen by immature audiences. That, however, is another subject entirely, and one for qualified psychiatrists to ponder. In my opinion Kubrick has made a movie that exploits only the mystery and variety of human conduct. And because it refuses to use the emotions conventionally, demanding instead that we keep a constant, intellectual grip on things, it's a most unusual—and disorienting—movie experience.

PAULINE KAEL

Review[†]

Literal-minded in its sex and brutality, Teutonic in its humor, Stanley Kubrick's *A Clockwork Orange* might be the work of a strict and exacting German professor who set out to make a porno-violent sci-fi comedy. Is there anything sadder—and ultimately more repellent—than a clean-minded pornographer? The numerous rapes and beatings have no ferocity and no sensuality; they're frigidly, pedantically calculated, and because there is no motivating emotion, the viewer may experience them as an indignity and wish to leave. The movie follows the Anthony Burgess novel so closely that the book might have served as the script, yet that thick-skulled German professor may be Dr. Strangelove himself, because the meanings are turned around.

Burgess's 1962 novel is set in a vaguely Socialist future (roughly, the late seventies or early eighties)—a dreary, routinized England that roving gangs of teen-age thugs terrorize at night. In perceiving the amoral destructive potential of youth gangs, Burgess's ironic fable differs from Orwell's *1984* in a way that already seems prophetically accurate. The novel is narrated by the leader of one of these gangs—Alex, a conscienceless schoolboy sadist—and, in a witty, extraordinarily sustained literary conceit, narrated in his own slang (Nadsat, the teen-agers' special dialect). The book is a fast read; Burgess, a composer turned novelist, has an ebullient, musical sense of language, and you pick up the meanings of the strange words as the prose rhythms speed you along. Alex enjoys stealing, stomping, raping, and destroying until he kills a woman and is sent to prison for fourteen years. After serving two, he arranges to get out by submitting to an experiment in conditioning, and he is turned into a moral robot who becomes nauseated at thoughts of sex and violence. Released when he is harmless, he falls prey to his former victims,

† "Stanley Strangelove," in *The New Yorker* 47.46 (January 1, 1972), 50–53. Reprinted in *Deeper into Movies* (Boston: Little Brown, 1973), 373–78. Reprinted by permission.

who beat him and torment him until he attempts suicide. This leads to criticism of the government that robotized him—turned him into a clockwork orange—and he is deconditioned, becoming once again a thug, and now at loose and triumphant. The ironies are protean, but Burgess is clearly a humanist; his point of view is that of a Christian horrified by the possibilities of a society turned clockwork orange, in which life is so mechanized that men lose their capacity for moral choice. There seems to be no way in this boring, dehumanizing society for the boys to release their energies except in vandalism and crime; they do what they do as a matter of course. Alex the sadist is as mechanized a creature as Alex the good.

Stanley Kubrick's Alex (Malcolm McDowell) is not so much an expression of how this society has lost its soul as he is a force pitted against the society, and by making the victims of the thugs more repulsive and contemptible than the thugs Kubrick has learned to love the punk sadist. The end is no longer the ironic triumph of a mechanized punk but a real triumph. Alex is the only likable person we see—his cynical bravado suggests a broad-nosed, working-class Olivier—and the movie puts us on his side. Alex, who gets kicks out of violence, is more alive than anybody else in the movie, and younger and more attractive, and McDowell plays him exuberantly, with the power and slyness of a young Cagney. Despite what Alex does at the beginning, McDowell makes you root for his foxiness, for his crookedness. For most of the movie, we see him tortured and beaten and humiliated, so when his bold, aggressive punk's nature is restored to him it seems not a joke on all of us but, rather, a victory in which we share, and Kubrick takes an exultant tone. The look in Alex's eyes at the end tells us that he isn't just a mechanized, choiceless sadist but prefers sadism and knows he can get by with it. Far from being a little parable about the dangers of soullessness and the horrors of force, whether employed by individuals against each other or by society in "conditioning," the movie becomes a vindication of Alex, saying that the punk was a free human being and only the good Alex was a robot.

The trick of making the attacked less human than their attackers, so you feel no sympathy for them, is, I think, symptomatic of a new attitude in movies. This attitude says there's no moral difference. Stanley Kubrick has assumed the deformed, self-righteous perspective of a vicious young punk who says, "Everything's rotten. Why shouldn't I do what I want? They're worse than I am." In the new mood (perhaps movies in their cumulative effect are partly responsible for it), people want to believe the hyperbolic worst, want to believe in the degradation of the victims—that they are dupes and phonies and weaklings. I can't accept that Kubrick is merely reflecting this post-assassinations, post-Manson mood; I think he's catering to it. I think he wants to dig it.

This picture plays with violence in an intellectually seductive way. And though it has no depth, it's done in such a slow, heavy style that those prepared to like it can treat its puzzling aspects as oracular. It can easily be construed as an ambiguous mystery play, a visionary warning against "the Establishment." There are a million ways to justify identifying with Alex: Alex is fighting repression; he's alone against the system. What he does isn't nearly as bad as what the government does (both in the movie and in the United States now). Why shouldn't he be violent? That's all the Establishment has ever taught him (and us) to be. The point of the book was that we must be as men, that we must be able to take responsibility for what we are. The point of the movie is much more *au courant*. Kubrick has removed many of the obstacles to our identifying with Alex; the Alex of the book has had his personal habits cleaned up a bit—his fondness for squishing small animals under his tires, his taste for ten-year-old girls, his beating up of other prisoners, and so on. And Kubrick aids the identification with Alex by small directorial choices throughout. The writer whom Alex cripples (Patrick Magee) and the woman he kills are cartoon nasties with upper-class accents a mile wide. (Magee has been encouraged to act like a bathetic madman; he seems to be preparing for a career in horror movies.) Burgess gave us society through Alex's eyes, and so the vision was deformed, and Kubrick, carrying over from *Dr. Strangelove* his joky adolescent view of hypocritical, sexually dirty authority figures and extending it to all adults, has added an extra layer of deformity. The "straight" people are far more twisted than Alex; they seem inhuman and incapable of suffering. He alone suffers. And how he suffers! He's a male Little Nell—screaming in a straitjacket during the brainwashing; sweet and helpless when rejected by his parents; alone, weeping, on a bridge; beaten, bleeding, lost in a rainstorm; pounding his head on a floor and crying for death. Kubrick pours on the hearts and flowers; what is done to Alex is far worse than what Alex has done, so society itself can be felt to justify Alex's hoodlumism.

The movie's confusing—and, finally, corrupt—morality is not, however, what makes it such an abhorrent viewing experience. It is offensive long before one perceives where it is heading, because it has no shadings. Kubrick, a director with an arctic spirit, is determined to be pornographic, and he has no talent for it. In *Los Olvidados*, Buñuel showed teen-agers committing horrible brutalities, and even though you had no illusions about their victims—one, in particular, was a foul old lecher—you were appalled. Buñuel makes you understand the pornography of brutality: the pornography is in what human beings are capable of doing to other human beings. Kubrick has always been one of the least sensual and least erotic of directors, and his attempts here at phallic humor are like a professor's lead balloons. He tries to work up kicky violent scenes, carefully estranging you from the victims so that you can *enjoy* the rapes and beatings. But I think one is more likely to feel cold antipathy toward the movie than horror at the violence—or enjoyment of it, either.

Kubrick's martinet control is obvious in the terrible performances he gets from everybody but McDowell, and in the inexorable pacing. The film has a distinctive style of estrangement: gloating closeups, bright, hard-edge, third-degree lighting, and abnormally loud voices. It's a style, all right—the movie doesn't look like other movies, or sound like them—but it's a leering, portentous style. After the balletic brawling of the teen-age gangs, with bodies flying as in a Western saloon fight, and after the gang-bang of the writer's wife and an orgy in speeded-up motion, you're primed for more action, but you're left stranded in the prison sections, trying to find some humor in tired schoolboy jokes about a Hitlerian guard. The movie retains a little of the slangy Nadsat but none of the fast rhythms of Burgess's prose, and so the dialect seems much more arch than it does in the book. Many of the dialogue sequences go on and on, into a stupor of inactivity. Kubrick seems infatuated with the hypnotic possibilities of static setups; at times you feel as if you were trapped in front of the frames of a comic strip for a numbing ten minutes per frame. When Alex's correctional officer visits his home and he and Alex sit on a bed, the camera sits on the two of them. When Alex comes home from prison, his parents and the lodger who has displaced him are in the living room; Alex appeals to his seated, unloving parents for an inert eternity. Long after we've got the point, the composition is still telling us to appreciate its cleverness. This ponderous technique is hardly leavened by the structural use of classical music to characterize the sequences; each sequence is scored to Purcell (synthesized on a Moog), Rossini, or Beethoven, while Elgar and others are used for brief satiric effects. In the book, the doctor who has devised the conditioning treatment explains why the horror images used in it are set to music: "It's a useful emotional heightener." But the whole damned movie is heightened this way; yes, the music is effective, but the effect is self-important.

When I pass a newsstand and see the saintly, bearded, intellectual Kubrick on the cover of *Saturday Review*, I wonder: Do people notice things like the way Kubrick cuts to the rival teen-age gang before Alex and his hoods arrive to fight them, just so we can have the pleasure of watching that gang strip the struggling girl they mean to rape? Alex's voice is on the track announcing his arrival, but Kubrick can't wait for Alex to arrive, because then he couldn't show us as much. That girl is stripped for our benefit; it's the purest exploitation. Yet this film lusts for greatness, and I'm not sure that Kubrick knows how to make simple movies anymore, or that he cares to, either. I don't know how consciously he has thrown this film to youth; maybe he's more of a showman than he lets on—a lucky showman with opportunism built into the cells of his body. The film can work at a pop-fantasy level for a young audience already prepared to accept Alex's view of the society, ready to believe that that's how it is.

At the movies, we are gradually being conditioned to accept violence as a sensual pleasure. The directors used to say they were showing us its real face and how ugly it was in order to sensitize us to its horrors. You don't have to be very keen to see that they are now in fact desensitizing us. They are saying that everyone is brutal, and the heroes must be as brutal as the villains or they turn into fools. There seems to be an assumption that if you're offended by movie brutality, you are somehow playing into the hands of the people who want censorship. But this would deny those of us who don't believe in censorship the use of the only counterbalance: the freedom of the press to say that there's anything conceivably damaging in these films—the freedom to analyze their implications. If we don't use this critical freedom, we are implicitly saying that no brutality is too much for us—that only squares and people who believe in censorship are concerned with brutality. Actually, those who believe in censorship are primarily concerned with sex, and they generally worry about violence only when it's eroticized. This means that practically no one raises the issue of the possible cumulative effects of movie brutality. Yet surely, when night after night atrocities are served up to us as entertainment, it's worth some anxiety. We become clockwork oranges if we accept all this pop culture without asking what's in it. How can people go on talking about the dazzling brilliance of movies and not notice that the directors are sucking up to the thugs in the audience?

CHRISTOPHER RICKS

Horror Show[†]

When Anthony Burgess published A Clockwork Orange ten years ago, he compacted much of what was in the air, especially the odd mingling of dismay and violence (those teen-age gangs) with pious euphoria about the causes and cures of crime and of deviance. Mr. Burgess's narrator hero, Alex, was pungently odious; addicted to mugging and rape, intoxicated with his own command of the language (a newly minted teen-age slang, plus poeticisms, sneers, and

[†] "Horror Show," in The New York Review of Books 18.6 (April 6, 1972), 28–29. Reprinted with permission from The New York Review of Books. Copyright © 1972 NYREV, Inc.

sadistic purring), Alex was something both better and worse than a murderer: he was murderous. Because of a brutal rape by Alex, the wife of a novelist dies; because of his lethal clubbing, an old woman dies; because of his exhibitionist ferocity, a fellow prisoner dies.

The second of these killings gets Alex jailed; word reaches him of the new Ludovico Treatment by which he may be reclaimed, and he seeks it and gets it. The treatment is to watch horrific films of violence (made by one Dr. Brodsky) while seething with a painful emetic; the "cure" is one that deprives Alex of choice, and takes him beyond freedom and dignity, and extirpates his moral existence. But the grisly bloody failure of his suicide attempt after his release does release him. Alex is himself again.

The novel was simply pleased, but it knew that aversion therapy must be denied its smug violences. And the early 1960s were, after all, the years in which a liberally wishful newspaper like the London *Observer* could regale its readers with regular accounts of how a homosexual was being "cured" by emetics and films.

"To do the ultra-violent"; Alex makes no bones about it. But the film of *A Clockwork Orange* does not want him to be seen in an ultra-violent light. So it bids for sympathy. There are unobtrusive mitigations: Alex is made younger than in the book. There are obtrusive crassnesses from his jailors: when Alex pauses over the form for Reclamation Treatment, the chief guard shouts, "Don't read it, sign it"— and of course it has to be signed in triplicate. (None of that in the book.) There are sentimentalities: where in the book it was his drugs and syringes that he was shocked to find gone when he got home, in the film he has been provided instead with a pet snake, Basil, whom his parents have wantonly and hypocritically done in. Above all, Alex is the only person in the film who isn't a caricature, the only person the film is interested in; whereas in the first-person-narrative of the book, Alex was the only person Alex was interested in.

One realizes that the film is a re-creation, not a carrying-over, and yet both Kubrick and Burgess are right to call upon each other in what they've recently written in defense of the film, Kubrick in *The New York Times*, February 27,[1] and Burgess in *The Listener*, February 17. The persistent pressure of the film's Alexculpations is enough to remind one that while *A Clockwork Orange* is in Burgess's words "a novel about brainwashing," the film is not above a bit of brainwashing itself—is indeed righteously unaware that any of its own techniques or practices could for a moment be asked to subject themselves to that same scrutiny as they project. Alex is forced to

---

1. Bernard Weintraub, "Kubrick Tells What Makes *Clockwork Orange* Tick," *New York Times*, January 4, 1972.

gaze at the Ludovico Treatment aversion films: "But I could not shut my glazzies, and even if I tried to move my glaz-balls about I still could not get like out of the line of fire of this picture." Yet once "this picture" has become not one of Dr. Brodsky's pictures but one of Mr. Kubrick's, then two very central figures are surreptitiously permitted to move "out of the line of fire of this picture."

First, the creator of the whole fictional "horrorshow" itself. For it was crucial to Burgess's *A Clockwork Orange* that it should include a novelist who was writing a book called *A Clockwork Orange*— crucial not because of the fad for such Chinese boxes, but because this was Burgess's way of taking responsibility (as Kubrick does *not* take responsibility for Dr. Brodsky's film within his film). Burgess's way of seeing that the whole enterprise itself was accessible to its own standards of judgment. The novelist F. Alexander kept at once a curb and an eye on the book, so that other propensities than those of Dr. Brodsky were also under moral surveillance. Above all the propensity of the commanding satirist to become the person who most averts his eyes from what he shows: that "satire is a sort of glass wherein beholders do generally discover everybody's face but their own." But in the film F. Alexander (who is brutally kicked by Alex, and his wife raped before his eyes) is not at work on a book called *A Clockwork Orange*, and so the film—unlike the book— ensures that it does not have to stand in its own line of fire.

Nor, secondly and more importantly, does Alex have to. The film cossets him. For the real accusation against the film is certainly not that it is too violent, but that it is not violent enough; more specifically, that with a cunning selectivity it sets itself to minimize both Alex's violence and his delight in it. Take his murders or woman-slaughters. The old woman in the novel with the cats and an ineffectual stick becomes in the film a professionally athletic virago who nearly stuns him with a heavy *objet d'art*; the killing comes after a dervishlike tussling and circling, and moreover is further protected, Alex-wise, by being grotesquely farcical. Alex rams her in the face with a huge sculpture of a penis and testicles, a pretentious art work which she has pretentiously fussed about and which when touched jerks itself spasmodically.

The film reshapes that murder to help Alex out. Similarly with the more important death of the novelist's wife. "She died, you see. She was brutally raped and beaten. The shock was very great." But the film—by then nearing its end—doesn't want Alex to have this death on our consciences, so the novelist (who is manifestly half-mad to boot) is made to mutter that the doctor said it was pneumonia she died of, during the flu epidemic, but that *he* knew, etc., etc. Or, not to worry, Alex-lovers.

Then there is the brutal killing within the prison cell, when they all beat up the homosexual newcomer:

> Anyway, seeing the old krovvy flow red in the red light, I felt the old joy like rising up in my keeshkas. . . . So they all stood around while I cracked at this prestoopnick in the near dark. I fisted him all over, dancing about with my boots on though unlaced, and then I tripped him and he went crash crash on to the floor. I gave him one real horrorshow kick on the gulliver and he went ohhhhh, then he sort of snorted off to like sleep.

No place for any of that in the film, since it would entail being more perturbed about Alex than would be convenient. No, better to show all the convicts as good-natured buffoons and to let the prison guards monopolize detestability. The film settles for a happy swap, dispensing with the killing in the cell and proffering instead officialdom's humiliating violence in shining a torch up Alex's rectum. None of that in the book.

"When the novelist puts his thumb in the scale to pull down the balance to his own predilection, that is immorality" (D. H. Lawrence). As a novelist, Burgess controlled his itching thumb (he does after all include within himself as much of a polemicist for Original Sin and for Christian extremity as his coreligionists Graham Greene and William Golding). But the film is not content with having a thumb in the pan—it insists on thumbs down for most and thumbs up for Alex. Thumbs down for Dr. Brodsky, who is made to say that the aversion drug will cause a deathlike terror and paralysis; thumbs down for the Minister of the Interior, who bulks proportionately larger and who has what were other men's words put into his mouth, and whose asinine classy ruthlessness allows the audience to vent its largely irrelevant feelings about "politicians," thus not having to vent any hostility upon Alex; thumbs down for Alex's spurious benefactors, who turn out to be mad schemers against the bad government, and not only that but very very vengeful—the novelist and his friends torture Alex with music to drive him to suicide (the book told quite another story).

But thumbs up for the gladiatorial Alex. For it is not just the killings that are whitewashed. Take the two girls he picks up and takes back to his room. In the book, what matters to Alex—and to our sense of Alex—is that they couldn't have been more than ten years old, that he got them viciously drunk, that he gave himself a "hypo jab" so that he could the better exercise "the strange and weird desires of Alexander the Large," and that they ended up bruised and screaming. The film, which wants to practice a saintlike charity of redemption toward Alex but also to make things assuredly easy for itself, can't have any of that. So the ten-year-olds become jolly dollies, no drink, no drugs, no bruises, just the three of them having a ball. And to make doubly sure that Alex is not dislodged from anybody's affection, the whole thing is speeded up so that it twinkles away like frantic fun from a silent film. Instead of the cold brutality of Alex's "the old in-out," a warm Rowan and Martin laugh-in-out.

Conversely, Alex's fight with his friends is put into silent slow motion, draping its balletic gauzes between us and Alex. And when one of those droogs later takes his revenge on Alex by smashing him across the eyes with a milk bottle and leaving him to the approaching police, this too has become something very different from what it was in the book. For there it was not a milk bottle that Dim wielded but his chain: "and it snaked whishhhh and he chained me gentle and artistic like on the glazlids, me just closing them up in time." The difference which that makes is that the man who is there so brutally hurt is the man who had so recently exulted in Dim's prowess with that chain:

> Dim had a real horrorshow length of oozy or chain round his waist, twice wound round, and he unwound this and began to swing it beautiful in the eyes or glazzies. . . . old Dim with his chain snaking whisssssshhhhhhhhh, so that old Dim chained him right in the glazzies, and this droog of Billyboy's went tottering off and howling his heart out.

The novel, though it has failures of judgment which sometimes let in a gloat, does not flinch from showing Alex's exultation. The movie takes out the book's first act of violence, the protracted sadistic taunting of an aged book lover and then his beating up:

> "You naughty old veck, you," I said, and then we began to filly about with him. Pete held his rookers and Georgie sort of hooked his rot wide open for him and Dim yanked out his false zoobies, upper and lower. He threw these down on the pavement and then I treated them to the old boot-crush, though they were hard bastards like, being made of some new horrorshow plastic stuff. The old veck began to make sort of chumbling shooms
> —"wuf waf wof"—so Georgie let go of holding his goobers apart and just let him have one in the toothless rot with his ringy fist, and that made the old veck start moaning a lot then, then out comes the blood, my brothers, real beautiful. So all we did then was to pull his outer platties off, stripping him down to his vest and long-underpants (very starry, Dim smecked his head off near), and then Pete kicks him lovely in his pot, and we let him go.

The film holds us off from Alex's blood-lust, and it lets Alex off by mostly showing us only the show of violence. The beating of the old drunk is done by four silhouetted figures with their sticks horribly violent in some ways, of course, but held at a distance. That distance would be artistically admirable if its intention was to preclude the pornography of bloodthirstiness rather than to preclude our realizing making real to ourselves Alex's bloodthirstiness. Likewise the gang fight is at first the frenzied destructiveness of a Western and is then a stylized distanced drubbing; neither of these incriminates Alex as the book had honorably felt obliged to do. The first page of the book knows that Alex longs to see someone "swim in his blood," and the book never forgets what it early shows:

> Then we tripped him so he laid down flat and heavy and a bucketload of beer-vomit came whooshing out. That was disgusting so we gave him the boot, one go each, and then it was blood, not song nor vomit, that came out of his filthy old rot. Then we went on our way.

> And, my brothers, it was real satisfaction to me to waltz—left two three, right two three—and carve left cheeky and right cheeky, so that like two curtains of blood seemed to pour out at the same time, one on either side of his fat filthy oily snout in the winter starlight.

The film does not let Alex shed that blood. But it isn't against bloodletting or hideous brutality, it just insists on enlisting them. So we see Alex's face spattered with blood at the police station, the wall too; and we see a very great deal of blood-streaming violence in the aversion therapy film which the emetic-laden Alex is forced to witness. What this selectivity of violence does is ensure that the aversion film outdoes anything that we have as yet been made to contemplate (Alex's horrorshows are mostly allowed to flicker past). It is not an accident, and it is culpably coercive, that the most longdrawn-out, realistic, and hideous act of brutality is that meted on Alex by his ex-companions, now policemen. Battered and all but drowned, Alex under violence is granted the mercy neither of slow motion nor of speeding up. But the film uses this mercilessness for its own specious mercy.

There is no difficulty in agreeing with Kubrick that people do get treated like that; and nobody should be treated like that. At this point the film doesn't at all gloat over the violence which it makes manifest but doesn't itself manifest. Right. But Burgess's original artistic decision was the opposite; it was to ensure that we should deeply know of but not know about what they did to Alex: "I will not go into what they did, but it was all like panting and thudding against this like background of whirring farm machines and the twittwittwittering in the bare or nagoy branches." I will not go into what they did: that was Burgess as well as Alex speaking. Kubrick does not speak, but he really goes into what they did. By doing so he ensures our sympathy for Alex, but at the price of an enfeebling circularity. "Pity the monsters," urges Robert Lowell: I am a man more sinned against than sinning, the film allows Alex to intimate.

The pain speaks for Alex, and so does the sexual humor. For Kubrick has markedly sexed things up. Not just that modern sculpture of a penis, but the prison guard's question ("Are you or have you ever been a homosexual?"), and the social worker's hand clapped hard but lovingly on Alex's genitals, and the prison chaplain's amiable eagerness to reassure Alex about masturbation, and the bare-breasted nurse and the untrousered doctor at it behind the curtains of the hospital bed. All of this may seem to be just good clean fun (though also most uninventively unfunny), but it too takes its part within that forcible reclamation of Alex which Kubrick no less than Dr. Brodsky is out to achieve.

The sexual farce is to excriminate Alex as a bit of a dog rather than one hell of a rat, and the tactic pays off—but cheaply—in the very closing moments of the film, when Alex, cured of his cure and now himself again, is listening to great music. In the film his fantasy is of a voluptuous slow-motion love-making, rape-ish rather than rape, all surrounded by costumed grandees applauding—amiable enough, in a way, and a bit like *Billy Liar*. The book ends with the same moment, but with an unsentimental certainty as to what kind of lust it still is that is uppermost for Alex:

> Oh, it was gorgeosity and yumyumyum. When it came to the Scherzo I could viddy myself very clear running and running on like very light and mysterious nogas, carving the whole litso [face] of the creeching world with my cutthroat britva. And there was the slow movement and the lovely last sighing movement still to come. I was cured all right.

The film raises real questions, and not just of the are-liberals-really-liberal? sort. On my left, Jean-Jacques Rousseau; on my right, Robert Ardrey—this is factitious and fatuous. When Kubrick and Burgess were stung into replying to criticism, both claimed that the accusation of gratuitous violence was gratuitous. Yet Kubrick makes too easy a disclaimer—too easy in terms of the imagination and its sources of energy, though fair enough in repudiating the charge of "fascism"—when he says that he should not be denounced as a fascist, "no more than any well-balanced commentator who read 'A Modest Proposal' would have accused Dean Swift of being a cannibal."

Agreed, but it would be Swift's imagination, not his behavior, that would be at stake, and there have always been those who found "A Modest Proposal" a great deal more equivocally disconcerting than Kubrick seems to. As Dr. Johnson said of Swift, "The greatest difficulty that occurs, in analyzing his character, is to discover by what depravity of intellect he took delight in revolving ideas, from which almost every other mind shrinks with disgust." So that to invoke Swift is apt (Alex's slang "gulliver" for head is not just Russian *golova*) but isn't a brisk accusation-stopper.

Again, when Burgess insists: "It was certainly no pleasure to me to describe acts of violence when writing the novel," there must be a counter-insistence: that on such a matter no writer's say-so can simply be accepted, since a writer mustn't be assumed to know so— the sincerity in question is of the deepest and most taxing kind. The aspiration need not be doubted:

> What my, and Kubrick's, parable tries to state is that it is preferable to have a world of violence undertaken in full awareness— violence chosen as an act of will—than a world conditioned to be good or harmless.

When so put, few but B. F. Skinner are likely to contest it. But there are still some urgent questions.

1. Isn't this alternative too blankly stark? And isn't the book better than the film just because it doesn't take instant refuge in the antithesis, but has a subtler sense of responsibilities and irresponsibilities here?

2. Isn't "the Judaeo-Christian ethic that *A Clockwork Orange* tries to express" more profoundly disconcerting than is suggested by Burgess's hospitable formulation? I think of Empson's arguments that Christianity marks itself out from the other great religions by holding on to an act of human sacrifice, and that it is a system of torture-worship. The Christian Church has always ministered to, often connived at, and sometimes practiced the fiercest and most insidious acts of brainwashing. The book in this sense takes its religion much more seriously—that is, does not think of it as somehow patently unimpeachable. "The wish to diminish free will is, I should think, the sin against the Holy Ghost" (Burgess). Those who do not believe in the Holy Ghost need not believe that there is such a thing as the sin against the Holy Ghost—no reassuring worst of sins.

3. Isn't the moral and spiritual crux here more cruelly unresolvable, a hateful siege of contraries? T. S. Eliot sought to resolve it:

> So far as we are human, what we do must be either evil or good; so far as we do evil or good, we are human; and it is better, in a paradoxical way, to do evil than to do nothing: at least, we exist. It is true to say that the glory of man is his capacity for salvation; it is also true to say that his glory is his capacity for damnation. The worst that can be said of most of our malefactors,

from statesmen to thieves, is that they are not men enough to
be damned.

But Eliot's teeth are there on edge, and so are ours; those who do
not share the religion of Eliot and Burgess may think that no primacy should be granted to Eliot's principle—nor to its humane
counter-principle, that it is better to do nothing than to do evil.

4. Is this film worried enough about films? Each medium will
have its own debasements when seduced by violence. A novel has
but words, and words can gloat and collude only in certain ways.
A play has people speaking words, and what Dr. Johnson deplored
in the blinding of Gloucester in *King Lear* is precisely the artistic
opportunity of drama, that we both intensely feel that great violence
is perpetrated and intensely know that it is not: "an act too horrid to
be endured in dramatic exhibition, and such as must always compel
the mind to relieve its distress by incredulity." But the medium of
film is an equivocal one (above all about how far people are really
part of the medium), which is why it is so peculiarly fitted both to use
and to abuse equivocations. *A Clockwork Orange* was a novel about
the abuses of the film (its immoralities of violence and of brainwashing), and it included—as the film of *A Clockwork Orange* does not—
some thinking and feeling which Kubrick should not have thought
that he could merely cut:

> This time the film like jumped right away on a young devotchka
> who was being given the old in-out by first one malchick then
> another then another then another, she creeching away very
> gromky through the speakers and like very pathetic and tragic
> music going on at the same time. This was real, very real,
> though if you thought about it properly you couldn't imagine
> lewdies actually agreeing to having all this done to them in a
> film, and if these films were made by the Good or the State you
> couldn't imagine them being allowed to take these films with-
> out like interfering with what was going on. So it must have
> been very clever what they call cutting or editing or some such
> veshch. For it was very real.
>
> The minds of this Dr. Brodsky and Dr. Branom . . . they must
> have been more cally and filthy than any prestoopnick in the
> Staja itself. Because I did not think it was possible for any veck
> to even think of making films of what I was forced to viddy, all
> tied to this chair and my glazzies made to be wide open.

The film of *A Clockwork Orange* doesn't have the moral courage
that could altogether deal with that. Rather, like Kubrick's *Dr.
Strangelove,* it has a central failure of courage and confidence,
manifest in its need to caricature (bold in manner, timid at heart)
and in its determination that nobody except Alex had better get a

chance. Burgess says: "The point is that, if we are going to love mankind, we will have to love Alex as a not unrepresentative member of it." A non-Christian may be thankful that he is not under the impossibly cruel, and cruelty-causing, injunction to love mankind; both Christians and non-Christians may think that though the angels may plead, they do not special plead.

PHILIP STRICK AND PENELOPE HOUSTON

Interview with Stanley Kubrick†

We met Kubrick last November at his home near Borehamwood, a casual labyrinth of studios, offices, and seemingly dual-purpose rooms in which family life and film-making overlap as though the one were unthinkable without the other. Despite his reputed aversion to the ordeals of interrogation, Kubrick proved an immensely articulate conversationalist, willing to talk out in detail any aspect, technical or theoretical, of his devotion to the cinema. When we came to transcribe our tapes, what indeed emerged was perhaps rather more of a conversation, covering a lot of ground, than a formal interview.

When A Clockwork Orange opened in London a few weeks later, Kubrick found himself in the front line of somebody else's war. The critics were up in arms about Straw Dogs,[1] in particular, and A Clockwork Orange became caught in the crossfire, especially after the Home Secretary's much publicised visit to the film. It was an extraordinary fuss (the novel was, after all, first published ten years ago), the more so for seeming to be about a Clockwork Orange that sounded like nothing much to do with the film Kubrick made. But it also meant that some of his replies to our original questions would have to be revised, to make due allowance for the arguments the film had caused. So what follows is to some extent a Kubrick rewrite of a Kubrick interview—in the interests, as always with Kubrick, of precision.

How closely did you work with Anthony Burgess in adapting A Clockwork Orange for the screen?

STANLEY KUBRICK   I had virtually no opportunity of discussing the novel with Anthony Burgess. He phoned me one evening

† From Sight and Sound 41.2 (Spring 1972): 62–67 (63–64). Reprinted by permission.
1. Straw Dogs (1971), a controversially violent film directed by Sam Peckinpah. See Charles Barr, "Straw Dogs, A Clockwork Orange and the Critics," Screen 13.2 (Summer 1972), 17–32.

when he was passing through London and we had a brief conversation on the telephone. It was mostly an exchange of pleasantries. On the other hand, I wasn't particularly concerned about this because in a book as brilliantly written as *A Clockwork Orange* one would have to be lazy not to be able to find the answers to any questions which might arise within the text of the novel itself. I think it is reasonable to say that, whatever Burgess had to say about the story was said in the book.

How about your own contributions to the story? You seem to have preserved the style and structure of the original far more closely than with most of your previous films, and the dialogues are often exactly the same as in the novel.

KUBRICK   My contribution to the story consisted of writing the screenplay. This was principally a matter of selection and editing, though I did invent a few useful narrative ideas and reshape some of the scenes. However, in general, these contributions merely clarified what was already in the novel—such as the Cat Lady telephoning the police, which explains why the police appear at the end of that scene. In the novel, it occurs to Alex that she may have called them, but this is the sort of thing that you can do in a novel and not in the screenplay. I was also rather pleased with the idea of 'Singin' in the Rain' as a means of Alexander identifying Alex again towards the end of the film.

How did you come to use 'Singin' in the Rain' in the first place?

KUBRICK   This was one of the more important ideas which arose during rehearsal. This scene, in fact, was rehearsed longer than any other scene in the film and appeared to be going nowhere. We spent three days trying to work out just what was going to happen and somehow it all seemed a bit inadequate. Then suddenly the idea popped into my head—I don't know where it came from or what triggered it off.

The main addition you seem to have made to the original story is the scene of Alex's introduction to the prison. Why did you feel this was important?

KUBRICK   It may be the longest scene but I would not think it is the most important. It was a necessary addition because the prison sequence is compressed, in comparison with the novel, and one had to have something in it which gave sufficient weight to the idea that Alex was actually imprisoned. The routine of checking into prison which, in fact, is quite accurately presented in the film, seemed to provide this necessary weight.

In the book there is another killing by Alex while he is in prison. By omitting this, don't you run the risk of seeming to share Alex's own opinion of himself as a high-spirited innocent?

KUBRICK   I shouldn't think so, and Alex doesn't see himself as a high-spirited innocent. He is totally aware of his own evil and accepts it with complete openness.

Alex seems a far pleasanter person in the film than in the book . . .

KUBRICK   Alex makes no attempt to deceive himself or the audience as to his total corruption and wickedness. He is the very personification of evil. On the other hand, he has winning qualities: his total candour, his wit, his intelligence and his energy; these are attractive qualities and ones, I might add, which he shares with Richard III.

The violence done to Alex in the brainwashing sequence is in fact more horrifying than anything he does himself . . .

KUBRICK   It was absolutely necessary to give weight to Alex's brutality, otherwise I think there would be moral confusion with respect to what the government does to him. If he were a lesser villain, then one could say: 'Oh, yes, of course, he should not be given this psychological conditioning; it's all too horrible and he really wasn't that bad after all.' On the other hand, when you have shown him committing such atrocious acts, and you still realise the immense evil on the part of the government in turning him into something less than human in order to make him good, then I think the essential moral idea of the book is clear. It is necessary for man to have choice to be good or evil, even if he chooses evil. To deprive him of this choice is to make him something less than human—a clockwork orange.

But aren't you inviting a sort of identification with Alex?

KUBRICK   I think, in addition to the personal qualities I mentioned, there is the basic psychological, unconscious identification with Alex. If you look at the story not on the social and moral level, but on the psychological dream content level, you can regard Alex as a creature of the id. He is within all of us. In most cases, this recognition seems to bring a kind of empathy from the audience, but it makes some people very angry and uncomfortable. They are unable to accept this view of themselves and, therefore, they become angry at the film. It's a bit like the King who kills the messenger who brings him bad news and rewards the one who brings him good news.

The comparison with Richard III makes a striking defence against accusations that the film encourages violence, delinquency and so on. But as Richard is a safely distant historical figure, does it meet them completely?

KUBRICK   There is no positive evidence that violence in films or television causes social violence. To focus one's interest on this aspect of violence is to ignore the principal causes, which I would list as:

1. Original sin: the religious view.
2. Unjust economic exploitation: the Marxist view.
3. Emotional and psychological frustration: the psychological view.
4. Genetic factors based on the 'Y' chromosome theory: the biological view.
5. Man—the killer ape: the evolutionary view.

To try to fasten any responsibility on art as the cause of life seems to me to have the case put the wrong way around. Art consists of reshaping life but it does not create life, or cause life. Furthermore to attribute powerful suggestive qualities to a film is at odds with the scientifically accepted view that, even after deep hypnosis, in a post-hypnotic state, people cannot be made to do things which are at odds with their natures.

Is there any kind of violence in films which you might regard as socially dangerous?

KUBRICK   Well, I don't accept that there is a connection, but let us hypothetically say that there might be one. If there were one, I should say that the kind of violence that might cause some impulse to emulate it is the 'fun' kind of violence: the kind of violence we see in the Bond films, or the Tom and Jerry cartoons. Unrealistic violence, sanitised violence, violence presented as a joke. This is the only kind of violence that could conceivably cause anyone to wish to copy it, but I am quite convinced that not even this has any effect.

There may even be an argument in support of saying that any kind of violence in films, in fact, serves a useful social purpose by allowing people a means of vicariously freeing themselves from the pent up, aggressive emotions which are better expressed in dreams, or in the dreamlike state of watching a film, than in any form of reality or sublimation.

Isn't the assumption of your audience in the case of *Clockwork Orange* likely to be that you support Alex's point of view and in some way assume responsibility for it?

KUBRICK   I don't think that any work of art has a responsibility to be anything but a work of art. There obviously is a considerable controversy, just as there always has been, about what is a work of art, and I should be the last to try to define that. I was amused by Cocteau's *Orphée* when the poet is given the advice: 'Astonish me'. The Johnsonian definition of a work of art is also meaningful to me, and that is that a work of art must either make life more enjoyable or more endurable. Another quality, which I think forms part of the definition, is that a work of art is always exhilarating and never depressing, whatever its subject matter may be.

In view of the particular exhilaration of Alex's religious fantasies, has the film run into trouble with clerical critics?

KUBRICK   The reaction of the religious press has been mixed, although a number of superb reviews have been written. One of the most perceptive reviews by the religious press, or any other press, appeared in the *Catholic News* written by John E. Fitzgerald, and I would like to quote one portion of it:

In print we've been told (in B. F. Skinner's *Beyond Freedom and Dignity*) that man is but a grab-bag of conditioned reflexes. On screen with images rather than words, Stanley Kubrick shows that man is more than a mere product of heredity and/or environment. For as Alex's clergyman friend (a character who starts out as a fire-and-brimstone-spouting buffoon but ends up the spokesman for the film's thesis) says: 'When a man cannot choose, he ceases to be a man'.

The film seems to say that to take away a man's choice is not to redeem but merely restrain him: otherwise we have a society of oranges, organic but operating like clockwork. Such brainwashing, organic and psychological, is a weapon that totalitarians in state, church or society might wish for an easier good even at the cost of individual rights and dignity. Redemption is a complicated thing and change must be motivated from within rather than imposed from without if moral values are to be upheld. But Kubrick is an artist rather than a moralist and he leaves it to us to figure what's wrong and why, what should be done and how it should be accomplished.[2]

2. John E. Fitzgerald, "More than a Product of Heredity," *Catholic News*, December 1971.

DON DANIELS

A Clockwork Orange[†]

Stanley Kubrick's films seem to provoke the kind of mindless praise and attack that is called 'controversy' these days. In the case of A Clockwork Orange, the responses have ranged from 'brilliant' to 'boring', with special attention to the film's depictions of violence. If the viewer responds to nothing else, he is sure to notice the sensational subject matter. Of course, violence is a difficult subject for visual treatment. The question must be, does the work provide a context that can safely hold such distracting materials? Kubrick has been careful to offer such a container. But if the viewer refuses it, he is left holding the inevitables—violence, sex, death—at least as far as chatter and film criticism are concerned.

A Clockwork Orange has a number of things to say about violence. It shows the victim's pain. Only the naturalistic details of suffering in Bonnie and Clyde are comparable in this respect to Kubrick's work, and Kubrick's is the more daring stylistically. The film also shows the joy of the attack, especially in the balletic gang-fight. But the parody there of bar-room brawls alerts us to the very special point of view even as we enjoy the feral grace. The beating of the tramp is nastiness seen darkly, peripherally. We all know it happens, but what to do? The attack on the HOME is the scene everyone will remember. Like Bonnie and Clyde's set-pieces of extempore chaos, part of the power of the scene is the anything-can-happen surprise of the visit. But Kubrick combines the gang's brutal improvisations with Alex's calculated song and dance: realistic detail and stylised action that reinforce one another and indicate the state of mind that is the subject of the film. Some have found only a technique of estrangement in the stylised violence. I find myself distanced and touched. Somehow the artificiality makes the violence more painful, Alex's coolly committed acts more evil.

Then there are those reviewers who have found Alex the only 'attractive' figure in the film. But surely evil is alluring; and ungenerous, too—an important point when the immediate vision we get is Alex's. Would the death of the rather attractively tart Catlady be the more appalling if it were not the obscene obliteration from Alex's ecstatic consciousness that the film records? Alexander De Large must not only conquer his world. He must unify it, no matter how distorted the final vision. His habit coincides with Kubrick's attempts to give a motion picture a complexity of visual coherence,

† In Sight and Sound 42.1 (Winter 1972–73): 44–46. Reprinted by permission.

to create a system of visual correspondences that will illuminate its theme. To complain of Alex's singular attractiveness is to indicate a naïveté about the role and to compliment Malcolm McDowell's rendering of evil's various charms. Kubrick's future society is 'Alexed' into a child's refuse-strewn playground.

The child keeps meeting fragments of himself in his career of crime; even his costume—white overalls, boots, bowler hat—looks borrowed from the technicians, guards and politicians he encounters. Alex is characterised not only by his actions against society, but in the actions of the State against Alex. The two are equated in the film, his charm reproduced in its durance, the principal difference—a perhaps considerable one—in the State's coarsely institutional and indiscriminately committed immoralities that Alex can only practise on a restricted scale. Those critics who find special pleading for Alex in the State's depredations against him ignore the equation, a real accomplishment in so carefully structured a work. Not only do each of the initial scenes of gang violence return in the retribution sequences at the end; they also set up the chief spheres of conflict throughout. The tramp is Alex's representative of an indifferent society; Billyboy's rival gang a prefiguration of Alex's mutinous droogs; and Mr. Alexander, in his very name, an indication of Alex's self-directed destructiveness. Just as Alex forces Mr. Alexander to watch the unspeakable, so Alex will be forced by the State. Both Alexanders are enemies of the State and share a name that means 'defender of men'. When Alex is interrogated by the quartet at the police station, he ironically invokes the law, just like the tramp at the mercy of his four tormentors. The martinet Chief Guard at the prison is Alex the gang-leader, and he inflicts inhumanities on Alex as Alex does on his victims. When Alex comically mimics him at the Medical Institute reception centre, he only punctuates the careful parallels of individual and State which we have seen all along.

The psychological mechanism behind Alex's unifying vision is that of 'projection'. All Alex's victims are outside society—the tramp, the gang, the radical—and when he punishes them, he unknowingly punishes himself. The 'mirror defence' of projection works to throw outward, to spit out, the consciously disowned aspects of the personality by ascribing them to others. The mechanism is itself unconscious. When Alex commits evil, he enjoys the pleasure of the act itself, the knowledge that it is considered wrong by society, and the unconscious justification of the act through projection. Thus, Alex rapes, ensures there is a witness to the rape, and punishes the 'complacency' of the victim. Evil is honoured, sharpened and justified. Alex levels the social ranks of his victims. A ballet of hoods implies a foregone conclusion: masculine power is questioned only to be affirmed. The drunk's rhetorical complaints are Alex's own: he hears just what he wants to hear. Throughout the film, figures of authority (Deltoid, the police, the Chief Guard, the doctors and the Minister of the Interior) are all versions of the gang leader.

As the equation is perfect but in one respect, Alex is conscious of his evil—horribly so—except in his need for self-justification. How reviewers could have missed the comedy of childish egotism is a kind of perfection in itself. The infantile fantasies show Alex's blindness to his own psychology through a masochistic dream in which he always triumphs despite indignity, torture and 'suicide'. Men court him, newspapers celebrate him, Hitler apes him. The lovely bird motif throughout the film—the Beethoven *frissons* in Bar and lair; the malchick screams at the Medical Institute's sinny; the gull over the Thames; and the growing boy eating from the Minister's hands—not only indicates the variety and integration Kubrick achieves through motivic relationships, but Alex's pathetic desire for freedom in the midst of blind dependence. Just an ordinary boy, with a stash, a pet and a love of Beethoven.

Kubrick has appropriated theme, character, narrative and dialogue from Anthony Burgess' novel, but the film is more than a literal translation of a construct of language into dramatic-visual form. Kubrick's film refashions the materials of the novel, and the rigour of the reworking gives the film a poetic compression and resonance that the novel lacks, despite its disturbing narrator, intricate structure and brilliant language. 'Nadsat' figures primarily in only the first third of the movie, but Kubrick has included much of Burgess' narrative invention, and as a result the Alexanders of film and novel conquer similar empires. The unifying parallels between citizen and State and the mechanism of projection are taken from the novel, although Kubrick finds new ways of communicating them visually.

There is a psychological name for the kind of ferocious insanity directed at the fabric of society that Burgess and Kubrick portray. It is 'Alexanderism', *agriothymia ambitiosa*, and it designates the desire to destroy nations. Alex is murderer, rapist, thief, hood—a Bad Bad boy. The film assumes the evil of his acts to be evident. What is condemned specifically is not the act but the mental dynamics that led to it. The shouts of the gang in their frolickings are mechanical, self-advertising, a bit joyless; obviously another kind of pleasure is being had in addition to simple sadism. When Alex moves to Rossini against the rival gang, or his own gang, or the Catlady, he mirrors his State's political conflicts. For the corrupt citizen and State, violent conflict is a necessary instrument of self-creation.

Burgess' novel is a fictional expression of this idea from the psychological writings of Franz Alexander, the neo-Freudian noted for his studies of psychosomatic diseases. Towards the end of his life,

Alexander studied the use of motion pictures to create stress in victims of hyperthyroidism (*Psychosomatic Medicine*, XXIII, No. 2, 1961, 104–14). But the generative materials of the novel can be found in the psychologist's earlier work, *The Psychoanalysis of the Total Personality*. The orange is clockwork because of what Franz Alexander would term the 'mechanism of neurosis'. For him, social expressions of violence mirror the conflict within the individual of ego, id and super-ego.

In the healthy personality, the super-ego aids the economy of the psyche with automatic, unconscious repression of the instincts. But in the neurotic, the super-ego is rigid and schematic in its automatic censorship, like an unbending totalitarian state. This unconscious part of the ego is formed by social laws and parental restraints. When the id threatens to invade the conscious mind with its anti-social desires, the super-ego represses without the ego's awareness of the repression. And in the neurotic, suffering becomes a method of obtaining instinctual release. The super-ego aids the id through over-severity. According to Alexander, 'Clinical experience taught me that the ego makes use of the satisfaction of the need for punishment in order to free itself from the super-ego and surrender itself to the repressed forces.' The corrupt State is 'a macrocosmic repetition of the ego-structure,' for as radical parties war for the sake of conflict, so do id and super-ego. Energy is expended internally rather than expressed. Violence becomes an end in itself. The neurotic drama of id, ego and super-ego is not just a metaphorical one for Alexander; he calls them 'part-personalities' and characterises the super-ego as a 'corrupt official', outwardly severe but privately bribeable. The super-ego conspires with the id and punishes the ego. The neurotic suffers in order to 'pay' for subsequent instinctual release. Punishment rids the ego of the prickings of conscience and adds zest to subsequent expression of instinctual desires.

In novel and film, Alex's career is an allegory of the disguise of instinctual impulse in neurotic symptom, of punishment endured to facilitate crime. By suffering, the ego absolves itself of sin and justifies its commission. Alex has learned the formula well that sees pain as part of pleasurable fulfilment; in fact, a licence to it. With Deltoid and the Minister the arrangement is as clear 'as an azure sky of deepest summer'. Each of Alex's triumphs is preceded or followed by defeat. The 'perfect evening' and the orgy must be paid for by Deltoid's visit and the mutiny of the gang in a series of pleasure-pain, manic-depressive rewards and punishments. Justice demands an eye for an eye. When Alex kills, he goes to prison. The Minister complains that the prisoners 'enjoy their so-called punishment' and counsels Alex on his way to the Medical Facility, 'Let's hope you make the most of it, my boy.'

The self-punishment is signalled in the film by the 'Adagio' from the *William Tell* 'Overture'. The home-coming scene is almost straight from the novel and beautifully played: Alex punishes himself, is punished by his parents (and Joe the Boarder, the Good Good Boy), and punishes Pee and Em in a family circle of guilt. Absolution comes in the near-drowning, nature's purifying rain, and Mr. Alexander's bath. When Alex's groans in the hospital are mixed with those of fornication, we hear Alex's pleasure-in-pain; the exorcism of restraint through punishment allows for masochistic delights as well.

Franz Alexander quotes Schiller's ballad 'The Ring of Polycrates': 'Therefore if thou desirest to ward off suffering, pray to the Invisible Powers that they add pain to happiness.' The universal sense of foreboding in the midst of joy is visualised in the film in the Last Supper that Kubrick has arranged for Alex—an ancient symbolic intimation of the pleasure-pain principle. Alex is the scapegoat (like the three condemned men in *Paths of Glory*), the sacrificial lamb, and his story is mythic—that of Osiris, Dionysus, and Christ. Death and suffering lead to absolution and resurrection. In the hospital, 'Eat me' on the fruit basket from Alex's parents is both obscene and sacramental. The film is Alex's masturbatory fantasy. When he listens to Beethoven, four suffering Christs dance. And he commits 'suicide' for his own ends. Alexander quotes Freud (*The Economic Problem in Masochism*): '. . . even self-destruction cannot take place without libidinal satisfaction.'

For Alexander, the Oedipus complex is 'the nuclear or root complex of all psychoneuroses.' The child must learn to sublimate the love and hate for his parents in tenderness, but there is always some destructive energy left over to be turned against society or against the self. The introversion of the death instinct Alexander sees as 'the primary process in the formation of the neurosis.' Alex provokes hatred in order to justify his anti-social acts and to punish himself. In the compulsion neurosis, Alexander suggests that the father is often identified with the strictness of the super-ego. Alex's parents have not only lost all authority; they have been raped and crippled at HOME. Alex commits symbolic incest (Kubrick carefully does not allow his crime to become matricide in the film) and, indirectly, patricide. With sets and lighting Kubrick has emphasised the rational realm of HOME. The conscious ego is unaware of the secret plans of the instincts. In fact, Kubrick allows Mr. Alexander to prompt his wife to let the forces in. When the 'father' is forced to watch the rape, it is the 'son's' revenge, the sinner watching his sin in all pride, and the id defining its power through the agency of the super-ego.

The Catlady is not so trusting. Her Health Farm is the very *locus* of the super-ego, all instincts honoured in domestication, like her cats and erotic art. Franz Alexander outlines the relationship of the super-ego with the id, both beyond the ken of the ego, but each aware of the other. The super-ego is not fooled by the disguises of desire. In the film, Kubrick has the Catlady call the police, unlike Mr. Alexander, thus allying her with the State and clarifying that the gang merely takes advantage of the call, having offered the attack on the Farm as a bribe to their tyrannical leader. Alex and the Catlady recognise each other immediately. Kubrick turns their fight into a dance in which the unconscious forces of the id (the phallus) battle the conscious personality (the bust of Beethoven). The bust is a symbol of instinct sublimated into the socially useful energy of artistic expression. When the Catlady strikes Alex, the ego is punished because of the id's threat of instinctual release. Having suffered, Alex can then overwhelm the personality and triumph.

Alex's roles are three. In attack he is the id's ever-renewing energies; in command he is the super-ego's ancient despotism; and in pain he is the neurotic ego. In the prison and final HOME sequences, Alex meets the leaders of the State's warring gangs—a new Mr. Alexander and Frederick, the Minister of the Inferior (his name, Kubrick's contribution, means 'peaceful ruler'). The ego is to the super-ego as a citizen of a totalitarian state is to his government. He is unaware of the government's machinations. And the State is indifferent to him. When Alexander De Large meets Frederick De Large in the prison, still another version of the crime-punishment contract is signed, to be honoured in Alex's conditioning and final rehabilitation. The coda between them in the hospital is another of Kubrick's scenes of duplicity and degraded language. Speech becomes a conspiratorial purr, a litany to console and corrupt, like Dr. Branom's promise, between injections, 'By this time tomorrow, you'll be healthier still,' delivered with that obsessional faith it is Kubrick's gift to record exactly.

Alex and Mr. Alexander, two 'victims', return again at the end of the film. Kubrick has Alex cripple Mr. Alexander, who becomes an enemy of the State and the very personification of the uninhibited instincts. By removing information about Mr. Alexander before the attack, Kubrick makes his politics and his madness seem even more its result. Having suffered, he derives his radical opinions from personal impotence and a liberated desire for revenge. Thus, Mr. Alexander's insanity reveals the same dynamic that is at the root of Alex's hatred of the world and himself. As Franz Alexander suggests, the outwardly directed destructive energies of the unconscious, when turned upon the self, become the super-ego's sadism. Like General Mireau's retaliations for military defeat in *Paths of Glory*, Alex and Mr. Alexander revenge themselves on each other.

Kubrick has combined in Mr. Alexander the various roles Alex alternates throughout the film. His Mr. Alexander is the crippled neurotic ego, the government of the super-ego, punishing Alex, and the power of the id, revolting against all order. Like Dr. Strangelove, he beautifully and boldly summarises the madness of the subject. I am thinking of his orgasm of pain and hatred upon recalling his crippler, and the final shot of him madly torturing with the 'Ninth' while surrounded by his co-conspirators.

Kubrick has compared Alex's craft and guile to that of Richard III. But the comparison cannot go very far, for Alex is unconscious of his clockwork. Free will necessitates self-knowledge. Alex is lost in the funhouse mirrors of the narcissist, in the doubles of his victims, in the mirrors of HOME, and in the water imagery throughout the film. There is that magnificent shot of Billyboy the pirate that leads to Alex's marine discipline of his droogs; and later the suicide thoughts by the Thames, the watery bit of corporal, the cleansing rain and bath. The socialist state is a little boy's playpen (Kubrick has made certain the prison doesn't look all *that* uncomfortable).

One of the director's crucial decisions was his very faithfulness to Burgess' narrative structure. The compression inevitably makes the psychological entrapment all the more obvious. In the novel the neurotic formula might possibly be overlooked. On screen, the hyperbolic structure undercuts and exposes the mechanism. The rhetoric is even more heightened than in the novel, but not coarsened. And Alex's litany, 'Clear as an azure sky', never seemed more desperate or ironic.

How ironic too that while Alex's masturbatory dreams are clips from Grade-B horrorshows, the Institute's sinnies look like parodies of 'realistic', Grade-A Hollywood (*Straw Dogs*, for example). While Alex comments on the realism of glorious Technicolor, Dr. Brodsky monitors the death of consciousness. When Walter Carlos' beautiful electronic transcription of the 'Joy' theme's 'Turkish' march variation that accompanies Alex through the Bootick re-enters beneath the 'unstaged' scenes of World War II devastation, the frame of the film widens startlingly. The mirror images multiply from the neurotic, to the gang, to the State, to the paths of glory. Consciousness and freedom lie in ruins.

Alex toasts us, fellow patrons of the Korova Milkbar, at the start of the film. The Vice needs his audience. Kubrick has visualised the ego's self-dramatising habit with actor-audience scenes throughout. Billyboy's near-rape is enacted on-stage. Alex then arranges a rape for an audience and later becomes an audience for rape. The State dramatises Alex's redemption at the Passing-Out ceremony (the Min of the Int: 'At this stage we introduce the subject himself'). An

Ascot audience applauds Alex's fantasy-rape at the end. And the film has as many eyes as *2001*, from eyelashes to cuff-links, to Alex's surgically clamped gaze.

Alex is seen as blind to the interdependence of the individual and society. The imagery of theatre and vision reveals that Alex insists on breaking down that unity to step aside for the voyeur's sense of power. The State punishes him for this separation, initiates him, but—if his vision can be trusted—into a corrupt society. In its punishment of the neurotic personality, the super-ego disrupts the unity of the psyche but preserves the integrity of the suffering ego. 'The world is one, life is one,' muses Dr. Brodsky in the novel. In the film, the newspapers champion 'Alex Burgess'. The citizen of a British borough is his own enemy.

The comparison to Richard III may be another Kubrick red herring (although Alex is recognisable in Richard's 'Shine out, fair sun, till I have bought a glass/That I may see my shadow as I pass'). The closer Shakespearian comparison that Burgess and Kubrick surely have in mind is Iago (the brainwashing technique *is* Ludovico's). Like Iago, Alex is guide, teacher, and 'playwright', even to conditioning. As in *Othello*, his chief victim goes mad for revenge. Alex acts out the violence of Iago's language. Both take pride in their evil. And the HOME rape may well be intended as a version of the Act IV, scene 1 playlet that Iago stages with Cassio and Bianca for a gullible Othello. Othello, after all, projects his fantasies on to Desdemona and luxuriates in self-torture. There is Stephen's description of the 'hornmad Iago' in *Ulysses*, 'ceaselessly willing that the moor in him shall suffer.' Both Alex and Iago are like Genet's Saints of Evil, creating self through crime—and utterly unpunishable. The Anti-Christ is vampire, lost in the bonds of theft.

The ending of novel and film leaves Alex free to choose new or old 'freedoms'. If we get a 'cleaner' Alex in the movie—no *pedophilia*, no 'matricide', no prison murder—it is because his first sin is against himself. The cause of much confusion among his critics has been Kubrick's ability to make us privy to Alex's vision, to show us its seductive beauty while carefully keeping all hands clean. More than a visual investiture of a novelist's or a psychologist's conceits, *A Clockwork Orange* is not a simple film. We watch with no little admiration as Alex demonstrates the coherence he can achieve with a hoodlum artist's exploitation of everything at hand to shape the self. We watch the Alexandrians attempt the formality of dance without ever truly achieving the Dionysian ecstasy that liberates, the 'fantasy' that frees. But the director—who has always been alive to the rhythms of structure—contrasts the locksteps of self-enslavement with the organic beauty of the movements of his film, to suggest something like true freedom from the very heart of fantasy and mechanism.

ALEXANDER WALKER

[Violence]†

* * *

* * * The intergang rumble vividly illustrates the nihilistic nature of Alex's commitment to life and also Kubrick's skill at the reduction of violence to movement, balletic movement, so that the incitement content of it is defused and it becomes a metaphor for violence. Nowhere in *A Clockwork Orange* does one find the "medical materialism," the gross addition to the drama of physical injury depicted with anatomical precision, which is characteristic of other violent films that appeared around the time of Kubrick's movie. Here the leaping, chopping, somersaulting combatants are edited into an acrobatic display and choreographed to the Rossini music of *The Thieving Magpie*. It is no more "offensive," though a lot more subtle, than the conventional saloon bar-brawl of any pre-Peckinpah Western. What really gives the sequence its dynamic aggressiveness is the note of adolescent celebration projected by the violent suppleness of the bodies. There might have been a rationale for the mugging of the tramp in the previous sequence—"It's a stinking world because it lets the young get onto the old"—but the only evident impulse here is the celebration of a primal will, a brutalized and debased will, all right, but existentially free. Like the ape colonies at one another's throats before the dawn of intelligence in *2001: A Space Odyssey*, Alex and his "droogs" represent the aggression and violence that will be bred into man, so-called *civilized* man, by natural selection in prehistory. The gang rumble is stylized into a barbaric ritual for another reason, too: so that the connection can be made much later on with the far more sophisticated violence inflicted on Alex, in order to extirpate his independent will, by a State that is itself contaminated by the evolutionary bad seed.

A Clockwork Orange never sets out to explore the moral issue of violence; this has been a misleading belief that has often caused the film to be branded as "conscienceless" by critics who fail to see where Kubrick's first priority lies, namely, with the moral issue of eradicating free will. It is not with "sin," an essential part of Anthony Burgess's Catholic conscience and Kubrick's probably agnostic scepticism, but with "cure" that the book and the film occupy themselves. It is pardonable, though, to miss this at a first viewing; one is so caught up in the demonstration of primitive savagery.

† From *Stanley Kubrick Directs* (New York: Harcourt Brace Jovanovich, 1972), 272–73, 293. Reprinted by permission.

* * *

In its scientific, not mythic, state, the Ludovico Treatment is a
peculiarly corrupt offshoot of behavioral psychology and conditioned-
reflex therapy, which operate on the assumption that man has no will
he can call his own but, on the contrary, is molded by his environment and the right kinds of stimuli administered to him in order to
make any socially undesirable behavior patterns conform to socially
approved ones. The film was well into its shooting schedule when B.
F. Skinner published his book *Beyond Freedom and Dignity*, a work
that argued, with almost blind faith in rationalism, that there was a
case for manipulating the causal relationship between man and his
environment for the good of society as a whole—indeed, for the
essential *survival* of society. *A Clockwork Orange* presents its own
diametrically opposed view of such a notion. The appearance of
Skinner's book and Kubrick's film at almost the same time is a fairly
consistent event with a director who, as I have pointed out already,
absorbs into his own interests, and then turns into the substance of
his art, much of what is happening in the world at large. And this
includes the progressively sinister development of such things as the
use of drugs to recondition scientifically certain types of criminals,
even the use of "psycho-adaptation" in some of the totalitarian countries that have learned to avail themselves of the less sensational (or
at least less publicized) forms of medicine as a means of political
control. From forcibly "referring" dissenters to be treated at State
psychiatric clinics to actually "reconditioning" them to return to
society is a short, tempting step. The "clockwork orange" world seems
tangibly close if, for example, one reads the account of Zhores Med-
vedev's ordeal in a Soviet clinic, recently published in the West under
the title *A Question of Madness*.

* * *

PHILIP FRENCH

[Juvenile Delinquency and Censorship]†

Despite the fact that it has not been seen in British cinemas since
the 1970s and has never been shown on TV or released here on
video-cassette, *A Clockwork Orange* remains vivid to those who
have seen it and is curiously known to those who haven't. Everyone
is familiar with the iconic opening shot—Malcolm McDowell as

† From "A Clockwork Orange," in *Sight and Sound* 59.2 (Spring 1990), 84–87. Reprinted
by permission.

Alex, an odd mixture of malevolence, menace and seductive charm, staring directly into the camera, grotesque false eyelashes on his right eye, a bowler hat on his head. It's a key image of the 1960s ethos turning sour.

The premiere of the Royal Shakespeare Company stage version at the Barbican in February, in a version by Anthony Burgess himself in collaboration with the director Ron Daniels, has provoked new discussion about Stanley Kubrick's film, the novel, censorship, political violence in authoritarian societies and the dramatic treatment of juvenile delinquency.

The theatre programme at the Barbican begins with a page of recent tabloid press stories about acts of senseless violence in our cities to demonstrate the work's continuing significance. The producers did not need to protest so much. The day the play opened, the London *Evening Standard* front-page headline read 'PUNISHMENT FOR THE 1990s—Jail the dangerous criminals, hard labour for the rest' (a report on the Home Secretary's latest 'reform package'), while on an inside page there was a story headed 'Fear that Stalks the Streets', a report on gang killings and muggings in north London. The day's other main story concerned revelations about an Establishment scheme of disinformation and dirty tricks back in the 1970s, aimed at discrediting radical politicians and known in Secret Service circles as 'Operation Clockwork Orange'.

The middle-aged and elderly have never had any qualms over intimidating the young, either directly or through their appointed agents—teachers, policemen, non-commissioned officers. When they themselves feel threatened by aggressive teenagers, alarms are sounded, questions asked in the House, commissions of inquiry set up. Consequently, middle-class adults have always been disturbed by movies that take a sympathetic view of juvenile delinquents and teenage gang-war. When Universal made *City Across the River* in 1949 (probably the first movie to feature high-school kids killing a teacher with a home-made zip-gun), the studio only got the film past the Hays Office by persuading the respected political columnist Drew Pearson to appear in a sober preface, presenting it as an urgent, responsible look at an important phenomenon.

Five years later the British censors banned *The Wild One* outright, arguing that local youths would imitate the activities of the ageing bikers led by Marlon Brando and Lee Marvin. The following year Clare Booth Luce, the US Ambassador to Italy, intervened to prevent *The Blackboard Jungle* (the film that introduced rock'n'roll to the general European public) being shown in competition at the 1955 Venice festival. Two years later *West Side Story* appeared on Broadway, romanticising gang warfare while at the same time neutralising it with music and the suggestion that life was ever thus, the Manhattan rumbles of the Jets and Sharks being no more than latter-day versions of the confrontations between Montagues and Capulets in the piazzas of Verona.

This cycle of juvenile delinquent (or JD) movies continued into the next decade with the appearance in 1961 of John Frankenheimer's *The Young Savages* and Robert Wise's film of *West Side Story*. The leader of the Puerto Rican delinquents in Frankenheimer's film was far removed from the tall, romantic figure George Chakiris played in *West Side Story*, and he anticipated Alex in *A Clockwork Orange*. He wore a stylish cloak and fedora and carried an umbrella; he killed without remorse; and he was touched by high culture, having found his hispanic roots in the paintings of Picasso, reproductions of which he displayed on the wall of his slum flat the way Alex made his bedroom a shrine to Beethoven.

In the mid-1950s, the distinguished *New York Times* foreign correspondent Harrison Salisbury returned to base after six years in Moscow to discover that gang warfare was rife in Manhattan. After following the youthful offenders around New York, he published in 1958 an earnest, widely discussed, now entirely forgotten book called *The Shook-Up Generation*. The book introduced into common parlance the underground terms 'gang bang' and 'circle jerk' and made what is now a familiar diagnosis—the ills derived from urban overcrowding, lack of opportunities for blue-collar youth, a decline of traditional moral sanctions, weakening of parental control and a general angst vaguely associated with the Bomb and the Cold War. It took another homecomer a few years later to make a deeper, more resonant analysis of the scene that confronted him.

In 1960, the 43-year-old Anthony Burgess, a victim of the end of Empire, returned from the newly independent Singapore where he'd been teaching, to an England he hadn't seen since the 1940s. Like Harrison Salisbury, he was confronted by a volatile, divided society where the last seedily elegant Teddy Boys were still on the streets, race riots periodically flared up, and the first seasonal conflicts were taking place at British seaside resorts between Mods and Rockers. Salisbury's response as a journalist was to get down among the kids and report on their lives, filtering their responses through his liberal prism. Burgess, as a Catholic novelist and linguist, took up the position of prophet and literary visionary. He believed (happily without justification) that he was soon to die and produced in rapid succession an immensely varied series of novels, a dozen within a couple of years, the most celebrated though not necessarily the best of which is *A Clockwork Orange*, first published in 1962.

* * *

Stanley Kubrick's film of *A Clockwork Orange* came nearly ten years after the novel, at a time when certain of the book's prophecies appeared to have come true. It propelled the articulate Burgess into the media limelight where he has remained ever since. The Vietnam War was raging, and following the riots in Watts and Detroit, the violence in the streets of Europe and North America sought to match that going on in the jungles of Indo-China. Publicly shown in January 1972 (though widely previewed in late 1971 to influence media 'opinion leaders'), *A Clockwork Orange* appeared in the immediate wake of three extremely violent movies that went on to break box-office records. Two of them—William Friedkin's *The French Connection* and Don Siegel's *Dirty Harry*—uncritically endorsed the use of maximum force by the state; the third—Sam Peckinpah's *Straw Dogs*—justified, indeed exulted in, retaliatory violence by a private citizen.

None of these three ran into serious censorship difficulties, but *A Clockwork Orange* was initially awarded an 'X' in America, the kiss of death for a big-budget film as most cinema chains refuse to exhibit 'X' movies and few newspapers accept display advertising for them. Kubrick was forced into negotiations with the MPAA and he made a token cut to bring about a reduction to an 'R' rating. At the time, this decision seemed outrageous.

Kubrick's highly stylised film, following Burgess' novel with some fidelity, was a clean-cut moral tale, joining *Dr Strangelove* and *2001, A Space Odyssey* to complete a trilogy of admonitory fables set in a bleak dehumanised future. What was objectionable, one supposed, was the implied politics and the probing of the connection between sex and violence. There was talk of it making gang life attractive, and indeed it does not shrink from demonstrating the pleasure derived from aggressive and destructive conduct. Not long after the film's release, newspaper stories began to appear about gangs imitating Alex and his droogs, though the actual evidence of this is hard to come by, as it is also for the crop of deaths from playing Russian roulette alleged to have occurred throughout Asia seven years later following screenings of *The Deer Hunter*.

The critical reception of *A Clockwork Orange* was mixed, but generally favourable. The serious reviewers in America were polarised between adulation (Hollis Alpert, Vincent Canby) and derision (Stanley Kauffmann, Pauline Kael). In Britain the least favourable national newspaper reviews came from Patrick Gibbs in the right-wing *Daily Telegraph* and Nina Hibben in the Communist *Morning Star*. The movie received Academy Award nominations for best picture, best screenplay and best direction. In the event all three Oscars in these categories went to *The French Connection* and its star, Gene Hackman, was named best actor.

Kubrick's picture did well enough, though not spectacularly, at the box office and went rapidly into profit. It then mysteriously disappeared from distribution in Britain, an absence not immediately noticed. Rumours began to circulate about the reasons for this, especially when no print was available for the National Film Theatre's 1979 Kubrick retrospective. The most persistent, and convincing, was that some lunatic had threatened to kill a member of Kubrick's family if it were to be screened. The director has denied this, though no official explanation has been offered for its withdrawal. The latest rumour is that he is re-editing the film.

Thus few people in this country under the age of 35 will have seen the film (unlike the four withdrawn Hitchcock Paramount pictures of the mid-1950s which were frequently shown by film clubs in bootleg prints before they eventually surfaced in 1984). The screenplay that Lorrimer published in 1972, the only script in the series to have been personally supervised by its director, has never been reprinted, but the absence of musical cues makes it a most misleading guide or *aide-mémoire* to the film.

What is most disturbing is that many younger filmgoers derive their view of the film from the most readily available verdict, that handed down by Leslie Halliwell in his *Film Guide*: 'A repulsive film in which intellectuals have found acres of social and political meaning; the average judgment is likely to remain that it is pretentious and nasty rubbish for sick minds who do not mind jazzed-up images and incoherent sound.'

* * *

THOMAS ELSAESSER

[Screen Violence and the Audience][†]

* * *

In what way might violence, considered as an aesthetic spectacle and a form of extreme emotional plenitude, serve the purpose of social control, in the way that representations of sexuality have become an instrument of manipulation in advertising? What is it, if anything, that screen violence could attempt to sell?

* * *

† From "Screen Violence: Emotional Structure and Ideological Function in *A Clockwork Orange*," in C. W. E. Bigsby, ed., *Approaches to Popular Culture* (Bowling Green, KY: Bowling Green U Popular P, 1976), 171–200. Reprinted by permission.

Can *A Clockwork Orange* serve as a model case for analysing the relation between emotional structure and ideological function in a popular movie? In many ways the film proved extremely baffling to critics and audiences alike. Was it a conservative film advocating a law-and-order stance against the permissiveness of the Welfare State? Was it a radical film celebrating the anarchic and subversive side of violence? Was it a proto-fascist film? Was its ethos a liberal-humanist one? Was Kubrick detached and 'objective'? Was it a satire, and if so, of what? Was it realistic, a fantasy or science fiction? Did it show a 'dehumanized society' in which the individual has to take a stand, if necessary, by resorting to violence, or were the hero and his gang 'demented laboratory rats'? These views and many more were expressed verbally and in print and they could hardly have been more contradictory. Surely, if a film is so confusing and equivocal in what it says on important issues, this must detract from its credibility? It would seem not, for the odd fact emerged that it was almost universally praised, and as the box-office returns proved to Kubrick, he had yet again hit the jackpot. How can a film full of 'gratuitous' violence, 'sadistic' rape, 'pornographic' drawings, physical and mental cruelty, be enjoyable to an educated audience, who, without a trace of cynicism, were apparently prepared to stand up and applaud, even if for their life they could not make up their minds what it was about? Not normally at a loss for a moral judgement when it comes to assessing the 'intentions' of a film, the reviewers in this case were happy to shift to an area where they felt on firmer ground: Kubrick's craftmanship, his technical virtuosity: ['justly deserves his reputation as the cinema's greatest perfectionist'; 'can select lighting and lenses with invincible authority'; 'not a single point is missed or miscalculated . . . each camera-movement and cut is exact and correct'; 'the whole thing works, yes, with the absolute precision of clockwork,' etc.] What, one may rightly wonder, has all this to do with the issue of sex and violence that brought the film notoriety? The censor spelled it out: 'in his [i.e. the censor's] judgement the use of music, stylization and other skills of the director succeeded in distancing audiences from the violence, which includes a gang fight, several scenes of beating up, and murder and rape, and keeping the effect within tolerable limits.'[1] The aesthetic apparatus surrounding the film, one is given to understand makes it acceptable: presentation and packaging give the commodity respectability.

☆   ☆   ☆

1. I am indebted for the quotations and for first suggesting the idea of writing about *A Clockwork Orange* to an article entitled '*Strawdogs, A Clockwork Orange* and the Critics', by Charles Barr, *Screen* 13, 2 (Summer 1972), 17–32.

One would want to go a step further and hazard the hypothesis that the film was successful precisely because it suggested to the spectator that he was having his cake and eating it. Could this constitute an ideological function? Raise controversial topics, acknowledge the existence of a political and social reality, but provide an emotional structure which somehow admits of a pleasing resolution which one cannot fault because one cannot get it firmly enough into one's grip. Is this the recipe for a successful and popular movie? And what role does violence play in this?

* * *

* * * For in so far as an audience judges a film to be 'good', it actively seeks the captivity, the engrossment that comes from being subject to an articulation and experience of time over which one has no control. Switched into the will of another being, the audience's awareness is at every moment controlled by the movement and angle of the camera, and the steady cadence of 24 frames a second. No possibility of going back to an earlier passage or skipping another, no possibility of a discursive, reflexive experience, no off-button to press or switching to another channel. A Clockwork Orange provides a graphic illustration of the position of the spectator: under the Ludovico treatment the hero is strapped into a cinema seat, straight-jacketed like a lunatic, and clamps are put on his eyelids to stop him shutting his eyes or averting his gaze. This, in effect is what a film does to its audience. Not with clamps and straight-jacket, for sure, but with what one might call the psychological equivalent of aggressive coercion. The irony here is that the audience pays and demands that their eyes and ears be 'riveted' and 'glued' to the screen.

* * *

Within this field of force, created out of expectation and familiarity, suspense and its release, surprise and gratification, the emotional contact with the main protagonist is of crucial importance because it provides the initial vector of responses. Much time is spent in a film on mapping the framework of orientation, and where it is not an actual or potential 'couple' sharing equally the audience's attention, a careful line of identification is build up with the central hero. There are countless ways in which this can be done effectively, and in this respect, the hero of A Clockwork Orange is doubly privileged: not only does Alex dominate by being continuously on screen and thus providing the narrative logic by which action and plot progress from one scene to the next, he is also present by means of a first-person narrative, a sort of running commentary, in which he confidentially and conspiratorially addresses the spectator in mock-heroic terms such as 'oh my brothers' and 'your humble narrator'. He is enlisting a subtle degree of jovial complicity that overtly appears to acknowledge his dependence on the audience's approval, while also efficiently ensuring the reverse, namely their desire to be led in their responses by his judgements and values. This double role—that of visually continuous presence and primary, organizing conscious-ness—is made necessary in *A Clockwork Orange* by the nature of the chief protagonist, who is of course a rather nasty piece of work, a young hooligan lacking precisely what one would normally regard as 'values'. The director (following the footsteps of the author) has to make sure, therefore, that the spectator is and stays interested, and he does so by showing the hero's awareness as obviously deficient, 'inferior' to that of the spectator, so that across the gap the mecha-nism of identification can energize itself. The careless assumption of superiority which lulls the spectator into a deceptively relaxed stance will eventually be turned against him with a vengeance and this is part of another strategy intended to enforce complicity. Iden-tification in the cinema is always a process which involves, besides recognition and confirmation of familiar stances and experiences, a fixation of affect, of a libidinous or aggressive nature, at a stage where it produces inhibition, anxiety and guilt, itself the result of a partial recognition whose blockage is overcompensated.

* * *

The scene in which the relaxed identification jackknifes and freezes the laughter comes when Alex rapes the wife of the writer while doing the song-and-dance routine from Gene Kelly's *Singin' in the Rain*. The apparently incongruous disjuncture between action and song, image and sound is pushed to an extreme where an uncanny recognition obtrudes itself on the spectator who suddenly discovers an unexpected congruence. The scene delves deeply into the nature of cinematic participation and the latent aggression which it can mobilize with impunity: what happens is that before one's eyes an act of brutal violence and sadism is fitted over and made to 'rhyme' with a musical number connoting a fancy-free assertion of erotic longing and vitalist *joie de vivre*. Kubrick is able to exploit the unde-fined, polyvalent nature of the emotion which the moving image generates, by running, as it were, two parallel cinematic contexts along the same track, or rather, short-circuiting two lines, both charged with emotional energy. What this demonstrates, I think, is the structure of the emotional circuit mentioned earlier, where the dynamics of love and violence, aggression and vitality are oddly aligned, for in effect they seem to share a common trajectory towards energy-projection and what Freud called cathexis. Primar-ily an articulation of musical or rhythmic elements, this pattern of energy not only comprises the soundtrack proper, but also speech, gesture, movement—including the movements of the camera. All aspects of the filmic process are therefore potential lines of energy which the narrative, by its selection or stylization, either discards or 'realizes' in the course of the action.

One of the significant implications of this would seem to be the probability, on one level at least, that a musical or a melodrama is as 'violent' as a gangster movie or any other kind of action picture; that besides the violence *on* the screen there exists the violence *of* the screen (or between screen and audience) and that of the two, the latter would seem the more 'insidious', if one were to argue in the language of the sex and violence debate. At all events, there appears to be an evident analogy between violent and erotic expenditure of affect, in the way it is portrayed in the cinema, and the intensity of that expenditure is most commonly scored by a musical or rhythmic notation that carries the kind of emotionality specific to film (and possibly opera). What makes the scene quoted somewhat special is not only the extremity of the contrast, but the fact that the effect is thematized in the film itself: normally a movie's emotional line is conveyed by the music on the soundtrack either in a manner made unobtrusive by convention (when a love scene gets the inevitable string accompaniment) or as a form of parody in order to force a distanciation (the Rossini overture mentioned above); here, however, it is the hero himself who cynically parodies the facile emotionality of film music. The theme, played in another key, so to speak, is provided by Alex's fondness, indeed passionate devotion to classical music, especially Beethoven's Ninth Symphony. What in the book is possibly intended as a satire on the fate of 'high culture', by pointing up the relation between violent music and violent action, i.e. what might be called the 'fascist' side of romantic and Wagnerian music, with its suspect cult of dionysiac frenzy (latterly Ken Russell's particular pitch), this the film apostrophizes with a possible critique of cinematic language as a language of manipulated emotions, as the medium of dynamism that essentially exploits sex and violence, eroticism and aggression because they are the two faces of emotionality.

But is it in fact a critique? As so often with this film, one must be careful not to mistake the intelligence of its maker for a sign of his integrity. The sick humour of the musical rape, while affording in retrospect an unusually transparent insight into the cinema's rhetoric, is actually used to tie the spectator in a kind of double bind to the hero: while Alex's violence is stylized into libidinal self-expression and his destructiveness becomes a manifestation of a self-assertion that promises a subversive, anarcho-individualist liberation, the spectator cannot help identifying—not with the victims themselves—but with their situation, the brutal and apparently unmotivated intrusion into 'innocent' and 'peaceful' people's homes by a gang of vandals and hooligans. After all, the latent fears of such an intrusion provide the basis for a good many horror movies, where the thrill consists in being made to identify with the threatened victims (though there as well, empathy is often deftly split between *belle* and *bête*—King Kong, Frankenstein, and even Dracula). In *A Clockwork Orange* the spectator is allowed to overcompensate by distanciation and parody for an identification with the victims which the film both invites and denies. This cuts considerably deeper than simple identification with either hero or victim, and one imagines that even the most hardened viewer will scarcely be able to protect himself from such a direct raid on his unconscious. * * *

* * *

The evidence adduced so far suggests that Kubrick's *mise en scène* is guided by one overriding principle: to maintain identification between hero and spectator at all cost. If this requires distanciation, modernist techniques of collage and pop-art, devices borrowed from slapstick comedy and the animated cartoon—so be it; but then again, if a more old-fashioned realism is called for that gets the spectator in the gut rather than appealing to his head, Kubrick is prepared to put up with what might otherwise appear a serious stylistic inconsistency. Clearly, what the critics admired when they talked about 'distancing', etc., was Kubrick's subservience to the needs of the spectator, in whom the voyeur is in turn gratified, exposed and justified: aggression and guilt, anxiety and frustration which an audience brings to a film that deals with so many powerful psychic fantasies, are carefully balanced and manipulated in terms of involvement and indifference, humour and empathy, cynicism and sentimentality.

Towards this end works a remarkable device in the novel: the hero's language, a form of teenage slang called 'nadsat', which Kubrick takes over. But in the film the distancing effect is much attenuated when compared with the book, where our perception of the violence that takes place is largely transmitted in nadsat. Two features are significant. First, the Russian origin of many of the words which gives them, when pronounced in English, the appearance of diminutives, of belonging to a kind of baby-talk: gooly, itty, lewdies, malenky. This is emphasized where the root word is English: baddiwad, jammiwam, guttiwuts, eggiweg. Secondly, the areas of experience where nadsat is most inventive describe the human body and its functions: rooker=arm, groodies=breasts, rot=mouth, litso=face, krovvy=blood, sharries=buttocks, etc. A sentence where Alex describes his encounter with the catlady, for instance, runs like this: 'you could viddy her veiny mottled litso going purplewurple where I'd landed the old noga.' The associations provoked by the words distract from the reality of the action, and the effect is a highly euphemistic language about the reality of physical violence. The film has to show this violence and therefore cannot rely on these pleasant circumlocutions, but not wishing to forego such an instrument of manipulation, Kubrick, as indicated, invents his own pop-art picturegrammes and uses them as inserts. Baby-talk is replaced by the strip cartoon.

* * *

[While] the overt logic of the plot argues in terms of 'you have done wrong, therefore we punish you' ('Violence is a very horrible thing. That's what you're learning now. Your body is learning it.'—'You've made others suffer. It's only right that you should suffer proper.'), the logic of the central fantasy reverses this order into 'I have been unloved, abandoned, robbed of my home and identity, therefore I have every right to avenge myself, by being in turn violent and helpless.' It is the latter logic that the film in its emotional structure exemplifies, and another reason why the audience seems prepared to forgive Alex any amount of violence. In this sense, the order of the narrative sequence reverses the logic of the fantasies. Cause and effect are inverted and what appears gratuitous is motivated, and vice versa. This is made plausible by the neat circularity which the end bestows on the film as a whole. On the level of the fantasies, the contradiction between loss of control and the need for security, between destructive aggression and affirmation of libido, has been resolved in terms of a sado-masochist bind, where the punishment that the hero metes out to the 'real people' and the victimization he is subject to in return are accepted as inevitable and recurrent phases of a circular movement. What is being carefully eliminated is the third term: who punishes the father-figures, the law, the monstrous guardians of society? With this question conveniently erased, the spectator is encouraged to project his aggression and introject his guilt-feelings, his desire for instinctual gratification and his fears about the consequences. In other words, where the plot installs a triumphantly ironic ending, the fantasies seem to confirm a (neurotic) internalization of conflicting demands.

This points directly to the nature of the political theme with which Burgess is concerned. Faithfully preserved by Kubrick in the film, the novel is focused on the argument about individual freedom and the dangerous forces that encroach upon it. However, the moral centre of the story is not represented by a character (in the book, at least, Mr Alexander and the prison chaplain together formulate an intentionally inadequate version of it; the film dispenses with that), but is, instead, displaced and distorted. Extreme variants of individualism, whether aggressive like Alex's or defensive like that of the people barricaded in their various 'homes', are pitted against each other or confronted with equally extreme forms of social control, interventionism and behaviourist social engineering. What is posited as an argument is that if libidinous individualism and post-Freudian laissez-faire has its way, social anarchy ensues, and the state will show its totalitarian fangs. In fact, as it emerges, the argument about the double invasion of privacy cleverly runs together several normally opposed ideological stances: it combines liberal misgivings about state control and state intervention with conservative demands for a strong government of law and order, while casting doubt in general on the viability of parliamentary democracy and its executive institutions. [. . .]

What seems probable in this ideological *jeu d'esprit* is that the target is the Welfare State and the idea of technology as a form of social planning—both associated in Britain with the brand of socialism which the Labour government tried to practice in the 1960s.

That the film is not a serious political analysis is clear, nor does it pretend to offer one. On the other hand, neither is it as innocently above politics as some critics have asserted. * * *

* * *

What does distinguish *A Clockwork Orange* and makes its popularity both more problematic and significant is the way the ideological aspects are brought to the surface. It boldly seems to confront overtly political and controversial material, in a spirited, authorative manner. Yet its language of violence effectively depoliticizes the issues by switching back to a rhetoric of affect and overdetermination, which on the level of formal elaboration shapes and sustains an aesthetics of ambiguity and whimsical paradox. In a movie appearing as a social and political satire this can only mean that the impulse to reveal is short-circuited, and replaced by a chain of displacements. The authoritative tone—the 'unflagging pace' of which one reviewer spoke—gives a semblance of commotion and energetic development, but this simply serves to disguise the fact that everything stays in place, or as the phrase goes, the 'status quo' is maintained, though as one can see, this does, nowadays, take some effort: in short, it requires 'violence'. To a forcibly dictated narrative logic of an either/or dualism that paralyses the intellect (though it pleases the senses with the neat formal patterns it generates out of heterogeneous material) corresponds a dense ideological smokescreen. The function of this exercise is to provide an emotional grid where frustration is allowed to surface and to be accommodated in the fictional narrative, only to be the more efficiently

displaced into areas where the real contradictions resolve themselves in witty incongruities and ironic parallels.

*   *   *

TOM DEWE MATHEWS
[Cinema Censorship]†

*   *   *

The press were alerted to *A Clockwork Orange* when Adrienne
Corri, who played one of the rape victims, gave an interview to the
Sunday Mirror which appeared two days after the critics' attack on
Straw Dogs in *The Times*. Corri, presumably in an attempt to boost
public interest in the film, revealed that she 'was scared to see it
herself' as 'this was violence beyond anything I ever imagined would
appear on screen.' The paper then asked, 'How much more violence,
sadism and rape is British film censor Stephen Murphy going to let
movie-makers get away with?'

Within days of *A Clockwork Orange*'s release other journalists
piled into the fray, the most pungent and pithy being Peregrine
Worsthorne, the deputy editor of the *Sunday Telegraph* who described
the film as 'muck in the name of art'. On the other hand, the same
paper's film critic, Margaret Hinxman, hailed the movie as 'a masterpiece'. Worsthorne, though, was a powerful player in the bureaucratic circles of censorship for he straddled two camps. As a member
of Lord Longford's committee on pornography he acted as a mouthpiece for the moralists, while as heir apparent to the editorship of
the *Sunday Telegraph*, a bastion of the establishment, he would have
been particularly wary of a film suggesting that Britain was sliding
into a police state.

Before the film opened Worsthorne had attended a specially
arranged screening—a print having been provided by a craven
British film industry—for Longford's commission along with Peter
Thompson and the curly, white, wing-haired peer. And although
Worsthorne subsequently commented that this was 'a sick film for
a sick society' both Longford and Thompson heaped praise upon
Kubrick. Thompson even informed the production company that,
'to someone who has committed violent acts and who has been
mentally ill, this film seems to have an awful lot to say to society.'
Not surprisingly, his convictions soon realigned themselves and

†   From Tom Dewe Mathews, *Censored* (1994), published by Chatto and Windus. Reprinted
    by permission of The Random House Group Ltd.

A Clockwork Orange was added to the Festival of Light's[1] black list, although this change of heart was less well publicised than Thompson's initial praise.

At last, the tide seemed to be turning for the Board, but then for the first time since the thirties the government intervened in film censorship, and the intervention did not favour the BBFC. Asked to comment on the connection between the rise in violent crime and violence in films, the Home Secretary Reginald Maudling replied that, yes, there probably was a connection. Film critics and historians have subsequently tried to explain away this response as 'rushed' or that Maudling was 'caught off guard', but the Home Secretary would have had time to collect his thoughts before he went on to tell the crowding journalists that, due to 'personal concern', he planned to see *A Clockwork Orange*—presumably for the purpose of examining it.

For a government minister to publicly single a film out for special scrutiny before it had even been released not only pre-judged *A Clockwork Orange* but, because of Maudling's responsibility for law and order, it gave the moral rearmament movement the stamp of political respectability. The local authorities needed no further prompting. In a reversal of their previous policy of not taking action against individual films, the GLC's vitally influential film viewing committee decided to examine *A Clockwork Orange*. They did not impose a London ban, but their chairman Mark Patterson did announce that his committee intended to 'keep a closer watch on controversial films, particularly those passed by the censor for public viewing'.

Then, in a latter-day echo of T. P. O'Connor's arguments in 1917 that the cinema should be a site of entertainment and not social comment, Patterson remarked that 'in the context of violent times' his committee 'had to consider the wide, general political and social implications of films, particularly those which reflected anarchy and did not provide answers'.

Until that moment the Board's mainstay, the British film industry, had held firm. They had ignored the warnings of MPs, the press, numerous councils and even a plan by the Festival of Light to set up an alternative censorship system. Now, however, when the battle was at its most intense, their unity broke. They could accept one or two films, such as *A Clockwork Orange* being banned by half a dozen councils; but if the GLC, after the Board the most important censor in the country, no longer followed BBFC decisions, then profits would fall in the ensuing chaos. A suitable offering to

---

1. The Nationwide Festival of Light was a movement initiated in the early 1970s by Christians in the UK, partly in response to the so-called permissive society. The TV-campaigner Mary Whitehouse (National Viewers' and Listeners' Association) was prominent in the movement's mobilization against the sexualization of TV and cinema. [Editor's note.]

appease the righteous wrath of the moralists had to be found, then sacrificed, which in turn would restore the trust of the local authorities in the film industry. Their eyes fastened on the new Secretary of the Board, Stephen Murphy.

Nearly twenty-five years before this a Secretary of the Board had lost his job because he had antagonised the industry; but in 1972 Stephen Murphy had not only lost the support of the BBFC's main sponsor, it was also during his regime that the councils had swung the censorship system in their own favour. Of course, it was not his fault that Trevelyan had woken up the municipal censors in the early sixties or that those censors felt pressurised to act by the myriad voices of the backlash. He just happened to be the censor in place who was, in the words of the distributor Jimmy Vaughan, supposed 'to reconcile the viewpoint of a London audience in Chelsea with that of a local councillor in Southend'.

But the time for reconciliation, of whatever kind, was already over. 'Murphy Must Go' screamed the front-page headline of the 11 March 1972 issue of *Cinema TV Today*. Below it the trade paper ran the following story: 'As the GLC calls for a Royal Commission into censorship Kenneth Rive, the showmen's President says "We've got the wrong man in the job . . ."' As President of the Cinematograph Exhibitors Association, Rive had in fact been a member of the committee which had unanimously appointed Murphy two years before. Now he remembered, 'the film industry appoints the censor,' but also, 'it's up to us to put our house in order by getting rid of him.' Murphy was too liberal and, according to Rive, too loath to cut. 'I think that films like *Straw Dogs* and *A Clockwork Orange* are brilliant pictures,' said the CEA President. 'But I don't think they would be any less brilliant with a little cutting.'

* * *

In the meantime the same charge of incitement to crime that had been laid against films in the Edwardian era was now being levelled at *A Clockwork Orange*. But whereas kids in 1910 committed burglary because of the 'flickers', in 1972 teenagers blamed their urge to mug old people on Kubrick's film, and as before the magistrates and judges indulged the easy excuse rather than the complex explanation. Pundits, such as the Labour MP Maurice Edelman, claimed that a 'clockwork cult' was taking hold in the nation's thoroughfares. 'The phallic dress of the "droogs" with their cod-pieces, will, no doubt become as widespread as the sub-Western gear in the High Street imitated from the Western film.' More calculatedly, the Conservative MP Jill Knight alleged that a link existed between Kubrick's film, which had recently been shown in her Birmingham constituency, and a murder committed there soon afterwards by a juvenile.

The director himself, who had made his home in England since 1961, defended his film first with the words: 'I'm very pleased with *A Clockwork Orange*. I think it is the most skilful movie I have ever made. I can see almost nothing wrong with it'; then when the tirade persisted he delayed the film's general release, which meant that for over a year it could only be seen in one cinema in London. Once it had had its initial run, Kubrick took what can only be described as his own personal revenge upon his adopted countrymen—he banned his own film. Because he owns the British distribution rights to *A Clockwork Orange*, Stanley Kubrick had—and still has—the legal power to outlaw the film within Britain. And this he proceeded to do by withdrawing the film from circulation in the summer of 1973. Unlike a BBFC-banned film, not even cinema clubs or film societies or media courses in universities or film schools are allowed to show this film. It is therefore the most effective banning in British film censorship.

Occasionally Kubrick's legal position is tested, most recently by the Scala Cinema which was fined £4,000 in the spring of 1993 for breaching Kubrick's copyright. In turn this resulted in the closure of the cinema, which, at the time, was one of only three outlets in London licensed to show non-certificated films. Thus the opportunity to discover what is being censored by the BBFC has been hindered by one individual's autonomous decision. For whereas official censors are occasionally, if rarely, called upon to explain their decisions, Kubrick's blackout has never been satisfactorily explained by the reclusive film-maker and censor. The listings magazine *Time Out* reported in December 1989 that Kubrick acted 'after he received death threats to his family and relatives'. But most film commentators think that a more likely motivation was provided by the politicisation of the film in which it was kicked between publicity-conscious MPs, a responsive press and the upholders of moral hygiene.

This cacophony of self-interest definitely distracted attention from the actual film, which, in the meantime, paradoxically still ticks away like a delayed-action bomb within the body of the BBFC. *A Clockwork Orange* is the most sexually violent film ever made for the commercial cinema. Just the single infamous image of Alex bearing down to sexually impale as well as physically destroy with the gigantic phallus would be rushed at with scissors in the feminist-friendly atmosphere of today's BBFC. In a confirmation of that policy the chief censor from 1975, James Ferman, has gone on record in asserting that he will cut 'deeply' into the film's two major rape scenes if Kubrick submits *A Clockwork Orange* for a video certificate in the foreseeable future.

* * *

JULIAN PETLEY

[Press Sensationalism and Copycat Violence]†

The British Board of Film Censorship may have cut or banned some worthwhile films in its time, but *A Clockwork Orange* wasn't one of them. Indeed, Stephen Murphy, the BBFC's secretary at the time of the film's release called it 'one of the most brilliant pieces of cinema, not simply of this year, but possibly of the decade,' while his predecessor, John Trevelyan, said that it was 'perhaps the most brilliant piece of cinematic art that I have seen'. After it (and he personally) had been subjected to a sustained campaign of vilification in the press, it was the film's director, Stanley Kubrick, who withdrew it from distribution in Britain, acting as the censor.

A Clockwork Orange appeared in Britain in January 1972 in the wake of a number of films—*Soldier Blue, The Devils, Witchfinder General, The Wild Bunch, Performance, Straw Dogs*—that had thoroughly shaken the guardians of official morality and, as ever, the pundits of Fleet Street. The critics tended to take a more tolerant, and certainly better informed, line. *Straw Dogs*, however, seems to have proved the last straw for most of them. They not only savaged it in their columns but 13 leading critics of the day took the unprecedented step of writing a letter to *The Times* in which they claimed: 'In our view the use to which this film employs its scenes of double rape and multiple killings by a variety of hideous methods is dubious in its intention, excessive in its effect and likely to contribute to the concern expressed from time to time by many critics over films which exploit the very violence which they make a show of condemning.' Although not an overt call for censorship, it could hardly have helped an increasingly beleaguered BBFC and certainly contributed to the growing climate of hysteria being whipped up by the moral entrepreneurs and their allies in the press.

It is a tribute to Stephen Murphy and the BBFC that they passed *A Clockwork Orange*, and uncut, in such a febrile atmosphere. Unfortunately they reckoned without the notorious pusillanimity of the British distributors and exhibitors, many of whom, particularly Sir John Davis of Rank, were horrified at what they perceived as a disturbing new trend in cinema and were more than prepared to add their weight to calls for stricter censorship (while, of course, profiting from the offending items in the meantime). And so, to *The Times* letter from the critics was added the even more extraordinary spectacle of the trade paper *Cinema TV Today* headlining its front

† From "Clockwork Crimes: Chronicle of a *Cause Célèbre*," *Index on Censorship* 24.6 (November/December 1995), 48–52. Reprinted by permission.

page of 11 March 1972 'Murphy Must Go'—because he was too loath to cut and ban films!

According to Rive, then president of the Cinematograph Exhibitors' Association, Murphy was 'the wrong man for the job', and he added that as 'the film industry appoints the censor, so it is up to us to put our house in order by getting rid of him. He has got completely out of touch with public opinion.' So out of touch, in fact, that in the 1972 list of top 20 box office hits *The Devils* came fourth, *A Clockwork Orange* eleventh (quite remarkable considering that Kubrick, disturbed by the campaign against the film, persuaded the distributor to delay considerably the film's release outside London), and *Straw Dogs* fourteenth!

The reason for the distributors' and exhibitors' craven attitude was, of course, their fear of the spectre of local censorship—to ward off which the BBFC had been formed in the first place. Alerted by lurid and sensational stories in the press, certain local authorities had now begun to ban films that had been passed by the BBFC—*The Devils* in particular falling victim to council public health and licensing committees, fire brigade committees and all sorts of other committees utterly unfitted to sit in judgement on films—let alone films that had been distorted out of all recognition by malicious and ill-informed press reports.

Local council moral entrepreneurship was given an undoubted boost, and a spurious legitimacy, by the stories of 'copycat crime' that rapidly attached themselves to *A Clockwork Orange*. Indeed, this scenario was laid out even before any such alleged crimes actually took place. In an article in the *Evening News* on 27 January 1972 entitled 'Clockwork Oranges Are Ticking Bombs', the Labour MP Maurice Edelman prophesied that 'when *Clockwork Orange* is generally released it will lead to a clockwork cult which will magnify teenage violence.' And, sure enough, by May the papers were alleging that the film had indeed led to violent crimes being committed. However, and not entirely unexpectedly, the stories simply do not bear close scrutiny. For example, the *Mail* of 8 May 1973 stated that 'a "Clockwork Orange" gang was being sought last night after the murder of a 50-year-old firewood seller' in Newton-le-Willows. However, the only 'evidence' that the paper adduces to link the murder to the film is the fact that it took place 24 hours after the film finished its run at a local cinema, and teenagers had been buying clothes and make-up similar to that worn by the droogs in the film.

Much more coverage was given to the case of Richard Palmer, who murdered a tramp in Bletchley. The *Mail* of 4 July headed its story 'Why "Clockwork Orange" Boy Murdered a Tramp', but then rather spoiled things by revealing that Palmer hadn't seen the film (as he was only 16 he wasn't entitled to do so anyway) but had simply read the book which, his mother is quoted as saying, had not affected him. The dubious *Clockwork Orange* comes in only because a consultant psychiatrist called by the defence opined that 'it seems to me the boy was acting a part which seemed very similar to the characterisations given by *A Clockwork Orange*: I believe the main theme of the book is this feeling of hostility from the younger to the older generation.' He is then echoed by the defence counsel who asks, somewhat rhetorically: 'What possible explanation can there be for this savagery other than this film?', although the answer, rather more prosaically, is actually 'robbery'. Once the notion of such crimes became firmly embedded in the news agenda it became increasingly tempting for defence counsel, especially when faced with a seemingly hopeless case, or a judge who appears to believe everything he reads in the papers, to push the *Clockwork Orange* button and hope for the best—or at least a lenient sentence on the grounds of mitigating circumstances.

As with so many British censorship *causes célèbres* it's hard not to read about the trials and tribulations of *A Clockwork Orange* without coming to the conclusion that the real villain of the piece is the British press with its uniquely awful combination of prurience and censoriousness. There's something particularly disturbing and outrageous about one section of the media calling for the censorship of another—particularly when, as the privacy debate over the past few years has shown, the press reacts to threats to its own considerable freedoms with howls of outrage and fury. It was only in Britain that *A Clockwork Orange* was subjected to a campaign of vilification in the press. It is only in Britain that Stanley Kubrick has decreed that the film may not be shown in cinemas. These two facts are not, presumably, unconnected.

Anthony Burgess: A Chronology

1917   John Burgess Wilson born in Manchester, UK.
1937   Begins bachelor's degree in English Literature at the University of Manchester.
1940   After graduation, enlists in Royal Army Medical Corps.
1942   Marries Llewela (Lynne) Jones.
1943   Posted to Gibraltar as lecturer in Speech and Drama.
1946   Demobilized, but continues work in Army education.
1950   English teacher at Banbury School.
1953   Writes *A Vision of Battlements*, his first novel, set in Gibraltar.
1954   Appointed Education Officer for Colonial Service, Malaya.
1956   Publishes *Time for a Tiger* under the pseudonym Anthony Burgess.
1958   Education Officer for Colonial Service, Borneo. *The Enemy in the Blanket* (novel).
1959   Invalided back to the UK. *Beds in the East* concludes the Malayan trilogy. Burgess, convinced he is terminally ill, begins a program of writing to secure his wife financially for widowhood.
1960   *The Doctor Is Sick*; *The Right to an Answer*.
1961   *The Devil of a State*; *One Hand Clapping* (as Joseph Kell); *The Worm and the Ring*. Travels to Leningrad.
1962   *A Clockwork Orange*; *The Wanting Seed*.
1963   *Honey for the Bears*. Publishes *Inside My Enderby* (as Joseph Kell), and reviews it as Anthony Burgess in the *Yorkshire Post*.
1964   *Nothing Like the Sun: A Story of Shakespeare's Love-Life*; *Language Made Plain* (as John Burgess Wilson).
1965   *Here Comes Everybody: An Introduction to James Joyce for the Ordinary Reader*; finally publishes *A Vision of Battlements*.
1966   *Tremor of Intent: An Eschatological Spy Novel*.
1967   *The Novel Now*. Lectures in the United States.
1968   *Enderby Outside*. In Hollywood to discuss script for film of his Shakespeare novel. Lynne dies. *Urgent Copy: Literary Studies*. Marries Liliana (Liana) Macellari.

1969   Writer-in-Residence at Chapel Hill. *A Shorter Finnegans Wake* (abridgement of Joyce's last work).

1970   Moves to Malta. Visiting Professor at Princeton.

1971   *MF*. Translates Rostand's *Cyrano de Bergerac* (with plans for Broadway musical). Film of *A Clockwork Orange*, written, directed, and produced by Stanley Kubrick, premiered in New York (19 December).

1972   *Stanley Kubrick's A Clockwork Orange* released in the UK (13 January) and the United States (February 2). Burgess in New York to accept New York Critics' Awards on behalf of Kubrick. Distinguished Professor, City College, New York. Kubrick asks Warner Brothers to withdraw the film from distribution in the UK in the wake of press coverage of "copycat" violence.

1973   *Joysprick: An Introduction to the Language of James Joyce.*

1974   *The Clockwork Testament: Or Enderby's End; Napoleon Symphony.*

1975   Starts teaching at the University of Iowa, where his Third Symphony is premiered.

1976   Settles in Monaco. *Beard's Roman Women.*

1977   *Abba Abba.*

1978   *1985.*

1979   *Man of Nazareth.*

1980   *Earthly Powers*, nominated for Booker Prize.

1982   *The End of the World News.*

1984   *Ninety-Nine Novels: The Best in English since 1939.*

1985   *The Kingdom of the Wicked.*

1986   *Homage to Qwert Yuiop: Selected Journalism.*

1987   *Little Wilson and Big God: Being the First Part of the Confessions of Anthony Burgess; A Clockwork Orange* (play with music).

1989   *Any Old Iron; The Devil's Mode* (short stories).

1990   *You've Had Your Time: Being the Second Part of the Confessions of Anthony Burgess. A Clockwork Orange—2004* premiered by the Royal Shakespeare Company.

1992   *A Mouthful of Air: Language and Languages, Especially English.*

1993   *A Dead Man in Deptford* (Burgess's undergraduate dissertation had been on this novel's literary protagonist, Christopher Marlowe). Anthony Burgess dies.

1995   *Byrne: A Novel* (verse).

2000   Following the death of Kubrick in 1999, *Stanley Kubrick's A Clockwork Orange* is screened again in the UK.

Selected Bibliography

• indicates works included or excerpted in this Norton Critical Edition.

Aggeler, Geoffrey. *Anthony Burgess: The Artist as Novelist.* Tuscaloosa, AL: U of Alabama P, 1979.

———, ed. *Critical Essays on Anthony Burgess.* Boston: Hall, 1986.

• ———. "Pelagius and Augustine in the Novels of Anthony Burgess." *English Studies* 55 (1974): 43–55.

Anderson, Ken. "A Note on *A Clockwork Orange.*" *Notes on Contemporary Literature* 2 (November 1972): 5–7.

• Biswell, Andrew. *The Real Life of Anthony Burgess.* London: Picador, 2005.

Bloom, Harold, ed. *Anthony Burgess: Modern Critical Views.* New York: Chelsea House, 1987.

Boytinck, Paul. *Anthony Burgess: An Annotated Bibliography and Reference Guide.* New York: Garland, 1985.

Brophy, Elizabeth. "*A Clockwork Orange,* English and Nadsat." *Notes on Contemporary English* 2.2 (March 1972): 4–5.

• Burgess, Anthony. *You've Had Your Time: Being the Second Part of the Confessions of Anthony Burgess.* New York: Weidenfeld, 1991.

• Cahn, Steven M. "*A Clockwork Orange* Is Not about Violence." *Metaphilosophy* 5.2 (April 1974): 155–57.

• Carson, Julie. "Pronominalization in *A Clockwork Orange.*" *Papers on Language and Literature* 12.2 (Spring 1976): 200–205.

• Chew, Shirley. "Mr. Livedog's Day: The Novels of Anthony Burgess." *Encounter* 38 (June 1972): 57–64.

Coale, Samuel. *Anthony Burgess.* New York: Ungar, 1981.

Craik, Roger. "'Bog or God' in *A Clockwork Orange.*" *ANQ: A Quarterly Journal of Short Articles, Notes, and Reviews* 16.4 (Fall 2003): 51–54.

Cullinan, John. "Anthony Burgess' *A Clockwork Orange*: Two Versions." *English Language Notes* 9.4 (June 1972): 287–92.

• Davis, Todd F., and Kenneth Womack. "'O My Brothers': Reading the Anti-Ethics of the Pseudo-Family in Anthony Burgess's *A Clockwork Orange.*" *College Literature* 29.2 (Spring 2002): 19–36.

De Vitis, A. A. *Anthony Burgess.* New York: Twayne, 1972.

Dix, Carol M. *Anthony Burgess.* Harlow, Essex: Longman, 1971.

Evans, Robert O. "The *Nouveau Roman,* Russian Dystopias and Anthony Burgess." *Studies in the Literary Imagination* 6.2 (Fall 1973): 27–37.

Fitzpatrick, William P. "Anthony Burgess's Brave New World: The Ethos of Neutrality." *Studies in the Humanities* 3.1 (October 1972): 31–36.

• Fowler, Roger. "Anti-Language in Fiction." In *Literature as Social Discourse: The Practice of Linguistic Criticism.* Bloomington: Indiana UP, 1981. 142–61.

Gladsky, Rita K. "Schema Theory and Literary Texts: Anthony Burgess' Nadsat." *The Language Quarterly* 30.1–2 (1992): 39–46.

• Goh, Robbie B. H. "'Clockwork' Language Reconsidered: Iconicity and Narrative in Anthony Burgess's *A Clockwork Orange.*" *The Journal of Narrative Theory* 30.2 (Summer 2000): 263–80.

Gorra, Michael. "The World of *A Clockwork Orange*." *The Gettysburg Review* 3.4 (Autumn 1990): 630–43.

Guetti, James L. "Voiced Narrative: *A Clockwork Orange*." In *Word-Music: The Aesthetic Aspect of Narrative Fiction*. New Brunswick, NJ: Rutgers UP, 1980. 54–76.

Hollinger, Veronica. "'A Language of the Future': Discursive Constructions of the Subject in *A Clockwork Orange* and *Random Acts of Senseless Violence*." In Andy Sawyer and David Seed, eds., *Speaking Science Fiction: Dialogues and Interpretations*. Liverpool: Liverpool UP, 2000. 82–95.

• Hutchings, William. "'What's It Going To Be Then, Eh?': The Stage Odyssey of Anthony Burgess's *A Clockwork Orange*." *Modern Drama* 34.1 (March 1991): 35–48.

• Jachimiak, Peter Hughes. "'Putting the Boot In': *A Clockwork Orange*, Post-'69 Youth Culture and the Onset of Late Modernity." In Alan R Roughley, ed., *Anthony Burgess and Modernity*. New York: Manchester UP, 2008. 147–64.

Jeannin, Marc. *Anthony Burgess: Music in Literature and Literature in Music*. Newcastle: Cambridge Scholars, 2009.

Jennings, C. Robert. "*Playboy* Interview—Anthony Burgess: A Candid Conversation with the Visionary Author of *A Clockwork Orange*." *Playboy* 21.9 (September 1974): 69–86.

• Johnson, Sam. "Deciphering Adolescent Violence and Adult Corruption in Anthony Burgess's *A Clockwork Orange*." In Emmanuel Vernadakis and Graham Woodroffe, eds. *Portraits of the Artist in* A Clockwork Orange. Angers: Presses de l'Université d'Angers, 2003. 27–39.

Lewis, Roger. *Anthony Burgess*. London: Faber and Faber, 2002.

• Lodge, David. *Working with Structuralism: Essays and Reviews on Nineteenth- and Twentieth-Century Literature*. London: Routledge, 1981. 152–53.

Madden, Deanna. "Women in Dystopia: Misogyny in *Brave New World, 1984*, and *A Clockwork Orange*." In Katherine Anne Ackley, ed., *Misogyny in Literature: An Essay Collection*. New York: Garland, 1992. 289–313.

Malko, George. "*Penthouse* Interview: Anthony Burgess." *Penthouse* 3.10 (June 1972). 82–84, 119.

• McCracken, Samuel. "Novel into Film; Novelist into Critic: *A Clockwork Orange* . . . Again." *The Antioch Review* 32.3 (June 1973): 427–36.

Mentzer, Thomas L. "The Ethics of Behavior Modification: *A Clockwork Orange* Revisited." *Essays in Arts and Sciences* 9 (1980): 93–105.

Morris, Robert K. *The Consolations of Ambiguity: An Essay on the Novels of Anthony Burgess*. Columbia: U of Missouri P, 1971.

Nehring, Neil. "The Shifting Relations of Literature and Popular Music in Postwar England." *Discourse: Journal for Theoretical Studies in Media and Culture* 12.1 (1989–90): 78–103.

O'Keefe, Vincent A. "The 'Truth' about Reading: Interpretive Instability in the Evolution of Anthony Burgess's *A Clockwork Orange*." *Reader* 41 (Spring 1999): 31–53.

• Parrinder, Patrick. "Updating Utopia? Burgess's Future Fiction." *Encounter* 56.1 (January 1981): 45–53.

• Petix, Esther. "Linguistics, Mechanics, and Metaphysics: Anthony Burgess's *A Clockwork Orange* (1962)." In Robert K. Morris, *Old Lines, New Forces: Essays on the Contemporary British Novel, 1960–1970*. Rutherford, NJ: Fairleigh Dickinson UP, 1976. 38–52.

Phillips, Paul. *A Clockwork Counterpoint: The Music and Literature of Anthony Burgess*. Manchester: Manchester UP, 2010.

• Rabinovitz, Rubin. "Ethical Values in Burgess's *A Clockwork Orange*." *Studies in the Novel* 11.1 (Spring 1979): 43–50.

———. "Mechanism vs. Organism: Anthony Burgess's *A Clockwork Orange*." *Modern Fiction Studies* 24.4 (Winter 1978–79): 538–41.

• Ray, Philip E. "Alex Before and After: A New Approach to Burgess' *A Clockwork Orange*." *Modern Fiction Studies* 27.3 (Autumn 1981): 479–87.

Roughley, Alan R., ed. *Anthony Burgess and Modernity*. New York: Manchester UP, 2008.

• Saunders, Trevor J. "Plato's Clockwork Orange." *The Durham University Journal* 68.2 (June 1976): 113–17.

• Schoene-Harwood, Berthold. "Anthony Burgess's *A Clockwork Orange*." In *Writing Men: Literary Masculinities from* Frankenstein *to the New Man*. Edinburgh: Edinburgh UP, 2000. 66–76.

• Sharpless, Geoffrey. "Clockwork Education: The Persistence of the Arnoldian Ideal." *Postmodern Culture* 4.3 (1994). http://muse.jhu.edu/journals/post-modern_culture/v004/4.3sharpless.html

Sheldon, Leslie. "Newspeak and Nadsat: The Disintegration of Language in *1984* and *A Clockwork Orange*." *Studies in Contemporary Satire* 6 (1979): 7–13.

Stinson, John J. *Anthony Burgess Revisited*. Boston: Twayne, 1991.

Tilton, John W. *Cosmic Satire in the Contemporary Novel*. Lewisburg, PA: Bucknell UP, 1977. 21–42.

Windle, Kevin. "Two Russian Translations of *A Clockwork Orange*, or the Homecoming of Nadsat." *Canadian Slavonic Papers/Revue Canadienne des Slavistes* 37.1–2 (1995): 163–85.

Wood, Michael. "A Dream of Clockwork Oranges." *New Society* 11.297 (June 6, 1968): 842–43.

• Zinik, Zinovy. "Dublin Dragomans." *Times Literary Supplement* (June 25, 2004): 12–13.